Dear Richie,

So you can read
a little sports history
before you make it!

Happy B-day,

Janet

A Century of Philadelphia Sports

A Century of

Philadelphia Sports

RICH WESTCOTT

Foreword by
Edward G. Rendell

TEMPLE UNIVERSITY PRESS
PHILADELPHIA

Temple University Press, Philadelphia 19122
Copyright © 2001 by Temple University
All rights reserved
Published 2001
Printed in the United States of America

♾ The paper used in this publication meets the requirements of the American
National Standard for Information Sciences—Permanence of Paper for Printed Library
Materials, ANSI Z39.48-1984

Library of Congress Cataloging-in-Publication Data

Westcott, Rich.
    A century of Philadelphia sports / Rich Westcott ; foreword by Edward G. Rendell.
      p. cm.
    Includes index.
    ISBN 1-56639-861-4 (cloth : alk. paper)
    1. Sports—Pennsylvania—Philadelphia—History—20th century.   I. Title.
GV584.5.P46 W47 2001
796′.09748—dc21   00-047978

CONTENTS

Nothing defines the City of Philadelphia more than its passion for sports. In fact, we are known nationally, somewhat unfairly, for being raucous fans who are often tough on our own.

Though it is true that we can hold our players to a high level of expectation, I believe we are truly a city of great sports fans. We are extremely knowledgeable and incredibly passionate. While we can be critical of our players and teams, we respect effort and have an almost infinite amount of patience if we believe a team is truly undergoing a rebuilding effort that is headed in the right direction.

And our passions. Oh my, you can never, ever discount the interest of Philadelphia sports fans. I have witnessed the passion time and time again and have seen it, in some cases, change the outcome of a game. In 1977 in the National League playoffs, the incredible noise from the crowd unnerved Burt Hooton and drove him from the game. In 1995 the fans literally willed the Eagles to make an amazing series of crucial fourth-down stops against the hated Barry Switzer–led Cowboys. And the excitement of a Villanova–St. Joe's or Penn-Princeton basketball game at the Palestra is raw emotion that creates a deafening crescendo unrivaled anywhere, even at Duke's Cameron Gymnasium, Phog Allen Fieldhouse, the Deandome, or Pauley Pavilion.

And we have had our champions to reward that loyalty. I know we are currently in a famine, but remember the great moments—as Rich Westcott so graphically reminds us—the incredible triumphs and the exhilarating wins. Remember the Whiz Kids of 1950, the World Champion "You Gotta Believe" Phillies of 1980, and the Krukker-led blue-collar gang of 1993.

Think back to Franklin Field in 1960 and remember Chuck Bednarik's tackle of Jim Taylor preserving the Eagles' NFL Championship. And who could forget Dick Vermeil almost willing our beloved Birds into Super Bowl XV. How about the glorious parades celebrating our still unbelievable Flyers' two Stanley Cups or the great Sixers led by Doc and, yes, Moses in the "four-five-four" run to the championship in 1983. And then there is Villanova's incredible run to the 1985 NCAA Basketball Championship. What great memories to treasure!

And our stars! We've had plenty. From Tom Gola to Dr. J, from Tommy McDonald to Reggie White, from Bobby Clarke to Eric Lindros, from Robin Roberts to Mike

Schmidt to Scott Rolen. Vic Seixas in tennis, Carl Lewis in track, Joe Frazier in boxing, and John B. Kelly in rowing: the whole world watched and saw their excellence.

It is safe to say that we fans have had plenty of magic moments in this century. We've had great friends to tell us about them—Bill Campbell, Les Keiter, By Saam, Al Meltzer, Harry Kalas, Andy Musser, Merrill Reese, Gene Hart, and Whitey. And in what other city could an Angelo make WIP so much a part of our lives or a Comcast SportsNet have such instant popularity?

Rich Westcott has successfully caught all this magic and put it in the proverbial bottle. He has adeptly chronicled the highs and the lows, the triumphs and the disasters (1964 Phils), and has wonderfully evoked the spirit of sports in Philadelphia. So sit back and enjoy.

Edward G. Rendell

A mong cities of the United States, none has had a more significant role or is more deeply immersed in American history than Philadelphia. The "Cradle of Liberty" in its more than 300 years of existence overflows with important historical events, places, and people.

The same kind of statement can be made about the city's sports history. Philadelphia has a long and illustrious background in sports that is second to none. New York, Boston, and maybe even Chicago have equally rich pasts, but at the risk of sounding a bit provincial, they don't outrank Philadelphia.

How could they? After all, this is a city where sports were played long before Philadelphia became the birthplace of the nation. It's a city where major events, prominent athletes, and spectacular performances—not to mention the woeful, the inept, and the calamitous—have been going on, it sometimes seems, forever.

Philadelphia sports have been especially prominent in the 20th century. From pro teams to college teams to independent teams, from champions to incompetents, from the great to the mediocre to the terrible, Philadelphia and its surrounding counties have had a little bit of everything during the century just past.

In the 20th century, the Philadelphia area produced four Heisman Trophy winners, five Sullivan Award winners, a two-time U.S. Open golf champion, 11 members of the Boxing Hall of Fame, and countless numbers of Olympic champions. Basketball players from Philadelphia have won 12 National Basketball Association (NBA) scoring championships and five national collegiate scoring titles. Twelve professional ice hockey teams, including a National Hockey League (NHL) team in 1930, have played in the city. Philadelphia is the only city ever to have Most Valuable Players in baseball in both the American and National Leagues in the same year, when Jimmie Foxx and Chuck Klein won the awards in 1933.

The Philadelphia area was the birthplace of the best tennis player (Bill Tilden), the best basketball player (Wilt Chamberlain), and the best rower (John B. Kelly, Sr.) of all time. The best race horse of all time (Man o' War) was raised here. Baseball's best third baseman, (Mike Schmidt), played here. So did the game's best second baseman (Eddie Collins). The first Olympian (Alvin Kraenzien) to win four gold medals in the same year, ran here. The last of pro football's 60-minute players and one of the greatest gridiron battlers of all time (Chuck Bednarik), performed here.

Numerous other great athletes such as Steve Van Buren, Carl Lewis, Robin Roberts, Tom Gola, Bobby Clarke, Joe Frazier, Anne Townsend, Julius Erving, Jay Sigel, Grover Cleveland Alexander, Paul Arizin, Willie Mosconi, Bob Montgomery, Syliva Wene Martin, Walt Bahr, Joe Verdeur, Vic Seixas, Eddie Plank, and many, many more either came from or played here. And a like number that ranges from Goose Goslin to Reggie Jackson, from Danny Murtaugh to Tom Lasorda, and also includes Earl Monroe, Franco Harris, Dawn Staley, Emlen Tunnell, Mickey Vernon, Leroy Kelly, Roy Campanella, and Tara Lipinsky were Philadelphia-area natives who went on to perform superbly in other places.

Legendary coaches and managers also made their marks in Philadelphia. Earle (Greasy) Neale, Alex Hannum, Jack Ramsay, Lon Jourdet, Cathy Rush, Jim (Jumbo) Elliott, Harry Litwack, Fred Shero, Herb Magee, Connie Mack, George Munger, John Chaney, Glenn Killinger, Gene Mauch, and Dick Vermeil were just a few of them. Philadelphia was the place where Eddie Gottlieb, Paul Owens, Keith Allen, Bert Bell, Bob Carpenter, and Ed Snider ran organizations with particular skill. And Bill Campbell, Harry Kalas, Byrum Saam, and Gene Hart in broadcasting, as well as Damon Runyon, Red Smith, Sandy Grady, Larry Merchant, and Bill Lyon in sportswriting all worked here for varying lengths, spinning their own particular brands of brilliance.

Philadelphia has been the home of six World Series winners, four NBA champions, four NFL titlists, and two Stanley Cup winners. It has two NCAA champions (La Salle and Villanova) and four NIT winners (Temple twice, La Salle, Villanova) in major college basketball, and scores of other national collegiate champs, including the pioneering three-time winner, Immaculata College. The city is the home of a nationally famous institution called the Big Five. Philadelphia area golf clubs have been the sites of some 50 national championship tournaments, including seven U.S. Opens. Haverford College played in the nation's first intercollegiate soccer game. In football, Penn played in the Rose Bowl and Temple in the Sugar Bowl. And there have been more than 50 professional teams calling Philadelphia home, including long-gone pillars such as the Athletics, the Warriors, the Ramblers, and the Frankford Yellowjackets, the city's first NFL championship team.

The Philadelphia area is where the Army-Navy game was played for 75 of its 100 years, where the Penn Relays, the Dad Vail Regatta, and the Devon Horse Show are held, and it was the home of some great Negro League baseball teams, including the Giants, the Daisies, and the Stars. It is where such legendary sports structures as Shibe Park, Baker Bowl, the Palestra, the Arena, Franklin Field, Convention Hall, Penmar Park, Garden State Park, Langhorne Speedway, and JFK Stadium have been located. The Schuylkill River is one of the world's major racing sites for rowers. The Manayunk Wall has become famous in professional bicycle racing. For the entire century, the city has been one of the most important centers of boxing in the country. In 1952 alone, there were three world championship fights in Philadelphia. At one time heavyweight champions Joe Walcott, Sonny Liston, Joe Frazier, and Muhammad Ali all lived in the Philadelphia area.

Philadelphia and its surrounding environs have produced the Mighty Mites and the Mighty Macs, the $100,000 Infield, the Destiny Backfield, and the Five Ironmen. The city provided the Whiz Kids, the Wheeze Kids, and Macho Row. It gave us Wham Bam, the Owl Without a Vowel, Dipper, Smokin' Joe, White Shoes, and Losing Pitcher. It even had its own mythical hero, the unforgettable Rocky Balboa.

Most of the world's greatest athletes have competed in Philadelphia. Jim Thorpe, Red Grange, Babe Ruth, Jack Dempsey, Bobby Jones, Ted Williams, Sugar Ray Robinson, Jesse Owens, Arnold Palmer, and Michael Jordan are just a few who have performed in the area. Many of them displayed their talent in especially memorable events here.

Philadelphia has also had its share of turmoil, heartbreak, and disaster, as well as artless klutzes and atrocious teams. The Phillies are the losingest team in the history of sports in the United States. They once went 31 seasons with just one winning team. They have had two former owners banned from baseball for life. One season they lost more consecutive games—23—than any team in baseball history. And then there was the infamous collapse of 1964, which left scars on the city's pysche for years.

The Athletics finished in last place a higher percentage of times (18 in 54 years) than any other baseball team. The Eagles once had 11 straight losing seasons, went 28 years without having anybody gain 1,000 yards in rushing, and haven't won an NFL championship in 40 years. In 1972–73, the 76ers had a 9–72 record, the worst mark in NBA history. The Flyers have bombed out of the Stanley Cup finals five disappointing times. Temple had just two winning seasons in football in the 20 years between 1979 and 1999. Villanova once went scoreless during an entire football season.

Disasters and tragedy have also shadowed Philadelphia's sports history. A balcony collapsed at Baker Bowl, sending 12 baseball fans to their deaths and injuring 232 others. Part of the roof blew off at the Spectrum. Garden State Park burned down. Connie Mack twice sold off pennant-winning teams, then a third time sold off the entire team, each time jilting fans who loyally followed his club. And in front of a national television audience, a railing collapsed at an Army-Navy game, plummeting nine students to the ground where they suffered various injuries and the city suffered excruciating embarrassment.

Scandal has been a part of the local scene, too. A point-shaving scandal involving three players from St. Joseph's and one from La Salle rocked college basketball in 1961. Villanova and La Salle in basketball and Temple in football had their seasons ruined by the improprieties of players or coaches. Drugs have played a role in local sports, most conspicuously involving Phillies players in the late 1970s. Nothing was more scandalous, though, than the Phillies' refusal to sign black players until nearly 10 years after Jackie Robinson had entered the major leagues.

Quite possibly, the worst of Philadelphia sports has been demonstrated by the conduct of some of the city's fans. In a city known nationally for its boo birds and poor behavior among fans, Philadelphia is a place where spectators have thrown snowballs and other objects not only at Santa Claus but at opposing players and coaches. They have cheered when opposing players were injured, booed home team players such as Del Ennis, Gus Zernial, and Dick Allen unmercifully, and become so unruly at Eagles games that a temporary court had to be set up on game days at Veterans Stadium.

Philadelphia has also been the home of colorful characters such as public address announcer Dave Zinkoff; exotic characters such as the Phillies' Jim Konstanty, who often summoned an undertaker friend to diagnose his pitching problems, and Athletics hurler Rube Waddell, who was known to leave the mound to chase fire engines; and silent characters, such as Steve Carlton, who refused to talk to the press through most of his career. It is a city where Joe Kuharich, Ben Chapman, Roy Rubin, William Baker, Norman Braman, and Mitch Williams would not be candidates for a local Hall of Fame. And it is a city about which Mike Schmidt made the often-quoted remark: "Philadelphia is a place where you have the ecstacy of winning, and the agony of reading about it the next morning."

Undoubtedly, that was not the case in earlier days of sports in Philadelphia. The city's first known athletic activity was recorded in 1732 when rowers sloshed along the Schuylkill River in crude shells. Crew continued to be a major athletic endeavor in the city for the next century, and in 1854 the first rowing club, known as the University Barge Club, was established for Penn oarsmen. Four years later, with 10 clubs in operation on Boathouse Row, the Schuylkill Navy of Philadelphia was founded. It is now the oldest amateur athletic governing body in the United States.

Another sport entered the local scene in the 1830s. Called base ball or town ball, it was first known to have been played in Philadelphia in 1833. By the 1850s the sport was becoming increasingly popular, and in the early 1860s amateur teams existed throughout the city. In one of the earliest recorded results, a team called Equity beat Pennsylvania, 65–52. Baseball teams manned by black players were numerous in Philadelphia in the 1860s and for the rest of the 19th century, among them the Excelsiors, the Pythians, the Mutuals, and the Orions. During the Civil War northern soldiers also played the game while encamped on a ball field later to be known as Recreation Park.

Philadelphia can lay claim to having the first professional baseball player when in 1865 a team called the Athletics signed a lefthanded second baseman named Al Reach to a contract that paid him $1,000. Reach, after he'd become the owner of a sporting goods company, would later become the first owner of the Phillies when the team moved in 1883 to Philadelphia from Worcester, Massachusetts, where it had been known as the Brown Stockings.

In 1871 another team called the Athletics won the first championship of the newly formed National Association, the first professional baseball league. Pitching for Philadelphia, Joe Borden, a resident of Yeadon and later West Chester, hurled the first known professional baseball no-hitter in 1875. After the National Association folded in 1875, a circuit called the National League was formed in 1876, and yet another team called the Athletics was among the charter members. Now pitching for Boston, Borden won the first National League game ever played, defeating Philadelphia, 6–5, at Jefferson Park. Still another team called the Athletics (all were different teams) joined the new American Association in 1882. Harry Stovey, the team's first baseman, led the league in home runs five times. In 1890 Philadelphia had three major league teams—the Phillies, the American Association Athletics, and the Quakers in the Players League—a circuit formed by players who temporarily quit the National League.

While baseball thrived in Philadelphia in the second half of the 19th century, other sports had also emerged. By the 1850s cricket had become a major sport. Germantown Cricket Club was formed in 1842 by a group of English hosiery weavers. Five more clubs opened in the following decade, including Philadelphia Cricket Club, which was founded on rented grounds in Camden in 1854 by William R. Wister, who has been called "the Father of American Cricket." Merion Cricket Club opened in 1865. By the mid-1870s some 120 cricket clubs existed in the Philadelphia area.

In 1857, Philadelphian Domick Bradley claimed the world's heavyweight boxing championship after defeating Sam Rankin of Baltimore in the 157th round of a bare-knuckled bout. Thereafter, boxing became increasingly popular and soon clubs sprouted all around the city. Polo and horse racing were also popular, with races often held in Fairmount Park, Nicetown, and Camden. Horse racing had been staged in the Philadelphia area since the 1770s.

Also gaining ground was football. Penn fielded its first team in 1876. Swarthmore followed in 1878, with Haverford and Pennsylvania Military College taking to the gridiron in 1879, La Salle and Ursinus in 1893, and Temple and Villanova in 1894. Penn, which opened its first formal playing facilities at 37th and Spruce Streets in 1885, played the world's first indoor football game in 1887 when it defeated Rutgers, 13–10, at Madison Square Garden. By then Penn was a national powerhouse. Quakers guard T. Truxton Hare made the All-American team four straight years from 1897 to 1900. The Quakers, under legendary coach George Woodruff, posted a 124–15–2 record between 1892 and 1901, registering marks of 12–0 in 1894, 14–0 in 1895, and 15–0 in 1897, each time being considered the top team in the nation.

Tennis was gaining a hold in Philadelphia, too. By the late 1870s, lawn tennis was popular at Germantown Cricket Club. An early proponent of the sport was Frederick Taylor, a fine player, who was a member of the winning U.S. doubles team in 1881 and an efficiency expert who invented time and motion studies while working at Midvale Steel Company. In 1883, Joseph Clark, father of the future Philadelphia mayor and U.S. senator, and his brother Clarence became the first Americans to play at Wimbledon. That year, Joseph won the first intercollegiate singles tournament, and he and Clarence captured the national doubles title. In 1887 the first U. S. Women's National Tennis Tournament was played at Philadelphia Cricket Club, and in 1894 the Pennsylvania Lawn Tennis Championship began at Merion.

Golf was also developing an avid following in the 1890s. In 1891, Philadelphia Country Club introduced golf to its members as an activity to be undertaken when they weren't watching tennis, cricket, or polo on the club's grounds then located in Bala Cynwyd. The first professional tournament in Philadelphia was held in 1898 at Huntingdon Valley Country Club with 10 players competing. That same year, Aronimink Country Club, then located at 52nd Street and Chester Avenue, hired what may have been the first club pro when it employed John Shippen, a black minister's son who had been raised on an Indian reservation on Long Island. Also in 1898, Bill Smith won Philadelphia's first Amateur Championship, a title he repeated in 1901 and 1902.

Basketball made its grand entrance in the 1890s with numerous local colleges fielding teams. In the first local intercollegiate game, Haverford defeated Temple, 6–4, in 1895. That year, while playing mostly a combination of club, YMCA, and high school teams, the Owls totaled 59 points to their opponents' 33 in 11 games.

Penn, which fielded its first baseball team in 1875, staged its first relay race in 1893, competing against Princeton. The Penn Relays were launched in 1895, the same year the Devon Horse Show began. The Army-Navy game was held for the first time in Philadelphia in 1899. By the turn of the century, sports had become an integral part of the social fabric in Philadelphia. It would get even better in the 20th century.

A Century of Philadelphia Sports is an attempt to describe the highlights of 100 years of the city's sports activities. Each chapter is devoted to a single 10-year period of that history. Within each chapter, I offer sketches on the major events or individuals of the decade, followed by a general, chronological discussion of other highlights of that period, and concluding with a brief profile of the top athlete of that decade. The top athletes were chosen from among those who participated during most of the decade.

To keep the book to a reasonable length, some parameters had to be established. First, this is not a critique of or commentary on the city's sports history but a factual presentation of its most prominent features. It was not possible to chronicle every athlete, every team, or every event of significance. Therefore, I have made some arbitrary choices, which I realize will not be met with unanimous agreement. So be it. I have also restricted the area of coverage to Philadelphia, the surrounding four counties (Bucks, Montgomery, Chester, and Delaware), and the nearby parts of South Jersey. In so doing, I have not included material about sports played in places that fall beyond the borders of those areas. Nor have I included high school sports except in a few instances of special significance.

What is included, though, is a summation of the major aspects of a city's marvelous sports history. What a grand and glorious history it has been.

ACKNOWLEDGEMENTS

A truckload of material and scores of people contributed to this project. I am deeply grateful for the various roles they played in the long, often tedious, and extremely difficult job of putting this book together.

There is a substantial body of material available on Philadelphia sports. Many fine books have been written on specific teams or sports in Philadelphia, and I recommend them for more in-depth reading. They include *Full Spectrum* by Jay Greenberg, *The Mackmen* by Rev. Jerome Romanowski (The Baseball Padre), *The Athletics of Philadelphia* by David Jordan, *Fight on Pennsylvania* by Dan Rottenberg, *Golf in Philadelphia* by James Finegan, *Pride of* the *Palestra* by Paul Zingg, *The Philadelphia Story* by Frank Dolson, *Fair Dealing and Clean Playing, the Hilldale Club and the Development of Black Professional Baseball, 1910–1932* by Neil Lanctot, *Sunday's Warriors* by Donald Campbell, *The Philadelphia Big Five* by Donald Hunt, *The Story of Philadelphia Tennis* by the International Tennis Hall of Fame, *The Phillies Encyclopedia* by Rich Westcott and Frank Bilovsky, and *Philadelphia's Old Ballparks* by Rich Westcott.

In addition, *The History of Penn AC* by Joe Sweeney, *The Negro Leagues* by the Society of American Baseball Research, *The Boxing Register, The Encyclopedia of Sports* by Frank Menke, *The Olympic Factbook, The Official NCAA Record Book,* Sports Illustrated's *Sports Almanac,* the Philadelphia Daily News's *Philadelphia's Record Breakers and Legend Makers,* and the *Baseball, Pro Football,* and *NBA Basketball* encyclopedias played a part in the preparation of this book. So, too, did the *Philadelphia Inquirer,* the *Daily News,* and the *Evening Bulletin,* as well as media guides from all of the pro and most of the college teams.

While it would almost fill another book to mention every one who has contributed to this effort, some must be mentioned. I offer my heartfelt thanks to the following for their special help: Marv Bachrad, Tony Berick, Frank Bilovsky, Bob Bloss, Jeff Brophy, Howard Bruno, Carola Cifaldi, Jon Caroulis, Skip Clayton, Brian Colgan, Gus Constant, Dave Coskey, Tom DiCamillo, Ray Didinger, John Douglas, Jay Dunn, Bob Ford, Jimmy Gallagher, Jan Giel, Brother Joseph Grabenstein, Zack Hill, Ed Hilt, Dave Johnson, Joe Juliano, Julie Kelly, Dean Kenefich, Brian Kerschner, Alan

Kravetz, Christen Langdon, Tony Leodora, Shawn May, John McAdams, Jack McCaffery, Bob Morro, Frank Phelps, Jack Scheuer, Jerry Schneider, Jen Shillingford, Larry Shenk, Al Shrier, Carla Shultzberg, Carl Smith, Joe Sweeney, Bob Tennant, Bob Vetrone, Sr., and Chris Westcott. Without their help, *A Century of Philadelphia Sports* would not have been even remotely possible.

Sports Play a Major Role in City Life

One could easily assume that as the 20th century dawned, Philadelphia was all work and no play. Nothing, however, could be farther from the truth.

To be sure, the city had become a major business and industrial center, and many of its nearly 1.3 million citizens spent long hours hard at work at the hundreds of companies, both large and small, that populated Philadelphia and its surrounding environs.

But Philadelphians also had time for sports. And at the turn of the century and throughout the first decade of the new millennium, local sports were a major part of the city's culture.

The local sports scene, was, of course, nothing like it is today. Professional teams and athletes were not in abundance. There was no pro football, no pro basketball, no ice hockey. Much of the focus of Philadelphia sports was on games and teams playing at the amateur level.

Nevertheless, at least to some extent, professional baseball was the dominant sport in Philadelphia in the first decade of the 20th century. The Phillies had by then become a respectable member of the National League, fortifying their position as great players such as Ed Delahanty made their marks. In 1901, with the formation of the American League, the Athletics not only entered the picture but, with Connie Mack launching what would become a 50-year career as the team's manager, would win two pennants in their first five years. Also new to the mix was a team called the Philadelphia Giants. Led by legendary figures Andrew (Rube) Foster and John Henry Lloyd, they would be crowned Colored World Champions twice in the decade.

In addition to these players, Eddie Plank, Rube Waddell, Chief Bender, Eddie Collins, and Frank Baker began Hall of Fame careers with the A's in the first decade of the 1900s. Shoeless Joe Jackson passed briefly through town. And Sherry Magee and Roy Thomas performed with an abundance of ability for the Phillies.

Professional boxing was also an important part of Philadelphia sports. Matches were held at no less than 14 fight clubs around the city, as well at Baker Bowl and Shibe Park. In the early 1900s, Philadelphia had its first champion when Jack O'Brien captured the light-heavyweight title. O'Brien would eventually enter the Boxing Hall of Fame after a long and glorious career.

Much of the rest of the attention of Philadelphia sports fans was directed at amateur sports. Football was played with enthusiasm and occasional examples of skill at Temple, Villanova, Swarthmore, Ursinus, and Pennsylvania Military College, and at the University of Pennsylvania, which in the first decade of the 1900s produced several top teams and All-American players. Basketball games in which the final scores often barely reached double digits were played at Penn, Temple, Drexel, Haverford, and Swarthmore.

Haverford also played a role of considerable importance in two other sports. Soccer was a major part of the college's active sports program. In 1901, Haverford fielded the nation's first intercollegiate soccer team. With a large contingent of English and Indian students, the Fords also went in heavily for cricket. So intent were the cricket players on keeping baseball from becoming part of the Haverford athletic program that they were known to have sawed bats in half whenever interest in baseball surfaced.

Swarthmore was a lacrosse powerhouse in the early 1900s, winning three national championships. Crew was another sport in the spotlight during the decade. Leading the way was Vesper Boat Club, which in both 1900 and 1904 put in eight-man crews that won Olympic gold medals.

Golf and tennis were also important to Philadelphians. The first of seven U.S. Opens held in the area was staged in 1907 at Philadelphia Cricket Club. Amateur golf had its avid followers among the country club set. In the early years of the 20th century, two women in particular—Frances Griscom and Norma Barlow—were highly successful players on a local as well as national level. Tennis was also an extremely popular game, and in the first decade Philadelphia had not only its first prominent national player in William Clothier, but also its first Davis Cup match.

Track and field also produced its share of Olympic gold medalists in the first decade. In a remarkable feat that was never equaled, Penn athletes captured eight gold medals in the 1900 Olympics, with Alvin Kraenzlein winning four of them. Baseball and men's field hockey were also sports played avidly at the college level.

The first decade saw the opening of Columbia Park and Shibe Park, and a tragedy at Philadelphia Base Ball Park. It saw player raids and court cases when the American League arrived, the first City Series game between the Phillies and the A's, and the brief existence of an insurgent professional baseball league. During the decade, the Army-Navy game become a fixture in Philadelphia, and the first auto race came to the city with an event held in Fairmount Park.

There was certainly no shortage of sports or major sports stories in Philadelphia in the early years of the 20th century. Even before the century was 10 years old, the city had become one of the leading sports centers in the country. And it was only going to get better.

A NEW BASEBALL TEAM COMES TO TOWN

Throughout the later part of the 1800s, professional baseball teams always seemed to be trying to establish a foothold in Philadelphia. The only one that managed to hang around for any length of time, though, was the Phillies.

That all changed in 1901 when a new franchise was established in Philadelphia. Called the Athletics, a name that had been used by several previous Philadelphia teams, it was viewed as one of the cornerstones of the newly formed American League.

The American League had previously been known as the Western League, a kind of minor league circuit composed of midwestern teams. Wishing to expand his operation into the more lucrative eastern market and determined to elevate his domain to big league status and compete with the National League, powerful league president Ban Johnson decided to set up teams in some of the big East Coast cities.

Philadelphia was a natural choice. The city had a reputation as a strong baseball town, and with a population that exceeded one million, a new team had an excellent chance of being a success.

To establish a team in Philadelphia, Johnson selected Connie Mack, a former National League catcher and manager who had been piloting the Milwaukee club in the Western League. Mack had played for 11 years with no particular distinction

Connie Mack launched the Philadelphia Athletics in 1901, and ran the team for 50 years.

in the big leagues, mostly with Washington and Pittsburgh. He had also managed the Pirates for a little more than two years without significant success.

Born Cornelius McGilicuddy, Mack came to Philadelphia in 1900. His assignment was to line up financial support, find a place to play, sign players, and ultimately run the team. For putting up a small sum of less than $10,000, Mack was awarded 25 percent ownership in the new team.

After enlisting the aid of local sportswriters Sam (Butch) Jones of the Associated Press and Frank Hough of the *Philadelphia Inquirer,* each of whom wound up with a 12½ percent share in the Athletics, Mack eventually found his sugar daddy. His name was Benjamin Shibe, who ironically was the partner of Phillies owner Al Reach in a flourishing sporting goods business. Encouraged by Reach to invest in the team, Shibe put up the money and became owner of 50 percent of the stock.

Mack's next job was to find a playing field. His choice was a plot of ground bordered by 29th Street, Columbia Avenue, 30th Street, and Oxford Street. Mack took a 10-year lease on the land, and then at a cost of $35,000 built a 9,500-seat ballpark. Named Columbia Park, it would be the Athletics' home for their first eight years.

Mack, who had moved into a house at 2932 Oxford Street, was also immersed in the job of signing players. He and Johnson made the Phillies their special target, raiding the club with a vengeance. Using higher salaries to lure players, the Athletics coaxed star infielder Nap Lajoie, top pitchers Chick Fraser, Bill Bernhard, and Wiley Piatt, and several lesser players away from the National League club. The invasion eventually landed in court, where an acrimonious legal battle severed relations between the two teams.

After the opener had been twice postponed because of rain, the Athletics finally began their maiden season on April 26, 1901. With an overflow crowd of 10,524 in attendance, including Mayor Samuel Ashbridge, the Athletics lost their first game to the Washington Nationals, 5–1, despite Lajoie's three hits.

The team went on to a fourth-place finish that season while drawing just 206,329 fans, the lowest the A's would attract to Columbia Park. Lajoie won the Triple Crown with 14 home runs, 125 RBI, and a still-standing American League record .422 batting average.

The Athletics were off and running. They would be a fixture in Philadelphia for 54 years.

PHILLIES FALL ON HARD TIMES

The first decade of the 20th century was not one that ranks among the Phillies' finest. The club was plagued with troubles and problems, both on and off the field.

The decade had started on a positive note when the Phillies opened the 20th century on April 18, 1900, with a 19–17 victory over the Boston Braves in 10 innings at Boston, overcoming a nine-run Braves ninth. The Braves outhit the Phillies, 25–19. The next day, the Phils made their home debut with a 5–4 win over Boston at Philadelphia Park.

The Phillies had three future Hall of Famers in the lineup, including first baseman Ed Delahanty, who hit .323 that year; second baseman Nap Lajoie, a .337 hitter; and outfielder Elmer Flick, who led the National League in RBI (110) and total bases (305) while finishing second in the league with a .367 batting average. Norristown native Roy Thomas led the league in runs scored with 131 after setting a still-standing record the previous year for most runs scored (137) by a rookie. Thomas, later the baseball coach at Haverford and Penn, also topped the circuit in walks for the first of seven times over an eight-year period.

The following year, with Delahanty hitting .354 and Flick .333, the Phillies fin-

Ed Delahanty was the first Phillies superstar and a
future Hall of Famer.

ished in second place, their highest finish since 1887. The club was even the recipient of its first no-hitter of the century, in 1903, when Chick Fraser blanked the
Chicago Cubs, 10–0.

All was not well with the Phillies, however. The arrival of the Athletics proved no
immediate benefit to them. Instead, attendance at Phillies games suffered as the A's
lured fans to Columbia Park. In 1902 the Athletics attracted 442,000 fans, while the
Phillies could draw only 112,000.

Worse yet, the Athletics raided the Phillies of some of their top players. The A's
tried to entice Delahanty to join them, but although that maneuver failed, they did
grab Lajoie, Fraser, Bill Bernhard, and Wiley Piatt for their first season in 1901. Then
they snatched Flick, infielder Monte Cross, and pitcher Bill Duggleby in 1902. Ultimately the Phillies filed suit in an attempt to regain their players. The case reached
the Pennsylvania Supreme Court, which ruled that the players either had to return
to the Phillies or they would be barred from playing in Philadelphia. Fraser and Duggleby chose to return to the Phils, while the other key players—Lajoie, Flick, and
Bernhard—went to the Cleveland Indians. In 1902 they were banned from playing
in Philadelphia when the Indians came to town. Unfortunately for the Phillies,
Lajoie went on to have one of the best five-year batting records in major league history, hitting .371 between 1901 and 1905.

Crippled by the raids, Phillies owners Al Reach and John Rogers had to borrow money to keep the team afloat. At the end of the '02 season they sold the team for $170,000 to a syndicate headed by broker and socialite James Potter. Reach and Rogers retained ownership of Philadelphia Park.

The Phillies' troubles continued in 1903, when a 100-foot long balcony collapsed during a game at Philadelphia Park, resulting in the death of 12 fans and injuries to 232 others. Fans had gone to the balcony, which hung over 15th Street, to observe a scuffle between a drunk and two young girls on the street below. Suddenly, the balcony gave way. Those standing on it plunged 30 feet to the street. People fell on top of other people, and, as reported in the *Philadelphia Inquirer,* "In the twinkling of an eye, the street was piled four deep with bleeding, injured, shrieking humanity struggling amid the piles of debris."

It was a tragedy of mammoth proportions. In the aftermath, more than 80 lawsuits were filed against ballpark owners Reach and Rogers and the Phillies, sending the club into a deep financial abyss. So overwhelming was the Phils' financial burden that the syndicate that had just bought the team was soon forced to sell it. Beset with problems, the Phillies had their first 100-loss season in 1904. It would be years before the club recovered financially and in the won-lost column.

HAVERFORD PIONEERS SOCCER

Among the many firsts in Philadelphia sports, one that had an especially lasting impact took place at Haverford College in 1901. That year, Haverford fielded the nation's first intercollegiate soccer team.

Soccer was by then a popular sport in other parts of the world, but it had generated little interest in the United States. That began to change, however, when a Haverford student named Richard Gummere proposed the sport as a genteel alternative to the more violent sport of rugby.

Gummere, who had been an avid soccer player in his native England, not only got the ball rolling, so to speak, but he also became the team's first captain. Within a few years, he would see Haverford play in the first intercollegiate game, launching a program that eventually made the Fords the winningest college team in the United States.

Soccer at Haverford appealed to the college's cricket players, who saw it as a way to keep in shape during the off-season. It also became popular with the student body, many of whose members had played the game at their Quaker prep schools.

After organizing a team and practicing for several months, Haverford embarked on a six-game schedule during the winter of 1902. The Fords' first game was played on January 4, 1902, against Germantown Cricket Club, and resulted in the first soccer game ever played by a U.S. college as well as a Haverford victory.

Haverford College's 1905 soccer team played in the sport's first intercollegiate game.

Haverford won three of its other five games, all against cricket club teams. Then, as in the next two years, Haverford officials refused to award varsity letters to the players because the team had not played against other colleges.

Haverford's first intercollegiate match, and the first intercollegiate game held in the United States, took place, April 1, 1905, when it met a team from Harvard, where Gummere had become a graduate student. Gummere set up two games with his alma mater, and Haverford won them both by 1–0 scores, defeating Harvard teams made up largely of former Haverford students.

Shortly thereafter, Haverford agreed to join Harvard in the first college soccer league. Penn, Princeton, Yale, Columbia, and Cornell also entered the league, which played games in winter and early spring. Haverford won the first league championship in 1905–06, then won it again in 1906–07, 1907–08, and 1910–11. For their efforts, the Fords were declared national champions.

The Main Line college won national championships again in 1915, one year after the season was switched to autumn, and in 1917 and 1926. That was Haverford's last national title, as greater numbers of colleges across the country began fielding teams. Haverford continued to field formidable teams. Between 1949 and 1970, under noted coach and former professional star Jimmy Mills, the Fords compiled a record of 122–90–21. Mills, coach of the 1956 U.S. Olympic team, had only three losing seasons.

Now, having won more than 700 games since it started fielding teams, Haverford has collected more soccer victories than any other college in the United States.

LACROSSE POWERHOUSE AT SWARTHMORE

Long after Native Americans invented the sport of lacrosse, the game finally arrived on college campuses. One of the first schools to embrace it was Swarthmore College.

Swarthmore embraced the sport so thoroughly, in fact, that in the opening decade of the 20th century, the Delaware County college became the first local lacrosse powerhouse, winning three national championships. While compiling a 43–9 record in the first six years of the new century, the Garnet had the best team in the country in 1901 and again in 1904 and 1905.

Swarthmore's finest team was easily the 1904 edition, which won 10 of 11 games, including a season-ending 4–2 triumph over the University of Toronto, the Canadian national champions. The Garnet had its only undefeated season of the decade in 1901 when it went 8–0. Swarthmore logged in at 7–1 in 1905.

The 1904 season was especially noteworthy, not only because of the victory over Toronto but also because Swarthmore clinched the national title with a resounding 8–2 victory over Johns Hopkins, the premier lacrosse team in that era as well as the entire century. With Phil Lamb, Henry Price, Percy Hoopes, and Bill Linton leading the offense and Harold Mowery in goal, Swarthmore outscored its opponents, 85–28.

Guided by first-year coach Bert Davis, a Canadian, and captain Archer Turner, Swarthmore opened the 1904 season with a 4–0 victory over Penn. That was followed by an 11–3 rout of Cornell and an 8–2 decision over Harvard. Swarthmore then went on to beat Columbia, Lehigh, Stevens Institute, Hobart, Hopkins, and Virginia (15–4), losing only to Crescent Athletic Club, a team made up mostly of former college players, 11–4.

With much the same team as it had in 1904—the only big difference being Pierre Seaman in goal—Swarthmore rolled to another national title in 1905, this time outscoring opposing teams, 67–28. The season began with a 9–0 shutout of Cornell, then continued with wins over Harvard, Penn, Mt. Washington (Baltimore) Club, Stevens, and Lehigh. In their next-to-last game of the season, the Garnet handed

The powerful Swarthmore College lacrosse team won the national championship in 1904, one of the squad's three national titles during the first decade.

Hopkins a stunning 16–4 thrashing. Swarthmore lost its only game in the season finale when it fell to Toronto, 7–4.

Although not as glittering as the two later winners, Swarthmore's 1901 team, coached by C. S. Powell and captained by Edward Williams, registered four shutouts while allowing just eight points all season. With goalie Ed Downing proving to be nearly impenetrable, Swarthmore's victories included a 5–0 win over Penn and a 3–0 victory over Columbia, plus wins over a Swarthmore alumni team, CCNY, Lehigh, Penn again, and Crescent. The season ended with Hopkins falling, 4–2.

Swarthmore had another winning season in 1906 (7–4), but in the final three years of the decade its best mark was 4–4 in 1908. The Philadelphia area's first dominant lacrosse team finished the decade with a 60–25–1 record.

GIANTS ARE THE CLASS OF BLACK BASEBALL

Black baseball teams started forming as soon as the Civil War ended. One of the first places where such teams existed was in Philadelphia.

Philadelphia's first black teams took the field in the late 1860s. Almost immediately the city became a hotbed of black baseball with the formation of a number of prominent amateur teams, which competed against each other as well as against white teams.

Eventually, black professional teams began to emerge around the country, and in 1902, Philadelphia got its first one. It was called the Philadelphia Giants, and its principal owner was Walter (Slick) Schlichter, a white man who doubled as sports editor of the *Philadelphia Item.*

Schlichter, who was well-connected in the black community, hired as his first manager (and shortstop) Sol White, one of the premier early black pro players, who was in the twilight of a marvelous career. White and Schlichter carefully put together a team that would win two "Colored Championships" in the first decade of the 20th century.

Although there was not yet a formal league, in 1902, the Philadelphia Giants met the Cuban X-Giants, a team from New York, in what was billed as the eastern half of the World's Colored Championship. Playing an eight-game series at various fields in Philadelphia, with huge crowds of black fans in attendance, the local team lost five games, including four to Andrew (Rube) Foster, a fast-rising young pitcher with tremendous talent.

Foster was lured to Philadelphia the following season in a move that proved highly worthwhile to the local team. Again, Philadelphia faced the X-Giants, this time in a three-game championship series in Atlantic City in September 1903. Bolstered by the likes of Grant (Home Run) Johnson and Charlie Grant—a light-skinned second baseman who John McGraw had once tried to sign for his New York Giants, passing him off as a Native American—the Philadelphia club won two out of three games. Foster was again the hero, getting out of a sickbed and striking out 18 to win the first game, 8–4, and hurling a two-hitter to gain victory in the third and deciding game, 4–2. Foster also led his team in hitting in the series with a .400 average.

Between 1903 and 1906, playing most of their home games at the Athletics' Columbia Park, the Giants claimed an overall record of 426–149. They beat the X-Giants again in 1904 in an unofficial championship series. In 1905 their record was said to be 134–21–3. The Giants won their next championship in 1906 in the initial season of the first formal black baseball league—the International League. Although the Giants were not originally invited to join the circuit because they were too good, they entered the league in July to help it out as it teetered on the edge of financial collapse. Foster, who claimed to have won 51 of 55 games the previous season, was getting paid the princely sum of $400 a month, and had become possessor of both a grossly inflated ego and body. Dan McClellan, who in his rookie season a year earlier had pitched the first recorded perfect game in black baseball while playing with the X-Giants, had a banner season, as did Johnson. After beating the X-Giants in 10 of 15 games during the season, Philadelphia met the Cubans again in a one-game battle for the league title. Playing at the Phillies Philadelphia Park with 10,000 fans in attendance, the Giants won easily to nail down the championship.

In 1907, Foster moved to Chicago, where he eventually became owner of the American Giants and then president and most powerful man in the league. Philadelphia, meanwhile, picked up a new star in shortstop John Henry (Pop) Lloyd, who would become one of the towering figures in early black baseball. But the Philadelphia team would win no more championships. The Giants continued to field teams in what had become the Negro National League through the 1912 season, but player raids by Foster and the departure of frustrated manager White had taken a heavy toll. Philadelphia dropped out of the league, although the team continued to play as an independent until 1917.

JACK O'BRIEN, PHILADELPHIA'S FIRST BOXING CHAMP

In the long line of great Philadelphia boxers, the first one in the 20th century was a colorful battler who fought under the name of Jack O'Brien. He never weighed more than 165 pounds, but he fought mostly as a heavyweight and light-heavyweight, while going up against some of the foremost pugilists of the era.

O'Brien, whose real name was James Francis Hagen, was not only a skillful boxer. He was also a showman and a shrewd self-promoter. He reigned as light-heavyweight champion from 1905 to 1912 and eventually gained a place in the Boxing Hall of Fame.

During a lengthy career, which began in 1896 with O'Brien fighting as an 18-year-old welterweight, the Philadelphia native rose through the ranks, moving as he matured to the middleweight division, then finally to the heaviest classes. He established his credentials in the fight game in 1901 when he sailed to England, fought 19 times, and won all 19, including 15 by knockouts. After sending press releases back to the United States extolling his prowess, O'Brien returned to a hero's welcome in

Philadelphia, where the mayor and a crowd of 10,000 greeted him at the dock. O'Brien then hit the lecture circuit with prominent Philadelphian, Major Anthony J. Drexel, who urged young fans to emulate the boxer's "muscular Christianity."

O'Brien's career record varies, depending on the source, but according to the *The Boxing Register*, the official record book of the International Boxing Hall of Fame, he fought 179 times with 100 wins, six losses, 16 draws, and 57 no decisions.

Unquestionably, O'Brien's finest hour came on December 20, 1905, when he met world light-heavyweightweight champion Bob Fitzsimmons in a bout in San Francisco. The 44-year-old Fitzsimmons also claimed the heavyweight crown because of the retirement of then-champ James J. Jeffries.

O'Brien had met Fitzsimmons once before in a nontitle fight. At the time, Fitzsimmons was also the middleweight champion. The two fought to a six-round no decision on July 23, 1904, at Philadelphia Park.

The 1905 battle raged for 12 rounds. Finally in the 13th, Fitzsimmons collapsed of a combination of exhaustion and O'Brien's relentless punches. The Philadelphia native was declared light-heavyweight champion of the world. Some also recognized him as heavyweight champion. Curiously, O'Brien never defended his light-heavyweight title, retiring with the crown intact in 1912. He did, however, fight numerous times for the heavyweight crown.

On November 28, 1906, having completed a vaudeville tour to capitalize on his

Jack O'Brien won the light-heavyweight boxing championship in 1905.

fame, O'Brien met Tommy Burns, the more widely recognized heavyweight champ, in a bout in Los Angeles. The match was declared a draw after 20 rounds. In a rematch May 8, 1907, Burns won a 20-round decision.

O'Brien had many other memorable fights. Twice in 1909 he fought middleweight champion Stanley Ketchel, losing once in New York and once in Philadelphia. In between Ketchel bouts, O'Brien met heavyweight champ Jack Johnson in a title fight in Philadelphia, fighting to a six-round draw.

After his retirement, O'Brien stayed close to boxing, running a gym in New York and often attending major bouts. He also gave violin concerts to appreciative audiences.

PENN'S NEARLY UNBEATABLE GRIDDERS

During its 125 years of football, Penn has enjoyed several periods when its teams were considered to be among the best in the nation. Few times, though, could match the Quakers' success in the first decade of the 20th century.

In the first 10 years of the new century, Penn had an amazing record of 100 wins, 17 losses and five ties. Nine of those losses came during the 1901 and 1902 seasons. In the first decade Penn had three undefeated seasons. Three other times the Quakers lost just one game. In 1904 and 1905, Penn had a combined record of 24–0–1. In those 25 games the Quakers allowed just 37 points.

Coached then by Dr. Carl Williams, an eye doctor and Penn captain in 1895 who led the Quakers to a 60–14–4 record during his six seasons at the helm (1902–07), Penn achieved unquestionably its finest season in 1904. That year, the Quakers posted a 12–0 record, 11 of the wins being shutouts. Penn did not allow an enemy touchdown the entire season while outscoring its opponents, 222–4.

The Quakers were led by three All-Americans—quarterback Vince Stevenson, guard Frank Pierarski, and running back Andrew Smith. Bob Torrey was the captain.

After beating Penn State, 6–0, in their opening game, the Quakers were scored on the only time all season when Swarthmore managed a field goal (which counted four points then) in a 6–4 Penn victory. Penn then reeled off shutout wins over Virginia, Franklin and Marshall, Lehigh, Gettysburg, Brown, Columbia, Harvard, Lafayette, Carlisle, and Cornell, the biggest margins of victory being 34–0 thrashings of F and M and Cornell. At the end of the season, Penn was declared co-national champion with Michigan and Minnesota.

The Quakers shared the national title again in 1905, this time with Harvard and Chicago. Penn again won 12 games, including a 42–0 victory over Villanova and a

Wild Bill Hollenbach was one of Penn's earliest football standouts.

39–0 rout of Ursinus, but had to settle for a 6–6 tie with Lafayette. Penn, led by All-Americans Torrey at center and Otis Lamson at tackle, outscored opponents, 259–33, while registering seven shutouts.

After going 11-1 in Williams' last year in 1907, Penn had another big season in 1908 under its 1903 captain, Sol Metzger. Wild Bill Hollenbach, an All-American selection in 1906 and one of the great players in Penn history, was the team's big gun and captain. A future National Football Hall of Fame inductee (1951), Hollenbach was a fullback on the 1908 All-American team, leading Penn to an 11–0–1 record. Penn's first five games were shutout victories. While totaling seven shutouts overall, the Quakers' biggest win was a 29–0 decision over Michigan at Ann Arbor. The only blemish on an otherwise spotless record was a 6–6 tie with Carlisle.

Penn, which had started the century going 12–1 under legendary coach George Woodruff, finished the decade with a 7–1–2 mark for Andrew Smith, the fourth coach of the decade. That would close out one of the greatest eras in Penn football.

THE CITY'S FIRST WORLD SERIES

In their fifth season of existence, the Athletics brought Philadelphia its first World Series. It was at that point the biggest sporting event the city had experienced.

The Phillies had been in town for 23 seasons, but had never won a pennant. It was a different story with the A's. They captured the flag and made it to the Series in 1905 in what would turn out to be the first of eight meetings with the National League.

The Athletics had won the American League pennant in 1902 in just their second year of operation, despite a court order that stripped them of most of the players who had been pirated away from the Phillies. But with Ralph (Socks) Seybold, who played the outfield wearing a first baseman's glove, claiming the home run title with 16, and Rube Waddell winning 24 games and Eddie Plank 20, the A's had finished five games ahead of the St. Louis Browns to capture the flag. Because of strained relations between the two leagues, however, there was no World Series that year. After the regular season ended, the Athletics had to be content with a huge parade down Broad Street with open carriages transporting the players and thousands of cheering fans lining the sidewalks.

Connie Mack's club finished second in 1903 and fifth in 1904. By 1905, Mack had done some remodeling with his roster, and with a fearsome pitching staff and a strong offense, the Athletics won 92 games while losing only 56. The second-place Chicago White Stockings also won 92 games, but playing in four more games than the A's, lost 60 to finish two games out of first place.

The Athletics' stellar mound crew featured future Hall of Famers Waddell (26–11), Plank (25–12), and Charles (Chief) Bender (16–10), a part Chippewa Indian, plus Andy Coakley (20–7). The staff gave up 2.19 earned runs per game while leading the league with 895 strikeouts and 20 shutouts.

The A's batting attack was anchored by first baseman Harry Davis, who led the league with 83 RBI, 92 runs scored, and eight home runs while hitting .283. The veteran Davis was in the midst of a streak in which he would top the circuit in homers four straight years, giving the A's six American League home run leaders in their first seven years.

In the World Series, the first one officially recognized by the National League, the Athletics were pitted against the mighty New York Giants of John McGraw. Winners of their second straight pennant, the Giants, who had refused to play in the Series the year before, had cruised to the 1905 flag with a staggering 105–48 record, finishing nine games ahead of the Pittsburgh Pirates. The Giants' strength rested with their pitching staff, a mighty coalition, led by the brilliant Christy Mathewson, owner of a 31–8 record that year, and including Red Ames (22–8) and Iron Man Joe McGinnity (21–15).

The Series was one of the most memorable ever played. McGraw outfitted his team in ominous black uniforms, and Mathewson blanked the A's on four hits in the opener at Columbia Park, winning, 3–0, over Plank. Bender came back with a four-hit shutout to best McGinnity in Game Two as the A's won, 3–0, in New York. After a one-day rain delay, the teams returned to Philadelphia, and Mathewson won again, 9–0, with another four-hitter as Coakley took the loss, although he allowed just two earned runs. McGinnity hurled a four-hitter to beat Plank, 1–0, the next day back at the Polo Grounds. Then the Giants clinched the Series in New York as Mathewson fired a six-hitter to beat Bender, 2–0.

Five games, five shutouts. Three of them were by Mathewson, who allowed just 14 hits, struck out 18, and walked only one in a masterful 27 innings of work. It was and remains to this day the greatest individual World Series pitching performance.

SHIBE PARK OPENS

Of all the dates in the first decade of the 20th century, perhaps no single date is more significant than April 12, 1909. That's the day the grand opening was held for what would become Philadelphia's most storied sports building.

No Philadelphia sports venue, whether a ballpark, an arena, a stadium, or a gymnasium, evoked more passion or held more major events than Shibe Park. For 62 years, it was the most significant athletic building in the city.

Shibe Park was the home of the Athletics for 46 years, the Phillies for 32½ years, and the Eagles for 17 years. It was the site of eight World Series, two All-Star Games, the first American League night game, an NFL championship game, and thousands of other sporting as well as nonsporting events.

Located at 21st Street and Lehigh Avenue, the stadium was built out of necessity. The Athletics originally played at Columbia Park, but as the team became increasingly successful, the 9,500-seat stadium was simply not big enough to accommodate all the A's fans. Team owners Ben Shibe and Connie Mack decided to build a bigger ballpark.

They settled on a 250,120-square-foot lot across the street from the rundown and soon-to-be-vacated Philadelphia Hospital for Contagious Diseases in a fairly rural part of Philadelphia. Seven parcels of land were purchased, a bond issue was floated, and eventually a ground-breaking ceremony was held April 13, 1908.

The park was built at a cost of $315,248.69. Using 500 tons of steel, it was the first steel and concrete stadium in the nation. Accessible by trolley car, it had a seating capacity of 23,000, which included 10,000 seats in a pavilion built in French Renaissance motif that ran between first and third bases. An additional 13,000 seats were

Shibe Park had a much different look when it opened in 1909.

set in uncovered bleachers that extended to the left and right field corners. There was also a standing-room area behind the seats for another 10,000. A special feature was the dome tower at the main entrance. The park also included a 12-foot- high wall that ran from the right field corner to dead center field.

The first of a series of 11 new baseball stadiums built in the next five years, Shibe Park officially opened with a lavish ceremony. Bands played and Mayor John Reyburn threw out the first ball as a huge assortment of city officials, celebrities, and baseball dignitaries watched. A crowd of 30,162—some of whom had arrived in the wee hours of the morning to stand in line—paid to get in. Another 5,000 attended on free passes.

The game was almost anticlimactic. Eddie Plank scattered six hits as the Athletics defeated the Boston Red Sox, 8–1. Right fielder Danny Murphy got four hits for the A's, while third baseman Simon Nicholls slugged three and scored four runs. The day, however, was marred by tragedy when A's catcher Maurice (Doc) Powers, a practicing physician, having eaten a cheese sandwich before the game, was stricken after the food failed to digest. Rushed to the hospital after playing the whole game, he later died of intestinal complications.

In its first year, Shibe Park drew 674,915. Over the years, the park would undergo many changes, including increasing the seating capacity to 33,500, adding 22 feet to the existing right field wall, taking in the Phillies, and having its name switched to Connie Mack Stadium. The last game at the park would be held in 1970. Later, it was partially destroyed by fire and eventually torn down.

While it existed, though, the park was Philadelphia's most fabled sports building.

ELSEWHERE AROUND THE CITY

As the first decade of the 20th century progressed, much of the focus of Philadelphia sports centered on the city's two major league baseball teams. With teams in both the National and American Leagues, the city was in an enviable position. There was almost always a game going on during the season. And there was almost always something to talk about.

Other sports, however, sometimes entered the picture. During the decade, there were many important stories, including those that follow.

In 1900, for instance, a relatively unknown woman golfer captured a share of the spotlight. Frances (Pansy) Griscom had become the first Philadelphia woman to

Frances Griscom was the first Philadelpia woman to win a national golf championship.

compete in a national championship when she qualified for a spot in the U.S. Women's Amateur Championship in 1897 just a few months after she bought her first set of clubs. Believed to be the first woman to own and operate a car in Philadelphia and later an ambulance driver in France during World War I, Griscom reached the semifinals both that year and the next before losing. She also played in the event in 1899.

In 1900 the Merion player again played in the tournament, and this time she progressed to the final at Shinnecock Hills, Long Island, after winning her semifinal match on the first hole of sudden death. In the final against Margaret Curtis, Griscom captured an impressive 6 and 5 victory to win the championship.

It was a big year in 1900 for Philadelphians, particularly Penn and Vesper Boat Club athletes, in the second modern Olympics games, held in Paris. Penn's Alvin Kraenzlein, a Milwaukee native, won gold medals in the 200-meter and 110-meter high hurdles, the 60-meter dash, and the broad jump, thus becoming the first male athlete in Olympic history to win four firsts in a single Olympics. Penn's Irvin Baxter won golds in the high jump and pole vault, Walter Tewksbury was first in the 200-meter low hurdles, and George Orton led the pack in the 2,500-meter steeplechase, setting a world record in the process. Orton also won a bronze medal in the 400-meter low hurdles.

Meanwhile, out on the Seine River, Vesper rowed to a gold medal in the eight-man crew with coxswain with a team comprised of Louis Abell, William Carr, Harry Debaeche, John Exley, John Geiger, Edward Hedley, James Juvenal, Liscoe Lockwood, and Edward Marsh. Vesper, one of the major boathouses in the country for much of the 20th century and winner of 93 national championships and 296 Schuylkill Navy races, would win another gold in the same event in the 1904 Olympics in St. Louis. Abell and Exley were the only returning oarsmen. The rest of the crew included Charles Armstrong, Frederick Cwiklinski, Joseph Dempsey, James Flannigan, Michael Gleason, Harry Lott, and Frank Schell.

In 1901, an Englishwoman named Constance (CMK) Applebee introduced the sport of field hockey in the United States while studying at Harvard College. Soon, she taught the sport to women at other U.S. colleges. Applebee joined the faculty at Bryn Mawr College in 1904, serving as field hockey coach and director of outdoor sports until 1929. In the 1920s she also started the Philadelphia and U.S. Field Hockey Associations, and launched the sport's first camp, held in the Poconos. Applebee lived until 1980 when she died at the age of 107.

The Army-Navy football game was held at Franklin Field in Philadelphia for the third time in 1901, and the game that year had a special guest. Theodore Roosevelt, who had recently been sworn in as President after the assassination of William McKinley, became the first Chief Executive to attend an Army-Navy game. The

Penn student Alvin Kraenzlein was the first athlete to win four Olympic gold medals.

Vesper Boat Club won its second straight Olympic gold medal in 1904 with an eight-man crew (shown rowing on the Schuykill River in front of the Philadelphia Waterworks) that included (from left) coxwain Louis Abell, stroke John Exley, Joseph Dempsey, Harry Lott, Charles Armstrong, James Flannigan, Frank Schell, Michael Gleason, and Frederick Cwiklinski.

Constance Applebee was a pioneer in U.S. field hockey and a coach at Bryn Mawr College.

former Vice President watched intently as Army quarterback Charles Daly kicked a field goal and ran back the second-half kickoff 95 yards for a touchdown to lead the Cadets to an 11–5 victory.

Penn played its first intercollegiate basketball schedule in 1902, opening with a 21–15 victory over Muhlenberg. In football that year, Connie Mack formed and coached what passed for a professional team called the Philadelphia Athletics. It lasted just one year. Ursinus had its only undefeated football team in the college's history when coach E. E. Kelley's squad posted a 9–0 record, including a season-opening 63–0 win over Muhlenberg and five other shutouts.

In 1903, Bucknell defeated Philadelphia College of Pharmacy in a basketball game, 159–5, and the Phillies and Athletics put aside their acrimonious relations to engage in their first City Series game. The teams would meet almost every year through 1954. Former Phillies great Ed Delahanty, just one year after leading the American League in batting with a .376 average for the Washington Nationals, was removed from a train while apparently drunk, and either was pushed, fell, or jumped off a bridge on the Canadian–United States border. His body was found several days later after it had washed over Niagara Falls.

En route to a berth in the Hall of Fame, eccentric A's pitcher Rube Waddell set a strikeout record in 1904 by fanning 349 batters. Waddell was famous for his offbeat antics. Often, he sent his outfielders to the dugout while he struck out the side in the ninth inning of a game. He loved to chase fire trucks, sometimes even leaving the ballpark in the middle of a game to follow them. A heavy drinker and womanizer, Waddell died of pneumonia in 1914 at the age of 37. His strikeout mark would stand for 42 years.

Merion Cricket Club played host to the U.S. Women's Amateur golf championship in 1904 with Georgianna Bishop of Bridgeport, Connecticut, winning. The tournament was held again in 1909 at Merion. Dorothy Campbell of Scotland won, defeating the host club's Norma Barlow. A native of Ireland who came to Philadelphia in 1898 with her husband and three children, Barlow became one of the top woman golfers in the area, winning nine Philadelphia Women's Championships and five Eastern Women's Golf Association titles.

Another top amateur golfer in the area was Harold McFarland. Playing out of Huntingdon Valley, he was a four-time Philadelpia Amateur champion and won numerous other local and state tourneys. Even more significant, McFarland was the first local player to regularly break 80 in competition.

A new organization entered the local scene in 1904. It was called the Philadelphia Sports Writers' Association, and nearly 100 years later, it was still going strong. Not only would it be led over the years by some of the most illustrious names in the business, but its annual banquet honoring local and sometimes national sports figures would become one of the top events of its kind in the country.

In 1905 a future member and president of that organization, Robert (Tiny) Maxwell, was in his second year as a guard on the Swarthmore College football team, having transferred from the University of Chicago. During the season, while Maxwell was earning a spot on the All-American team, a newspaper ran a picture of him battered and bloody after a game against Penn. Somehow, the photo came to the attention of President Roosevelt, who was shocked and angered by the violent image the picture portrayed and concerned about the uncommonly large number of deaths that had occurred that year on the gridiron. Roosevelt said that if such rough play continued, he would abolish the game. That winter the football rules committee, thus prodded to save its sport, instituted several major changes in the rules of the game, including ones that reduced the amount of violence and the legalization of the forward pass.

The massive, 250-pound Maxwell became one of the towering figures among early sportswriters in the city, working for the *Public Ledger,* then one of seven daily

After winning All-American honors in football at Swarthmore College, Robert (Tiny) Maxwell became a prominent Philadelphia sportswriter.

newspapers in Philadelphia, He also formed what later became known as the Maxwell Club. With its membership consisting of avid football fans and former players, it grew into a thriving organization that annually presents an award to the top college football player of the year.

Another prominent athlete with ties to Swarthmore was tennis player William Clothier. A native of Sharon Hill and son of the cofounder of Strawbridge and Clothier department store, Clothier had studied at Swarthmore before going on to Harvard, where he won both the singles and doubles intercollegiate titles in 1902. In 1906 he made his mark on the national scene by winning the U.S. Lawn Tennis championship. Clothier reached the finals of the national tournament three other times during his career. He competed at Wimbledon once, and in 1905 and 1909 was a member of his country's Davis Cup team. Clothier was ranked in the top 10 nationally 11 times between 1901 and 1914, including first in 1906, second in 1904 and 1909, and third in 1903 and 1913.

While Philadelphian J. Barton King, regarded as the greatest all-around cricket player ever produced in the United States, was setting a national record with 344 runs, two new developments occurred in the Army-Navy game in 1906. That year marked the debut of the forward pass. In what was the first successful pass in the history of the service academy games, Homer Norton unloaded a 25-yard toss to Jonas Ingram to help Navy to a 10–0 victory. The game also featured the debut of what would become the Navy theme song, *Anchors Aweigh.*

Another innovation surfaced in Philadelphia in 1907. Philadelphia played host to its first U.S. Open when Alex Ross shot a 72-hole 302 to win the tournament at Philadelphia Cricket Club. John Miskey of Philadelphia won the first national squash championship, then repeated the following year and again in 1910. In 1908 the city also had its first auto race. Held on a 7.8-mile course in Fairmount Park, the race was won by George Robertson driving a Locomobile. Philadelphia also got another professional baseball league when a team calling itself the Quakers joined the newly formed Union League. Playing home games at a field at 62nd and Walnut Streets, the Quakers lasted until June when the eight-team league folded.

Shoeless Joe Jackson joined the Athletics as an unvarnished rookie out of the woods of South Carolina in 1908. Lost and lonely in the big city, the illiterate farm boy went home early in the season. He returned to Philadelphia the following year, only to experience the same problems. Connie Mack gave up on him and traded him to Cleveland, where team officials took a more insightful approach and helped Jackson put into gear a career that would earn him accolades as one of the finest hitters ever to play baseball.

Also in 1908, Philadelphia native Jack Norworth forever etched his name in baseball lore. Inspired by a poster urging fans to ride New York City's new subway to the Polo Grounds to watch a baseball game, the vaudeville entertainer and songwriter dashed off the lyrics to a song he called *Take Me Out to the Ballgame* as he rode a Manhattan train. Writing on a scrap of paper, it took Norworth just 15 minutes to write the song. Ironically, Norworth had never seen a baseball game, but his song—one of 2,500 he wrote, including *Shine on Harvest Moon*—became one of the three most frequently sung songs in the United States (along with *The Star Spangled Banner* and *Happy Birthday*).

Philadelphian Harry Lewis knocked out Frank Mantell in the third round to win the world welterweight championship in 1908 in New Haven, Connecticut. Lewis, who along with Jack Blackburn was one of Philadelphia's most prominent early-20th century boxers, ended his career many years later with a 110–36–24 record. Also that year, John Baxter Taylor, who had graduated from Central High, Brown Prep, and Penn, became the first black athlete ever to win an Olympic gold medal when he ran on the winning 1,600-meter relay team. Taylor, a veterinary school graduate, died of typhoid fever before the year was over. Penn runner Nathaniel Cartwell was a member of the winning 4 × 400-meter relay team at the Olympic

Games in London. Phillies lefthander Harry Coveleski earned the nickname "Giant Killer" after defeating the New York Giants three times in six days late in the season to knock John McGraw's club out of the pennant race. And Penn, on its way to winning its second Eastern Intercollegiate basketball championship in three years, lost two of its first three games, then won 23 straight. In a special East-West playoff, the Quakers, led by Charles Keinath, Philadelphia's first College Player of the Year, who was called at the time an "electrifying dribbler," lost to the University of Chicago, 21–18. In a rematch, Chicago won again, 16–15, giving it claim to the national championship.

In 1909, St. Joseph's College fielded its first basketball team. The Phillies had a third baseman named Eddie Grant, a Harvard graduate who in 1918 would become the first major league player killed in World War I when he was shot while leading his battalion in battle in the Argonne Forest. And the first Davis Cup match held in Philadelphia took place in 1909 at Germantown Cricket Club with the United States defeating Great Britain, 5–0, in the qualifying round. It was the first of 10 Davis Cup matches held in the Philadelphia area between 1909 and 1939.

Eddie Plank, the 20th Century's First Great Southpaw

Philadelphia baseball teams have been richly endowed with great pitchers in the 20th century. The first one to make a mark on the local scene was hard-throwing Athletics lefthander Eddie Plank, who had the rare distinction in that era of being a professional athlete with a college degree.

Plank was more than the best pitcher of his era. He was the finest athlete in the entire city.

There were, of course, many other excellent athletes in Philadelphia. Boxer Jack O'Brien, tennis player William Clothier, Penn football player Bill Hollenbach, and Phillies outfielder Sherry Magee were among the best. So, too, were Athletics second baseman Eddie Collins, third baseman Frank Baker, and pitcher Rube Waddell, although none of them played the entire decade.

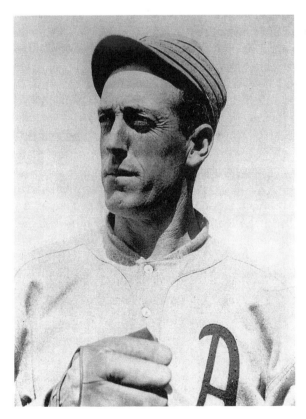

Eddie Plank was a seven-time 20-game winner during a Hall of Fame career with the Athletics.

Plank began with the Athletics in 1901, fresh out of Gettysburg College. A native of Gettysburg, where he lived his entire life, Plank was an immediate success with the A's, posting a 17–13 record in his rookie season.

Over the next six years, he was a 20-game winner five times. The one year he didn't win 20, he was 19–6. Overall, Plank was a 20-game winner seven times with the A's, his best mark being 26–6 in 1912.

During his 14 seasons with the Athletics, Plank had a 285–171 record. His log was 187–120 during the first decade of the 20th century, when he was the top hurler on a club that won two American League pennants.

The 5–11, 170-pound hurler was especially durable, five times during the decade reaching the 300 mark in innings pitched. Four times he pitched in more than 40 games in a season, and five times he numbered more than 30 complete games in one year.

Plank was noted for his pinpoint control. He almost always struck out twice as many batters as he walked. A sidearm thrower, he also excelled at firing shutouts, and currently ranks fifth on the all-time list in that category.

Other players called Plank the team's best all-around athlete. Eddie Collins once said that Plank was a combination of good temperament, savvy, control, and courage.

Plank won only two of seven decisions in World Series play. In his only outings in the first decade, he lost by 3–0 and 1–0 scores to the New York Giants.

In 1915, Plank left the Athletics to join the Federal League. He won 21 games for the St. Louis Terriers that season, then returned to the American League for the final two years of his career to toil with the St. Louis Browns. He concluded his career in 1917 with a 327–193 record and a lifetime 2.34 earned run average. In 4,505⅓ innings, Plank allowed 3,956 hits, struck out 2,246, and walked 1,072.

For many years after his retirement, Plank owned the most wins of any lefthanded pitcher in baseball. His mark was eventually passed by Warren Spahn and Steve Carlton. To this day, Plank still holds the major league record for most complete games (412) by a lefthander, as well as American League marks for wins (306) and shutouts (63) by a southpaw.

Eddie was elected to the Baseball Hall of Fame in 1946, some 20 years after his premature death at the age of 51 in Gettysburg.

CHAPTER 2

Baseball Dominates the City

Never before and never since has baseball played as dominant a role in Philadelphia sports as it did in the second decade of the 20th century. While several other sports—particularly golf and tennis—flourished, baseball at the professional level was the city's unchallenged leader, and it ruled the spotlight with remarkable brilliance.

Baseball was elevated to its lofty pedestal by the performances of the city's two major league teams, the Athletics and the Phillies. Five times during the decade, the World Series visited Philadelphia. Three times, a Philadelphia team walked away as the winner.

The Athletics won American League pennants in 1910, 1911, 1913, and 1914, capturing the World Championship in each year but the last. The Phillies claimed the National League flag in 1915 before finishing second the next two years.

During that glorious period, Philadelphia was blessed not only by the presence of outstanding teams, but also by great players. Future Hall of Famers Eddie Collins, Frank Baker, Eddie Plank, Chief Bender, and Herb Pennock graced the A's roster along with such other stars as Jack Coombs, Joe Bush, Stuffy McInnis, Rube Oldring,

Amos Strunk, Harry Davis, and Danny Murphy. On his way to the Hall of Fame, Grover Cleveland Alexander led a talented Phillies team that included future Hall of Famers Dave Bancroft and Eppa Rixey as well as excellent players such as Gavvy Cravath, Fred Luderus, Dode Paskert, and Erskine Mayer.

With the Athletics playing in the new Shibe Park and the Phillies housed just seven blocks down Lehigh Avenue at the newly renamed Baker Bowl, North Philadelphia was at the center of the nation's baseball stage through much of the decade. Elevating the temperature of the city's baseball climate were several fine professional Negro League teams, first the Philadelphia Giants and later the Hilldale Daisies. Although the Giants faded out of the picture in the early part of the second decade, the Daisies would become one of the most storied franchises in black baseball.

Unfortunately, the decade of the 1910s would end dismally for both Philadelphia major league franchises. After his team lost the 1914 World Series, Athletics part owner and manager Connie Mack unceremoniously broke up his team and, in one year it plummeted to last place, the first time a big league club ever dived from first to last in one year. Down the street, Phillies owner William Baker, fearing his star pitcher would be drafted into World War I, traded Alexander. Without the cornerstone of the franchise, the Phillies would also soon career to the bottom of the standings where both they and the A's would live a dreary existence for many of the ensuing years.

Although professional baseball attracted much of the attention, including the unusual circumstance of Phillies owner Horace Fogel getting banned for life from the game and the damaging invasion of the Federal League, there was no shortage of major occurrences in other sports in Philadelphia in the 1910s. In boxing, a popular young Philadelphian who fought under the name Battling Levinsky captured the world's light-heavyweight title and held it for four years, while a young promoter named Herman Taylor staged his first fight, a practice he would continue for the next 63 years.

Philadelphia continued to be one of the nation's leading tennis hotbeds. That repuation was enhanced during the 1910s with the emergence of Richard Norris Williams II as one of the world's outstanding players. Wallace Ford Johnson was another fine player with national credentials.

Golf had one of its most memorable decades in Philadelphia in the 1910s. In what became one of the most captivating stories of triumph and tragedy in Philadelphia sports, the city produced a two-time U.S. Open champion in West Philadelphia's Johnny McDermott. The area had winners of the first PGA championship in Jim Barnes and of the U.S. Women's Amateur championship in Florence Vanderbeck. Merion East and Pine Valley were opened. Bobby Jones made his national debut at the former. And J. Wood Platt, a young player from Roxborough, first attracted notice to what would become a legendary career.

Penn's football team played in a Rose Bowl game. Swarthmore College had an excellent decade of football. Penn's Lon Jourdet became the first successful basketball coach in the area. Ted Meredith added his name to the growing list of local Olympic heros with two gold medals and two world records. The Army-Navy game moved out of Philadelphia. The first major auto race in the city was held. The Penn Relays continued to grow. And Philadelphia rowers remained among the best in the country.

Late in the decade, three natives of the Philadelphia area began to gain prominence on a national level. By the time their careers ended, oarsman Jack Kelly, Sr., tennis player Bill Tilden, and racehorse Man o' War would be ranked among the finest ever produced in their respective sports.

ATHLETICS BUILD A DYNASTY

Connie Mack relied on friends, scouts, and ex-players to find young ballplayers with whom to stock his teams. For much of the first three decades of the 20th century, that system worked well.

By the beginning of the second decade, Mack's Athletics had already won two American League pennants. Soon, they would win four more in what became major league baseball's first real dynasty of the century. It was all because Mack's large collection of tipsters had fed him a steady stream of good, young players.

As the 1910s got under way, the Athletics had an excellent team in place. The A's last pennant had been in 1905, but there were few remnants of that team left. Instead, Mack had restocked his squad with players such as Eddie Collins, arguably the best second baseman who ever played the game; third baseman Frank (Home Run) Baker, who would lead the league in home runs four straight years from 1911 to 1914 and in RBI in 1912 and 1913; and first baseman Stuffy McInnis, a fine hitter who with Collins, Baker, and shortstop Jack Barry would form what became known as the $100,000 infield.

The A's also featured a pitching staff led by Eddie Plank, Chief Bender, and Jack Coombs. Rube Oldring, and Philadelphia-area natives Danny Murphy, Bris Lord, and Amos Strunk manned a formidable outfield, with sturdy Ira Thomas and later Wally Schang catching.

It was a powerful team that dominated the American League through the first half of the second decade, beginning in 1910 when the Athletics opened the season in Washington with President William Howard Taft becoming the first chief executive to throw out the opening day ball. After starting slowly, the A's caught fire and romped to the flag with a 14½-game lead over the second-place New York Highlanders. Coombs won 31 games and Bender 23, with Collins (.322), Oldring (.308), and Murphy (.300) leading the club in hitting as the A's became the first American League team to win 100 games, winning 102.

Because the National League ended its season one week later than the American League, to keep his team sharp Mack scheduled a five-game series with a team of AL all-stars that included Ty Cobb, Tris Speaker, Walter Johnson, and Ed Walsh. Although the A's lost four of the five games and Oldring suffered a season-ending injury, the plan worked. In the World Series, the Athletics cruised to an easy four-games-to-one victory over the Chicago Cubs as Coombs won three games and Collins hit .429 and Baker .409. Bender beat the Cubs with a three-hitter, 4–1, in the opener, then Coombs, pitching two days apart, won 9–3 and 12–5, the latter coming with the help of Murphy's three-run homer. After Bender dropped a 4–3 verdict in Game Four, the A's came back to clinch victory with a 7–2 decision behind Coombs.

The Athletics went over the 100 mark again in 1911, winning 101 to finish 13½ games ahead of the Detroit Tigers. Coombs won 28, and Plank nailed down 23, while Collins (.365), Baker (.334), Murphy (.329), McInnis (.321), and Lord (.310) all had big years at the plate.

Going against the vaunted New York Giants of John McGraw in the World Series, the A's bowed to old nemesis Christy Mathewson in the first game, 2–1. Baker's two-run, sixth-inning homer gave the Mackmen and Plank a 3–1 victory in Game Two. In the third game, Baker again performed the heroics, clubbing a ninth-inning homer that sent the game into extra innings with the A's finally winning, 3–2, in the 11th as Coombs went the distance. As a result of the homers, Baker was given the nickname "Home Run," a sobriquet that stuck with him the rest of his life.

Bender beat Mathewson, 4–2, in the fourth game. Then, despite Oldring's three-run homer, the Giants came back to win Game Five, 4–3. The sixth and deciding game went to the Athletics as Bender won again, 13–2, the A's turning the game into a rout with a seven-run seventh inning.

The Athletics' juggernaut took a break in 1912, the club finishing second behind New York. But it was business as usual in 1913 as the A's won 96, good for a 6½–game margin over the Washington Senators. With Coombs out the entire season with typhoid fever, Bender (21) and Plank (18) were the big winners. Collins (.345), Baker (.336), and McInnis (.326) provided the heavy stickwork.

That fall, the Athletics won the third straight World Series in which they partici-pated, squashing the Giants in five games. The only New York win came in the sec-ond game when Mathewson topped Plank, 3–0, in 10 innings. Bender won 6–4 in Game One with the help of a Baker homer and 6–5 in Game Four. Joe Bush grabbed an 8–2 verdict in the third game, and the 37-year-old Plank won the clincher with a sparkling two-hitter over Mathewson, 3–1.

The Athletics had one more pennant left in them, and they won it in 1914 when, despite the loss of Murphy to the new Federal League, they wheeled home 8½ games ahead of the Boston Red Sox. While winning 99 games, the A's had seven pitchers with wins in double figures, although none won as many as 20. The leader was Bender with 17, followed by Bob Shawkey and Bush, each with 16. Collins had another marvelous season, hitting .344 and winning the Chambers Award, an equivalent of today's MVP, while Baker (.319) and McInnis (.314) lent their support.

The World Series, though, proved to be a disaster. Facing the Boston Braves, dubbed the Miracle Braves because they had been in last place in the National League on July 21, the Athletics dropped four straight games. Bender and Plank lost at home, 7–1 and 1–0, respectively, the former bowing after Strunk misplayed a fly ball with two outs in the ninth. Then, playing at the Red Sox' Fenway Park because their own park was too small, the Braves took the next two games, 5–4, in 11 innings and 3–1, as catcher Hank Gowdy proved to be the batting star with a .545 average and Dick Rudolph won the clincher with his second complete game of the Series.

The Braves' stunning upset put a decisive end to what had been a spectacular run for the Athletics. The dynasty was over. Mack would soon break up his glorious team, and it would be quite some time before the A's tasted success again.

EDDIE COLLINS, BASEBALL'S GREATEST SECOND BASEMAN

During the best years of the Philadelphia Athletics, the cornerstone of the franchise was a lithe second baseman whose virtuoso performances carried into every aspect of the game. Eddie Collins could hit, run, field, and throw with such magnificent skill that in more than one century of major league baseball, there has never been a better second baseman. Collins was simply the best there ever was.

Elected to the Baseball Hall of Fame in 1939, Collins played in the big leagues for 25 years—a record for second basemen—compiling a career batting average of .333. Spraying hits to all fields, he hit over .340 10 times, and his 3,311 hits rank as the ninth-highest total in major league history. While leading the American League in runs scored three times, he crossed the plate 1,821 times during his career, a figure that ranks 12th on the all-time list

Collins was more than a great hitter, though. He led American League second basemen in fielding nine times. He once stole six bases in a single game and 81 bases in a season, and his career 744 pilfers are the seventh-highest total ever compiled. And when he wasn't beating opponents with his arms or legs, he beat them

Eddie Collins led the Athletics to four pennants and three World Series victories.

with his brain. Collins was considered one of the smartest players ever to take the field.

Extremely aggressive, confident, and even cocky, Collins played for the Athletics from 1906 to 1914 and again from 1927 to 1930. In his first stint with the club, playing as a member of the team's legendary $100,000 infield, he helped the A's win four American League pennants and three World Series. He also played in two other World Series and had a career postseason batting average of .328.

A native of Millerton, New York, Collins was a quarterback and shortstop at Columbia University when spotted by a part-time A's scout named Billy Lush. Collins, then 19 years old, signed with the A's during his junior year. To protect his eligibility at Columbia, he played at the end of the 1906 season with the A's under the name of Eddie Sullivan. The ploy was uncovered, however, and Collins was declared ineligible for his senior year at Columbia, although he remained at school as a nonplaying captain.

Originally a shortstop with the A's, Collins was switched to second base in 1908. He stayed there the rest of his career.

A resident of Lansdowne while he played with the A's, Eddie was in the prime of his career between 1911 and 1914, hitting .365, .348, .345, and .344. At the start of the 1914 campaign he signed a three-year contract calling for an annual salary of $14,000. At the end of the season, he was the recipient of the Chambers Award, the equivalent of today's MVP. But in the start of a stunning destruction of his great team, Connie Mack sold Collins in December to the Chicago White Sox for $50,000.

Collins played 12 years in Chicago, participating on two pennant winners. He was one of the honest members of the 1919 Black Sox, the infamous team that threw the World Series to the Cincinnati Reds. In 1920, Collins batted a career-high .369 while collecting 222 hits. He also managed the Chicago team from 1924 to 1926, after which he became a coach and part-time player with the A's. Collins served as vice president and general manager of the Boston Red Sox from 1932 until his sudden death in 1951. During that tenure, he was credited with signing future Hall of Famers Ted Williams and Bobby Doerr.

JOHNNY MCDERMOTT WINS TWO U.S. OPENS

The story of Johnny McDermott is an amazing tale of triumph and tragedy. It is also one of the most incredible yet least known stories in Philadelphia sports annals.

McDermott grew up playing golf in West Philadelphia, caddied at Aronimink, then located near his home, and by the time he was 16 years old, had become the pro at Merchantville Country Club in New Jersey. Two years later in 1910 he won his first Philadelphia Open. That year, unknown and unheralded, he entered the U.S. Open at Philadelphia Cricket Club, and to the amazement of all he finished the regulation 72 holes with 298, which put him in the first three-way tie for first place in Open history. In an 18-hole playoff with British brothers Alex and Macdonald Smith, McDermott shot 75 to finish second, two strokes behind Alex.

McDermott's strong performance catapulted him into the limelight. He was soon hired as head pro at Atlantic City Country Club. After successfully defending his Philadelphia Open title and gaining more fame by issuing a challenge to all comers, in 1911 he again entered the U.S. Open at Chicago Golf Club. Again, the 130-pound Philadelphian, just 19 years old, landed in a three-way playoff after tying in regulation with Mike Brady and George Simpson, each with a 307. This time,

Johnny McDermott nearly won three straight U. S.
Open golf titles.

though, McDermott emerged victorious, shooting 80 to finish in front of Brady by
two strokes and Simpson by five. The win made McDermott the youngest player and
the first American ever to capture an Open title.

As defending champ, McDermott held center stage in the 1912 Open, played at
the Country Club of Buffalo. He responded with another win. There was no playoff
this time as McDermott, playing the last 16 holes of the tournament in three under
par, carded 294 for 72 holes to win by two strokes over Tom McNamara.

McDermott then finished fifth in the British Open, won his third Philadelphia
Open, and defeated a field that included British greats Harry Vardon and Ted Ray
in a tournament at Shawnee-on-the-Delaware. Moving on to the 1913 U.S. Open at
Brookline Country Club in Massachusetts, McDermott suffered a stunning defeat
when he shot 308 to finish four strokes off the lead and in eighth place.

Johnny recovered to win both the Western Open at Memphis and the North and

South Open at Pinehurst. But those would be his final victories. Distracted by heavy investment losses, suffering the effects of a shipwreck in the English Channel, and showing an alarming lack of the self-confidence that had always been a major part of his demeanor, he was never in contention in the 1914 U.S. Open.

Shortly afterward, McDermott collapsed in his shop at Atlantic City. Early in 1915 he was diagnosed as having had a severe "nervous breakdown." Over the next 16 months he spent time in several institutions for the insane. Finally, in 1916, at the age of 24 and suffering from chronic schizophrenia, he was committed to the State Hospital for the Insane at Norristown.

McDermott spent the rest of his life there. Occasionally a family member took him to a golf banquet or tournament. On Sundays one of his sisters drove him to church and often to nearby Valley Forge Golf Course, where he would play a round by himself. He was visited by Walter Hagen and various other golfing greats, and even briefly attempted to get his game back in shape, playing in a few local tournaments

As the first great American-born champion, Johnny was elected to the Golf Hall of Fame in 1941, just the sixth player to be enshrined. He died in 1971 at the age of 80, a forgotten hero.

MAKE ROOM FOR TWO CLASSIC COURSES

It is generally acknowledged among golf aficionados that two of the nation's finest courses reside in the Philadelphia area. Perhaps somewhat ironically, the two were built within a few years of each other.

The East Course at Merion in Ardmore and Pine Valley near Clementon, New Jersey, have taken vastly different paths to attain their lofty status as premier golf courses. But they are undeniably similar in terms of magnificent holes and storied histories, and to this day, both annually rank among the top 10 courses in the United States.

Merion East opened for play in 1912, less than two years after construction began. Built as a replacement for the too small Merion Cricket Club course in Haverford, it cost $181,000, which included the purchase of real estate and the erection of a clubhouse. Merion originally measured 6,235 yards from the back tees.

The driving force behind the construction of Merion was 31-year-old Hugh Wilson, a Philadelphia amateur golfer and insurance salesman who also designed Cobbs Creek, the city's first municipal golf course. Wilson spent seven months studying some of the great courses of England and Scotland, then returned to design a Merion course that he hoped would be both challenging and beautiful.

Wilson supervised construction of the course, being especially careful to incorporate the contour of the farmland on the 125-acre tract. When he finished the job, Merion had some of the most noteworthy holes in golf. Among many prominent holes is the now-legendary 16th where a shot to the green must pass over an abandoned quarry.

Since it opened, Merion East, followed two years later by the construction of Merion West—built to accommodate the club's rapidly increasing membership—has been the site of many important events. Its first big tournament was the U.S. Amateur championship in 1916, and it has held that event five more times. It has also played host to four U.S. Opens, most recently in 1981, and 16 national United States Golf Association (USGA) championships altogether.

While Merion has been much more in the eye of the public, the opposite is true of Pine Valley. Its owners have made a particular effort to avoid major tournaments, holding only two Walker Cup matches 50 years apart. Yet it, too, ranks as one of the nation's great courses.

Planned and overseen by avid Philadelphia golfer and entrepreneur George Crump, the course was built on a heavily wooded, 195-acre section of the South Jersey Pine Barrens. Some 22,000 trees were felled to make way for the course.

Crump, who sold shares of stock to friends, including Connie Mack, to raise seed money, lived alone on the site, supervising construction, for five years. The first 11 holes were opened in 1914, but the full 18 holes were not open until 1919, one year after Crump died suddenly at the age of 46.

Pine Valley's layout became noted for its rugged terrain and ultradramatic holes. It is an extremely difficult course, as many of the nation's leading players would attest after succumbing to its rigors. Bobby Jones in his first outing on the course shot an 88.

In its early days, a guest could play Pine Valley for greens fees of $2.

MACK DISSOLVES A DYNASTY

Having won four pennants and three World Series in five years and six flags since 1902, the Athletics by the middle of the second decade of the 20th century had established themselves as the premier franchise in all of baseball. There was seemingly no end in sight to the A's winning habits.

But Connie Mack had other ideas. And those ideas would inflict heavy damage on the psyche of Philadelphia baseball fans for years to come.

Mack was understandably disappointed by the Athletics' shocking upset in the 1914 World Series. It didn't help his mood when some fans and members of the press tried to claim that the club had "laid down" during the Series, even though the charges were never substantiated. Nor did it help that the one-year-old Federal League was making attractive overtures to certain A's players.

Given that atmosphere, Mack decided it was time to break up the dynasty. Sell off his top players and start over again, he concluded.

Although any good businessman should have been able to turn a winning team into a perpetual fan favorite and a big moneymaker, Mack tried to justify his logic with an assortment of excuses. The fans were getting bored with a repeated winner and attendance had dropped, he said. Players on winning teams always demanded more money, and so salaries would be going up, he claimed. Better to have a team in contention all season to maintain fan interest, and finish in second place where players wouldn't be as able to make big salary demands, he rationalized. "When your club is fighting for the top, the fans come out to the park," Mack alabied. "But pennant winners soon get to be an old story." Most significantly, he postured, the club simply needed money.

Mack's credentials as an administrator were highly suspect in other ways, too. It was Mack, who had let Christy Mathewson get away when the great pitcher had originally signed a contract with the Athletics, who had given up on the illiterate Southern farm boy Joe Jackson, trading him away when he found big-city life difficult, and who had turned down an offer from the minor league Baltimore Orioles to purchase for some $20,000 a young pitcher whose name was Babe Ruth.

The much-revered Connie may have been a good manager, but off the field he was far from perfect. And so, the dismantling began. The 1914 season was hardly over when he asked waivers on pitchers Eddie Plank, Chief Bender, and Jack Coombs (the first two winding up in the Federal League and Coombs with the Brooklyn Dodgers). Soon afterward, he peddled his great second baseman Eddie Collins to the Chicago White Sox. Then, refusing to meet Frank Baker's offer from the Federal League, he watched in disbelief as the home run champ elected to sit out the entire 1915 season—playing for a semipro team in Upland, Delaware County—before eventually selling him to the New York Yankees.

Connie wasn't through yet. In mid-1915 he sold future Hall of Famer Herb Pennock (from Kennett Square) and Jack Barry to the Boston Red Sox, Bob Shawkey to the Yankees, and Jack Lapp and Danny Murphy, who had returned from the Federal League, to the White Sox. In short order Mack had decimated his great team. And the destruction showed in the standings. The A's became the first major league team to fall from first to last place in one season, finishing the 1915 campaign with a staggering 109 losses and only 43 wins.

The Athletics had now embarked on the worst run of seasons in Philadelphia baseball history. They ended up with the worst record in club history at 36–117 in

1916. It was a season in which young rookie shortstop Whitey Witt made an incredible total of 78 errors and three pitchers—Joe Bush (15–24), Elmer Myers (14–23), and Jack Nabors (1–20)—each lost 20 or more games. The A's finished in last place every year through 1921. Five times in those seven years they lost 100 or more games.

Along the way, Mack's fire sale continued as he unloaded Bush, Amos Strunk, Wally Schang, and Stuffy McInnis after the 1917 season. The A's were left with a team of unknown youngsters, castoffs, and over-the-hill veterans, sorry representatives of a once-proud franchise.

Crushed by the destruction of their team, fans stayed away in droves. Sadly, it would not be the last time that Mack left them holding an empty bag. He would pull the same trick, using the same reasons, after pennant-winning years in 1929, 1930, and 1931. But even that wouldn't be the last time he jilted Philadelphia baseball fans. The ultimate insult would come in 1954 when he sanctioned the move of the A's from Philadelphia, casting 54 years of occasionally glorious baseball aside forever.

PHILLIES WIN THEIR FIRST PENNANT

It took the Phillies 32 seasons to win their first pennant, but when they finally did, the timing couldn't have been better. Nor could the achievement have been much easier.

Philadelphia had just endured the breakup and swift demise of the Athletics. Although each team had its own set of fans, the city craved a winner. The Phillies gave it to them with a stirring performance in which they ran away with the National League pennant.

The Phillies had begun to come together a few years earlier, and by 1913 they were one of the leading teams in the league. A second-place finish that year, coupled with the Athletics' American League pennant, brought Philadelphia as close as it ever came to an all-city World Series, gave impetus to the feeling that the Phils were now ready for a real run for the flag.

It didn't happen in 1914, however, as raids by the Federal League deprived the Phillies of several of their best players. The team finished a disappointing sixth, despite a sparkling 27–15 season by superstar pitcher Grover Cleveland Alexander and the second of six home run titles during the decade by slugging outfielder Gavvy Cravath.

The Phillies changed managers for the 1915 season, elevating coach and former backup catcher Pat Moran to the skipper's chair. "This is not a sixth-place team," Moran insisted. The wily Moran arranged three key trades that jettisoned star outfielder Sherry Magee, third baseman Hans Lobert, and former manager and catcher Red Dooin, bringing in outfielder Possum Whitted, third baseman Milt Stock, pitcher Al Demaree, and second baseman Bert Niehoff. Moran also changed some of the team's routines in spring training and installed young Dave Bancroft at shortstop.

The result was a solid although not overpowering team whose focal point was the great Alexander. Exceeding the 20 mark in wins for the fourth time in five years, the brilliant righthander embarked in 1915 on one of the most spectacular three-year stretches ever fashioned by a big league pitcher with the first of three straight 30-win seasons.

The Phillies won 11 of their first 12 games. Stationed in first place from the start of the season until May 22 and then for 41 of the next 50 days, they took the lead for good on July 13. Along the way, Alexander pitched three one-hitters. Ol' Pete, as he was called, added a fourth one-hitter in the pennant-clinching game September 29 as the Phillies wrapped up the flag with a 5–0 win over the Boston Braves, cruising home first with a 90–62 record and a seven-game lead over the defending world champs.

Alexander finished with a 31–10 record while leading the National League in wins, ERA (1.22), strikeouts (241), innings pitched (376), and complete games (36). He got strong support from Erskine Mayer who won 21 games and Demaree who won 14. Cravath led the league with 24 home runs, 115 RBI, and 28 outfield assists while batting .285. It was the third of his six home run titles, and his 24 homers would stand as a record until Babe Ruth broke it with 29 in 1919. First baseman Fred Luderus hit .315 and fielded a sparkling .993.

The Phillies' first trip to the World Series was greeted with widespread enthusiasm, but the joy would be short-lived. Facing the Red Sox in the second straight Philadelphia-Boston World Series, the Phillies won the opener, 3–1, at Baker Bowl as Alexander went the distance to get the win. In the ninth inning, Babe Ruth made his World Series debut with a pinch-hit appearance.

The second game was attended by President Woodrow Wilson, who became the first chief executive to throw out the first ball in a World Series game. The Phillies, however, bowed, 2–1, with Boston pitcher Rube Foster tossing a three-hitter and driving in the winning run off Mayer in the ninth inning. The loss would be the first of seven straight one-run World Series losses for the Phillies.

Moving to Boston, where in a departure from the previous year's World Series, the games were played at the new Braves Field, the Phillies lost their next two games also by 2–1 scores. Duffy Lewis singled home the winning run in the ninth inning to

Baker Bowl at Broad and Lehigh was the site of the Phillies' first World Series.

beat Alexander in the third game, and he also drove home the winning run to get the decision for Ernie Shore in Game Four.

Back at Baker Bowl for the fifth game, the Phillies got the unhappy news that Alexander was unable to start because of a sore arm. The Phils, however, took a 4–2 lead into the eighth, but Rixey, pitching in relief of Mayer, couldn't hold it as Lewis tied the score with a two-run homer. Then Harry Hooper won it, 5–4, in the ninth for Boston with his second home run of the game. Both Hooper hits were ground-rule homers that bounced into the temporary center field bleachers that the Phillies had installed to increase the size of the crowd.

It was a bitter end to an otherwise marvelous season for the Phillies, whose owner William Baker was loudly criticized for putting the temporary stands across the playing field in order to increase the size of the financial pot. The Phils had hit just .182 as a team in the Series.

Afterward, the club had two more respectable seasons, finishing second each time. But then it would drop into a long and dismal abyss in which the Phillies encountered the worst period in club history. It would be another 35 years before the team returned to the World Series.

DICK WILLIAMS, A TITANIC SURVIVOR

To say that Richard Norris Williams II lived a charmed life would be a massive understatement.

Dick Williams, as he was called, was one of the lucky ones. He survived the sinking of the *Titanic*. He made it through World War I and the Second Battle of the Marne. Ultimately, this son of a wealthy Philadelphia family became one of the world's great tennis players.

Williams's finest years on the tennis court came during the second decade of the 20th century. From 1913 to 1915 he was ranked the second-best player in the country. In 1916, he made it to the top as the number-one-ranked player.

Although his family had retained its U.S. citizenship, they lived for a time in Geneva, Switzerland, where Dick was born. Williams began playing tennis at an

Dick Williams survived the sinking of the *Titanic* to become a world class tennis player.

early age. He progressed so rapidly that by 1911, at the tender age of 20, he won both the Swiss and French indoor championships.

In 1912, Williams and his father were returning to the United States where Dick planned to enroll at Harvard. Like several thousand others, they had made the mistake of booking passage on the maiden voyage of the supposedly unsinkable new ship, the *Titanic*. That decision cast Williams into a role in one of the largest disasters in maritime history after the ship hit an iceberg in the North Atlantic.

Williams's father, Charles, a prominent attorney, was struck and killed by a collapsing funnel. Dick survived the catastrophe by jumping into the frigid ocean and clinging to a waterlogged raft for six hours. When finally rescued, Williams's legs were frozen, and he faced almost certain amputation. He saved his legs, restoring circulation to them by painfully hobbling for hours around the deck of the rescue vessel.

Distraught over the loss of his father, Williams diverted his energy almost entirely to tennis, and in late 1912, he teamed with Mary Browne to win the U.S. mixed doubles championship. Then he won the U.S. clay court championship, as well as three other major tournaments, and in 1913 he was named number-two player in the country.

After enrolling at Harvard, Williams captured the U.S singles title in both 1914 and 1916, each time defeating the defending champion to win. He also won the 1913 and 1915 national intercollegiate and the 1915 U.S. clay court championships. In his senior year at Harvard in 1916, Williams was ranked as the nation's number-one player.

World War I and a stint as an Army officer, during which he won the Legion of Honor and the Croix de Guerre for his heroism in the Second Battle of the Marne, interrupted Williams's tennis career. But in 1919 he returned to the court and quickly picked up where he'd left off.

From 1919 through 1925, Williams, by now a full-time resident of the Philadelphia area where he worked as a statistician for an investment company, ranked third in the nation twice and no lower than sixth every year except one. He became especially proficient in doubles matches. Dick teamed with Chuck Garland to win the doubles title at Wimbledon in 1920; he won two U.S. doubles crowns with Vinnie Richards; he won the mixed doubles gold medal with Hazel Hotchkiss Wightman in the 1924 Olympics; and four times he won Davis Cup challenge round victories, teaming once with Bill Tilden, twice with Richards, and once with Watson Washburn.

Williams served as captain of the U.S. Davis Cup team from 1921 to 1926 and again in 1934. Four of those teams defeated Great Britain for the Cup. He continued to play tournament tennis into the late 1930s, even winning the Pennsylvania state doubles title with Washburn in 1936 at the age of 46.

During World War II, Williams, ever the patriot, donated all his trophies to a scrap metal drive. He was elected to the Tennis Hall of Fame in 1957. For many years, he served as director and librarian at the Historical Society of Pennsylvania.

SOME OTHER IMPORTANT EVENTS

By the start of the second decade of the 20th century, Philadelphia was undergoing some major changes. Numerous high-rise buildings were being constructed, the first section of the subway had been opened, and several important new highways were being built. Most significantly, before the decade ended, the city's population would reach 1.5 million, and there would be in excess of 100,000 motor vehicles traveling city streets.

Unlike the city itself, though, sports in Philadelphia had not undergone many changes from the previous decade. Baseball was still the city's top sport. Golf, tennis, and boxing remained popular with certain segments of the citizenry. And football continued its large following at some of the local colleges.

In terms of teams or whole sports, however, nothing really new had been added to the local sports scene. The only difference was that with all their cars and with ever-growing public transportation, Philadelphians now had easier access to local sporting events.

That was particularly true among the baseball teams. The Phillies, for instance, experienced a huge increase in attendance in the second decade, even passing the 500,000 mark for the first time in 1916. That achievement was doubtless largely attributable to the team's excellent performance on the field, but it helped that fans could get to the ballpark with greater ease.

Of course, attendance figures for both the Phillies and the Athletics dropped as quickly as they had risen, once the teams tumbled to the lower levels of the standings. As the fans so clearly stated, nobody likes a loser.

There were plenty of winners around town, though, particularly in the early part of the decade. Among the most prominent occurrences, in 1910, Athletics pitcher Chief Bender fired the first no-hitter at Shibe Park, beating the Cleveland Naps, 4–0. Phillies outfielder Sherry Magee, one of the most overlooked stars in the club's history, won the National League batting championship with a .331 average. One year later, Magee stamped a huge blemish on an otherwise fine career when he punched umpire Bill Finneran during a game in Philadelphia. Magee was fined $200 and ultimately served a 36-day suspension. Ironically, he later became a National League umpire.

Penn football had several reasons to celebrate in 1910. The Quakers became the first gridiron team ever to wear numbers when a team manager, Edward Bushnell, whitewashed figures to the backs of players' jerseys. Unfortunately, it rained the day of the game, and the numbers were mostly washed away. During the season, Penn gained a major victory when it defeated a Carlisle Indian team led by Jim Thorpe, 17–5. Leroy Mercer was in his first of two years as an All-American fullback for Penn. Later named to the College Football Hall of Fame, he also was a member of the 1908 and 1912 Olympic track teams.

Also in 1910 the Ursinus football team, led by All-American tackle Kerr Thompson, had its fourth straight winning season and was ranked one of the best squads in the nation after running up a 6–1 record and outscoring opponents 157–8, including a 53–0 victory over Temple. Penn hired Douglas Street as its soccer coach. When he retired in 1942, he had compiled a 236–109–42 record with 11 championships.

In 1911, Athletics third baseman Frank Baker won his first of four consecutive American League home run titles. As they had done throughout the early part of the 20th century, A's hitters would continue to hold a prominent spot in home run races as outfielder Tilly Walker tied the Boston Red Sox' Babe Ruth for the AL home run lead with 11 in 1918.

Philadelphia staged its first major auto event in 1911 with a one-time-only 202.5-mile road race in Fairmont Park. Four racing classes, divided according to size of the cars' engines, performed simultaneously over the 8.1-mile course. Averaging 60.8 miles per hour, Erwin Bergdoll won in the biggest class.

A lot happened in Philadelphia in 1912, not all of it good. Phillies president Horace Fogel, a former Philadelphia sports editor and writer, who, backed by the Taft family of Cincinnati, had put together a group to purchase the team in 1910, was barred for life from baseball by other owners after making disparaging remarks about the 1912 National League pennant race, claiming it was fixed.

The Philadelphia Giants bowed out of the Negro National League. In one of the most bizarre big league games ever played, the Athletics defeated a team called the Detroit Tigers, 24–2, at Shibe Park. The Tigers were actually a team made up of Philadelphia-area college and sandlot players hastily put together by Connie Mack after the real Detroit players refused to take the field in protest of the suspension of Ty Cobb. Three days earlier, Cobb had jumped into the stands in New York and pummeled a heckler, who turned out to be a cripple. The Tigers faced a fine of $5,000 per game for not playing. Taking the loss for baseball's first "replacement" team was Aloysius Travers, the manager of his college baseball team, who never pitched either before or after his one big league outing. A future priest, Travers earned $25 for going the distance and allowing 26 hits. Another member of the "Tigers" was an infielder who played under the name of Billy Maharg. Later, he boxed under his real name of Graham (Maharg spelled backward), but he drew more attention as the bagman in the infamous Black Sox scandal in 1919.

Ted Meredith performed spectacularly in the 1912 Olympics.

Nineteen-year-old schoolboy Ted Meredith from Chester Heights in Delaware County made his presence felt in the Oympics when he set a world record and won a gold medal in the 800-meter race at Stockholm, Sweden. A student at Mercersburg Academy who enrolled at Penn following the Olympics, Meredith captured another gold, running a leg of the winning 1,600-meter relay team, which also set a world record. In boxing, two gyms that would become major elements of the local fight scene were opened. Herman Taylor purchased Broadway Athletic Club at 15th and Washington Streets and began promoting fights. Taylor, who would become a member of the Boxing Hall of Fame, promoted fights for the next 63 years, the longest of anyone in the sport's history. Olympic Athletic Club was also opened at Broad and Bainbridge.

Wallace Johnson, a Wayne native and member of Merion Cricket Club, reached the final of the 1912 U.S. singles tennis championship before losing to Californian Maurice McLoughlin. Johnson, who was ranked in the top 10 nationally nine times between 1908 and 1924, including number three in 1909 and 1912, would lose again in the U.S. singles final in 1921 to Bill Tilden. During a distinguished career, Johnson won his only Davis Cup match in 1913 against Germany's Oscar Kreuzer. He won more than 30 local and state tournaments as well as four U.S. mixed doubles titles, three times with Hazel Hotchkiss Wightman and once with Mary K. Browne, before retiring in 1929 to become tennis and squash coach at Penn, a position he held until 1960.

The Phillies had a new owner in 1913. Former New York City police commissioner William F. Baker became the majority stockholder in the franchise and promptly changed the name of the club's ballpark from Philadelphia Park to Baker Bowl. The Phillies finished second that year, but in one game fans in the bleachers flashed mirrors in the eyes of New York Giants batters. When they refused to stop, umpires forfeited the game to the Giants (although the decision was later rescinded). Under the reign of the penny-pinching Baker, the Phillies had just one truly successful season (1915), but otherwise mostly wallowed in the depths of the National League standings during his 17-year stewardship.

The Phillies' status wasn't helped by the formation in 1914 of the Federal League. No team was hit harder by Federal League raids than the Phillies, who lost standout pitcher Tom Seaton, second baseman Otto Knabe, shortstop Mickey Doolan, and pitcher Ad Brennan.

That same year, Oxford University became the first foreign team to compete in the Penn Relays, which for the first time the year before had used a baton in relay races. Local fight promoter Johnny Burns began staging the city's first outdoor boxing matches at the Cambria, a fight club at Frankford and Cambria. And after eight straight and 14 of the last 15 games in Philadelphia, the annual Army-Navy gridiron tussle left the city, returning just once (in 1922) over the next 13 years.

Innovation was often a hallmark of Philadelphia sports, and in 1915, Penn flexed its creative juices again when Quaker basketball coach Lon Jourdet invented what was thought to be the first version of a zone defense. It worked well for the Quakers, who won six Eastern Intercollegiate League championships under Jourdet. In coaching stints from 1914 to 1920 and 1930 to 1943, Jourdet's 227 wins rank as the most of any Penn basketball coach. In the three seasons between 1917 and 1920 his teams posted a combined record of 56–4. Penn was also aided in that era by the play of Ed McNichol, who was named All-American three times between 1915 and 1917. Another Quaker, Howard Berry, became prominent in that era when he won three straight national decathlon championships between 1915 and 1917.

Golf continued to be a major part of the Philadelphia sports scene in the second

Lon Jourdet is the winningest coach in Penn basketball history.

half of the second decade. In 1915, Florence Vanderbeck, playing out of Philadelphia Cricket Club, won the U.S. Women's Amateur championship played in suburban Chicago. The following year, Cricket's Mildred Caverly finished second in the same tournament in suburban Boston when Vanderbeck was unable to defend her title. En route to the Squash Hall of Fame, Philadelphian Stanley Pearson won the first of three straight U.S. squash championships. Later, he again won the title three years in a row between 1921 and 1923, giving him six crowns in seven years (there were no title matches in 1918 and 1919). The only match the Germantown Cricket Club player lost between 1915 and 1923 was the national championship in 1920.

Jim Barnes, a 6-foot, 3-inch Englishman, who served as head pro at Whitemarsh Valley from 1914 to 1916, won the first PGA championship and the first-place prize of $500 when he beat Jack Hutchinson by one stroke at Bronxville, New York. A member of the Golf Hall of Fame, Barnes later won the PGA again in 1919 and twice lost in the final round to Walter Hagen (1921—when he won the U.S. Open—and 1924). And in his national debut in 1916, 14-year-old Bobby Jones entered the first big tournament held at Merion East, the U.S. Amateur championship. Chick Evans of Chicago won the event, becoming the first golfer to win it and the U.S. Open in the same year.

Battling Levinsky was a name that area boxing fans were hearing repeatedly as the second decade progressed. On January 1,1915, the Philadelphia native, whose real name was Barney Lebrowitz, began the New Year in grand style, engaging in three fights in the same day. He fought a 10-round bout in the morning in Brooklyn and a 10-rounder in the afternoon in New York City, then ended his day with a 12-round match at night in Waterbury, Connecticut. The day before Christmas in 1916, Levinsky—apparently partial to holiday bouts—defeated Jack Dillon in 12 rounds

Battling Levinsky won 192 fights during a 24-year boxing career.

in Boston to win the light-heavyweight title. Levinsky had lost to Dillon in 15 rounds in a title bout the previous April.

A veteran of more than 600 fights, although his career record is listed as 192–52–34, Levinsky fought most of the greats during a career that stretched from 1906 to 1929. He was knocked out in the third round in 1918 in a fight with an up-and-coming Jack Dempsey. After holding the title for four years, Levinsky lost his light-heavyweight crown to Georges Carpentier by a fourth-round knockout in 1920. Two years later, he fought and lost in 12 rounds to Gene Tunney in a light-heavy title match.

The 1917 sports season was kicked off in grand style when Penn's football team became the only one from the Philadelphia area ever to play in the Rose Bowl. After posting a 7–2–1 record during the regular season in 1916, beating Penn State and Michigan and losing only to Pittsburgh and Swarthmore, the Quakers met Oregon on New Year's Day. Confidently but perhaps unwisely, Penn coach Bob Folwell had invited Beavers coach Hugo Bezdek, also the manager of the Pittsburgh Pirates baseball team at that time and later head football coach at Penn State, to watch the Quakers practice. Bezdek watched carefully, and a little later Oregon emerged a 14–0 winner.

Swarthmore, meanwhile, was in the midst of an excellent decade of football during which it rang up a 50–23–5 record. Villanova football was unspectacular during the decade, the Wildcats waging three seasons in which they didn't win a single game. Temple was almost as bad, and after a winless 1917 season, the Owls canceled football for the next four years.

Outdoor boxing had become extremely popular in Philadelphia, and in 1917 in the first big fight staged under the stars, Benny Leonard successfully defended his lightweight title by knocking out featherweight champ Johnny Kilbane in the third round at Shibe Park. James C. Kirk became the only Philadelphian in the 20th century to win the U.S. croquet championship. Also in 1917, the Hilldale Giants, an amateur baseball team since its formation in 1910, became a professional team, a status it held with distinction into the 1930s. Formed and operated by local black baseball entrepreneur Ed Bolden, the team, which was later also called the Daisies, played all of the top eastern black teams at Hilldale Park in Yeadon. One of Hilldale's first paid players was a young infielder from Wilmington. His name was William (Judy) Johnson, and he would become one of the outstanding players in Negro League history and a member of the Baseball Hall of Fame.

One who didn't make it to the Hall of Fame but got a top grade for perseverance was Phillies pitcher John (Mule) Watson. In 1918, Watson pitched all 21 innings of a game with the Chicago Cubs but wound up losing, 2–1, while giving up 19 hits. It was the longest game ever hurled by a Phillies pitcher. Another Phillies pitcher also

Judy Johnson began a legendary career with Hilldale in 1918.

earned a mark of distinction one year later. When he joined the team in 1919, Lee Meadows was the first major league player ever to wear eyeglasses while playing.

Local sports also had another oddity that year. In the quarterfinals of the U.S. Amateur golf championship at Oakmont, an unheralded 20-year-old from Roxborough with no credentials except victory in the 1918 Philadelphia Junior championships beat the famous golfer Francis Ouimet in a driving rainstorm on the 38th hole of what has been described as one of the greatest matches in golf history. Although J. Wood (Woody) Platt would suffer a letdown and lose, 7 and 6, the next day in the semifinals to Davy Herron, who went on to beat Bobby Jones in the finals, the match helped to launch a marvelous career. One of the great Philadelphia-born golfers, Platt later won seven Philadelphia Amateur titles, capping a fine career by winning the first U.S. Senior Amateur championship in 1955, four years before his death.

How good was the fabled Platt, whose name to this day is attached to a widely known local scholarship fund for caddies? Once, while playing a round at the treacherous Pine Valley course, he went birdie, eagle, ace, and birdie on the first four holes for an astonishing six under par. Passing the nearby clubhouse at the fifth tee, Platt decided to stop for a quick drink. He never returned to the match, choosing

After an upset victory in the U. S. Amateur championship, Woody Platt became one of Philadelphia's most successful amateur golfers.

to stay in the clubhouse while his partners continued on. Asked why he didn't resume such a potentially awesome round, Platt had a ready reply. "Why go on?" he said. "I couldn't do any better."

Grover Cleveland Alexander, One of a Kind

In 1910, while Grover Cleveland Alexander was pitching for a minor league team at Syracuse, the Phillies made a prudent decision. They decided to check for prospects in the New York State League.

A contact was made with Patsy O'Rourke, a native Philadelphian, part-time Phillies scout, and manager of Albany in the same league. "See anything up there you like?" O'Rourke was asked.

Grover Cleveland Alexander was a 30-game winner in three straight years with the Phillies.

"You bet I do," came the reply. "A fine pitcher. He's one of the greatest pitching prospects I've ever looked at. You better grab him before somebody else does."

With that piece of advice, and despite the fact that they had originally been more interested in another pitcher named George Chalmers, the Phillies bought the contract of the 23-year-old Alexander for $750. It was the best purchase the club ever made.

Alexander, or Ol' Pete as he came to be called, went on to become quite possibly the finest pitcher in Phillies history, as well as one of the best hurlers ever to pull on a uniform. And, in an era in which tennis player Dick Williams, boxer Battling Levinsky, and baseball players Eddie Collins, Frank Baker, and Gavvy Cravath were also top Philadelphia athletes, Alexander ranks as the city's finest player of the second decade.

Alexander won 28 games in his rookie season in 1911, and from then on never stopped winning during his seven years with the Phillies. Twice more he was a 20-game winner (22 and 27) and three times in a row he won 30 (31, 33, 30). Over that period, as one of the few moundsmen able to work consistently well at tiny Baker Bowl, he had an overall record of 190–88.

Between 1911 and 1917 he led the National League in wins, complete games, shutouts, and strikeouts each five times, in innings pitched six times, and in ERA three times, each time under 2.00. Possessor of exceptional control, he tossed four one-hitters in 1915, and the following year set a record that still stands with 16 shutouts.

In 1915, Alexander, after leading the Phillies to a pennant with a 31–10 record and a 1.22 ERA during the regular season, won the first game of the World Series against the Boston Red Sox. The Phillies didn't win another Series game until 1980.

With World War I under way and Americans getting called into military service, Phillies owner William Baker worried that Alexander might get drafted. Deciding he didn't want to risk losing Alex to a war injury, he traded him to the Chicago Cubs for two virtual unknowns in unquestionably the worst swap in Phillies history. After serving less than one unscathed year in the war, Alexander came back to pitch brilliantly for another decade, eventually winding up with 373 wins, tied for the third highest in major league history. Saddled with drinking and health problems, Alex returned to the Phillies to pitch briefly in 1930 before retiring.

The great pitcher was one of the earliest players elected to the Baseball Hall of Fame, voted into the Cooperstown shrine in 1938. Ironically, the pitcher who was named for a U.S. president was the subject of a 1952 movie, *The Winning Team,* with Ronald Reagan playing Alexander.

1920s

Big Names Leave Their Marks

It has often been suggested that sports mirror society. If that contention is true, there was no better example of it than during the riveting decade of the 1920s.

The Roaring '20s . . . it was a time when the unusual—in many cases, the outrageous—took precedence. Flamboyance reigned. Life was often unpredictable, but it was surely seldom dull. Variety, innovation, and a fondness for excess were in style.

Sports in general and Philadelphia sports in particular followed this pattern, too. Sports figures—Babe Ruth, Red Grange, Jack Dempsey, Bobby Jones, Bill Tilden— were almost bigger than life on a national level. And all played major parts in the sports history of Philadelphia, which had an abundance of its own important figures, teams, and events.

None was more important than the city's very own Tilden, a native of Germantown and the greatest tennis player of his or perhaps any other era. But there were lots of other homegrown talents to join him. Man o' War left his paddock in Delaware County to became the greatest racehorse of all time. Jack Kelly, Sr., of East Falls rowed from the Schuylkill River to worldwide fame in crew. Tommy Loughran fought his way from the streets of Philadelphia to the top of the boxing world. Philadelphian Peter DePaolo drove out of the city and into auto racing glory, capped by victory in the Indianapolis 500. And Eddie Gottlieb parlayed a shrewd mind and a hankering for action into a long career as a sports entrepreneur.

Among others from the area, Paul Costello picked up a boatload of Olympic gold medals in rowing, and Betty Becker Pinkston as well as several other localites also collected golds during the decade. Ray Leech of Coatesville also won an Indianapolis 500. Max Marston won the U.S. Amateur championship, and Helen Stetson earned the U.S. Women's Amateur title in golf. Lew Tendler carved a spot in boxing annals for his toughness. Goose Goslin won an American League batting title.

Many others came to Philadelphia to join in the festivities. Chuck Klein, Jimmie Foxx, Mickey Cochrane, Lefty Grove, and Al Simmons arrived in town to launch Hall of Fame careers in baseball. Cy Williams added his name to the city's already large number of home run champs. Glenna Collett Vare took up residence while emerging as the nation's best woman golfer. Benny Bass brought Philadelphia another boxing title. Judy Johnson established his credentials as the best third baseman never to play in the major leagues. And the ubiquitous Damon Runyon spent much of his time traveling in local boxing circles while he penned some of the most brilliant prose ever to appear on a sports page.

But there was more, much more. When the Frankford Yellowjackets joined the National Football League, Philadelphia got its first real professional football team, and soon thereafter, its first professional football championship. The city also landed its first professional ice hockey team as the Arrows took up residence at the Arena. The SPHAS fielded their first basketball team. Villanova launched a men's basketball team, and Temple became the first local college to field a women's basketball team while also resuming football. And the Phillies took part in the first radio broadcast of a baseball game.

The Yellowjackets weren't the only Philadelphia team that won a championship in the 1920s. The Hilldale Daisies, playing in Yeadon, captured three straight eastern Colored League titles. The Philadelphia Football Club became the first of many local teams to win soccer crowns. Penn clinched two national basketball championships. The Athletics finally emerged from the ashes to win another World Series. And Philadelphia's rowing clubs continued to win national championships.

Spectacular events of nationwide significance were also taking place with regularity in the 1920s in Philadelphia, not the least of which was the legendary Jack Dempsey–Gene Tunney fight, one of several title fights held in the city during the decade. Bobby Jones won his first U.S. Amateur championship at Merion. Red Grange played in a memorable game against Penn. At Shibe Park, Babe Ruth hit some of the longest home runs ever seen.

The 1920s had one other major component. There was a proliferation of construction unlike any other in the 20th century. Sesquicentennial Stadium was built. The Palestra was built. The Arena was built. Temple and Villanova Stadiums were built. An upper deck was added to Shibe Park. And a new stadium was built to replace the old one at Franklin Field.

Of course, there was a downside to all the good things that were happening in Philadelphia sports. The Phillies were terrible during the decade. With six last-place and two seventh-place finishes, and playing in dingy Baker Bowl under the unbearably cheap owner William Baker, the team experienced its most dismal period. For a while, the Athletics were pretty dreary, too, buried in the second division until 1925 after Connie Mack had demolished his powerhouse team 10 years earlier.

Mainly, though, Philadelphia in the 1920s enjoyed one of its most prosperous eras in sports. If it hadn't been before, Philadelphia was now one of the nation's leading sports centers. It had the facilities. It had the teams and the athletes. And it had all of the ingredients that made the Roaring '20s such a remarkable period.

The Name Sounds Familiar

When the Penn football team took the field in 1920, its coach was John Heisman. The name may ring a bell. The widely celebrated Heisman Trophy, the preeminent award in college football, is named after him.

Heisman, who had played his final two years as a tackle at Penn after transferring from Brown, was in his first of three seasons as head coach of the Quakers. A career coach, he had previously guided teams at Oberlin, Akron, Auburn, and Georgia Tech, where he won a national championship in 1917. He compiled a 16–10–2 record at Penn before moving on to Rice and then Washington and Jefferson, where he concluded his coaching career with a Rose Bowl trip and an overall 162–64–14 mark.

After retiring as a coach, Heisman became athletic director at the Downtown Athletic Club, a New York City organization that annually presented an award to the top college football player in the East. When Heisman died in 1936, while serving as Downtown AD, the club renamed the award after him and moved to give it to the top player in the nation.

Heisman was just one of many people found in surprising places in Philadelphia sports during the 1920s. In 1920 and until he was traded in 1921, Casey Stengel was the regular right fielder for the Phillies. Much later, he would become baseball's most successful manager, winning 10 pennants and seven World Series with the New York Yankees.

Another Phillies outfielder who we would meet again spent part of 1921 with the team after coming in a trade with the Cincinnati Reds, for whom he played in the infamous 1919 World Series. His name was Earle (Greasy) Neale, and in due time he would return to Philadelphia to lead the Eagles into three straight NFL championship games and to two NFL titles.

A 1920 Penn graduate who had been the Quakers starting quarterback and a four-year letter winner later emerged as the owner of the Eagles. Still later, Bert Bell led the NFL to stability as its highly successful commissioner.

In 1923, Philadelphia Textile hired a new coach for its struggling, four-year-old basketball program. Eddie Gottlieb led the team for two years, then returned for the 1930–31 season. He would be heard from many times later, as a promoter of Negro League games but most significantly as one of the founders of the NBA and original owner of the Warriors.

Villanova received a considerable amount of attention in 1925 when it hired Harry Stuhldreher as head football coach. Stuhldreher, who over the next 11 seasons compiled a 65–25–9 record to rank first in winning percentage (.702) and second in wins among Villanova football coaches, had been a member of Notre Dame's legendary Four Horsemen.

Another coach with a good pedigree came to Drexel in 1927. Hired as athletic director and coach of the basketball team, his name was Walter Halas, brother of the Chicago Bears' George Halas. Walter coached the Dragons through 1934, compiling a 52–78 record.

The Athletics got into the act of hiring familiar names in 1927 when they signed Ty Cobb. One year later, they added another future Hall of Famer, Tris Speaker. Cobb, who tried unsuccessfully to purchase the Phillies in 1929, played two years with the A's, and Speaker performed for one.

BIG RED WAS INVINCIBLE

People who saw Man o' War for the first time were almost always stunned. He was so big. He looked so strong. He had an absolutely magnificent physique.

The huge chestnut colt affectionately called Big Red had a vastly different appearance from the lean, silky thoroughbreds to which the horse racing fraternity was accustomed. He stood higher (16.2 hands), weighed more (1,125 pounds), and strode longer (25 to 28 feet) than normal racehorses. He ran faster, too.

Man o' War won 20 of the 21 races in which he ran. He set five American records

Man o' War (with Clarence Kummer up) came out of the Riddle stable to win 20 of his 21 races.

during his career. He earned more money ($249,465) than any other horse up to that time. Once he won a race by 100 lengths. Another time he carried 138 pounds and still won. Three times he went off at odds of 1–100. He won the Preakness and Belmont in 1920.

Generally considered the greatest racehorse of all time, Man o' War was bought in New York as a yearling for $5,000 by Samuel Riddle, a wealthy Delaware County native who ran a family-owned woolen mill in Lenni. Although the colt's original owner, August Belmont, had told Riddle, "You don't want him," Riddle felt otherwise. "As soon as I saw him, he simply bowled me over," he said.

Riddle brought the horse to his estate in Glen Riddle, just south of Media, and there Man o' War got his early training while eating 12 quarts of oats a day. Soon the horse was on the track. Under the guidance of trainer Louis Feustel, he won his first race by six lengths. His winning streak reached six before it was stopped in the Sanford Stakes at Saratoga. Backing up when the race began, Man o' War finally got going, was blocked in, had to go to the outside, and ultimately lost the race to a horse named Upset by one-half length. It was the only loss in the career of Big Red, who later beat Upset six times.

After finishing 1919 with wins in nine of 10 races, Man o' War won all 11 races in 1920, including the Preakness, where he edged Upset, and the Belmont, which he won by 20 lengths, both times with jockey Clarence Kummer in the saddle. Riddle refused to enter his horse in the Kentucky Derby that year, claiming he didn't believe in racing three-year-olds so early in the season.

Although he was born in Kentucky and died there, Man o' War spent much of his early years in the Philadelphia area. As a colt, he was often seen romping in the paddock at Riddle's stable in Delaware County, where a hospital now stands. Man o' War swept through the rest of the 1920 season virtually unchallenged. In one race, he was ridden by the great jockey Earl Sande in his only trip on Big Red. "That day," Sande said, "I knew I was riding the greatest horse ever bred for running."

According to Riddle, the great horse was pulled up in every race except the one he lost. In his final outing of 1920, Man o' War ran a match race against the 1919 Triple Crown winner, Sir Barton, at Kenilworth Park in Windsor, Ontario. Big Red won the race by seven lengths, earning a total purse of $80,000.

By then Man o' War was spending most of his time at Riddle's stable in Lexington, Kentucky. In late 1920 Riddle brought the horse to Rose Tree Hunt Club near Media for the annual fall race. Some 30,000 people showed up to get a glimpse of the racing giant, but Big Red fell getting out of the truck and hurt his leg. That injury, coupled with the fact that Riddle had been informed that his horse would have to carry more than 138 pounds as a four-year-old, prompted the owner to make an announcement. "Man o' War will never race again," he said. "I am going to retire him to stud. He will be my gift to the American turf."

The great horse went back to Lexington, and in the ensuing years he sired 386 colts and fillies, who won more than 1,200 races with earnings of more than $3 million. Included in the illustrious group were 1937 Triple Crown winner War Admiral; another Kentucky Derby winner, Clyde Van Dusen; and Battleship, the winner of England's 1938 Grand National Steeplechase.

At one point, Riddle was offered $500,000 for Man o' War. When he refused the bid, Riddle was offered a blank check and urged to write in any amount he wanted. Again, the owner declined. "Then you can go to hell," he was told.

Man o' War lived to the ripe old age of 30. When he died in 1947, he lay in state for two days. Since then more than 700,000 horse lovers have visited his grave. Although his life was long, his career had been short. Nevertheless, during his two years on the track, he etched his name in horse racing circles as the greatest thoroughbred of the century.

JACK KELLY ROWS TO GOLD

There is a perfectly logical reason that the road that runs along the east side of the Schuylkill River is called Kelly Drive. For almost as long as anybody can remember, the name Kelly has been synonymous with the sport of rowing, and in Philadelphia, the Schuylkill River is where rowing takes place.

John B. Kelly, Sr.,—Jack to everyone who knew him— was undeniably the foremost rower ever to dip an oar into the Schuylkill. He was the dominant oarsman of his day on a national level, and after his career was over and his son Jack was ably following in his father's wake, he continued to be a major force in the sport for the rest of his life.

Kelly reached the apex of his extraordinary career in the 1920 Olympics at Antwerp, Belgium, when he won the gold medal in single sculls, beating England's Jack Beresford by one second. He then teamed with his cousin Paul Costello to win another gold in doubles competition, crossing the finish line ahead of Italy and France. At the time, Kelly and Costello were rowing for Vesper Boat Club.

Jack Kelly, Sr., won three Olympic gold medals, and with his son Jack, Jr. (left) made the family name the most prominent in local rowing history.

The two followed that performance with a repeat gold medal victory in the 1924 Olympics in Paris. Now rowing for Penn AC after having left Vesper because of a disagreement, the two glided to victory on the Seine River in front of France and Switzerland. Costello, who had won the national single sculls championship in 1919 and 1922, would go on to win the gold again in the 1928 Olympics at Amsterdam, teaming with Charley McIlvaine to beat Switzerland and Austria.

By then Kelly's career as an international competitor had wound down. A native of a tough section of East Falls, Jack had begun rowing in 1908. East Falls at the time was a rowing hotbed, and many of the young oarsmen from that section of the city were members of Vesper on Boathouse Row.

Vesper then, as it would be for many years to come, was the dominant rowing club in Philadelphia. Its eight-man crew had won gold medals in the 1900 and 1904 Olympics and it would win one again in 1964. Along the way, the club won 93 national championships and 296 Schuylkill Navy races.

Kelly, possessor of huge amounts of energy and stamina, became Vesper's shining star. At one point, he won 126 consecutive races. He won the national single sculls championships in both 1919 and 1920 and numerous other championships throughout the country. But there was one race he couldn't win. In 1920, Kelly was denied entry into the prestigious Diamond Sculls race at the Henley Regatta in England. The reason: Kelly worked with his hands, a thinly veiled attempt at saying the East Falls bricklayer was not a gentleman.

Nothing was farther from the truth. Outraged by the insult, Kelly's friends in the Schuylkill Navy raised $2,000 and used the money to buy a gold trophy. It was presented to Kelly as "the world singles champion" after he won the Olympics.

Kelly's son Jack would later avenge the Henley snobbery by winning two Diamond Sculls races.

Ultimately Kelly, Sr., reached the point where he could buy and sell most of the Henley bluebloods. His brick business flourished, and he became one of the wealthiest and most powerful men in Philadelphia

Kelly, whose children also included the Oscar-winning actress Grace—later to become the Princess of Monaco—rejoined Vesper in 1945. For many years, he was the club's principal sponsor.

DAISIES BLOOM IN YEADON

While white professional baseball in Philadelphia offered virtually nothing to get excited about through the early to mid-1920s, the sport didn't come to a complete standstill. There were the Hilldale Daisies.

Few white Philadelphians knew much about them. Even fewer had ever seen them play. The team wasn't covered by the local newspapers, except the *Philadelphia Tribune*. And its players were hardly familiar names. But to the black population of the Philadelphia area, the Hilldale Daisies were the best thing on the local sports docket.

Hilldale, headquartered in Darby and sometimes known as the Giants, won Eastern Colored League championships in 1923, 1924, and 1925. In 1925, Hilldale also won the Colored World Series, beating the Kansas City Monarchs, a team that had beaten it in the same series the year before.

Although they sometimes engaged in exhibition games at Baker Bowl, Shibe Park, or other area fields, the Daisies played most of their regular-season home games at a well-manicured field known as Hilldale Park, opened in 1914 and located at Chester and Cedar Avenues in Yeadon. Crowds of between 6,000 and 8,000 often attended games.

The Daisies had been around since 1910 when they were formed by Ed Bolden as an amateur team made up mostly of young men from Darby and Southwest Philadelphia. In 1917, with the strong-willed Bolden, a post office employee, directing the team, they became "professional" and played strong independent teams, many of them made up of white players. Outfielder Otto Briggs was the Daisies' first professional player.

In 1920, Hilldale played a series of games against a team of major league all-stars that included Babe Ruth. With some of the games at Baker Bowl, the Daisies lost four of the five contests. At the end of the 1921 season, Hilldale met the American Giants of Chicago, a Negro National League powerhouse, in a six-game series in Philadelphia. With the first three games at Baker Bowl and the last three at Hilldale Park, the Daisies laid claim to being the best black team in baseball after winning three, losing two, and tying one.

After feuding with the NNL for several years and filing several lawsuits, Bolden became the driving force in the formation of the Eastern Colored League in 1923. One of the charter members, the Daisies under manager Frank Warfield featured Judy Johnson, a Wilmington youngster who would go on to a legendary career that would lead him into the Baseball Hall of Fame at Cooperstown; Biz Mackey, one of the finest catchers in Negro League history; the aging but once-brilliant shortstop John Henry (Pop) Lloyd; spitball pitcher Phil Cockrell; fireballing hurler Nip Winters; Clint Thomas, a slugger who hit 28 homers in 1924; and wily veteran Louis Santop.

With such a star-studded lineup, Hilldale easily captured the pennant with a 32–17 record. Actually, some records show that the Daisies had an overall record of 137–43–6, which included exhibition games and five wins in a six-game series at

Negro League pioneer Ed Bolden was the driving force behind the remarkable success of the Hilldale Daisies.

the end of the season against a team made up mostly of players from the Philadelphia Athletics.

There was no postseason series that year. But in 1924, after the Daisies ran away with the flag again with a 47–22 mark (112–51–9 overall), they met the Monarchs in the first official Colored World Series.

Kansas City, led by the brilliant pitcher Bullet Joe Rogan, was the dominant team of the era and had won the Negro National League pennant with a 55–22 record. The World Series was, to say the least, unusual. The first two games were played at Baker Bowl with the largest crowd being about 8,600 and each team winning one game. The next two games were played in Baltimore; then the teams traveled to Kansas City for three games. The last three games were held in Chicago with the Monarchs winning the final game, 5–0. The Monarchs had won the series with five wins to Hilldale's four with one tie.

The same teams met again in 1925 after Hilldale (52–15) and Kansas City (62–23) won their respective league titles. This time, the Daisies prevailed, winning five of the six games played, including the last two at Baker Bowl, with Rube Currie winning his second outing of the series, 2–1, in the fifth game and veteran hurler Cockrell getting a 5–2 win in the final game. The winning Hilldale players were awarded $69 per man.

The Daisies finished third in 1926 and fifth in 1927. The Eastern League disbanded after the 1927 season, and Hilldale played an independent schedule before joining the American Negro League in 1929. Even with future Hall of Famer Oscar Charleston in the lineup, the team came in fourth. The ANL also dissolved, and again the Daisies returned to an independent schedule. Dispirited and out of money, Bolden left the team and focused full-time on his job at the post office after the 1930 season. Hilldale continued to operate in 1931 under new management, and although considered the best team in the East after compiling a 42–13 record, the Daisies folded at the end of the season.

A BUILDING BINGE

For anyone involved in the construction of stadiums, there was no better time to be in that business than in the 1920s in Philadelphia. The decade saw the greatest proliferation of sports venues the city has ever experienced.

Prior to the 1920s, Philadelphia's sports teams were extremely limited in the number of places they could play. Shibe Park and Baker Bowl held most of the major outdoor events. If teams had to play somewhere else, it was often on an open lot or in a dingy gym.

During the third decade of the 20th century, however, no less than five major new sports palaces were built. They included the Arena, the Palestra, Sesquicentennial Stadium, Temple Stadium, and Villanova Stadium. In addition, the old Franklin Field was knocked down, and a new one was built in its place, and an upper deck was added to Shibe Park. The building binge continued into the early 1930s with the opening of Convention Hall.

The Arena was the first building off the drawing board. Located at 45th and Market Streets, it was originally called the Philadelphia Auditorium and Ice Palace when it opened in 1920. The first event was an ice hockey game in which Yale defeated Princeton, 4–1.

Seating 5,226 for most events—although 2,000 floor seats could be added for boxing and wrestling matches—the Arena was the home of Philadelphia's early professional ice hockey teams, as well as a site for basketball games, roller derbies, and nonsporting events. The Warriors often met NBA opponents there, and even in the 1960s the 76ers occasionally played there. The Arena burned down in the 1980s.

In 1922 the wooden Franklin Field, opened in 1895 and rebuilt as an enclosed, brick-walled stadium in 1903, was demolished and replaced by a steel and concrete stadium on the same site at 33rd and Spruce Streets on the Penn campus. The seating capacity was doubled to 54,500. Three years later a second deck was added, expanding the seating capacity to 78,205.

As the home of Penn teams, Franklin Field has been the site of more college football games than any other stadium in the country. It was also the first two-tiered college stadium and the site of the nation's first scoreboard. In 1922 it played host to the first football game ever broadcast on radio. In 1939 it was the site of the first football game ever televised.

Over the years, Franklin Field has been the stage for many major sporting events in addition to Penn football. The first Army-Navy game in Philadelphia was held at the original Franklin Field in 1899. Over the following years, whenever it was played in Philadelphia, the annual military classic was held at Franklin Field through 1935. The Penn Relays have also been held at Franklin Field since their inception. The Eagles called it their home field from 1958 to 1971.

Another stadium addition occurred in 1925 when the Athletics extended the upper deck from first base to right field and from third base to left field at Shibe Park. Previously, the park had only an upper deck in the area from third to first bases.

The new deck added 10,000 seats to the ballpark, bringing its total capacity to 33,500. Some 750 more seats were added to the park in 1928 when a mezzanine was built between the upper and lower decks behind home plate. One year later, 3,500 more seats were added to the grandstands.

The Sesquicentennial Stadium opened for business in 1926 on a 61.5-acre site at Broad Street and Pattison Avenue. Built for the Sesquicentennial Exposition, which celebrated the nation's 150th birthday, the stadium had a permanent seating capacity of 86,443, but temporary seats were sometimes used to expand the number to more than 100,000. Army-Navy games held there annually drew 102,000, and the Dempsey-Tunney fight, the stadium's first major sporting event, attracted a crowd of more than 130,000.

The stadium underwent several name changes while it existed. It was called Municipal Stadium, then Philadelphia Stadium, and finally John F. Kennedy Stadium. In its day it was one of the major outdoor arenas in the country, housing numerous important boxing matches, as well as Eagles games, stock car races, and an assortment of other football games. The stadium was demolished in 1992 to make way for the First Union Center.

The next important sports building to go up was the Palestra on the Penn campus at 33rd and Walnut Streets. Dedicated New Year's Day, 1927, it had a seating

Municipal Stadium (originally called Sesquicentennial Stadium) was once one of the largest outdoor arenas in the nation.

capacity of 8,700. Despite its listed capacity, a crowd of 20,000 packed the building to watch Penn beat Yale, 26–15, on that first day.

Palestra, meaning "outer court" in Greek, would become one of the most storied basketball buildings ever built. The home of not only Penn basketball, but the Big Five, it has played host to 52 games in 20 NCAA tournaments. Today, it is the fifth-oldest Division I college arena in the country.

Villanova joined the building frenzy in 1927 with the opening of Villanova Stadium. Originally seating 5,400, it has since been expanded to hold 12,000. In the first game at the new stadium, the Wildcats defeated Lebanon Valley, 32–7. The stadium has enjoyed continuous use for 73 years.

The following year, Temple Stadium, also known as Beury Stadium and later Owl Stadium, opened in West Oak Lane on a site previously known as Vernon Park. The

Owls beat St. Thomas College of Scranton, 12–0, in the first game. Counting mobile field seats, the stadium originally held 34,200. Its permanent capacity was slightly in excess of 20,000. It would be the home of not only Owls football but also several high school teams until it was knocked down in the 1980s.

While Temple Stadium represented the last major sports construction in the 1920s, one more building went up shortly after the decade ended. In 1931, Convention Hall opened on 34th Street. With seats for 12,000, it became a major arena for professional and college basketball, as well as ice hockey, boxing, and numerous nonsports activities.

TUNNEY STUNS DEMPSEY

In the highly decorated history of Philadelphia boxing, numerous matches of particular significance have taken place. There is one, though, that ranks above all the others.

It was the match in which Jack Dempsey lost his heavyweight championship to Gene Tunney on September 23, 1926, in the first event held at the new Sesquicentennial Stadium.

Few fights anywhere have been more famous. Certainly, none ever held in Philadelphia topped it. It was a bout that was remembered through the 20th century as one of the city's most memorable sporting events.

At the time of the fight, Dempsey was the world's most renowned boxer. A former barroom brawler who had emerged from the tough little Colorado mining town of Manassa to turn pro in 1914, Dempsey, called the Manassa Mauler, was a relentless battler. On his way up the ladder, he ruthlessly beat opponents into senselessness; "187 pounds of unbridled violence," as sportswriter Red Smith described him.

Dempsey captured the heavyweight title in 1919 when he battered the mammoth defending champ, 6-foot, 6-inch, 245-pound Jess Willard. Several noteworthy title fights followed, but in 1923, Dempsey decided a long vacation was in order. He took the next three years off, traveling around the world with his actress wife, Estelle Taylor.

By 1926 the 31-year-old Dempsey was ready to resume his boxing career. A title fight was scheduled against light-heavyweight champ Gene Tunney, a classy former Marine from New York City, a strong but much more sophisticated boxer who frequently quoted Shakespeare. The fight, originally scheduled to be held in New York, was moved to Philadelphia by promoter Tex Rickard to take advantage of the brand new Sesquicentennial Stadium.

A crowd of 125,732 paid a total of $1,895,733 to see the fight with another 7,000 watching for free, making it the largest gathering ever to attend a boxing match. Stadium officials installed 40,000 extra seats and hired 148 ticket takers and several thousand ushers. Some 2,500 police were on duty, and more than 300 writers from around the world covered the event.

It rained virtually throughout the fight. But in a stunning upset, Dempsey proved no match for the 28-year-old Tunney. Gentleman Gene, as he was called, turned the champ's face into a bloody mess, winning a unanimous 10-round decision.

Back at his hotel after the fight, the badly battered Dempsey was asked by Taylor, his second of four wives, what happened. "Honey," Dempsey said, "I forgot to duck."

Tunney gave Dempsey another chance one year later in another legendary fight in Chicago. Again Tunney prevailed with another 10-round decision that was made famous by the "long count" in which the defending champ got the benefit of some extra time after being knocked down by Dempsey, who failed to go to a neutral corner right away.

Gene Tunney is against the ropes, but he came back to defeat Jack Dempsey in a stunning upset in Philadelphia.

Dempsey retired after that fight, although he tried a comeback in the early 1930s. He finished with a career record of 64–9–10. Tunney, who retired with the crown in 1928, had a lifetime mark of 65–1–1.

THE YELLOWJACKETS LAND

It may come as a surprise to some followers of modern pro football, but the Eagles were not the first National Football League team in Philadelphia. Nor were they the city's first NFL champions. That distinction goes to the Frankford Yellowjackets, a long ago team that holds a place as the grandfather of all pro football in Philadelphia.

Originally formed around the turn of the century as an independent team, the Yellowjackets, sponsored by a nonprofit group called the Frankford Athletic Association, had become highly successful after World War I. Most of the team's roster consisted of former high school and college players from the area who found it difficult to resist the urge to play football on weekends. There was always plenty of competition because the Philadelphia area was loaded with independent teams in that era.

Ultimately the Yellowjackets got so good that in 1924 they joined the NFL. Playing at 12,000-seat Frankford Stadium, or Yellowjacket Stadium as it was sometimes called, the team was forbidden to play on Sundays because of Pennsylvania's blue laws, which prohibited sports contests from being held on that day. Thus the Yellowjackets had to play home games on Saturdays when they had to compete for fan support with high school and college teams.

Nevertheless, the Yellowjackets drew large crowds. Several times during their tenure, the Yellowjackets played at Baker Bowl against a traveling team of Native American football players led by Jim Thorpe. Sometimes the team played a home game on Saturday, then would hop a train and head to another city to play a Sunday contest. For that reason, the Yellowjackets often played more games in a season than any other NFL team.

Frankford finished its first season in the 18-team NFL in third place with an 11–2–1 record, which included a 12–7 win that stopped a 30-game winning streak of the Canton Bulldogs. Not bad for starters, but the club's directors felt the team could do better. They hired player-coach Guy Chamberlain, a future member of the Pro Football Hall of Fame who had just won three straight NFL titles (with Canton in 1922 and 1923 and the Cleveland Bulldogs in 1924).

Chamberlain brought with him several players from the Bulldogs, and his team finished sixth with a 13–7 record in 1925. Then, in 1926, the Yellowjackets ran away with the title. Posting a 14–1–1 record while scoring 236 points to their opponents' 49, Frankford was by far the class of a league that included teams such as the Chicago Bears, New York Giants, and Green Bay Packers. The Yellowjackets' record for number of wins was not surpassed until 1984 when the San Francisco 49ers went 15–1.

In the championship game, the Yellowjackets defeated the unbeaten Bears, 7–6, at Shibe Park. After Chamberlain, an end, blocked the Bears' extra-point attempt, the Yellowjackets rallied with Houston Stockton passing to Henry Homan for a touchdown and Ernie Hamer kicking the game-winning extra point. Stockton was the grandfather of Utah Jazz basketball star, John Stockton.

The Yellowjackets never won another NFL title. After slipping to 6–9–3 in 1927, they finished second with an 11–3–2 record in 1928. By 1929 many of team's players had either retired or jumped to other teams that paid higher salaries. When the Depression struck, the Yellowjackets were further stymied by a shortage of funds. More players left, and the team's stadium fell into disrepair. The Yellowjackets went 9–4–5 in 1929 and 4–13–1 in 1930. In 1931, after only eight games (1–6–1), the team folded. It was a sad end to what was briefly a proud franchise.

In their eight years, the Yellowjackets won more games than any other NFL team of the era, compiling a record of 69–45–14. Two years after its demise, the team's debts were assumed by the new Philadelphia Eagles as a condition of their joining the NFL.

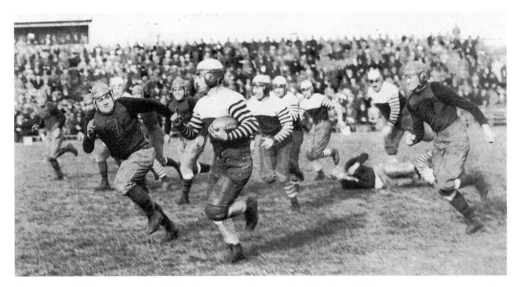

Wearing striped shirts, the Frankford Yellowjackets won the city's first NFL title in 1926.

TOUGH, TALENTED TOMMY LOUGHRAN

Once upon a time, Philadelphia was a place where nearly every street corner in the inner city had kids who wanted to grow up to become boxers. They were tough kids who learned at an early age to use their fists, and many of them parlayed that skill into careers in the ring.

Boxing was big in those days. It appealed to kids who had nothing else on which to hook a dream. As a result, many of them pursued careers in the sport, and collectively they gave Philadelphia a reputation as a city that produced scores of outstanding boxers.

An especially fertile period was during the third decade of the 20th century. In the 1920s, Philadelphia produced enough good boxers to fill a boxcar.

The best of a talented group was unquestionably Tommy Loughran, one of the cleverest and most gifted boxers in the sport's history. Possessing an uncommonly strong lefthanded punch (developed after he broke his right hand) and noted for his footwork and brilliant defense, Loughran came off the streets of Philadelphia to battle his way to the world's light-heavyweight championship and eventually a place in the Boxing Hall of Fame. Tommy was arguably the best Philadelphia native ever to step into the ring.

Loughran began his career as a middleweight and ended it as a heavyweight. Throughout the late 1920s, he dominated the light-heavyweight division. In a career that went from 1919 to 1937, Tommy fought 172 times, winning 94. He had 23 losses, nine draws, and 46 no decisions.

Loughran was undefeated in his first 43 bouts. In 1922 he had no-decision fights with the fierce Harry Greb as well as Gene Tunney. He beat the Frenchman Georges Carpentier in Philadelphia in 1926, a year in which he served as a sparring partner for Jack Dempsey as he prepared for his first bout with Tunney.

The 5-foot, 11-inch Irishman captured the light-heavy title in 1927 when he decisioned Mike McTigue for the vacant crown in a bruising 15-round bout in New York. Loughran, who dominated the fight, went on to defend his title six times over the next two years, including one winning bout with middleweight champ Mickey Walker.

In 1929, Tommy gave up his crown to pursue the heavyweight title, which had become vacant with the retirement of Tunney. In a fight before 45,000 at Yankee Stadium, Loughran was knocked out in the third round of a championship bout with Jack Sharkey.

Over the next four years, Loughran beat several top heavyweights, including Max Baer and Sharkey in a rematch. He got another title shot in 1934 against Primo Carnera.

In a career that covered 19 years, Tommy Loughran was possibly Philadelphia's greatest fighter.

Seven inches shorter and 86 pounds lighter—the biggest weight differential in heavyweight title fight history—the game Loughran suffered a broken toe when the lumbering Carnera stepped on it. Tommy wound up losing a 15-round decision.

Loughran fought for another three years, but never again challenged for the title. He retired to become a sugar broker. Tommy died in 1982 just short of his 80th birthday.

ATHLETICS ARISE FROM THE ASHES

Fifteen years after their last pennant, the Athletics returned from the dead to win again. Another dynasty was under way.

It had been a long, gloomy period of ineptitude after Connie Mack had unceremoniously scattered a great team to the winds after the A's had won four American League pennants in five years between 1910 and 1914. Mack's shredding had turned baseball's most dominating team into a farce, resulting in seven straight last-place finishes, five of those A's teams losing 100 or more games, including a record-setting 117 in 1916.

In 1922, however, the A's finally emerged from the cellar and began a move upward. From seventh to sixth to fifth they went, even though they lost a then-record 20 straight games in 1923. Then, in 1925, the team jumped all the way to second place.

By then the penny-pinching Mack had begun gathering top players again. They were all young, so they came cheap. Al Simmons and Bing Miller were already on board. In 1925 the team added a hotheaded pitcher named Lefty Grove, a muscular kid from Maryland known as Jimmie Foxx, and a rock-solid young catcher named Mickey Cochrane. The trio, along with Simmons, all had tickets to the Baseball Hall of Fame.

The A's dipped to third in 1926, but with the addition of future Hall of Famers Ty Cobb and Zack Wheat rebounded to finish second the following season, although Philadelphia was 19 huge games behind the mighty New York Yankees. Then in 1928, adding another future Hall of Famer, Tris Speaker, the Philadelphians again finished second to the Yanks, but this time just 2½ games back as Grove led the league with 24 wins and Simmons hit .351.

Foxx was still not a regular, although he had now been with the team for four seasons. But in 1929, Mack finally put him in the starting lineup, and the big kid responded with a .354 batting average, 33 home runs, and 117 RBI. Simmons hit .365 and led the league with 157 RBI, while Cochrane hit .331 and Miller .325. Grove, who led the league in strikeouts in each of his first seven years, won 20, but the big winner was Swarthmore College graduate George Earnshaw, who had 24 wins. Rube Walberg added 18.

As a result of all these sparkling numbers, the Athletics ran away with the pennant, posting a 104–46 record and finishing 18 games ahead of the Yankees. It was not only the best A's team ever fielded, but one of the best clubs in baseball history.

In a memorable World Series, the A's had little trouble with the Chicago Cubs, a heavy-hitting crew led by Rogers Hornsby (.380), Riggs Stephenson (.362), Kiki Cuyler (.360), and Hack Wilson (.345). The Cubs under Joe McCarthy, a native of the Germantown section of Philadelphia who would become the fifth-winningest manager in baseball history with 2,125 victories, had romped to their first National League pennant since 1918 with a 98–54 record and a 10 ½-game lead over the Pittsburgh Pirates. But they lost four out of five to the Athletics.

Mack surprised the Cubs—and everyone else—by sending aging veteran Howard Ehmke to the mound in the first game, held at Wrigley Field. Winner of only seven games during the season, the seldom-used Ehmke set a Series record with 13

The Athletics returned to the World Series in 1929 after a long absence. Among the stars in that Series were (from left): the Chicago Cubs' Rogers Hornsby and Hack Wilson from Leiperville, Delaware County, and the A's Al Simmons and Jimmie Foxx.

strikeouts, beating the Cubs, 3–1, with the help of Foxx's solo homer and a tie-breaking two-run ninth-inning single by Miller.

Homers by Foxx and Simmons got the A's and Earnshaw a 9–3 win in the second game. Guy Bush beat Earnshaw two days later, 3–1, at Shibe Park for Chicago's only win. Then, in one of the most memorable World Series games ever played, the A's overcame an 8–0 deficit with a 10-run seventh inning to gain a 10–8 victory. Simmons homered leading off the inning, and Wilson lost two balls in the sun, including Mule Haas's drive that turned into a three-run, inside-the-park homer.

After that, the shell-shocked Cubs bowed again in the fifth game. Trailing 2–0, the A's rallied off 22-game winner Pat Malone for three runs in the bottom of the ninth on a two-run homer by Haas and an RBI double by Miller that gave Philadelphia a 3–2 victory and the Series.

It was the start once again of something big for the A's. With their minidynasty, they would win two more pennants and one more World Series before Mack once again destroyed a good thing.

ROARING THROUGH THE ROARING 20S

If there was one word that characterized Philadelphia sports in the 1920s, it was variety. The city had a little bit of everything.

Big names, big events, and lots of teams—some of them very good, some of them very bad—shared the attention. It was a decade in which so much was going on that no one area of sports dominated the action.

While the Delaware River Bridge (now the Ben Franklin Bridge), the Broad Street Subway, the Frankford El, the Free Library, and the Philadelphia Museum of Art were all opened in the 1920s, Philadelphia sports kept pace with many new developments of its own. Some of the best of them included the following:

In 1920, Penn, in the midst of four straight Eastern League basketball championships, won the national title in a best-of-three series with the University of Chicago. In the third and deciding game, played at neutral Princeton, Bill Graves got out of a sickbed to lead the Quakers to a 23–21 victory, giving Penn a record of 22–1 in the final year of Lon Jourdet's first tenure as coach. Villanova fielded its first basketball team, beating Catholic University in its initial game, 43–40, before registering an 8–7 record for the season under coach Michael Saxe. And Oxford and Cambridge universities, their ranks depleted by World War I, sent a combined team to the Penn Relays. The team created such high interest that a record crowd of 30,000 attended the meet with another 5,000 being turned away.

The 1920s were a great decade for rowing in Philadelphia. Not only were Jack Kelly and Paul Costello attracting worldwide attention for their individual and combined efforts, but the clubs on Boathouse Row were hugely successful, too. Vesper, Penn AC, Malta, Bachelors, Undine, and Pennsylvania Barge clubs all won national championships in various categories. From 1920 to 1938, a Philadelphia club won the national double sculls championship every year. Philadelphia clubs won national four-oared with coxswain titles 10 times between 1920 and 1932, and eight-oared shells crowns eight times between 1923 and 1934.

Phillies outfielder Cy Williams won the National League home run title in 1920 with 15, giving the club seven home run crowns in eight years. Williams would also win the crown in 1923 with 41 homers and in 1927 with 30. He was one of the few bright spots in an otherwise bleak Phillies decade. During the first two years of the decade, the club traded two future Hall of Famers, shortstop Dave Bancroft and pitcher Eppa Rixey, getting little in return. The Phils then embarked on a decade in which they finished in eighth place six times and in seventh twice.

In 1921 the Phillies achieved some small measure of distinction when they participated in the first radio broadcast of a major league baseball game. With Harold Arlin, grandfather of a future Phillies draft choice, pitcher Steve Arlin, handling the play-by-play for Pittsburgh station KDKA, the Phillies dropped an 8–5 decision to the Pirates at Forbes Field. Philadelphia got another first that year when the first of three straight U.S. Men's Singles Tennis Championships was held at Germantown Cricket Club, with Bill Tilden defeating Wallace Johnson in the finals. Tilden then defeated William Johnston each of the next two years.

It was a big year in Philadelphia sports in 1922. The Philadelphia Football Club gave the city its first major independent soccer championship when it finished first in the American Soccer League. Football resumed at Temple, and after winning only two games in their first three years, the Owls hired former Penn star Henry (Heinie) Miller, who in eight seasons between 1925 and 1932 never had a losing campaign. In the only Army-Navy game of the decade played in Philadelphia, the Cadets came from behind to gain a 17–14 decision. The Phillies lost a 26–23 shootout to the Chicago Cubs at Wrigley Field in a game that still stands as a major league record for most runs by two teams.

In golf, Glenna Collett won her first of six U.S. Women's Amateur championships, her first of six Eastern titles, and the North and South women's tournament, launching a career that would land her in the women's Golf Hall of Fame. Originally from Rhode Island, Collett, after marrying and becoming Glenna Vare, moved to Philadelphia in 1928, eventually becoming known as "the Bobby Jones of women golfers." Glenna dominated women's golf through most of the 1920s and 1930s, capping a spectacular career by beating Patty Berg in 1935 for her sixth Women's Amateur title. Vare, who once hit a drive that was measured at 307 yards, played on every Curtis Cup team from 1932 to 1950 and competed in local tournament golf into the 1960s. The Vare Trophy, given annually to the LPGA player with the lowest scoring average for the year, is named in her honor.

Golf was big news again in 1923 when Max Marston, a member of Merion and Pine Valley, beat tourney favorite Bobby Jones in the second round of the U.S. Amateur championship, then defeated Francis Ouimet in the semifinals. In the finals, Marston, an investment banker, cashed in on the grand prize by beating defending champion Jess Sweetser on the second extra hole at Flossmore Country Club in suburban Chicago. Marston, who helped the United States win the Walker Cup in both 1922 and 1923, lost in the semifinals of the U.S. Amateur in 1924.

Temple fielded the area's first women's collegiate basketball team in 1923, going

Glenna Collett Vare (right) was the top woman golfer during most of the 1920s and 1930s.

12–0 under coach Blanche Voorhees. Swarthmore piloted by Leroy Mercer embarked on a streak of seven straight winning seasons in football, something that would never happen to the Garnet again. In his only year as head coach, Herchel Mosler led West Chester's football team to its first undefeated season with the Rams, in their fourth year of football, winning seven games and outscoring opponents, 205–0. Villanova had one of the worst records in collegiate football history, not only going winless (0–7–1), but also going scoreless for the entire 1923 season. Penn's Carl Fischer won the U.S. intercollegiate tennis championship and ranked seventh in the nation. The Phillies lost a 20–14 decision to the St. Louis Cardinals in a game in which the teams combined for a record 10 home runs. And in an unusual piece of baseball history, two no-hit games were pitched against the Athletics at Shibe Park three days apart. One was by Sam Jones of the New York Yankees, and the other by Howard Ehmke of the Boston Red Sox. Ironically, these were the only times in their 54 years in Philadelphia that the A's were no-hit at home.

At Baker Bowl during a Phillies game, something new happened when Reuben Berman, an 11-year-old fan, caught a foul ball and refused to throw it back, as was always done in those days. Berman was placed in a house of detention for the night and brought before a local judge the next morning. The judge ruled that the boy had not committed larceny, as charged, but had yielded to a natural impulse to catch the ball, and was therefore allowed to keep it as a souvenir. From then on, baseball fans in every professional ballpark were permitted to keep balls that they caught.

The Phillies were involved in a vastly different kind of story in 1924. Late in the season, Phils shortstop Heinie Sand got a message from New York Giants outfielder Jimmy O'Connell. "Take it easy on us," O'Connell urged while implying that Sand and his teammates might earn extra cash if they helped the Giants in their torrid pennant race with the Brooklyn Dodgers and Pittsburgh Pirates. Sand reported the attempted bribe, and after an investigation O'Connell and Giants coach Cozy Dolan, who was in on the scheme, were banned from baseball for life.

Bobby Jones, the 1923 U.S. Open winner, was back in the picture in 1924 when he won his first of five U.S. Amateur championships, in a tournament played at Merion. The 22-year-old Jones, a recent Georgia Tech engineering graduate, waltzed through the field to win easily. That year, Merion's Dorothy Campbell Hurd won the U.S. Women's Amateur championship, and Joe Coble of Cobbs Creek won the U.S. Public Links crown.

While he was welterweight champ, Mickey Walker had two title defenses at Baker Bowl. The future mayor of New York City defeated Lew Tendler in 10 rounds in one bout and kayoed Bobby Barrett in the sixth round in the other. The former was one of five title shots given to Tendler, the ex–South Philadelphia newsboy who was often considered the greatest lefthanded boxer of all time and one of the most feared punchers of his era. Starting as a bantamweight and then moving up to light-weight and welterweight, Tendler fought from 1913 to 1928, facing the best opponents in the game. "Any fight of his had to be exciting," noted fight critic Damon Runyon once said. Lew, knocked out just once during his 167 bouts, fought a 12-round no-decision match with lightweight champ Benny Leonard in 1922 and lost a brutal 15-round decision to Leonard in 1923 before a crowd of 60,000 at Yankee Stadium. Tendler, who ran a local restaurant for many years, never won a title, but his marvelous talent earned him a spot in the Boxing Hall of Fame in 1998.

Philadelphian Betty Becker won a gold medal in springboard diving and a silver in platform diving in the 1924 Olympics in Paris. And starting in 1924, the challenge round of the Davis Cup was held four straight years at Germantown Cricket Club with Bill Tilden and William Johnston leading the United States to victories over Australia once and France twice before bowing to France in 1927.

The following year, a legend in the making came to town and left his mark. Red Grange had an extraordinary game against Penn as he set an NCAA record, rushing

Lew Tendler was considered one of the best lefthanded boxers of all time.

for 237 yards (while gaining 331 yards overall) in ankle-deep mud in a 24–2 upset victory for Illinois. After the game, the Franklin Field crowd gave Grange a standing ovation.

The 1925 season was the first for the Pottsville Maroons in the NFL. That was also the year the first big football game was played at Shibe Park. With two weeks left in the season, the Maroons had a 10–2 record, good for first place in the league. With an open weekend, Pottsville had scheduled an exhibition game against a squad mainly

Playing at Germantown Cricket Club, the 1926 Davis Cup team was led by (from left): Dick Williams, Vince Richards, William Johnston, and Bill Tilden.

composed of the 1924 Notre Dame team, including the legendary Four Horsemen, as sportswriter Grantland Rice had dubbed the Fighting Irish backfield. Scheduled to play an NFL home game the same day, the Frankford Yellowjackets filed a protest, claiming the Maroons game violated their territorial rights. NFL commissioner Joe Carr upheld the protest and told the Maroons they couldn't play. They did anyway, and with 10,000 watching, won a 9–6 decision when ex-Lafayette College star Charlie Berry, at the time also a rookie catcher with the A's and later an American League umpire, drop-kicked a 30-yard field goal for the winning margin. There was a price, though. The second-place Chicago Cardinals were given the NFL title by a 12–2 vote of league owners, Pottsville's record was frozen, and the Maroons were expelled from the league. Cardinals owner Chris O'Brien refused to accept the title, but the NFL awarded it to his team anyway. Pottsville returned to the league the following year and played in it through 1929.

In 1925, Philadelphia also got its first Indianapolis 500 winner. Peter DePaolo, piloting a Duesenberg, became the first Indy driver to average more than 100 miles per hour when he won the Memorial Day race while averaging 101.127 mph. It would be another five years before another driver exceeded the 100-mph barrier. DePaolo, who had ridden as a mechanic in the 1920 500 with his uncle, Ralph DePalma, one of the great early drivers, had first driven at Indy in 1922. Altogether, he raced there seven times, finishing as high as sixth in 1924 and fifth in 1926. DePaolo was named national driving champion by the U.S. Auto Racing Club in 1925 and 1927.

By the mid-1920s soccer was beginning to take hold as a quasi-professional sport in Philadelphia. The original Philadelphia Football Club had moved to Bethlehem, but a new team of the same name had formed in 1922 and would play in the American Soccer League until 1927. That year, a team called the Philadelphia Celtics joined the ASL, but folded after their 10th game. Philadelphia Football Club

Philadelphian Peter DePaolo became the first Indianapolis 500 winner to average more than 100 miles per hour.

returned to action in 1928 and fielded a team for two more years before disbanding again.

Also creeping into the local picture was a form of professional basketball. After leaving his post at Philadelphia Textile, the young and enterprising Eddie Gottlieb had begun to branch out into a number of different areas. He had become involved in promoting local baseball games, and he would eventually become a key promoter of Negro League contests. Since basketball was played mostly by young Jewish men at the time, he was also heavily involved in that sport, and in the mid-1920s formed a team called the South Philadelphia Hebrew Association (SPHAS). The SPHAS played originally as an independent team, but by the early 1930s had joined the professional Eastern League. Later they switched to the American Basketball League where they would play until 1949.

In 1926, Philadelphia had another fine woman golfer move to the forefront when Helen Stetson, who lived near West Chester, returned the U.S. Women's Amateur title to the Philadelphia area with a win at Merion. The first American Legion baseball World Series was held that year at the new Sesquicentennial Stadium, and Philadelphia had an entry in the new American Football League with a team called the Quakers. The Quakers had been playing as an independent team since the early 1920s. Many of their players performed for the Quakers on Saturdays, then raced to Buffalo where they played professionally on Sundays. The conflict created such a dispute that it led to the first contracts that bound players to one team. The Quakers won the first championship of the nine-team league with an 8–2 record after beating Red Grange and the New York Yankees twice in three days. The Quakers won a 13–10 decision before 22,000 at Yankee Stadium in a game in which Grange hurt his hip. Two days later, with Grange unable to play, the Quakers collected a 13–6 victory in Philadelphia. The celebration, however, was short-lived. The league folded after its maiden season.

A problem of a different kind arose at Baker Bowl in 1927. When fans overloaded a covered area of the lower deck in an attempt to escape a rainstorm during a Phillies-Cardinals game, two sections of the grandstand bearing close to 1,000 people collapsed. Players raced to the stands to help as fans screamed with panic. Fifty fans were injured and one man died later of a heart attack. Umpire Frank Wilson called off the game with the Phillies leading, 12–3. "Baker Bowl is the worst constructed place I ever saw," fumed a city official after the accident. It cost the Phillies $40,000 to repair the damage. While the park was being fixed, the Phillies played 12 games at Shibe Park.

Philadelphia got its first pro ice hockey team in 1927 with a team called the Arrows. Playing in the Canadian-American League, the Arrows' top scorer was Bryan

Hextall, whose grandson Ron would many years later be an outstanding goalie for the Flyers. The Arrows existed until 1935, when they became known as the Ramblers and played two more years in the CAL as a farm team of the New York Rangers.

Temple recorded what might be the most lopsided win in college football history when it defeated little Blue Ridge College, 110–0. Tucker (Swede) Hanson, one of the Owls' all-time gridiron greats, scored five touchdowns and Grover Wearshing added three. With the Owls leading 78–0 at halftime, the coaches agreed to limit the game to an eight-minute third quarter and a six-minute fourth period. By the end of the game, several Temple players had switched jerseys and were filling in for the hapless Blue Ridge team.

Adopted Philadelphian Benny Bass, who had emigrated from Russia as a youth, won the vacant featherweight championship in 1927, coming back from two knockdowns to capture a hard-fought 10-round decision over Red Chapman at Sesquicentennial Stadium. Bass, who resided at Second and Vine Streets, was one of the most prolific fighters in boxing history, entering the ring an estimated 500 times during a career that stretched from 1919 to 1940. His official record lists him as having 227 bouts with 176 wins, 38 losses, 10 draws, and three no decisions. In his first title defense

Goose Goslin of Salem, New Jersey, won the American League batting title in 1928 en route to a berth in the Hall of Fame.

The Philadelphia area got its second Indy 500 winner when Ray Keech of Coatesville drove to victory in 1929.

against Tony Canzoneri at Madison Square Garden, Bass suffered a broken collarbone in the third round, yet held on before losing in 15 rounds. Five months later Benny came back to win the junior lightweight crown by knocking out Tod Morgan in the second round. Bass held that title for more than two years, beating Lew Massey in 10 rounds in one title fight at the Arena in 1931, then losing the crown to Kid Chocolate in a seventh-round kayo at Baker Bowl later that same year. That fight was one of only two in which Bass failed to go the distance, the other being a match with Henry Armstrong in 1937 when Benny became one of the great fighter's 27 straight kayos.

One of Bass's more memorable bouts occurred in 1928 when he kayoed Harry Blitman in the sixth round before a crowd of 26,000 at Shibe Park in a fight billed as a grudge match between two Jewish rivals. At the time Blitman was unbeaten and had just defeated the extremely tough Canzoneri in a nontitle fight at Baker Bowl. Blitman, a Central High School graduate, was regarded as one of the toughest fighters of the era.

Another local guy who made good strutted his stuff in 1928. Leon (Goose) Goslin, who came out of Salem, New Jersey, to carve out a splendid big league baseball career, won the American League batting championship with a .379 average. Playing mostly with the Washington Senators during an 18-year career that also included stops with the St. Louis Browns and Detroit Tigers, Goslin was one of the finest hitters of his day. His .316 lifetime average carried the stellar outfielder into the baseball Hall of Fame in 1968.

Although the Goose was out of town, the Phillies brought a power hitter into town when they called up Chuck Klein from the minors. The big slugger hit .360 for new manager Burt Shotton's 109-game losers. The next year, another new Phillies slugger, Lefty O'Doul, led the National League with a remarkable .398 batting average while setting a record with 254 hits. Six Phillies regulars—also including Klein, Pinky Whitney, Don Hurst, Fresco Thompson, and Denny Sothern—hit over .300 that year to help boost the club to fifth place, its highest finish since 1917.

Betty Becker, now Betty Pinkston, was back in the Olympics in 1928, just two years after giving birth to twins. Again she won a gold medal in platform diving. Another Philadelphian, Geoffrey Mason, also came home with a gold medal during the winter Olympics after being part of the winning U.S. five-man bobsled team.

The 1929 season had one other glittering achievement. The Philadelphia area got its second Indianapolis 500 winner when Ray Keech of Coatesville drove his Simplex Special to victory with an average time of 97.58. Keech, who led for 46 laps, had been fourth at Indy in 1928.

Bill Tilden Dominates Tennis

Of all the athletes who have performed in Philadelphia in the 20th century, none dominated a sport any more than Bill Tilden did tennis in the 1920s. Tilden was by an overwhleming margin the best tennis player in his era, and quite possibly the best of any era.

From 1920 through 1929 the Germantown native was ranked number one in the nation. He won seven U.S. tennis championships, six U.S. clay court titles, three Wimbledon crowns, 17 of 22 Davis Cup matches, and numerous doubles championships both nationally and internationally.

Called the "Colossus of Courts," he dominated tennis with passion and fervor during a decade when a handful of sports figures ranked among the biggest names in the

Bill Tilden was a dominant figure on tennis courts throughout the world.

world. Big Bill, as he was also called, was not only a brilliant player, but one of the most theatrical athletes as well, a temperamental and dramatic showman with an eye for self-promotion. He was also one of the most tragic.

Tilden, standing 6 feet, 1½ inches and weighing 155 pounds, was swift, nimble, and graceful. He possessed a punishing serve, had a variety of shots, and could volley with deadly accurate speed and power. Rare was the opponent who could keep up with him during his long and spectacular career.

Unquestionably, Tilden was Philadelphia's finest athlete of the 1920s, despite competition from an immensely talented group that included Jack Kelly, Sr., Tommy Loughran, Man o' War, Benny Bass, Lefty Grove, Al Simmons, Mickey Cochrane, Cy Williams, and Glenna Collett Vare.

Born into a wealthy family, Tilden began playing tennis at the age of seven. Later, he attended Germantown Academy and Penn, after which he became a reporter for the *Philadelphia Evening Ledger,* a job he held through much of his amateur playing career. Tilden's career gained momentum while he served as a private in the Army. After his discharge, he won 82 of 86 matches and attained rankings in both 1918 and 1919 as the number-two player in the nation. In 1919 he reached the final of the U.S. championship at Forest Hills before losing to William Johnston.

That loss would be Tilden's last defeat in that event for a while. Beginning in 1920, he captured six straight U.S. championships, winning every match. He won again in 1929 while also winning five U.S. doubles titles. He triumphed at Wimbledon in 1920 and 1921, then after not competing there from 1922 to 1926, won again in 1930 at the age of 37. Along the way, Tilden also led the United States to seven straight Davis Cups, winning 13 consecutive singles victories.

Tilden turned professional in 1930 and won U.S. pro titles in 1931 and 1935. He toured until 1937, but played competitively into the mid-1940s, participating in exhibitions to help the war effort. An admitted homosexual, Tilden fell on hard times in the late 1940s and was twice arrested when police found him engaged in sexual activities with young boys. Broke after failed attempts to become an actor and a playwright, Tilden was jailed both times and shunned after his release. Living then in Hollywood, he earned a meager living by giving tennis lessons. A tragic figure, Tilden died of a heart attack in 1953 at the age of 60.

1930s

Somber Era Had a Bright Side

Quite possibly, the true value of sports was never revealed more fully than it was during the 1930s. While the nation was locked in the grip of the Great Depression, the world of fun and games was one of the few activities that offered an escape from the somber realities of the day.

Americans could forget their troubles, if only for a few hours. They could lose themselves in the joys of rooting for the home team. Sports, striding undauntedly onward, provided an important diversion, which is really what their main function was always supposed to be, anyway.

That function was profoundly evident in Philadelphia, where the local citizenry immersed itself in the sports scene. With good reason, too. Sports in the 1930s in Philadelphia absorbed people's attention for numerous reasons. And even if many fans couldn't scrape up the money to buy a ticket, they still followed the city's teams and players at least as avidly as those of any previous generation.

They had a lot to follow. In the 1930s Philadelphia gave birth to a new professional football team called the Eagles. Although the team was hardly an instant success, the foundation would be laid for a franchise that would stir the passions of local sports fans for most of the next 70 years.

Philadelphia also got its first National Hockey League team. The Quakers didn't last long, but before the decade was over, an assortment of ice hockey teams with such names as Arrows, Comets, and Ramblers took up residence in the city, laying the groundwork for the sport's future popularity.

Pro basketball also took root in the city in the 1930s with the formation of the South Philadelphia Hebrew Association (SPHAS) team, basically the forerunner of the next decade's Warriors and winner of several league championships. At the college level, basketball burst emphatically from its status as a crude and not very popular minor sport as Temple won the first National Invitational Tournament (NIT), Villanova went to the Final Four in the NCAA tourney, and St. Joseph's and its fabled Mighty Mites put together a four-year run of some of the finest teams in the college's history.

Temple also sent a football team to the first Sugar Bowl. La Salle began not only a football team, but also a basketball team. The Army-Navy game returned to Philadelphia. And led by its Destiny Backfield, Penn enjoyed another glorious era in football.

In baseball, the Athletics won two more American League pennants and one World Series, after which Connie Mack waved his machete once again and, with the same excuse that he had no money, destroyed his last great team by peddling future Hall of Famers Jimmie Foxx, Lefty Grove, Mickey Cochrane, and Al Simmons, among others. The Philadelphia A's would never be a strong pennant contender again.

The Phillies, meanwhile, struggled through another depressing decade, although at one point they managed to break out of the second division for the only time during a 32-year period. The club did finally escape from the dreary confines of Baker Bowl, however, while taking part in several historic baseball firsts. Undeniably, the best news of the decade for the Phillies was the performance of slugger Chuck Klein, a future Hall of Famer and one of the finest hitters the club ever had. Klein and Foxx even won the Triple Crowns in their respective leagues in 1933, the only time two players from the same city ever did so in major league baseball.

Philadelphia got a new Negro League team in the Stars, a club that not only won a pennant but also became a fixture in the league for nearly two decades. Auto racing came to the Philadelphia area on a regular basis with the opening of Langhorne Speedway. And the Dad Vail Regatta began, although in a different city.

The city also had its share of nationally important events. Bobby Jones won the Grand Slam of golf by triumphing in the U.S. Amateur at Merion, after which he retired at the age of 28. Sam Snead, in one of pro golf's most famous collapses, shot an eight on the last hole to lose the U.S. Open at Philadelphia Country Club. And 22-year-old Ben Hogan made his Philadelphia debut.

Joe Louis and Primo Carnera had major fights in Philadelphia, which also played host to six championship bouts during the decade. At Baker Bowl, Babe Ruth played his last major league game. The Baseball Hall of Fame opened with former Philadelphia players Grover Cleveland Alexander, Eddie Collins, and Nap Lajoie being among the first group inducted. And Philadelphia held its 10th and most famous Davis Cup match.

Athletes from Philadelphia gained national prominence, too. The city had two Sullivan Award winners in track and field star Barney Berlinger and rower Joe Burk. Kelly Betillo became the third Philadelphian to win the Indianapolis 500. Anne Townsend was in her prime as perhaps the area's greatest woman athlete. Bill Carr set world records while winning two Olympic gold medals in track, and several other Philadelphians won gold medals during the decade, while Eulace Peacock became famous for his string of classic races against the legendary Jesse Owens. War Admiral, Man o' War's son, won the Triple Crown of horse racing. Midget Wolgast and Johnny Jadick captured boxing titles. The German-Americans won the national soccer championship. And Penn AC's eight-oared crew won the world title on the way to becoming known as the greatest rowing team in the first half of the century.

The decade of the 1930s was also noteworthy for its proliferation of outstanding coaches. Temple had Glenn (Pop) Warner in football and Jimmy Usilton in basketball with a young assistant named Harry Litwack on the way up. Jim (Jumbo) Elliott in track and Al Severance in basketball got their starts at Villanova. In football, George Munger at Penn, Glenn Killinger at West Chester, and Lew Elverson at Swarthmore launched lengthy careers. At St. Joseph's, Billy Ferguson's long basketball career was just getting under way.

Other names also became a familiar part of the area's sports lexicon. Eddie Gottlieb. Lud Wray, Bert Bell, Herb Gardiner, Gerry Nugent, Burt Shotton, and Byrum Saam all carved special niches in the 1930s. Pulitzer Prize–winning *New York Times* columnist Red Smith was in the early stages of his career covering baseball and other sports at the *Philadelphia Record*. And along with all the others, this group helped to make the decade one in which the local sports scene was far brighter than the world surrounding it.

GRAND SLAM AND OUT

If going out while you're at the top is the ideal way to end a career, Bobby Jones made the perfect exit. And he did it in Philadelphia in 1930 in dramatic fashion.

It had been 14 years since Jones made his national debut while playing at the age of 14 in the U.S. Amateur championship at Merion. Over the next 13 years, he had won virtually every major tournament in sight, including four U.S. Amateurs, three U.S. Opens, and two British Opens. But neither he nor anyone else had ever won all four major tournaments—which including the British Amateur championship, then constituted the Grand Slam of golf—in the same year.

That, however, would change in 1930. The great Georgia golfer claimed his first big victory of the season in the British Amateur at St. Andrews in Scotland. Two weeks later, he walked off with the British Open at Royal Liverpool. A ticker-tape parade greeted Bobby's return to New York. Jones then captured the U.S. Open with a birdie on the last hole in Minneapolis.

Just one win away from the Grand Slam and victory in the world's four major tournaments, Jones came to Philadelphia in search of a clean sweep. The U.S. Amateur tournament was held again that year at Merion, a course with which Jones was extremely familiar and which was one of his favorites.

A heavy favorite to win, Jones easily captured the medal with a two-round score of 142 to advance to the championship matches. As he strolled down the Merion

On his way to the U.S. Amateur crown at Merion in 1930, Bobby Jones (left) accepts congratulations from Jess Sweetser.

fairways, Jones was accompanied by a group of Marines serving as bodyguards to fend off the hero-worshipping crowd.

The idol of the masses defeated former Canadian Amateur champion Sandy Somerville and Fred Hoblitzel in the first two rounds of match play, each 5 and 4. Then in 36-hole matches, Jones beat Fay Coleman, 6 and 5, on Thursday and 1922 Amateur champ Jess Sweetser, 9 and 8, in the semifinal on Friday.

The final pitted Jones against 22-year-old Gene Homans of Englewood, New Jersey. Jones shot 72 to go up by seven holes after the Saturday morning match. Then with the crowd swelling to 18,000, Bobby was up by eight after 10 holes in the afternoon match. He closed out the match with a par on the 11th hole. The win gave Jones the coveted Grand Slam, making him the only golfer ever to accomplish that feat. It was Jones's 13th major championship, a record that would stand for more than 40 years.

Two months later, Jones, just 28 years old and at the height of his game, stunned the sports world in which he was such a towering figure by announcing his retirement. There were no worlds left for him to conquer, Bobby explained. He would play no more tournament golf.

Except for his annual appearance in the Masters on the Augusta course that he helped design, Jones was true to his word. He focused on course design and his law practice in Atlanta, and would never again play in such conditions as those in that final, famous tournament in Philadelphia.

PHILADELPHIA GAINS AN NHL TEAM

Long, long ago, in the dank, dark ages of professional ice hockey, Philadelphia had an entry in the National Hockey League. The team, like so many other Philadelphia sports teams, was called the Quakers.

Most followers of local ice hockey today have never heard of the Quakers. In fact, most of them would say that the city's first NHL team was the Flyers. To some extent, they may be right. It's debatable whether or not the Quakers were really a team.

The Quakers had a brief and inglorious stay in Philadelphia. Before their sudden arrival in the city in 1930, they had been known as the Pittsburgh Pirates. Competing in the NHL, which had begun in 1917, the Pirates had struggled in Pittsburgh, hardly able to win many games and even less able to attract many fans.

Seeing opportunity elsewhere, the team's owner, former light-heavyweight boxing champion Benny Leonard, brought the Pirates to Philadelphia. The ex-pug figured that ice hockey was gaining in popularity around the country, and Philadelphia would be a good place to station a team. Benny changed the name of his team to Quakers and set up shop at the Arena.

By then Philadelphia had been introduced to pro ice hockey, compliments of the Arrows, a team that played in the Canadian-American League beginning in 1927. What Leonard didn't figure on, though, was that the minor league Arrows would outdraw his NHL team.

That was mainly because the Quakers were absolutely putrid. During the 1930–31 season they played 44 games and won just four of them. Eventually, Leonard, having lost $80,000, was forced to fold the team.

The Quakers were never heard from again. Meanwhile, minor league ice hockey flourished in Philadelphia with teams playing at the Arena. Former NHL standout and eventual Hall of Famer Herb Gardiner coached most of the teams between 1929 and 1947. After finishing last in their first season in 1927–28, the Arrows became one of the better teams in the C-AHL, even winning the league title in 1932–33 with a 29–12–7 record.

After dropping back to last place in 1934–35, the Arrows folded, only to resurface the following season as the Ramblers, a farm team of the NHL's New York Rangers. The Ramblers won the C-AHL championship with a 27–18–3 record in 1935–36. After that season the C-AHL folded. The Ramblers joined the American Hockey League and played in it until 1941.

Philadelphia also had one other pro ice hockey team in the 1930s. The Comets played in 1932–33 in the TriState Hockey League, which dissolved at the end of the season. None of the minor league teams, however, could match for futility the record of the Quakers, Philadelphia's first NHL team.

A's GET THE AX AGAIN

Connie Mack builds a powerhouse team full of great players. The team does nothing but win. Connie Mack dismantles the team. The Athletics quickly decline into pathetic losers and stay that way for a long time. Philadelphia baseball fans are jilted again.

Sound like a familiar story? It should be. It's an exact repeat of a story that happened two decades earlier. The only difference was that this time Mack dug the A's such a deep hole that they never escaped and were eventually forced to move out of town.

Nowhere in the history of sports was a championship team so thoroughly demolished as the Athletics were—not once, but twice. The second time came after a run of three straight American League pennants and victories in two World Series.

After winning the Series in 1929, the A's of 1930 were essentially the same star-spangled unit. They had exceptional pitching, with Lefty Grove winning 28 and George Earnshaw 22. After a prolonged holdout during which he missed all of spring training, Al Simmons gave the A's their first batting champion since 1901 with a .381 average while clubbing 36 home runs and driving in 165. Jimmie Foxx went .335–37–156, and Mickey Cochrane hit .357, Bing Miller .303, and Havertown native Jimmy Dykes .301.

The 1930 A's went over 100 wins for the second straight year, posting a 102–52 record and winning the pennant by eight games over the Washington Senators. In the World Series the A's faced the St. Louis Cardinals, who had just edged the Chicago Cubs by two games to win the National League flag.

Grove, with home run support from Simmons and Cochrane, won the first game, 5–2. Cochrane homered again in the second game to help Earnshaw to a 6–1 victory. But then Wild Bill Hallahan blanked the A's, 3–0, in the third game, and Jesse Haines pitched a four-hitter to gain a 3–1 decision in Game Four as the Cards tied the Series at two wins apiece.

Pitcher Lefty Grove (left) and catcher Mickey Cochrane were two of the top players when the Athletics won three straight pennants and two World Series.

That was it for the Cardinals. Foxx's dramatic two-run ninth-inning homer broke a 0–0 tie and gave the A's a 2–0 win in the fifth game, with Earnshaw getting the win in relief of Grove. Then the A's clinched the Series as Simmons and Dykes homered and Earnshaw, pitching on one day's rest, hurled a five-hit, 7–1 victory.

The Athletics came back in 1931 to set a club record in wins while posting a 107–45 (.704) mark and becoming one of only eight teams in major league history to finish with a winning percentage over .700. The A's romped home 13½ games ahead of the New York Yankees as Simmons again led the league in hitting with a .390 average, climaxing a magnificent five-year spurt during which he hit .376 overall. Cochrane hit .349, Mule Haas had a .323 average and Foxx went .291–30–120. Named to an early version of the Most Valuable Player Award, Grove had one of the finest seasons any pitcher ever had with a dazzling 31–4 record, while Earnshaw won 21 and Rube Walberg copped 20.

The Series had a different outcome this time. Again facing the Cardinals, winners by 13 games over the New York Giants, the A's fell in seven games as outfielder Pepper Martin hit .500 and ran wild on the bases for St. Louis. Grove was brilliant, winning the first game, 6–2, and the sixth game, 8–1, but the only other A's victory came on Earnshaw's 3–0 shutout in Game Four. Earnshaw, who had lost Game Two, lost again in the seventh game when he gave up a two-run homer to George Watkins that sparked St. Louis to a 4–2 victory.

The Athletics finished second to the Yankees in 1932 and 1933. Foxx led the league in home runs with 58 and in RBI with 169 in 1932, and he won the Triple Crown in 1933 with .356–48–163. Grove won more than 20 games for the seventh straight year.

But following the 1932 season, Mack, who had a reported annual salary of $50,000, began to sabotage his team again. Saying the team needed money and using the same weak excuses—"Pennant winners get to be an old story" was one of them—he traded Simmons, Haas, and Dykes to the Chicago White Sox. Then, after the 1933 campaign, he swapped Grove, Walberg, and shortstop Max Bishop to the Boston Red Sox, as well as Cochrane on the same day to the Detroit Tigers. He followed up in 1935 by shipping Foxx to the Red Sox.

Having received little in return but cash in the trades, the A's had suddenly become a team mostly made up of youngsters and washed-up veterans. They dropped into fifth place in 1934, and in 1935 they fell all the way to eighth, a spot they held for nine of the next 12 years, while fielding some of the most embarrassing teams ever to pose as big leaguers.

Mack, who was already at retirement age but, because he controlled the team, held on for nearly 20 more years, once again had turned a formidable club into a joke. Although they developed a few good players in the 1930s—notably Doc Cramer, Wally Moses, Bob Johnson, Sam Chapman, and Elmer Valo—the A's never really recovered, and because the fans ultimately lost interest, the long-term effect of Mack's folly was that the A's eventually were forced to find another home. It was a sad way to lose a ball club.

KLEIN CARRIES THE PHILLIES

Of all the batters who passed through Philadelphia trying to apply a wooden stick to a speeding, darting small round sphere, one of the most successful was Chuck Klein, a big, rawboned slugger from Indiana. It could be argued not only that Klein was one of Philly's finest, but that he might have been the best the Phillies ever had.

Klein came to the Phillies midway through the 1928 season and hit .360. His first five full seasons were the best with which any batter ever began a big league career. From 1929 through 1933 he recorded batting average, home run and RBI figures of

Hard-hitting Chuck Klein was one of the greatest players in Phillies history.

.356–43–145, .386–40–170, .337–31–121, .348–38–137, and .368–28–120, the last being the year of his Triple Crown. He was named the league's Most Valuable Player in 1932.

Chuck, who spent three different stints with the Phillies before retiring in 1944, led or tied for the lead in the National League in home runs four times, in runs scored three times, in RBI twice, and in batting once. In 1933 he became the only Phillies player and one of just five National League players in the 20th century to win the Triple Crown. That year, his totals included 223 hits and 44 doubles, and he hit for the cycle for the second time. In 1933, Klein was also named the National League's starting right fielder in the first All-Star Game.

Although Klein's Triple Crown elevated him to the ranks of the premier National League hitters of all time, he may have had his best year in 1930 when he hit .386. Chuck finished third in the batting race that year, but led the circuit in doubles (59), total bases (445), and runs scored (158). His totals for hits (250), home runs (40), RBI (170), and slugging percentage (.687) all ranked second in the league, but his numbers for RBI, total bases, and long hits (107) established league records that still stand for lefthanded batters. He even set a record for assists by an outfielder when he threw out 44 base runners that year.

With a bat that simply devoured opposing pitching, Klein was one of the few bright spots during an otherwise dreary decade for the Phillies. Although the team played poorly, at least Chuck always gave the fans something to cheer about. Klein's exploits kept the struggling franchise afloat.

The slugging right fielder did his best hitting at Baker Bowl where the right field wall stood just 280 feet down the line. Klein's feats were sometimes belittled because it was so easy to hit balls against or over that wall. On the other hand, many of Klein's doubles against the wall might have been home runs in other parks.

The penny-pinching Phillies traded Klein to the Chicago Cubs after the 1933 season, but he returned to Philadelphia in 1936 and promptly became only the second Phillies player to hit four home runs in one game when he pumped a quartet out at Forbes Field in Pittsburgh.

Klein was sold to the Pirates in 1939 but came back to the Phillies the following year and finished his career as a player-coach. When he retired, Chuck held—and still holds—numerous league and club records. With a career batting average of .320, 300 home runs, and 1,201 RBI, he was elected to the Baseball Hall of Fame in 1980.

EAGLES JOIN THE NFL

It took professional football a while to gain a foothold in Philadelphia. But when it finally did, it became as solidly entrenched as any sport in the city.

The road to that path began in 1933 with the formation of the Eagles. Previously

Philadelphia had had a brief fling with pro football, most notably with the Frankford Yellowjackets. But they disbanded in 1931, leaving a huge void in the city's sports ranks.

Fortunately, an enterprising young man named Bert Bell had a burning desire to fill that gap. Bell had been a quarterback at Penn before graduating in 1920. He had long been interested in establishing a pro football team in Philadelphia, but pro football was not terribly interested in Philadelphia because of the blue laws that banned sports teams from playing on Sunday, the most desirable day to play pro football games.

"We'll put a franchise in Philadelphia if the city scraps its blue laws," National Football League officials told Bell. Bert got the message. Along with leaders of other Philadelphia sports, he led a drive that took him to Pennsylvania governor Gifford Pinchot. The group persuaded Pinchot to issue a bill that allowed local electorates to vote on whether or not they wanted to permit sports on Sunday. Soon afterward, Philadelphia decided to put the ban to a vote in the November election.

Bell, who headed a syndicate that also included Lud Wray (the former coach of the NFL's Boston Braves), former Phillies president Jack Potter, and Fitz Eugene Dixon, Sr., was then awarded a franchise on July 8, 1933. The cost was $2,500, plus an agreement to assume some of the Yellowjackets' NFL debts.

Using the symbol for the New Deal's National Recovery Act, the club was named the Eagles. Wray was installed as the head coach and general manager with Bell serving as president and assistant coach. The team would play its home games at Baker Bowl.

The first training camp was held at Bader Field in Atlantic City. The Eagles played a series of exhibition games against semipro teams. Eventually, a squad of 25 players, few of them with much ability, was selected.

The first Eagles regular-season game was held October 16 against the New York Giants at Yankee Stadium. Philadelphia was annihilated, 56–0. Incredibly, the Eagles played their first home game two days later at night using temporary lights, losing to the Portsmouth Spartans, 25–0, before a Baker Bowl crowd estimated to be 1,750.

In their third game, after a three-day bus trip to Green Bay, the Eagles finally scored their first touchdown, with Roger Kirkman combining with former Temple star Swede Hanson on a 35-yard pass during a 35–9 loss to the Packers. In their next outing, the Eagles registered the franchise's first win with a 6–0 victory over another new NFL entry, the Cincinnati Reds. Two days later Philadelphians voted overwhelmingly to permit Sunday sports, and in the first Sunday football game on November 12, the Eagles tied the soon-to-be NFL champion Chicago Bears, a team featuring Red Grange, Bronko Nagurski, and Wild Bill Hewitt, 3–3, before a crowd of 20,000 at Baker Bowl.

The Eagles then defeated the new Pittsburgh Pirates, 25–6, and Cincinnati again, 20–3, before ending their first season with a 3–5–1 record and a fourth-place finish in the Eastern Division. Hanson finished the season as the NFL's fifth leading ground-gainer.

It was a start, but it would be a long journey toward respectability for the Eagles. They posted losing seasons in their first 10 years, three times winning only one game all season. After doing no better than 9–21–1, Wray was fired after his third season. Bell took over as head coach from 1936–1940, but posted only a 10–44–2 record.

A NEW TEAM OF STARS

Negro League baseball was an important part of the local sports fabric for almost the entire first half of the 20th century. During that time, no team enjoyed more longevity or had a bigger following than the Philadelphia Stars.

Formed in 1933, two years after the demise of the Hilldale Daisies, the Stars held a prominent place in black baseball until 1952, a year that roughly corresponded with the end of the Negro Leagues. The Stars were bankrolled and run by local sports impresario Eddie Gottlieb, with Ed Bolden, who had put together the Daisies many years earlier, serving as the figurehead leader. They played originally at Passon Field, at 48th and Spruce Streets. Later, they moved to Penmar Park, a 6,000-seat, enclosed field built in the 1920s by the Pennsylvania Railroad at 44th and Parkside. They also played occasionally at Baker Bowl and Shibe Park, attracting as many as 25,000–30,000 at the latter for a Sunday game.

The Stars played quality baseball. One of their top players was outfielder Gene Benson, an excellent hitter who many said could have played big league baseball if only his skin had been of a lighter hue. Benson was the last Negro League roommate of Jackie Robinson when both played with the Kansas City Monarchs in 1945. Catcher Bill (Ready) Cash; pitchers Stuart (Slim) Jones, Barney Brown, and playing-manager Webster McDonald; third baseman Jud Wilson; and left fielder Red Parnell were some of the top-of-the-line Stars. Over the years Negro League aces such as Oscar Charleston, who also managed the team, Buck Leonard, Biz Mackey, and Boojum Wilson played briefly with the Stars. Outfielder Harry (Suitcase) Simpson was one of several Stars players who reached the major leagues.

The Stars entered the Negro National League in 1933 and one year later won the league championship. After finishing first in the second half and fashioning an overall record of 23–13, the Stars defeated the Chicago American Giants in a hotly contested seven-game playoff to win the title.

There would be no more pennants for the Stars. The team finished regularly in the middle of the pack, playing respectably but not quite well enough to be serious contenders. At Penmar Park, where overflow crowds sometimes numbered as high as 10,000 for a Sunday doubleheader, Stars games were often noteworthy less for the game itself than for the smoke and cinders from nearby locomotives that would rain down on the field and stands, sometimes forcing temporarily delays of games.

The Stars played in the Negro National League through the 1948 season. When the league merged with the Negro American League, the Stars switched to the new division where they remained until 1952. Financial trouble and the integration of major league baseball, which removed many top players from the Negro Leagues, forced the Stars to disband after the 1952 season. It was the last year an all-black professional team ever played in Philadelphia.

During their two decades, though, the Stars played a prominent role in baseball in the city. And it wasn't determined only by how they performed on the field. In an era when baseball was still weighted by the shackles of segregation, they were the main rooting source for legions of fans.

ANNE TOWNSEND IN A LEAGUE OF HER OWN

Nearly 70 years after Anne Townsend dashed across athletic fields with a fervor seen few times before, her name is still mentioned with a kind of reverence usually reserved for very special people. The awe that is expressed is not without justification.

Townsend was indeed very special. She ranks among the best women athletes ever to come from the Philadelphia area. In fact, in *The Encyclopedia of Sports,* she is credited as being "the greatest American field hockey player."

It is generally acknowledged that she is Philadelphia's greatest field hockey player. But she was also a marvelous lacrosse player. A member of Merion Cricket Club near where she grew up, Townsend made All-American in both sports. Moreover, she was an outstanding player in tennis, squash, and golf as well.

In an era when women's sports were relegated so deeply to the bottom of the heap that they were barely noticeable, Townsend attracted attention because she was so good. "She was very quick and very smart," recalled Alice Willetts, an All-American player in the 1940s and 1950s.

One of the first members inducted into the U.S. Field Hockey Hall of Fame, which is housed at Ursinus College, Townsend's career spanned two decades, starting in the early 1920s. In 1924 she was named to the U.S. Field Hockey Association's first team, an honor comparable today to being selected as an All-American. Versatile

Anne Townsend has been called "the greatest American field hockey player."

enough to play both center halfback and left fullback, Townsend was named to that team every year through 1938.

From 1923 to 1936 she was captain of the U.S. team, an honor accorded the ranking player in the country. In 1924 she captained an all-star team that toured England. She also captained a touring team in 1936 that played in Copenhagen, Denmark.

While she was excelling in field hockey, Townsend was also one of the nation's leading lacrosse players. She was named to the All-American team in 1933, 1934, 1936, and 1938 while playing for club teams in Philadelphia.

After her playing career ended, Townsend continued an active role in sports and served as president of the U.S. Field Hockey Association. During her tenure in that position, field hockey undertook numerous innovations, the result being that the sport was modernized considerably. A commanding presence at hockey conferences throughout the country, Townsend was heavily involved in the sport well into the 1960s.

TEMPLE'S TIME

If there was one college whose sports program was particularly prominent in the 1930s, it was Temple. Although other colleges enjoyed some measure of success, the fourth decade of the 20th century belonged to the Owls.

Temple football first under former Penn star Henry (Heinie) Miller and then the fabled Glenn (Pop) Warner had an extremely prosperous decade, climaxed by a trip to the Sugar Bowl. Owls basketball with Jimmy Usilton at the helm and Harry Litwack serving as an assistant also flourished, ranking first in the nation, with the crowning achievement being the championship of the first National Invitational Tournament. It was surely the best decade in Temple sports history.

Warner, one of the great college football coaches of all time, had come to Temple in 1933 after developing enormously successful programs at Pittsburgh and Stanford. Lured back to the East Coast, Pop Warner (whose name a nationwide boys' football program would later bear) replaced Miller, who had won 20 of 28 games in the first three years of the 1930s, compiling an overall 50–15–8 mark during his eight seasons at Temple.

With the exception of Penn State, however, the Owls under Miller played a mostly weak schedule. Warner upgraded the schedule, and in his second year, with games against Virginia Poly, Texas A&M, Indiana, West Virginia, and Holy Cross, Temple finished with a 7–1–2 record. The Owls beat Virginia, 34–0, and Texas A&M, 40–6 in their first two games, and by the end of the season, playing before capacity crowds at Temple Stadium, had only ties with Indiana and Bucknell marring their record.

Led by All-American running back Dave Smukler, captain and future Temple coach Pete Stevens, and linemen Stan Grayson and Chet Messervey, the Owls for the first and only time in their history gained national stature in football. They were rewarded at the end of the season with an invitation to the inaugural Sugar Bowl. The game, played in New Orleans, matched Temple against unbeaten Tulane.

With 28,000 in the stands, Temple's Danny Testa scored in the first quarter on a pass from Glenn Frey to record the Sugar Bowl's first touchdown. Smukler, often called one of the finest football players in Temple history, played the entire 60 minutes of the game, added another six-pointer on a 25-yard run, and kicked his second extra point to give the Owls a 14–0 lead in the second quarter.

The Owls, however, could not score again. Tulane All-American Monk Simons returned the kickoff 80 yards for a touchdown to cut Temple's lead at halftime to 14–7. Then, with Dick Hardy scoring on a 42-yard pass play in the third period and on a 25-yard run in the fourth, the Green Wave pulled to a 20–14 victory.

Although Temple's season ended in defeat, the Owls still had plenty of good football left. Adding teams such as Michigan State, Iowa, Mississippi, Vanderbilt, and

Running back Dave Smukler (left) and
head coach Glenn (Pop) Warner led Temple to the first Sugar Bowl after the 1934
season.

Boston College to the schedule, Temple remained a national power over the next
two years, posting records of 7–3 and 6–3–2. The Owls then went 3–2–4 and 3–6–1
in Warner's last two years, twice beating Florida. Warner's Temple career came to
a close after the 1938 season with the future Hall of Fame member compiling a
31–18–9 record.

Meanwhile, Temple basketball had entered a period of spectacular success. Usilton had taken over the Owls in 1926 and led them to winning seasons in his first
seven years. In a four-season spurt from 1927 to 1931, Temple had won 68 of 84
games with Litwack serving as team captain in two of those years.

Each season the Owls, playing either at Mitten Hall on the main campus, at the
Arena, or at Convention Hall, faced a schedule packed with nationally prominent
teams, often including Notre Dame, Ohio State, Michigan, NYU, CCNY, and Stanford.
After their first losing season under Usilton in 1933–34, Temple went on to 17–7, 18–6,
and 17–6 records over the next three seasons. Then, in 1937, the Owls hit the top.

In their third game of the season, the Owls defeated national powerhouse Stanford, 35–31. Assistant coach Litwack devised a defense that became known as the
box-and-one that completely shut down Stanford All-American Hank Luisetti, the

first great one-handed set shot artist. Temple then went on to win 20 of 22 games, losing only to Georgetown and Villanova, and beating St. Joseph's, 40–34, in the final game before a record crowd of 12,000 at Convention Hall.

The Owls featured a starting unit known as The Five Ironmen. High-scoring forward Don Shields, 6-foot, 6-inch, two-hand set shooter Mike Bloom, Howard Black, and guards Ed Boyle and Don Henderson all stood over six feet tall, and all usually played the entire 40 minutes of each game.

Based on their regular season record, the Owls were offered a spot in the first NIT ever held (there was no NCAA tournament then). Playing at New York's Madison Square Garden, Temple beat Bradley in the opening round, 53–40, and Oklahoma A&M in the semifinal, 56–44. That victory vaulted the Owls into the final, and before a packed house of 15,000, Temple crushed Colorado, 60–36, for the tournament title, finishing the season with a 23–2 record. The 6-foot, 5-inch Shields was named the tourney's most valuable player.

The NIT title ended a glorious era for Temple basketball. The Owls fell to 10–12 the following year. That turned out to be the last year for Usilton, who retired with a 205–79 record. But unlike football, there would be many other special seasons for Temple basketball.

Coached by Jimmy Usilton (top left), Temple won the inaugural NIT in 1938. The Owls' starters were Howard Black, Ed Boyle, Don Shields, Mike Bloom, and Don Henderson (seated, second to sixth from left).

PHILLIES FUTILITY PERSISTS

Throughout much of the 1930s, baseball in Philadelphia was excessively poor. Sure, the Athletics had their run in the early part of the decade, and the Phillies careened all the way up to fourth place one year. But other than those fleeting moments of prosperity, there was precious little that a fan could get excited about.

When Burt Shotton pushed the Phillies into the first division in 1932, it was the club's highest finish since 1917. The Phils would not place that high again until 1949.

During the 1930s the Phillies had four last-place and four seventh-place finishes. And that was with some pretty decent hitters. Chuck Klein, Johnny Moore, Pinky Whitney, Don Hurst, Ethan Allen, and various others always managed to hit for high averages, thanks in part to the inviting right field wall at Baker Bowl. The trouble was, the Phillies' pitching was usually atrocious.

How bad was it? In 1930, for instance, the Phillies hit .315 as a team but still lost 102 games. The pitching staff had a combined ERA of 6.71 and didn't pitch a single shutout at Baker Bowl, where the Phillies were outscored for the season by an average of 8–7.

In the 1920s, and especially in the 1930s, semipro baseball thrived in Philadelphia with several top-level leagues in operation, such as the Philadelphia and the Quaker City baseball leagues. Teams were sponsored mostly by local businesses, which gave the players daytime jobs. A number of players were good enough to play with the Phillies, but most of them refused because the overall pay was better where they were.

Also refusing to cooperate were the fans. Sometimes as few as 500 would show up for a game at rickety old Baker Bowl. Many of them were gamblers who sat in the stands and bet on every pitch. The fans often got so disgusted with the Phillies' performance that they'd throw seat cushions onto the field in what was one of the early demonstrations of discontent among local sports followers. Play had to be stopped while ushers scurried across the field to retrieve the cushions.

Under owner William Baker, the Phillies were notoriously cheap. Baker died suddenly in 1930, and two years later the team was taken over by Gerry Nugent, who ran the club with his wife Mae, the first woman executive in professional baseball. The Nugents had little money and would often have to sell players just to finance road trips or spring training. Once, the couple even had to sell the office furniture.

Good players didn't stay long in Philadelphia. Such was the case with Germantown native Bucky Walters, Dolph Camilli, and Claude Passeau, three excellent players who the Phillies swapped in deals that brought them much-needed cash. All three went on to become top-level stars in the National League, the first two being MVP award winners with Walters posting a 27–11 record to lead the Cincinnati Reds to the pennant in 1939.

Even Kensington native and former Phillies catcher Jimmie Wilson couldn't pull the club out of the doldrums when he was hired as manager. All was not a total loss, though. The Phillies were finally permitted to play Sunday home games in 1934. Predictably, they lost their first Sunday game of the regular season to the Brooklyn Dodgers, 8–7. In 1938, the Phils at long last escaped from Baker Bowl, leaving their decrepit and collapsing stadium of 51½ years to become tenants of the Athletics at Shibe Park. The Phillies played their first game there on July 4, losing the opener of a doubleheader with the Boston Braves, 10–5, then winning the nightcap, 10–2.

NO SHORTAGE OF ACTION

Despite the gloom of the Great Depression, Philadelphia was hardly a city at a standstill in the fourth decade of the 20th century. The city was now the third largest in the nation with a population of more than 1,950,000. New buildings included the 30th Street Station, the PSFS Building and Convention Hall. And the city retained its position as one of the major sports centers in the nation.

Sports in Philadelpia in the 1930s were especially successful at the amateur level. Athletic programs at a number of colleges flourished, and the city produced many fine amateur athletes. There were also numerous innovations on the local sports scene. New teams and new ideas surfaced with uncommon regularity, making the decade one that left an indelible mark on the city's sports history.

One of the most significant developments to occur at the start of the decade was the emergence of pro basketball in the city. In the mid-1920s, Eddie Gottlieb had organized and played for a traveling semipro team called the SPHAS, which stood for South Philadelphia Hebrew Association. The club, with its uniforms purchased by the Young Men's Hebrew Association located at Fourth and Reed Streets, barnstormed throughout the East and Midwest. Eventually, the SPHAS joined the Eastern Basketball League, then one of the top professional circuits in the country. SPHAS players, all of whom were local, were paid between $5 and $30 per game. The team played its home games on Saturday nights at the Broadwood Hotel at Broad and Vine Streets. Women were admitted free, and dances followed the games. For away games, eight players and a coach traveled in a seven-passenger Ford.

One of the great early pro basketball teams, the SPHAS, featuring a running and passing game, won the league championship during the 1931–32 season and again in 1933–34, 1935–36, and 1936–37. When they weren't playing league games, the SPHAS barnstormed against independent clubs such as the Original Celtics and the Harlem Globetrotters. Among the SPHAS star players were Harry Litwack, Petey Rosenberg, Cy Kasselman, Edwin Black, and Chuck Passon. The team's public address announcer was a little man with a booming voice who was paid $5 a game and answered to the name of Dave Zinkoff. A close lifetime friend of Gottlieb's, The Zink, as he came to be called, would go on to a legendary career as a PA announcer. He specialized in Warriors and later 76ers games, but he was a familiar voice at sporting events throughout the city, even including a brief stint doing baseball games at Shibe Park.

The SPHAS joined the American Basketball Association in 1937, remaining there until the team folded in 1949. By then Gottlieb was heavily involved in his new team, the Warriors, which had joined a new professional basketball league. The SPHAS, though, had earned a place as the father of pro basketball in Philadelphia.

Also new at the start of the decade was full-time auto racing. Langhorne Speedway opened for business in 1930, and in its first major event, a 100-mile race, Bill Cummings, a nationally prominent driver and veteran of the Indianapolis 500, won what was billed as a national championship event. Averaging 77.3 miles per hour in his Miller, Cummings drove what was believed to be the first car with a supercharger. Indy winner Billy Arnold won the race the following year in a Duesenberg, and in 1932, Mauri Rose, later to become a three-time 500 winner, won a 50-mile race.

Langhorne was then a dirt track catering primarily to stripped-down versions of street cars. Because of its circular configuration, the track was considered extremely dangerous. Crashes were frequent. Yet, Langhorne prevailed as the leading auto racing track in the Philadelphia area until the early 1970s. The city also had its own track, Yellowjacket Speedway at G and Luzerne Streets, which was in its prime in the 1930s and 1940s.

Boxing also left its mark in Philadelphia during the 1930s. In the city's second largest gate up to that time, a sellout crowd of 30,000, bringing in total receipts of $180,000, watched Italy's Primo Carnera defeat George Godfrey of Leiperville, Delaware County, in a controversial heavyweight fight at Baker Bowl. Godfrey, one of the top black heavyweight fighters of his day, was far ahead on points when he was disqualified for too many low blows. Godfrey was banned for life for the offense, but the lumbering Carnera would go on to win the heavyweight title in 1933.

Future Hall of Famer Hack Wilson, who lived much of his life in Leiperville, set a National League record with 56 home runs for the Chicago Cubs. The record would stand until 1998. Another local resident of considerable prominence was Fred Luehring. He moved to Swarthmore in 1931, when he became director of intermural programs at Penn, and lived there until he died at the age of 99 in 1981. Luehring had a storied career in which he played football for Amos Alonzo Stagg at the University of Chicago, was Princeton's first basketball coach in 1912, was athletic director at the University of Minnesota when Bronko Nagurski played there, was head linesman in the first Notre Dame–Army football game played at the Polo

Grounds, and was a member of the U.S. Olympic committee for 12 years and chairman of the swimming committee in 1932 and 1936.

Philadelphian Midget Wolgast defeated Black Bill in 15 rounds in New York to win the flyweight title in 1930 en route to a career record of 150–36–15. That year, Ruth Hall Banks won the national women's squash championship, and Penn AC's eight-oared crew won the world championship at Liège, Belgium, with a record time of 5:18.8 that still stands for 2,000 meters. Voted the greatest crew of the first half century, the Penn AC team, which included Charley McIlvaine, Tom Curran, Jack Bratten, John McNichol, Myrlin James, Joe Dougherty, Dan Burrows, Chet Turner, and Tom Mack, was in the midst of a streak in which it won 31 straight races between 1929 and 1931.

Two more additions to the city's sports scene in 1931 came when La Salle fielded its first football and basketball teams, both coached by Philadelphian Tom Conley. The Explorer gridders defeated Brooklyn College, 26–0, in their first game before

The eight-oared crew of Penn AC was named the best of the first half-century. It included (from left) coach Frank Miller, Chet Turner, Dan Burrows, Joe Dougherty, Myrlin James, John McNichol, Jack Bratten, Tom Curran, and Charley McIlvaine.

going on to a 4–3 record for the season. With assistant coach Marty Brill, a former Penn Charter star from Norwood, replacing his former Notre Dame teammate Conley in 1933 and piloting the squad through 1939, La Salle had only one losing season during the decade, and in 1934, led by 140-pound dynamo Wink Gallagher, had the only undefeated season in the school's history with a 7–0–1 mark. In basketball, La Salle dropped its first intercollegiate game to Delaware, 33–25, but sparked by co-captains Mort Gratz and Ray Bab, finished the season with a 15–8 record. The Explorers, so named because a sportswriter in the early 1930s incorrectly wrote that the college was named after the French explorer, also had only one losing season during the decade, with Len Tanseer coaching the team from 1933 on.

The Sullivan Award, first presented in 1930 when Bobby Jones was the winner, came to Philadelphia for the first of five times in 1931 when Penn's Barney Berlinger won the honor, which went to the top amateur athlete in the nation. Berlinger had just won his

Tom Conley (left) and Marty Brill (right) flank La Salle president Brother Alfred as they sign on as coaches of the first Explorers football team in 1931.

Decathlon champ Barney Berlinger was the first of Philadelphia's five Sullivan Award winners.

third straight decathlon at the Penn Relays and was regarded as the nation's premier performer in that event. In 1934 he would win the national decathlon championship.

Philadelphia athletes made news in the 1932 Olympics in Los Angeles. Penn sprinter Bill Carr won gold medals in the 400-meter race and the 1,600-meter relay. World records were set in both events. Jean Shiley from Haverford High School and Temple set a world record and won a gold medal in the high jump after being declared the winner over Babe Didrikson, who was disqualified because she dived over the bar. Joe Schauers of Drexel and Charles Kiefer of La Salle with Ed Jennings as coxswain combined to win a gold in pairs rowing with a coxswain, and Bill Gilmore of Wayne and Ken Myers of Norristown teamed to win gold in double sculls. In winning, Myers, who had captured silver medals in the 1920 and 1928 Olympics in fours and single sculls, respectively, became only the fourth American to win three rowing medals in the Olympics.

The Army-Navy game returned to Philadelphia in 1932 for the first time since 1922 with the Cadets marching to a 20–0 victory. The game would be moved from

Franklin Field to Municipal Stadium in 1936, and except for a three-year disappearance during World War II, would be held in Philadelphia every year until 1983. And in boxing, Philadelphian Johnny Jadick captured won a 10-round decision over Tony Canzoneri at the Arena to win the junior welterweight title. Six months later, Jadick, who had an 85–57–9 career record, won another 10-round decision over Canzoneri in a rematch at Baker Bowl.

The big news in 1933 was the winning of the Triple Crown by the Phillies' Chuck Klein and the Athletics' Jimmie Foxx. It was the only time two players from the same city achieved that distinction in their respective leagues. Klein in right field and teammate Dick Bartell at shortstop were National League starters in the first All-Star Game that year. No Athletics started in the game won 4–2 by the American League at Comiskey Park in Chicago, although Lefty Grove pitched in relief.

In two fights at the Arena in 1933, Kid Chocolate successfully defended his junior lightweight title with a 10-round decision over Johnny Farr, but lost the crown seven months later when he was knocked out in the seventh round by Frankie Klick. Boxing thrived in Philadelphia during that era, especially after the opening of Convention Hall and the staging of top cards at the Olympia in South Philadelphia and the Met in North Philly under new owner Jimmy Toppi.

With trains bringing them to sidings on South Broad Street, West Point Cadets head to Municipal Stadium to attend the Army-Navy game.

Roy Coffin and Neil Sullivan, II, two of the top squash players in Philadephia, teamed to win the U.S. men's doubles championship in 1933, the first of five consecutive titles the two would win. Sullivan also won the national men's singles crown in 1934. At that time, squash was a prominent sport in the Philadelphia area. Anne Page won the national women's singles title in 1936, 1937, 1939, and 1947, as well as two national doubles championships. Cecile Bowes captured the singles crown in 1938, and again in 1940, 1941, and 1948.

The U.S. Open golf tournament returned to Merion in 1934, and in his first Open, 22-year-old Ben Hogan missed the cut. An unhearalded Olin Dutra became the first Californian to win the event as he defeated Gene Sarazen by one stroke. It was the only major tournament victory for the 6-foot, 3-inch, 230-pound Dutra, who shot a 13-over par 293 to win.

In 1934 the Dad Vail Regatta began with the first race pitting Rutgers, Manhattan, and Marietta at Marietta in Ohio. The Phillies and Athletics, meeting in the City Series, played in the first Sunday baseball game in Philadelphia. Steve Hamas, a five-sport athlete from Penn State, upset Max Schmeling in a heavyweight fight before 14,000 at Convention Hall. Joe Carter caught four touchdown passes to lead the Eagles to a 64–0 thrashing of the Cincinnati Reds. And in a shocking upset, Ursinus defeated Penn, 7–6, at Franklin Field as Herman (Reds) Bassman returned an interception 45 yards for a touchdown. It was one of the biggest wins for the Bears, who hadn't beaten or even scored on Penn since 1910.

A legendary coaching career was launched in 1934 at West Chester State when Penn State's first All-American football player (1921), a former triple-threat quarterback named Glenn Killinger, took a job as head football, basketball, and baseball coach. A former minor league baseball player and manager and head football coach at Rensselaer and Moravian, Killinger went on to post a 146–39–12 record in 23 seasons in football, never having a losing season and recording undefeated campaigns in 1945, 1952, and 1957. Between 1945, when he returned to the Rams after three years of military service, and 1953, Killinger compiled a 66–9–1 record. Killinger, who was credited with converting Otto Graham from a tailback to a T-formation quarterback when he coached a military team during World War II, also registered a 340–167 record in 32 years as head baseball coach.

Nineteen thirty-four was also the first year of St. Joseph's Mighty Mites, so named because of their lack of height. Under coach Billy Ferguson, the Hawks in their first major splash on the local basketball scene began a four-year run in which they won 54 of 71 games. Matt Guokas, Sr., was the team's star. Ferguson's coaching career, during which he posted a 309–208 record, extended from 1928 to 1953, longest of any Hawks mentor.

Babe Ruth, playing for the Boston Braves, ended his storied career in Philadel-

Glenn Killinger (attending to a player) began a brilliant coaching career at West Chester State College in 1934.

phia in 1935 when he left the field after the first inning of the first game of a Memorial Day doubleheader at Baker Bowl. After botching a play in left field, Ruth waited until the inning ended, then tucked his glove under his arm and sprinted to the clubhouse in center field. Fans, sensing it might be Ruth's final appearance, gave him a standing ovation.

That year the Phillies met the Cincinnati Reds at Crosley Field in the major leagues' first night game. With President Franklin Delano Roosevelt pressing a key at the White House to turn the lights on, the Phils dropped a 2–1 decision before a crowd of 20,422. On the bench for the losing team was rookie reserve infielder Jose (Chile) Gomez, the first Hispanic ever to play with the Phillies.

Kelly Betillo became the latest Philadelphian to make a name for himself in auto racing when he won the Indianapolis 500 in 1935. Driving a Gilmore Special, Betillo set a new 500 record with an average speed of 106.24 miles per hour. Betillo, who also won a 100-mile race at Langhorne Speedway, climaxed the year by being named the U.S. Auto Club's national champion.

Billy Ferguson, talking with (from left) Jim O'Neill, Al Guokas, and Ed O'Halloran, led the Mighty Mites of St. Joseph's during one of the Hawks' finest eras.

A human racing machine named Eulace Peacock also performed superbly. During the 1935 track season the Temple sprinter defeated Jesse Owens in seven of 10 meetings, and in the AAU national championships he beat Owens in the 100-meter dash and the long jump, two events in which Peacock set world records. A sophomore from Union, New Jersey, Peacock tore a hamstring in the 1936 Penn Relays and was thus denied a chance to compete in the Berlin Olympics, made famous by Owens's capturing four gold medals in front of a chagrined Adolph Hitler. Peacock recovered in time to conclude a banner career at Temple in 1937. He won six national pentathlon titles between 1933 and 1945, and later ran a meat-packing business in New York with his old friend and rival Owens.

Another Philadelphia champion in 1935 was the German-American team, which captured top honors in the American Soccer League. No champion was Connie Mack, who grew tired of losing gate receipts because fans sat on rooftops of houses

Eulace Peacock and Jesse Owens (left) met many times in 1930s races with the Temple sprinter usually finishing first.

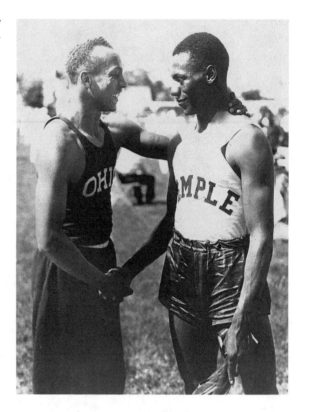

on 20th Street to watch the Athletics play. When other efforts tried to stop that practice failed, he added 22 feet to the existing 12-foot-high right field wall. Having lost their view, fans took Mack to court in an attempt to get the wall torn down. Mack, represented by a young lawyer named Richardson Dilworth, won the case, and what had become known as "the spite wall" stayed.

The Eagles made a different kind of news in 1935 when they signed defensive lineman Alabama Pitts, recently paroled from Sing Sing Prison. Pitts played for just one season, which happened to be one in which the Eagles began with a night game against the Pittsburgh Pirates before a crowd of 20,000 at Temple Stadium.

Faced with another weak group of players, Eagles coach and president Bert Bell made a proposal in 1936 that had an immeasurable impact on pro football. To resolve the vast inequities in talent on different teams, Bell, who had become sole owner of the Eagles after buying out his partners for $4,000, suggested an annual draft of college players with the weakest team selecting first. The proposal was adopted on May 19, and the downtrodden Eagles got the first pick. They chose running back Jay Berwanger, the Heisman Trophy winner from the University of Chicago. Berwanger, however, refused to sign with the Eagles, who then traded him to the Chicago Bears. Berwanger's demand for a two-year, $24,000 contract was rejected by the Bears, ending his pro football career before it got started.

The 1936 Eagles needed all the help they could get. After switching home games to Municipal Stadium, they beat the New York Giants, 10–7, in the season's opener. But, scoring only 41 points and just six touchdowns all season, they then lost 11 straight to finish with a 1–11 record, the worst in NFL history. Meanwhile, across town, La Salle's football team, sparked by the exciting play of quarterback Joe Sciaretta, moved back to the campus to play in its new McCarthy Stadium. Penn had its finest football season of the decade as it won seven of eight games. It was the final year for the Quakers' famed Destiny Backfield, a stellar group led by All-American Franny Murray and including Lew Elverson, Bill Kurlish, and Ed Warwick. To accommodate larger crowds, the Army-Navy game was shifted to Municipal Stadium, and the Middies won the first game there, 7–0.

Philadelphian and future Penn coach Jack Medica won a gold medal in the 400-meter freestyle and silvers in both the 100-meter freestyle and the 4 × 200-meter freestyle relay while swimming for the University of Wisconsin in the Olympic Games in Berlin. Some 55,000 fight fans went to Municipal Stadium to see Joe Louis, just three months after being knocked out by Max Schmeling but now on his way to becoming the greatest heavyweight boxer of all time, knock out Overbrook's Al Ettore in the fifth round. In the only shutout ever recorded in Walker Cup competition, the United States, led by nonplaying captain Francis Ouimet, scored nine points to zero by both Great Britain and Ireland in a one-sided golf match at Pine Valley. And Al Severance led his team to a 15–8 record in his first season as basketball coach at Villanova. The Wildcats would go on to post a 75–15 record in Severance's first four years, and he would become Villanova's winningest coach, compiling a 413–241 mark in 25 seasons.

Another coach who would become prominent joined the ranks at Villanova in 1937. Jim (Jumbo) Elliott became the Wildcats' track and field coach. During a career that would carry into 1981, Elliott established himself as one of the nation's greatest track coaches.

War Admiral, owned by Delaware County racing squire Sam Riddle and sired by the great Man o' War, won the Kentucky Derby, the Preakness, and the Belmont Stakes to become only the fourth horse in history to win the Triple Crown of racing. That fall, future Green Bay Packers coaching legend Vince Lombardi, playing for the Eastern College All-Stars, appeared in a preseason exhibition game against the Eagles at Temple Stadium. A crowd of 25,000 saw the Eagles—in the midst of a 14-game regular season losing streak—triumph, 14–6. Weightlifter Dave Mayor of Philadelphia was named the world's strongest man. And Villanova made its first postseason appearance in football when it tied Auburn, 7–7, in the Bacardi Bowl in

Havana, Cuba, the first bowl game ever played outside the United States. The Wild-cats, in their first year under Maurice (Clipper) Smith, took a 7–2 record into the contest. Trailing late in the fourth quarter, Villanova gained a tie when lineman Matt Kuber recovered a blocked Auburn punt and scored from the two-yard line, after which Bill Christopher kicked the extra point.

Penn hired George Munger to coach its football team in 1938. In 16 seasons, the longest of any Penn football coach, Munger would guide the Quakers to an 82–42–10 record and nine Ivy League titles, and 14 of his players would become All-Americans. During Munger's reign, which included just one losing season, Penn enjoyed its last great era in football. Playing at Franklin Field before sellout crowds, the Quakers led the nation in attendance every year between 1938 and 1942, pack-ing 1,780,500 fans into the stands during that five-year period.

Another coach making his debut in 1938 was Lew Elverson, the former Penn back, who took over at Swarthmore College. Except for time out during World War II, Elverson would faithfully lead the Garnet through 1972 and again in 1974, com-piling a 96–129–8 record in 32 seasons, by far the longest of any Swarthmore coach. Still another newcomer on the scene appeared in a Philadelphia broadcast booth for the first time. Calling the home games of the Phillies and Athletics, Byrum Saam would broadcast more than 8,000 games—more losing games than any other broadcaster, it was said—before retiring in 1975. In his familiar Texas drawl, Saam would become noted for his informed play-by-play as well as his frequent misuse of the language, some examples of which rate as all-time classics.

The Eagles finally got a draft choice that they could count on in 1939 when they made quarterback Davey O'Brien the first choice. A Heisman Trophy winner out of Texas Christian, the All-American first team selection signed for a $12,000 salary and a percentage of the gate. He was worth it. In his rookie season the 150-pound O'Brien played both ways, and on offense he set an NFL passing record with 1,324 yards while completing 99 of 220 tosses. Despite the presence of O'Brien, along with top players Bill Hewitt, Joe Carter, and Dave Smukler, the Eagles could still do no better than a 1–9–1 record. But with Alan Walz at the mike for NBC, they did play in the first televised pro football game, losing, 23–14, to the Brooklyn Dodgers at Ebbets Field.

Another first in 1939 came when the Athletics played in the American League's first night game, after lights had been installed at Shibe Park. Although they lost, 8–3, to the Cleveland Indians, it was a victory of sorts for the A's, who had to with-stand protests and threatened lawsuits from 20th Street residents who were upset by the intrusion the lights would make in their evening lifestyles. Soon after that game, the Phillies made their nighttime debut at the park in a 5–2 loss to the Pitts-burgh Pirates.

Joe Carter was one of the Eagles' top players during the 1930s.

It was a big year for Philadelphia sports in 1939. In the midst of winning 37 straight races, Penn grad and future Quakers coach Joe Burk became the first oarsmen to win the Sullivan Award. Rowing for Penn AC, Burk had become only the second American to win the Diamond Sculls in the Henley Regatta in 1938, and he repeated the victory the following year. He was a four-time winner of the national sculls championships.

The first NCAA basketball tournament was held in 1939, and Villanova went to the Final Four. After beating Brown, 42–30, the Wildcats advanced to the Eastern Division final at the Palestra against Ohio State. With 3,000 watching, the taller Buckeyes proved too much, defeating the Wildcats, 53–36. While Villanova, led by Johnny Krutulis, ended the season with a fine 20–5 record, Ohio State eventually lost to Oregon, 46–33, in the title game.

The Baseball Hall of Fame opened at Cooperstown, New York, and former Philadelphia players Nap Lajoie (elected in 1937), Grover Cleveland Alexander

(1938), and Eddie Collins (1939) were among the first group inducted. Former New York Yankees outfielder Sam Byrd, now running the golf shop at Philadelphia Country Club, won the Philadelphia Open. He would also win the first *Philadelphia Inquirer* Charities tournament for touring pros in 1944. In one of the most memorable college football games ever played in Philadelphia, 70,000 fans jammed Franklin Field to see Penn take on second-ranked Michigan, led by All-American and future Heisman winner Tom Harmon. The Quakers lost, 19–17, but Penn's star running back Frank Reagan gained 356 total yards to outshine Harmon.

Philadelphia's last and 10th Davis Cup match in which the United States was involved was held at Merion Cricket Club in 1939. Four previous Davis Cup rounds had been played in the area during the 1930s—in 1930 and 1932 at Philadelphia Cricket Club, and in 1936 and 1938 at Germantown Cricket Club—with the United States defeating Canada once and Australia twice and losing to Australia another time. This challenge round proved to be the most memorable of the group as a U.S. team led by Wimbledon champion Bobby Riggs, Frank Parker, and high school student Jack Kramer lost, 3–2, to Australia, the last match coming shortly after Great Britain had declared war on Germany.

In another memorable event held in the final year of the decade at Philadelphia Country Club, Sam Snead bogied the 17th hole, then shot eight on the 18th to blow certain victory in the U.S. Open. Snead wound up two strokes off the lead as Byron Nelson, Denny Shute, and Craig Wood ended in a first-place tie with scores of 284. In an 18-hole playoff Sunday afternoon, Nelson and Wood tied to force another 18-hole playoff the next day. This time, Nelson, after rolling in an eagle with a one-iron shot on the fourth hole, scored 70 to beat Wood by two strokes and win his only major championship.

Jimmie Foxx, Philadelphia's Greatest Hitter

When it came to raw talent, few hitters had more than Jimmie Foxx. Double XX, or The Beast, as he was sometimes called, packed 200 pounds of muscle over a 6-foot frame, and if a pitched ball happened to get in the way of his bat, it was often good-bye baseball.

The Philadelphia Athletics' slugger hit them long and he hit them often. Next to Babe Ruth, he was the premier home run hitter of his era. When Foxx retired after a

Jimmie Foxx was a devastating slugger who ranked second only to Babe Ruth.

20-year career, only the New York Yankees basher had more home runs than Jimmie's 534.

Double XX won four home run crowns. His 58 homers in 1932 were the most anyone other than Ruth had ever hit in one season. Foxx wasn't just a home run hitter, though. He won two batting titles and hit over .300 on 11 occasions after he became a regular, once going as high as .364. He also won three RBI crowns and led the American League in slugging percentage five times while posting a career batting average of .325 with 2,646 hits, 1,921 RBI, and 1,751 runs scored. He was elected to the Hall of Fame in 1951.

Based on such lusty hitting, Foxx, who hit more long shots at Shibe Park than any other player, has to be regarded as Philadelphia's finest hitter of the 20th century. Without question, he was the city's top athlete in the 1930s, although he gets strong competition from Chuck Klein and teammates Lefty Grove, Mickey Cochrane, and Al Simmons.

Jimmie joined the A's in 1925, a strong 17-year-old kid from Sudlersville, Maryland. Connie Mack didn't believe in farm systems and got many of his players through tips from friends, would-be scouts, and ex-players. Foxx came on the recommendation of former A's star Frank (Home Run) Baker, who at the time was managing an Eastern Shore League team at Easton where Jimmie played. Foxx was mostly a catcher at the time, but he could run, field, and oh, could he hit.

Foxx played sporadically for the A's over the next four years, learning the big league game and coming off the bench to play first base, third base, and catcher. He never hit below .300 in a part-time role. In 1929, Mack moved Foxx to first base and made him a regular. Jimmie hit .354 with 33 home runs and 117 RBI.

From then on, Foxx terrorized enemy pitching. While the A's were winning three straight pennants, Jimmie was the bulwark of the club's offense. Then, in 1932, he registered a .364–58–169 and was voted the league's Most Valuable Player. He repeated that honor in 1933, going .356–48–163 and becoming only the third AL player to win the Triple Crown (which Chuck Klein also won in the National League, making Philadelphia the only city ever to have two such winners in the same season).

Unfortunately, Mack, as he did with all his stars, traded Foxx to the Boston Red Sox after the 1935 season, getting virtually nothing in the way of players but $150,000 in cash. Jimmie continued his heavy hitting for six seasons with the Bosox, and in 1938 he won two legs of the Triple Crown with a .349 batting average and 175 RBI.

Foxx came back to Philadelphia in 1945 to finish his career as a part-time pitcher and infielder with the Phillies. Later, he managed in the All-American Girls' League (the character portrayed by Tom Hanks in the movie *A League of Their Own* was loosely based on him) and served as a coach with the A's. Having fallen on hard times after retiring as a player, Jimmie died in 1967 in Miami, Florida.

Pro Football, Pro Basketball Go Big Time

For Philadelphia sports, the decade of the 1940s was one that underwent a major transformation. It was the decade in which professional football and professional basketball finally arrived on the scene as major forces.

In earlier times, professional baseball had always been the dominant team sport in Philadelphia. Some college teams flourished, too. But pro football and pro basketball were never really more than minor league operations, attracting small clusters of fans and seldom rising to a level of prominence in the city.

That changed in the 1940s when the Eagles ended a more than decade-long struggle as a hand-to-mouth operation and won two of three National Football League championship games, and a new team called the Warriors became a charter member of the fledgling Basketball Association of America, promptly winning the league's first title.

The emergence of the Eagles and Warriors as bona fide pro teams made Philadelphia one of the few cities that fielded major league teams in each of the top three sports. But the city's reputation as a hotbed of sports activity was primarily fueled during the latter part of the decade. During the first half of the 1940s, a different kind of situation existed. It was known as World War II. At no other time during the entire century did an external influence have such a major impact on sports.

In Philadelphia the effects of the war were reflected in numerous ways. Professional as well as college athletes went off to fight, leaving their teams to be manned by what Philadelphia author Harrington (Kit) Crissey called "teenagers, graybeards and 4-Fs." The roster shortages were so severe that the Eagles had to combine with the Pittsburgh Steelers one year to field a team called the Steagles. The Phillies and Athletics stayed close to home for spring training. Events were canceled or scaled down.

When the war was finally over, another unusual phenomenon occurred. Fans, striving to put some fun back in their lives, flocked to sporting events in greater numbers than ever before. War heroes and grizzled veterans of battles on foreign soil returned to the lineups. And a feeling of euphoria swept across the world of fun and games, just as it did through much of the real world.

The Eagles stood at the top of the list of local post-war success stories. They had started to end a long history of losing the minute they drafted running back Steve Van Buren out of Louisiana State University. Van Buren, who was destined to become one of the NFL's greatest ball-carriers, was surrounded by a talented array of teammates playing under a future Hall of Fame coach, Earle (Greasy) Neale. By the late 1940s the Eagles not only had finally gained acceptance among the city's football fans, but had also become the most powerful team in the league.

Almost as successful were the Warriors, who brought professional basketball out of the dance halls and into the major leagues. The Warriors had the deadly shot-maker Joe Fulks, the BAA's first scoring champion. Coached by Eddie Gottlieb, they won the first BAA championship in 1946–47, then lost in the final round the following year. Few years would pass after that when the Warriors weren't among the premier teams in the league.

There was nothing premier about Philadelphia's major league baseball teams. Through the first half of the decade, the Phillies and Athletics were uniformly awful. The Phillies finished in last place in five of the first six years of the decade, losing not only more than 100 games four times, but also two owners, one to insolvency, the other banned by the league for life for betting. Only toward the end of the decade when the Whiz Kids started coming together did the Phillies finally end more than 30 years of losing. The Athletics, meanwhile, had a record that was no better. Still suffering from the decimation of the team that had been perpetrated by Connie Mack in the 1930s, the A's endured six last-place finishes in the first seven years of the decade, losing 100 games in three of those seasons. The A's surfaced as a contender in 1948, but prosperity was brief, and ultimately the team settled back into its familiar role in the second division.

The decade had plenty of other high spots, though. A new track for thoroughbred horse racing opened in Cherry Hill, New Jersey. Called Garden State Park, it quickly became one of the nation's most prominent racetracks. Another track, Langhorne Speedway, staged NASCAR and midget races for the first time. Philadelphia also had a highly popular minor league ice hockey team called the Rockets, and the first PGA tournament was held in the area.

Penn football was in the midst of another splendid era, producing sellout crowds and All-Americans almost every year. The Quakers also had a stellar basketball player in Herb Lyon. La Salle hoopsters went to the finals of the NIT tournament, and Villanova went to the Final Four in the NCAA tournament. Temple women had three straight undefeated seasons in basketball. Villanova sent two football teams to bowl games. Several Army-Navy games, one of which featured Doc Blanchard and Glenn Davis, were dramatic, memorable battles. And professional soccer was dominated by Philadelphia teams.

Philadelphia was the site of more championship boxing matches in the 1940s than in any other decade. Eight were held in the city, including the only local title defense by Joe Louis and three bouts by Trenton resident Ike Williams. Fighting twice in these matches was an adopted son of the city, Bob Montgomery, who held the lightweight championship for parts of four years.

The city also had another Indianapolis 500 winner in Bill Holland. Jack Kelly, Jr., was the nation's dominant oarsman of the decade, and in 1947 he gave Philadelphia its third Sullivan Award winner. Willie Mosconi launched a magnificent career in which he would capture 15 world billiards titles. Helen Sigel Wilson and Dorothy Germain Porter dominated women's amateur golf. And St. Joseph's George Senesky and Villanova's Paul Arizin led the country in scoring in basketball.

Mickey Vernon of Marcus Hook won an American League batting title. La Salle's Joe Verdeur, the best swimmer in the nation, won an Olympic gold medal. Hunter Lott and Charles Brinton were two of the best squash players in the country. While Charlie Sifford played golf at Cobbs Creek, Skee Riegel of Upper Darby won the U.S. Amateur championship. Browning Ross became Villanova's first NCAA track champion. Max Patkin got his start doing baseball comedy.

Overall, despite lean years at the start, the 1940s were a splendid decade for sports in Philadelphia. The Eagles and Warriors arrived. There were many outstanding performances by other teams and players. There was no question where Philadelphia stood in the world of sports.

GARDEN STATE OPENS FOR HORSE RACING

In the early decades of the 20th century horse racing in the Philadelphia area was a sport largely reserved for people who lived in mansions and drove fancy cars. Most races were held at local hunt clubs where the rich and sometimes famous would convene for a day of frolicking between the intermittent competitions.

Occasionally a race was held at Belmont Plateau in Fairmont Park. But there was no track for the masses, a fact which was somewhat understandable because betting on horses was illegal in Pennsylvania. In New Jersey, where betting was also banned, there had been no thoroughbred racing since 1897, the last race having been held at Gloucester Race Course.

That deficiency was remedied in the early 1940s when Eugene Mori of Vineland, New Jersey, convinced the state to reinstate legal betting and built Garden State Park. Plans were announced on December 31, 1941, and construction began shortly thereafter on land just east of Camden in what was then Delaware Township but would soon be called Cherry Hill.

Because World War II had just begun, steel was in short supply. The park was built mostly of wood and stone. The only steel used came from a dismantled rail line in New York City. Because of the hectic building schedule, several grandstand sections were built in Glassboro at a Works Progress Administration site. Construction costs totaled $1.5 million, and when it was completed, the park had a clubhouse and grandstand capacity of 19,148.

Although its construction was opposed by religious groups, patriotic organizations, and the Camden newspaper, Garden State opened for business on July 18, 1942. Despite the war, a boycott by taxi drivers, gasoline rationing, and insufficient alternate transportation, an overflow crowd of 31,682 jammed every inch of available space to celebrate the park's grand opening.

A steady stream of horse-drawn carriages and double-decker buses brought patrons to the track. General admission was $1.65. It rained off and on during the day, creating deep mud on the track and on the unpaved surfaces where patrons had to walk. Signs throughout the premises advised people that "Air Raid Shelters Are Directly Under the Grandstands." Beer and liquor had not been sanctioned by local politicians and were not on sale. And, because of a government ban on the dissemination of race results via wire communication, the results were dispatched from the press box to newspapers and Western Union offices by hordes of carrier pigeons and a team of motorcycle-riding messengers.

Spanish Sun, ridden by Porter Roberts, won the first race. Boysy, going off at 10–1, won the featured Camden Handicap by two lengths. And Garden State was off and running toward a long and colorful existence.

Ultimately, it became one of the most prominent courses for thoroughbred racing on the East Coast. Numerous major races—including the track's most notable race, the Jersey Derby—were held there. Over the years, most of the nation's leading horses ran at Garden State.

A little more than one month after Garden State opened, the great horse Whirlaway, a Triple Crown winner and horse of the year in 1941, won the track's inaugural running of the 1½-mile Trenton Handicap. Citation, Nashua, Bold Ruler, Carry Back, Kelso, Secretariat, and virtually all the other great horses of the midcentury raced at Garden State. Citation, fresh from victories in the Kentucky Derby and Preakness, won the Jersey Stakes by 11 lengths at Garden State in 1948. He won 19 of 20 starts that year.

Garden State had a singular hold on the area's thoroughbred racing for only a short time. In the late 1940s a group headed by Philadelphian Leon Levy opened Atlantic City Race Course. Delaware Park below Wilmington followed soon after.

WILLIE MOSCONI, MASTER WITH THE CUE

Whenever great billiards players are discussed, one of the first names always mentioned is the master shooter from South Philadelphia, Willie Mosconi. As anybody familiar with the sport can attest, Mosconi was as good as anybody who ever wielded a pool cue.

Willie Mosconi, a 15-time world pocket billiards champion, gives a demonstration to fellow players, including Jimmy Caras (left) of Springfield.

There was, of course, Willie Hoppe. Ralph Greenleaf. Luther Lassiter. And Ralph (Minnesota Fats) Wanderone. South Philly Willie was right there with them.

Between 1941 and 1957, Mosconi won the world pocket billiards championship 15 times. No one ever topped that figure. He won every major professional national and international tournament there was. It's safe to say that Willie never met an opponent he couldn't beat.

Mosconi grew up at Eighth and Wharton Streets, and by the time he was seven years old he was giving billiards exhibitions at pool halls in South Philly. After his brief fling as a child prodigy, Willie laid off the game for about 10 years. He resumed playing in the early 1930s, and in 1933, at the age of 20, he was so good that he was invited to go on a cross-country exhibition tour with the top player of the day, the great Ralph Greenleaf, eventual winner himself of 13 world titles. They played 107 games, and Willie won exactly 50 of them, an amazing total for a young upstart.

At the time, billiards was extremely popular in the United States. In fact, Mosconi was fond of pointing out that in Chicago in the 1930s, he drew more spectators to one of his Saturday night matches than the pro football Bears attracted the next day at Soldier Field.

Mosconi won his first world championship when he was 28 years old in 1941. He then won 14 more times before retiring from active competition in 1957.

At the height of his career, Mosconi played as many as 500 matches each year, counting exhibitions. He set a number of world records for competitive play, one of which was running 306 balls in a row. He once ran 526 straight shots in an exhibition match.

Mosconi went into full-time exhibition play after 1957. In 1968 he was one of the first players elected to the Billiards Hall of Fame.

Willie, who wrote several books on the art of shooting pool, lived much of his adult live in Havertown and Haddonfield. As recently as 1988, five years before his death, he was still playing, participating that year in a nationally televised match with Fast Eddie Parker.

PORTER, WILSON WERE FRIENDLY RIVALS

Throughout much of the 20th century, the Philadelphia area has been the home of many excellent women golfers. From the days of Glenna Collett Vare and her contemporaries to the present with the great touring pro Betsy King, (from Berks County), women from the region have been extremely successful not only on a local level but nationally as well.

Dorothy Germain Porter (left) and Helen Sigel Wilson were friendly rivals for more than five decades of championship golf.

Fine women golfers were particularly in abundance in the Philadelphia area during a period that began in the 1940s. Two of the finest of that and any other era were Dorothy Germain Porter and Helen Sigel Wilson. Both came from privileged backgrounds, both belonged to local country clubs, and both won dozens of tournaments, often at the expense of the other.

Dorothy Germain was a Drexel Hill native and member at Llanerch Country Club. She began playing golf at the age of 12, and within one year she had won her first tournament. While still a student at Upper Darby High School, she had already won three straight Philadelphia Junior Girls championships.

As a 17-year-old, Germain competed in 1941 in her first U.S. Women's Amateur championship, losing to Sigel on the third hole of sudden death in the third round. Two years later, as a freshman at Beaver College, she lost in the semifinal of the Women's Western Open, then won the Women's Western Amateur in Evanston, Illinois.

In 1944, Germain lost in the final of the Western Open to Babe Didrickson Zaharias, but six weeks later successfully defended her Western Amateur title. In

1945, Germain lost two more times to Zaharias—in the Open final and in the Amateur semifinal.

Now married, the 25-year-old wife of Mark Porter claimed her greatest victory in 1949 when she won the U.S. Women's Amateur championship at Merion East. Playing while two months pregnant, she defeated Dot Kielty, 3 and 2, for the victory. Three years later, she was the low amateur with a four-round score of 300 in the U.S. Women's Open at Bala Golf Club in a tournament won by Louise Suggs with a 284.

For the next four decades, Porter, who became a member at Riverton Country Club, remained one of the top female golfers ever to come out of the Philadelphia area. She won three Pennsylvania Women's Amateur titles and nine Philadelphia Women's crowns, the last coming in 1992 at the age of 68. She was a winner four times of the U.S. Senior Women's Amateur championship, the last one in 1983 at Rolling Green in Springfield. And she played on the 1950 Curtis Cup team and was nonplaying captain of the 1966 Curtis and 1984 Women's World Amateur teams, all three of which won.

Helen Sigel was a top athlete at Eden Hall Academy in Torresdale but didn't take up golf until after her senior year. After she did, though, she learned the game quickly and, playing out of Philadelphia Country Club, soon became a contender in top local tournaments.

Sigel won her first Philadelphia Women's tournament in 1940. It would be the first of 12 such victories. The following year, after defeating Germain, she lost to Elizabeth Hicks Newell in the final of the U.S. Women's Amateur in Boston. In the same tournament, Sigel lost in the semifinal to Zaharias in 1946, and in the final to Grace Lenczyk in 1948.

Helen got her big breakthrough in 1949 when she won the Women's Western Amateur in Wilmette, Illinois, beating Peggy Kirk. But in 1950, after beating Betsy Rawls in the quarterfinal, she lost yet another U.S. Women's Amateur after bowing to Mae Murray in the semifinal.

Having launched a successful restaurant in center city and married Charles Wilson in the early 1950s, Helen continued her sparkling golf career into the 1980s. By the time she retired, she had won five Pennsylvania Women's titles and two Women's Eastern amateur crowns, and at the age of 47 in 1965 she was the low amateur (fifth overall) with a record 296 in the U.S. Women's Open at Atlantic City. A member of the 1966 Curtis Cup team, she was nonplaying captain of that team in 1978. And in 1981, Helen captured first place in the Philadelphia Women's Seniors tournament for the eighth time.

Both Wilson and her friendly rival Porter represented the Philadelphia area with exemplary golf over more than five decades. Hardly anyone ever played the game any more exquisitely.

PHILLIES FINALLY GET A LEADER

Ownership in the first four decades of the 20th century was not one of the Phillies' strong points. Not that they had many strong points, anyway, but after Al Reach sold the club in 1903, the string of clumsy men who owned and ran the Phillies generally performed no better than the sorry efforts the team usually put forth on the field.

This state of affairs reached a head in the 1940s when a series of calamities occurred. First, Gerry Nugent had to throw in the towel. Nugent, an honest man with a good mind for baseball but with barely two dimes to rub together, had taken over the club in 1932, two years after the death of penny-pinching William Baker. With his wife Mae as his top aide, Nugent had tried valiantly to keep the club afloat, but with no financial base, the task proved to be impossible. Finally, in 1942, the beleaguered club president—having been unable to put together various deals to sell the team to such interested buyers as Milton Hershey, John B. Kelly, Sr., Branch Rickey, Moe Annenberg, Dan Topping, and Alexis Thompson, and having withstood an attempted coup by other Phillies stockholders—met defeat.

Out of options, out of money, out of anything to sell, and in debt to the National League for loans and to the Athletics for the rental of Shibe Park, Nugent stood by helplessly as the league in an unprecedented action took over his team. Trustees were appointed to run the club, but their services were only temporary. Waiting in the wings to buy the club was William D. Cox, a friend of Rickey and National League president Ford Frick. (It was later reported but never substantiated that Bill Veeck wanted to buy the team and stock it with top players from the Negro League, but was rejected in his bid by Commissioner Kenesaw Mountain Landis.)

Cox, a New York lumber company president, headed a 30-man syndicate that included Fitz Eugene Dixon, Jr. The group put up $190,000 in cash, plus a $50,000 note, and on March 15, 1943, it took over the team. Calamity number two was now on its way.

Before the season was barely half over, Cox had fired new manager Bucky Harris. A future Hall of Famer and ultimately the fourth-winningest skipper in baseball history with 2,157 career victories, Harris had encountered constant interference from the team president. Subsequently, Harris made it known that Cox had bet on Phillies games.

An investigation by the commissioner's office followed. It dragged on for months, but finally, in November, Commissioner Landis announced that he was banning Cox from baseball for life. Cox appealed, but the original verdict stood. And the Phillies had to seek their third owner in one year.

Fortunately, he arrived quickly. Robert R. M. Carpenter, Jr., with solid family con-

nections to the wealthy du Pont family of Wilmington, took over the team after his
father, a vice president at Du Pont Company, put up the $400,000 needed to buy the
team. At 28, Bob Carpenter was the youngest president in baseball history.

At long last the Phillies had stability at the ownership level. Carpenter hired Kennett Square native and former pitching great Herb Pennock as the team's first general manager, and together the pair slowly put the Phillies on their feet for the first
time in almost 30 years.

By 1944 the club had begun to build its first farm system. It had started to sign
good, young players. And by the end of the decade, with such players as future Hall
of Famers Robin Roberts and Richie Ashburn, as well as Del Ennis, Granny Hamner, Curt Simmons, Willie Jones, and various other youngsters in the fold, the
Phillies had shed the cloak of a perennial loser and were contenders for the
National League pennant.

Carpenter would preside over the Phillies until 1972, never scrimping on money
and always trying to make the club better. He had some flaws—he refused to sign
black players until long after most teams had, and he had a penchant for signing

Bob Carpenter (right) got the Phillies
back to respectability with the help of
players such as Olney High grad Del
Ennis.

big, strong pitchers whether or not they were bona fide prospects. But overall Carpenter not only brought the Phillies out of a long and unhappy funk, but he elevated them far above the levels of his predecessors and made them respectable. It was an effort worthy of the highest commendation.

THE EFFECTS OF WAR

While World War II raged across two oceans, there was no limit to the turmoil it caused back home. Philadelphia sports were no exception. In one way or another, the war touched nearly every aspect of local athletic life.

The war's most conspicuous impact on local sports involved manpower. Rosters of all sports teams were depleted as players marched off to join the armed forces. The spots were filled mostly by a collection of untested youth, washed-up veterans, and part-time cripples who couldn't pass the military's physical exams.

This crisis was particularly evident in pro football, where the Eagles had such a shortage of manpower that they had to merge with the equally depleted Pittsburgh Steelers during the 1943 season to form a team that became known as the Steagles. The Eagles provided 20 players, while the Steelers supplied 11. One of the players was a former Eagle, Wild Bill Hewitt, who had last played in 1939 but was coaxed out of retirement. The team, codirected by the teams' coaches, Greasy Neale and Walt Kiesling, played four home games at Shibe Park and two at Pittsburgh's Forbes Field, fashioning a 5–4–1 record, good for third place in the NFL's Eastern Division.

On the Phillies, pitcher Hugh Mulcahy in 1941 became the first major league player inducted into military service. That began a long parade of Phils to draft boards, resulting in patched-together lineups that were sometimes almost comical. At one point in 1944 the Phillies had a roster that included 16-year-old Putsy Caballero, 17-year-old Granny Hamner, and assorted nobodies who were never heard from again. One player was Lee Riley, the father of noted pro basketball coach Pat Riley. Another player, George Hennessey, was only available for home games because he held a full-time job as an airplane mechanic in Trenton. And aging, overweight Jimmie Foxx came out of retirement to lumber around the diamond and even pitch on occasion.

Spring training was another matter. With gasoline rationed and teams forbidden to travel the long distances to sunny Florida, it was necessary to train close to home. The Athletics once went all the way to Wilmington, Delaware, and twice to Frederick, Maryland. The Phillies worked out at Hershey, Pennsylvania, once and Wilmington twice. The New York Yankees trained at Atlantic City and the Boston Red Sox at Pleasantville, New Jersey.

Philadelphia had its first All-Star Game in 1943 at Shibe Park. So that fans who were hard at work during the day, many engaged in the war effort, could attend the event, baseball commissioner Kenesaw Mountain Landis ordered the game to be played under the lights. The start of the game was delayed 65 minutes while city officials practiced a blackout. Eventually, the American League won the first All-Star night game, 5–3.

Many college teams played abbreviated schedules, mostly against nearby opponents, including service teams. In one such game, in 1943, Penn defeated Lakehurst (a naval air base), 74–6. Ursinus played only four games that year, including a 6–0 loss to Willow Grove Naval Air Station, while West Chester didn't play at all in 1943 and 1944.

Many amateur events that would have otherwise been held were canceled. Major league baseball games often began at 3:30 P.M. so that war-time workers could get to the ballpark. Most of them had to travel to the games by public transportation because gasoline was rationed and cars were idled. Golf and tennis tournaments

Two heros of World War II were Athletics pitchers Lou Brissie (left) and Phil Marchildon, joined by Connie Mack.

were held to raise money for the war effort. The Army-Navy game left Philadelphia for three years. Langhorne Speedway was shut down completely.

The effects of the war continued to be felt even after it was over. Some veteran athletes never regained the form they had before they left. Others came back hurt or scarred. Two notable examples were Athletics pitchers Phil Marchildon and Lou Brissie. A member of the Royal Canadian Air Force who was shot down over enemy-occupied territory, Marchildon spent nearly three years as a German prisoner of war before returning to baseball with frayed nerves and weakened physique, but he became 19-game winner in 1947. Brissie survived a mine explosion that nearly cost him a leg, coming back to baseball following 23 operations, a leg pieced back together with wire and metal, and many months of recovery. He won 30 games for the A's in 1947 and 1948.

ARMY, NAVY HAVE THEIR OWN WAR

During the first 100 years of their rivalry, Army and Navy met 75 times in Philadelphia. For sheer drama, it's doubtful if there were any better games than the ones played in the mid-1940s.

After a long absence in which the game had been played only once in Philadelphia between 1915 and 1931, the rivalry had taken up permanent residence in the city in 1932. Because of World War II, however, it was played between 1942 and 1944 at Annapolis, West Point, and Baltimore, but in 1945 it was back in the city.

Because of the war, both service academies virtually had their pick of the nation's top athletes. For that reason, Army and Navy each fielded powerhouse teams that were as good as any they ever put together. When they met at the end of the season, the games were of titanic proportions.

That was especially true in 1945 and 1946. In 1945 undefeated Army entered the big game at Municipal Stadium ranked number one in the nation. Unbeaten and once-tied Navy, which had opened the season with three straight shutouts, was number two. The game figured to be a magnificent battle.

But Navy had not faced a team as strong as Army. Nor had it encountered anybody like Felix (Doc) Blanchard or Glenn Davis, the Cadets' brilliant All-American running backs. Nicknamed Mr. Inside and Mr. Outside, the two were the biggest names in college football, and their reputations were easily matched by their talent.

Blanchard, who would win the Heisman Trophy that year, played the game of his life. He scored two touchdowns to push Army to a 20–0 lead in the second quarter before Navy came back with a 39-yard TD pass from Bruce Smith to Clyde (Smack-

All-American running backs Glenn Davis (left) and
Doc Blanchard performed spectacularly during the
1945 Army-Navy game in Philadelphia.

over) Scott to cut the deficit to 20–7 at halftime. Then, in the third quarter, Blanchard intercepted a pass and returned it 52 yards for his third touchdown of the day. Although Scott intercepted a pass by Davis to set up Navy's second touchdown, the Cadets clinched victory when Davis atoned for his miscue by racing 28 yards for the final Army tally. Army walked off the field with a stunning 32–13 victory. A little while later, coach Earl (Red) Blaik's Cadets would be crowned national champion. Navy was ranked second.

The Cadets were back in the limelight in 1946 when they took a number-two ranking into the big game with only a 0–0 tie with top-ranked Notre Dame spoiling their record. Army hadn't lost a game since it was beaten by Navy in the last game of the 1943 season, and although Blanchard and Davis had departed, the Cadets again had a powerful team. The same could not be said for Navy that year. The Middies had won only one of eight games and were hardly expected to give Army much of a battle. Oddsmakers made them a 30-point underdog.

But battle they did. With President Harry S. Truman in the stands, Army romped to a 21–6 lead at halftime. Then the Middies took over. Bill Hawkins scored from the two-yard line, Reeves Baysinger passed to Leon Bramlett for another touchdown, and suddenly, Navy trailed by just three points.

As the clock wound down, the Middies, who had missed all three extra points, were driving deep into Army territory. The game ended in a sea of confusion as Navy players argued that the clock should have been stopped, claiming that running back Pete Williams had gone out of bounds on the last play. But as fans poured onto the field, time ran out with Navy on Army's three-yard line. Had Navy won, it would have been one of college football's greatest upsets.

History nearly repeated itself two years later. After Army had rolled to an easy 21–0 victory in 1947, the Cadets entered the 1948 game with a perfect 8–0 record. Navy was an imperfect 0–8 and a 20-point underdog.

Army held a 14–7 lead at halftime. Then, after Navy's Hawkins and Army's Arnold Galiffa traded touchdowns, Hawkins scored again in the fourth quarter, and Navy had a 21–21 tie. The game ended with that score, making it an extraordinary comeback for the Middies, and one final magnificent Army-Navy game of the 1940s.

THE WARRIORS DELIVER

If there was one thing that Philadelphia needed in the 1940s to complete its status as a major league sports town, it was pro basketball. The city had big league baseball and football. And in 1946 it got big league basketball.

By then basketball had started to blossom in the city. College basketball had gained considerable stature, and the SPHAS had their group of followers. When the new Basketball Association of America was formed in 1946, Philadelphia received a franchise.

The new franchise was the product of efforts by Eddie Gottlieb, a local entrepreneur and one of the founders of the BAA. Called the Warriors, the new team would play its home games at the Arena, which was the property of the team's original owner, Pete Tyrell. Gottlieb was the coach and general manager.

The Warriors hit paydirt right away when they signed for $8,000 a 24-year-old ex-Marine from Kentucky named Joe Fulks. "You've probably never heard of him," Gottlieb told the press, "but I believe he has the potential to be a great scorer."

The slim, 6-foot, 5-inch, 190-pound graduate of Murray State proved his coach right. Specializing in one-handed shots and driving layups, Fulks became the first pro superstar, and in his rookie year led the BAA with 1,389 points for an astonishing 23.2 average. His total was more than 400 points higher than his closet rival. With

Joe Fulks was the first pro basketball superstar in Philadelphia, leading the league in scoring as a rookie.

his uncanny scoring ability, Fulks, who ranked second in the league in points in each of the next two years, had changed the game of basketball forever.

Fulks was sometimes criticized for shooting too much. "They give me the ball, and I shoot. That's all there is to it," he would respond. In his first year, Fulks set a BAA record with an unheard of 41 points in one game.

Joined by star guards Howie Dallmar from Stanford and Penn, George Senesky from St. Joseph's, and Angelo Musi from Temple, Jumpin' Joe led the Warriors to a second-place finish in the Eastern Division in 1946–47. Posting a 35–25 record, they finished 14 games behind Red Auerbach's Washington Capitols.

While the Caps were upset by the Chicago Stags in the first round of the playoffs, the Warriors advanced to the championship round after beating the St. Louis Bombers and the New York Knickerbockers in the opening rounds, each two games to one. The Warriors' opponent in the final was the Stags, led by high-scoring Max Zaslofsky.

Fulks poured in 37 points in the opener to lead the Warriors to an easy victory at the Arena. The Warriors won the next two games but, with Fulks in foul trouble and scoring only 21 points, lost the fourth game of the series. They came back to clinch the title with an 83–80 victory before a sellout crowd of 8,221 at the Arena as Fulks bagged 34 points to finish the series with a 26.2 average. Each Warriors player received $2,000.

Injuries sidelined Fulks part of the 1947–48 season, but he still finished second in the league in scoring with 949 points. Dallmar led the league with 120 assists, and the Warriors edged the Knicks by one game for first place in the East. In the play-offs the Warriors beat St. Louis, four games to three, to advance to the final. But this time, after losing three games by a total of eight points, they lost in six games to the Baltimore Bullets, including an 88–72 defeat in the last game.

Fulks set a career high with 1,560 points (26.0 average) in 1948–49, but he would win no more scoring titles after the first one. In 1949, however, he set a new record with 63 points in a 108–87 victory over the Indianapolis Jets. Joe hit 27-for-56 from the field and 9-for-14 from the line. He retired after the 1953–54 season, two years before the Warriors' second and last title.

PHILADELPHIA'S GREATEST FIGHT

There was no better era for boxing in Philadelphia than in the 1940s. The city was home to numerous high-level fighters, and important matches were frequent, including no less than eight championship bouts, the most ever staged in the city in one decade.

Of those bouts, one stood out far above the rest. It pitted Philadelphian Bob Montgomery against Trenton's Ike Williams in a match for the lightweight title at Municipal Stadium. The 1947 bout is generally considered the greatest in the city's long boxing history.

Montgomery is regarded as one of Philadelphia's finest boxers. Born in Sumter, South Carolina, he had come to the city at the age of 15, and for the rest of his life he made Philadelphia his home.

Bob began his professional boxing career as a 19-year-old in 1938. By the time he retired from the ring in 1950, he had won 75 fights and lost 19 with three draws. He was elected to the Boxing Hall of Fame in 1995.

By 1941, Montgomery was ranked a top lightweight contender after having split two nontitle bouts with reigning champion Lew Jenkins. Bob then dropped two decisions in 1942 in nontitle matches with the new champ, Sammy Angott. His first title fight finally came in 1943 when he met the great Beau Jack at Madison Square Garden. Montgomery won a bruising 15-round decision to capture the New York-World lightweight crown.

Montgomery lost the title back to Jack later in the year, but regained it in 1944 on

Bob Montgomery is regarded as one of the finest boxers in Philadelphia history.

a 15-round split decision. Six weeks earlier he had pummeled Williams unmercifully in a savage bout in which Ike was knocked out for the first time in his career in the 12th round. The bout fueled the two fighters' intense dislike for each other, their hatred so strong that it carried over into the press.

Williams was also a superior fighter, considered by some experts to the greatest lightweight who ever boxed. A native of Brunswick, Georgia, who relocated to Trenton, he had been boxing professionally since 1940. After losing to Montgomery, he would win the National Boxing Association lightweight title in 1945. (There were then two organizations that recognized champions.)

The feud between Montgomery and Williams simmered for three years with charges and countercharges flying back and forth. Twice Montgomery successfully defended his title in 1946, knocking out Allie Stolz in the 13th round and winning an eighth-round TKO over Wesley Mouzon. Finally, on August 4, 1947, with each still holding a lightweight title, Montgomery and Williams met for the undisputed world championship at Municipal Stadium.

No fight was ever more vicious. Ignoring the art of boxing, the two went at each other with everything they had, right from the opening bell. By the third round, Montgomery, nicknamed the Bobcat, had opened a sizable cut over Williams's eye. Sensing he had Williams in trouble, Montgomery hacked away at the cut time after time. But Williams battled back, and in the sixth round he knocked Montgomery over the ropes. Dangling like a sack of potatoes, Montgomery somehow managed to recover before the count of 10.

But his return was brief. Again Williams knocked him down. This time referee Charley Daggert had seen enough. He stopped the fight at 2:37 of the sixth round, ending an incredibly brutal slugfest and making Williams the winner of a title he would successfully defend five more times and would hold until 1951.

The grudge match between two future Hall of Famers was over. And so, basically, was Montgomery's illustrious career. Bob had two more fights, then did not enter the ring at all in the next two years. In 1950 he attempted a comeback, but after losing his fourth fight and sixth in a row, he retired for good. While he fought, though, Montgomery was not only one of the best lightweight boxers of all time, but also participant in the most rousing match ever held in Philadelphia.

CHUCK BEDNARIK, LAST OF THE GREAT TWO-WAY PLAYERS

In a century of Philadelphia football players, none performed the game harder, with more intensity, or with greater enthusiasm than Chuck Bednarik. And as far as the city is concerned none played the game any better, either.

Bednarik was the quintessential gridiron warrior, a ferocious battler whose blood-and mud-splattered uniform, crooked nose, and gnarled fingers were proud trademarks of the cause. He plied his trade in Philadelphia for 18 years, first as a two-time All-American at Penn, then as the anchor of some of the finest Eagles teams ever fielded.

Chuck was the last of the great two-way players. He played center on offense and linebacker on defense. Even when football had changed almost entirely to a two-platoon system, Bednarik was still going both ways at the age of 35, playing virtually the full 60 minutes of each game. He also was a master of booming kickoffs.

A standout baseball and football player in his native Bethlehem, Pennsylvania, Bednarik was a gunner on 30 bombing missions over Germany during World War II, before enrolling at Penn at the age of 20. He joined the Quakers in 1945, and over a four-year period, one of the most storied eras of Penn football, he led them to a 24–7–1 record. He was first-team All-American in 1947 and 1948, a year in which he

Philadelphia's best football player was Chuck Bednarik, who starred for George Munger (left) at Penn and with the Eagles.

also became the first offensive lineman to win the Maxwell Award as the nation's outstanding college player.

Bednarik was the Eagles' first draft choice in 1949, and as a 24-year old rookie, he helped the Eagles win the NFL title. Chuck really came into his own in the 1950s, when he not only played both ways, but was regarded as the premier center and linebacker in the league. He was named to eight Pro Bowls, and in 1954 he was the game's most valuable player.

Concrete Charley had his finest moments in 1960 when he led the Eagles to another NFL championship. Two particular tackles he made still stick in the minds of Eagles fans. He not only stopped Frank Gifford but knocked him out in a key drive-ending play in a late-season Eagles victory over the New York Giants. Then he squashed Jim Taylor at the Eagles' eight-yard line on the final play of the championship game, preserving his team's 17–13 victory over the Green Bay Packers. Bednarik played 58½ minutes of that 60-minute game.

"I held him and watched the last five seconds run off the clock." Bednarik said. "Then I said, 'You can get up now, you son-of-a-gun. This game is over.'"

Bednarik retired after the 1962 season, having played in 253 of a possible 256 games during his 14-year pro career. Elected to both the College and Pro Football halls of fame, he was, upon his entry into the latter in 1967, only the third player voted to both bodies. He was also selected as the center for the NFL's first 50-year team, as well as the nation's lineman of the decade in the 1950s.

No player in the city's football history is as decorated as Bednarik. He was without question the finest home team player ever to grace a Philadelphia gridiron.

EAGLES' FINEST ERA

After 10 miserable seasons plus a one-year aberration as the Steagles, the Eagles finally arrived as a legitimate pro football team in the 1940s. By the time the decade was over, they were the dominant team in the National Football League, with three straight division titles and two league championships.

During their first 10 years the Eagles had won the grand total of 20 games while losing 84 and tying five. But in 1941, one year after the Eagles moved from Municipal Stadium to Shibe Park, Earle (Greasy) Neale, a one-time Phillies outfielder and a highly successful college coach, was hired as head coach. In 1944, one year after the Steagles' only season, the club made running back Steve Van Buren its first draft choice. After a 28–7 opening-day win over the Boston Yanks at Fenway Park, the Eagles had their first winning season (7–1–2) since the team began in 1933.

They followed that with 7–3 and 6–5 records, the latter including a win over the New York Giants that drew a record crowd of 40,059 to Shibe Park. Then, in 1947, the Eagles went 8–4, good for a tie with the Pittsburgh Steelers for first place in the Eastern Division. In their first playoff game in history, the Birds won the right to meet the Chicago Cardinals in the NFL title game as Tommy Thompson threw touchdown passes to Jack Ferrante and Van Buren, and Bosh Pritchard ran a punt back 79 yards to lead the Birds to a 21–0 victory over the Steelers.

A sheet of ice covered Comiskey Park, where the championship game was held. Unprepared for such conditions, the Eagles wore cleats that could barely dig into the frozen turf. Meanwhile, wearing sneakers, the Western Division champs had no trouble with their footing and captured a hard-fought 28–21 victory for the title, despite a remarkable performance by Thompson in which he completed 27-of-44 passes for 297 yards.

The Eagles, though, were not to be denied the following year. After an opening-day loss to the Cardinals and a tie with the Los Angeles Rams, they beat the New

York Giants and Washington Redskins by identical 45–0 scores, then reeled off six more wins in a row. By the time the season was over, the Eagles had scored 45 points four times and 42 points once, and posted a 9–2–1 record while cruising to the Eastern title. Van Buren, quarterback Thompson, end Pete Pihos, and tackle Al Wistert were all named to the All-Pro first team, and Van Buren was the NFL's Most Valuable Player.

Weather conditions marred the championship game again in 1948. This time, the Eagles met the Cardinals in a raging snowstorm at Shibe Park. It had snowed through most of the previous night, and snow shoveled off the field was piled deep along the sidelines. Convinced that the game wouldn't be played, Van Buren had stayed at his Lansdowne home until a call from Neale routed him out of the house. Steve had to take public transportation to get to Shibe Park, arriving 30 minutes before game time. With 28,864 shivering fans in the stands, the Eagles prevailed, 7–0, scoring on Van Buren's five-yard plunge four plays after guard Bucko Kilroy had recovered a fumble at the Cardinals' 17 yard line.

As defending champs, the Eagles didn't rest on their laurels. In 1949, having

Head coach Earle (Greasy) Neale celebrated the Eagles 1948 championship with (front from left) Tommy Thompson, Ben Kish, and Steve Van Buren.

made Chuck Bednarik their top draft choice and with Vince McNally taking over as general manager for a team of new owners, the Eagles started with a 38–0 victory over the College All-Stars before 93,780 at Soldier Field in Chicago in their first of three appearances in that annual game. (They lost 17–7 in 1950 and won 28–14 in 1961.) The Birds then flew away with an 11–1 record, their best ever. The only setback was a 38–21 loss to the Chicago Bears in the fourth game of the season. The Eagles won most of their games with ease, and at one point placekicker and guard Cliff Patton broke the old NFL record of 72 straight extra points, while Clyde Scott set a team mark with the longest punt return (70 yards). At the end of the season, Van Buren, Pihos and tackle Vic Sears were named first-team All-Pro.

The NFL championship game this time pitted the Eagles against the Rams at the Los Angeles Coliseum with the Birds traveling to the West Coast by train. With Van Buren gaining an amazing 196 yards rushing, Thompson passing to Pihos for one touchdown, and rookie Leo Skladany recovering a blocked punt in the end zone for another, the Eagles blasted to a 14–0 victory in rain and mud, giving the Birds two straight shutout championship wins.

In the final two years of the decade the Eagles were the NFL's premier team. They outscored opponents 761–290 in 1948 and 1949, and overall won 22 games while losing only three and tying one in that period. The Eagles had an enormously talented team that along with those already mentioned included receiver Neil Armstrong, tackles Jay MacDowell and Mike Jarmoluk, centers Vic Lindskog and Alex Wojciechowicz, and backs Russ Craft, Joe Muha (also the punter), Ben Kish, and Frank Reagan. Van Buren, Pihos, Bednarik, Wojciechowicz, and Neale all have been inducted into the Pro Football Hall of Fame.

It was a great era for the Eagles, the best one they ever had. But it was quickly over. After 1949 they settled into a long period of mediocrity that lasted until 1960.

A SLOW START, BUT A FAST FINISH

Despite the fact that nearly half the decade was obliterated by World War II, the 1940s turned out pretty well in Philadelphia sports. Not only did a substantial amount of activity take place, but much of it, including some of the events about to be described, was of considerable significance.

During the four main war years from 1942 to 1945, Philadelphia sports, like those everywhere in the country, existed in a weakened condition, suffering in quality and in some cases barely holding on. And although the first two years of the decade were nothing special either, the last four provided the city with as much excitement as it's ever had. It could be said, in fact, that the modern, multifaceted era of Philadelphia sports was born in 1946.

One of the biggest stories of the early part of the decade was once again Penn football. Frank Reagan was winding up a brilliant college career in 1940, and in one game, a 46–28 victory over Princeton, he had a spectacular outing when he scored five touchdowns and an extra point while rushing for 200 yards. That year Reagan, along with center Ray Frick, was first-team All-American. Penn's 13–2–1 record in 1940 and 1941 launched its last great football decade. With huge crowds jamming Franklin Field and winning seasons occurring every year, the Quakers also featured a first-team All-American nearly each season. End Bert Kucynski, who pitched briefly for the Athletics in 1943, made it in 1942. He was followed by halfback Bob Odell, who also won the Maxwell Club Award as the outstanding college player in the nation and was second in the Heisman voting. Tackle George Savitsky made the team four years in a row, center Chuck Bednarik was named twice, and halfback Skipi Minisi and guard John (Bull) Schweder were Penn's other All-American selections during the decade.

The 1940 season also saw the career of Eagles quarterback Davey O'Brien come to an abrupt end. After playing only two seasons, the 5-foot, 9-inch, 151-pounder quit football to join the FBI. O'Brien went out with a bang in the last game of the season, setting records with 33 completions in 60 attempts for 318 yards in a 13–6 loss to the Washington Redskins. O'Brien played more than 59 minutes of the game. Despite a 1–10 record, the Eagles also had a stellar performance from rookie end Don Looney, who led the NFL with a record 58 pass receptions.

After the season, one of the most unusual and complicated moves in pro sports occurred when Art Rooney sold the Pittsburgh Steelers to Alexis Thompson with Rooney buying one-half interest in the Eagles and Bert Bell becoming part owner of the Steelers. The Eagles and Steelers swapped players, then Rooney returned to Pittsburgh and Thompson took over ownership of the Eagles.

Far less confusing was the emergence of the Rockets as Philadelphia's latest ice hockey team. In 1940 the Rockets became members of the American Hockey League. They lasted for two years before folding, only to return to the same league in 1946. With Phil Hergesheimer and Wally Stefaniw leading the way, the Rockets opened with a 5–52–7 record. They folded again in 1949, having registered a 42–141–17 record in three years.

In 1940, Betty Shellenberger was named to her second straight U.S. Field Hockey Association first team. The Philadelphia native would make the first team every year through 1955 and again in 1958 and 1960. The U.S. women's tennis team defeated Great Britain to win the Wightman Cup at Merion Cricket Club. Penn AC had the best rowing club in the country with national titles in virtually all of the top events. In college basketball Villanova posted a glittering 17–2 record, and in the pro ranks

Phil Hergesheimer (left) and Maurice Comteau were key players on the 1940s Rockets ice hockey team coached by Hall of Famer Herb Gardiner (center).

the SPHAS broke through to win their first championship of the American Basketball League. Eddie Gottlieb's team would become the dominant one in the league, winning titles again in 1941, 1942, 1943, and 1945 with a team led by Art Hillhouse, Ozzie Schecktman, and Petey Rosenberg.

Philadelphia professional soccer teams were also dominant. During the decade a number of teams represented the city in the American Soccer League. The Philadelphia Americans were especially strong, winning league titles in 1942, 1944, 1947, and 1948. The Philadelphia Nationals won in 1949. The Philadelphia Passons and the German-Americans also competed in the league in the 1940s.

The 1941 season had a landmark event in baseball. Boston Red Sox left fielder Ted Williams, ignoring his manager's suggestion to sit out a doubleheader on the last day of the season so his .3996 average would become .400, went 6-for-8 against the Athletics at Shibe Park to finish with a .406 mark, making him baseball's last .400

No Philadelphia-area field hockey player was better than Betty Shellenberger, a first-team All-American 19 times.

hitter. Also that season, the A's Sam Chapman had a banner season with a .322 average, 25 home runs, and 106 RBI. Negro League great Oscar Charleston took over as manager of the Philadelphia Stars, a position he would hold through 1950. Edgar Smith of Burlington, New Jersey, was not only the Chicago White Sox' winning pitcher in the All-Star Game, but was the pitcher who gave up the first hit in Joe DiMaggio's 56-game hitting streak. And a plucky kid from Chester named Danny Murtaugh made his big league debut as the Phillies' second baseman and led the National League in stolen bases with the now-unheard-of total of 18.

Heavyweight champ Joe Louis, in his only title defense in Philadelphia, continued his "Bum of the Month" tour by knocking out local fighter Gus Dorazio in the second round before 15,425 at Convention Hall. Meanwhile, Southwark's Tommy Forte, having upset champion Lou Salica in a nontitle fight the previous year, lost twice in title bouts with Salica, each time losing a 15-round decision, once at the Arena and once at Shibe Park.

The first PGA tournament, which had a total purse of $5,000 and included some of the country's top amateurs, was held in 1941 at Torresdale-Frankford Country Club. Sam Snead nailed down first place. The following year, Snead won the PGA again, this time at Seaview near Atlantic City. The next day he enlisted in the Navy. Jane Vaughan, representing Philadelphia Skating Club, won the U.S. Women's Figure Skating championship, a title she repeated in 1942. Her brother Arthur Vaughan won the men's title for PSC in 1943, and from 1946 to 1949, Dick Button represented the Philadelphia club when he won national crowns.

Philadelphian Clara Marie Schroth dominated women's gymnastics like no others have ever done after launching a career in 1941 by winning her first of 11 straight national titles on the balance beam. By 1952, Schroth (later Lomady) would win 39 national titles, including six all-arounds and five on the flying rings, plus a bronze medal in the 1948 Olympics. Future Hall of Famer Charles Brinton of Merion Cricket Club, widely considered the nation's best player of the decade, won his first U.S. Men's Squash championship. He would win again in 1942, 1946, and 1947 while teaming for the national doubles title in 1946 with Don Strachan and in 1948 with Stan Pearson. After going 17–6–1 in its last three seasons, La Salle football was halted after the 1941 campaign because of World War II. Meanwhile, Temple and Villanova were having mediocre seasons through most of the 1940s.

Eagles coach Greasy Neale did the unthinkable in 1942 when he suffered a heart attack during a game but remained on the sidelines in a 14–0 loss to the New York Giants. That year, Philadelphia got its second ice hockey team when a group called the Falcons entered the Eastern Hockey League, where they would play without distinction through the 1946 season. Richard DiBatista of Penn became the only Philadelphia-area college player ever to win two NCAA wrestling championships when he captured his second straight 175-pound title while pacing the Quakers to an eighth-place tie in the tournament, the highest any local college ever finished.

Hall of Famers Hunter Lott (left) and Charles Brinton were two of the nation's finest squash players.

Phillies left fielder Danny Litwhiler became the first major league outfielder to field a perfect 1.000 for the season. Philadelphians Hunter Lott and Bill Slack won their fifth consecutive U.S. Men's Doubles title in squash. Lott, playing out of Cynwyd Club, would team with G. Diehl Mateer to win three more national crowns in 1949, 1950, and 1953, while also winning the singles title in 1949. Both Lott and Mateer were elected to the Squash Hall of Fame in 2000.

As the war escalated, sports activity slowed. One of the top stories in 1943 was the performance of St. Joseph's guard George Senesky, who led the nation in scoring with a 23.4 average while winning the Helms Foundation Award as the country's top college player. Temple's women's basketball team behind the high-scoring efforts of Grace Shuler began a run of three straight undefeated seasons during which it would compile a 27–0 record between 1942–43 and 1944–45. And having just been discharged from the Army, the Eagles' Jack Hinkle lost the NFL rushing title by one yard, losing that yard on an uncorrected mistake by the official scorer.

Richard DiBatista of Penn was the only Philadelphia-area collegian to win two NCAA wrestling titles.

Temple's basketball team reached the NCAA tournament for the first time in 1944 in its second season under coach Josh Cody. After posting a 13–8 record during the regular season, the Owls, led by Jerry Rullo, lost to Ohio State, 57–47, in the first round at Madison Square Garden. In a setup vastly different from today's, Temple then defeated Catholic University, 55–35, to gain a share of third place in the Eastern Regionals. Also that year, Phillies pitcher Ken Raffensberger became the club's first winning pitcher in an All-Star Game when he got the decision in the National League's 7–1 victory at Forbes Field.

In 1945, in the second year of the *Philadelphia Inquirer* Charities professional golf tournament, Byron Nelson shot a 63 in the final round for an overall 269 to take first place at Llanerch in his sixth of a record 11 consecutive PGA victories. Herman Barron, Bobby Locke, Johnny Palmer, and Joe Kirkwood won the tournament in subsequent years before it ended in 1949. Athletics pitcher Dick Fowler, just three weeks after being discharged by the Canadian army, hurled a no-hitter for his only win of the season. The 1–0 victory over the St. Louis Browns was accomplished

Before becoming a backcourt star with the Warriors, George Senesky led
the nation in scoring while playing at St. Joseph's.

in one hour, 15 minutes, the fastest no-hit game in modern times. Gymnast Marion
Twining (Barone) won the national women's championship on the horse vault and
uneven bars, a title she would capture twice more. The largest crowd ever to watch
a pro football game in Philadelphia jammed 90,218 strong into Municipal Stadium
to see the Eagles defeat the Green Bay Packers, 28–21, in an exhibition game. Just
one year later, that mark was broken when 92,800 watched the Chicago Bears beat
the Eagles, 24–12, in another exhibition game at Municipal Stadium. That year Bert
Bell also became commissioner of the NFL.

Mickey Vernon, who came out of Marcus Hook to carve a splendid 50-year career
in baseball as a player, coach, scout, and manager, won his first of two American
League batting titles in 1946 when he hit .353 for the Washington Senators. Vernon,
who still holds numerous records for first baseman set during his 20 years as a

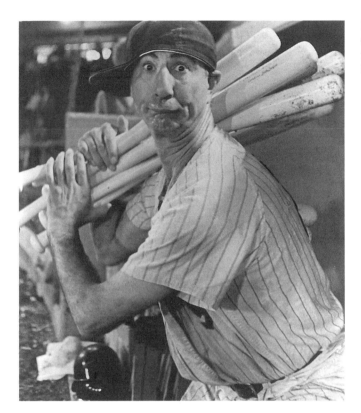

For more than 50 years, Max Patkin entertained baseball fans throughout the nation with his unique brand of humor.

player, won the crown again in 1953 with a .337 mark. Another long career was launched in 1946 when Cleveland Indians owner Bill Veeck signed Philadelphian Max Patkin as a part-time coach and full-time comedian. The colorful prankster went on to spend more than 50 years performing one-night stands mostly at minor league ballparks throughout the country, serving up his brand of humor as "The Clown Prince of Baseball."

Del Ennis came out of Olney High and a stint in the service to earn Rookie of the Year honors in the National League. The Phillies also hired Edith Houghton, the first woman scout. On another baseball front, Connie Mack, who in 1941 had bought for $42,000 the remaining shares in the Athletics that were owned by the Shibe family and thus become sole owner of the team, made the first of two trades that would help nail the lid on the A's coffin: Mack traded promising third baseman George Kell to the Detroit Tigers. Before the decade was over, he would swap second baseman Nellie Fox to the Chicago White Sox. Mack's double folly would bring him virtually nothing of use in return. Even worse, both Kell and Fox would go on to Hall of Fame careers that surely would have benefited the A's had they remained in town.

Auto racing resumed at Langhorne Speedway in 1946 with the big event being an annual 100-mile championship race featuring Indianapolis cars and drivers. Rex Mays won the first one. Others who finished first in the decade would include Indy winners Bill Holland and Johnny Parsons. Holland became the fourth Philadelphia-area driver to win the 500 when, after being runner-up in 1947 and 1948, he won the event in 1949, driving his Blue Crown Special to victory at a record speed of 121.327 miles an hour. Holland was runner-up at Indy again in 1950.

One year after it reopened, Langhorne introduced racing for the new NASCAR organization, which featured late-model stock cars. In a 200-mile race, Bob Flock won while averaging 68 mph. By then smaller tracks were also beginning to operate, some holding events that varied from the standard kind of auto race. One such event was the Demolition Derby, started by George Marshman of Yerkes at tracks he owned in Hatfield and Sanatoga.

Golf made a big splash in Philadelphia during the summer of 1947. The National Negro Open was played at Cobbs Creek. It was won by resident Cobbs ace Howard Wheeler, a five-time winner of the Open who played cross-handed. Coming in second was a shipping clerk at the Nabisco plant on Roosevelt Boulevard who had moved to the Philadelphia area seven years earlier. His name was Charlie Sifford, and he would go from a legendary status hustling golfers at Cobbs to becoming the first African-American on the professional golf tour, where he would have a long and colorful career.

Another colorful figure in golf gained national prominence in 1947 when Upper Darby native Robert (Skee) Riegel won the U.S. Amateur championship at Pebble Beach shortly after he had led the U.S. Walker Cup team to victory at St. Andrews in Scotland. In a 36-hole final, the first eight holes being played in dense fog, the 32-year-old Riegel defeated the favored Johnny Dawson, 2 and 1, to win the tournament. Soon afterward, Riegel, who had won numerous other major amateur tournaments, turned pro. Although he would play in 11 Masters, 16 U.S. Opens, and various other top tournaments during his career, his time as a touring pro was relatively short. Skee left the tour in the early 1950s and returned home to become a club pro, a job he held at several area courses until his retirement.

The man who is generally considered the city's greatest swimmer also made his first big splash in 1947. By the time he was a senior at North Catholic High School, Joe Verduer had already set one world record. After a stint in the Navy, he enrolled at La Salle College, and in 1947 he won the NCAA 200-yard butterfly. In 1948 he not only won that title again, but also captured a gold medal and set a world record in the 200-meter breaststroke in the Olympics at London. He won the NCAA title in the 150-meter medley in 1949. By 1950 the Kensington native was a four-time All-American, had won four NCAA championships and 19 AAU titles, and had set 19 world records.

Joe Verduer was a four-time All-American swimmer and an Olympic champion at La Salle College.

The year 1947 was also important for still another of Philadelphia's finest athletes. Jack Kelly, Jr., of East Falls avenged the snub of his father at the Royal Henley Regatta by winning the world's top rowing race, the Diamond Sculls. The victory helped Kelly capture the Sullivan Award as the country's top amateur athlete. Kelly, who had won his first U.S. single sculls championship in 1946 and would repeat that title seven more times, won the Diamond Sculls again in 1949, during a 10-year period in which he was the best rower in the country. Rowing for Vesper Boat Club, the nation's dominant rowing house in the late 1940s, the Penn grad competed in the 1948, 1952, 1956, and 1960 Olympics, just missing out on a medal in photo finishes in the first two and claiming a bronze medal in 1956. Kelly also won two gold medals in the Pan-American Games and six Canadian single sculls championships. He died suddenly in 1985, three weeks after he had been named president of the U.S. Olympic Committee.

In 1947, Harry Walker won the National League batting title with a .363 average after coming to the Phillies in a trade in May. Early in the season, southern-born

Phillies manager Ben Chapman and others on the team had ridden rookie Jackie Robinson, the century's first Afro-American player, unmercifully during the Phils' first meeting with the Brooklyn Dodgers at Ebbets Field. The ugly encounter was followed by a Phillies threat to boycott the Dodgers when they appeared for the first time that season at Shibe Park. Eventually, wiser heads prevailed, the weekend series went on, and in a Sunday doubleheader, the largest crowd (41,660) in Shibe Park history—many of whom were there to see the pioneering Robinson—showed up to watch the Phillies win both games behind the pitching of Schoolboy Rowe and Dutch Leonard.

Playing second base for the Dodgers that year was Eddie Stanky from Kensington. His backup was Eddie Miksis from Burlington, New Jersey. Both would have long, solid careers in the big leagues. Across town, Satchel Paige, pitching for the Kansas City Monarchs against the Philadelphia Stars at Penmar Park, tossed a perfect game for eight innings. In the ninth, he intentionally walked the first three batters, then ordered the seven fielders behind him to sit down. Paige then struck out the next three hitters on nine pitches.

After losing to Army by scores of 62–7, 61–0, and 34–7 in its three previous encounters, Penn managed a 7–7 tie with the Cadets en route to its first undefeated record (7–0–1) since 1908. With George Blanda passing for one touchdown and kicking three extra points, Villanova bowed to Kentucky, 24–14, in a battle of Wildcats in the Great Lakes Bowl in Cleveland's Municipal Stadium. After going 10–0 during the season, West Chester bowed to Missouri Valley, 26–7, in the Cigar Bowl in Tampa.

In the 1948 Olympics, weightlifter Frank Spellman of Paoli won a gold medal in the middleweight class and diver Bruce Harlan of Lansdowne took the gold in the springboard. Browning Ross became Villanova's first NCAA champion with a victory in the 3,000-meter steeplechase. Eagles quarterback Tommy Thompson led the NFL with 25 touchdown passes. Ike Williams knocked out Beau Jack in the sixth round at Shibe Park in a lightweight title fight. And Warriors guard Howie Dallmar led the BAA in assists with 120, after which he was named head basketball and baseball coach at Penn for the following season while still performing one more year for the Warriors. At the time the Quakers' top gun was a smooth shooter named Herb Lyon. Penn's first big scorer, Lyon led the team in scoring four different years between 1945 and 1950.

La Salle entered its first post-season tournament with a bid to the NIT. Led by South Philadelphia's Larry Foust, who would go on to a distinguished 12-year career in the NBA with Fort Wayne, Minneapolis, and St. Louis, the Explorers lost, 68–61, to Western Kentucky in the final. The Explorers, however, would be heard from many times again. Between 1946 and 1955 they would ring up a remarkable

206–47 record, which included five NIT appearances and two NCAA tournament berths.

The 1948 season turned out to be the last hurrah for the Athletics. After a sorry succession of second-division finishes, the A's finally fielded a solid lineup, led by outfielders Sam Chapman and Elmer Valo, infielders Ferris Fain, Eddie Joost, and Hank Majeski, and catcher Buddy Rosar. In a torrid five-team race, the A's moved in and out of first place from early July until mid-August before getting knocked out of the race. The A's ended the season in fourth place, their first first-division finish since 1934. Never again, though, would a Philadelphia Athletics team be a pennant contender.

A pennant contender was on the way, however, for Philadelphia's other baseball team. After only one first-division finish (1932) since 1917, the Phillies finally shed the weight of years of dismal teams by finishing third in 1949. Featuring a nucleus of young, enthusiastic players and a sprinkling of solid veterans, the Phillies were about to become not only the favorite team of the city's fans but a pennant-winner as well. During the season popular first baseman Eddie Waitkus was shot in a Chicago hotel room by a crazed teenage stenographer named Ruth Ann Steinhagen. Although critically injured, Waitkus would recover in time for the 1950 season. Also in 1949, the Phillies tied a major league record with five home runs in one inning in a 12–3 victory over the Cincinnati Reds. Andy Seminick hit two homers, and Ennis, Rowe, and Jones each one.

Philadelphia had a new basketball sensation in Villanova's Paul Arizin. Cut from his La Salle High School team, "Pitchin' Paul" entered Villanova but didn't join the Wildcat varsity until his sophomore year after coach Al Severance spotted him playing in a gym league. In 1948–49, Arizin averaged 22 points per game, and in one game he scored 85 points against a team from the Navy Air Material Center. Villanova, in the middle of a three-year spurt in which it posted a combined 73–15 record, gained a berth in the NCAA tournament and reached the Final Four before losing in the semifinal to Alex Groza–led Kentucky, the eventual champion, 85–72. The Wildcats then downed Yale, 78–67, for third place. A master jump-shot artist, Arizin had a banner season in 1949–50 when he led the Wildcats to a 25–4 record while leading the nation in scoring with 735 points (25.3 average). That year, he became the first Villanova player to score 1,000 career points and was named first-team All-American and college player of the year. Arizin went on to a Hall of Fame career with the Warriors during which he twice led the NBA in scoring, won an MVP award, and was named to 10 All-Star teams.

On New Year's Day 1949 coach Jordan Oliver's Villanova's football team, led by Pete D'Alonzo with two touchdowns, defeated Nevada, 27–7, before 20,000 in the Harbor Bowl at San Diego. Temple won the men's NCAA gymnastics championship as coach Max Younger's squad beat Minnesota, 28–18, for the title with Bob Stout finishing first in the horizontal bar and Joe Berenato winning the pommel horse. The first midget auto race was held at Langhorne Speedway with Bill Schiendler winning the 150-mile test with an average speed of 78.5 mph. Margaret Osborne DuPont and Doris Hart led the U.S. team to a 7–0 victory over Great Britain in the Wightman Cup at Merion. In a pair of title matches, Sugar Ray Robinson won a 15-round decision over Kid Gavilan in a welterweight fight at Municipal Stadium, and Ike Williams decisioned Freddy Dawson in 15 rounds in defense of his lightweight crown at Convention Hall. The St. Joseph's Field House was opened with the Hawks losing to Rhode Island, 62–46, after which they launched a streak of 23 home wins in a row. And Eagles owner Alexis Thompson sold the team to a 100-man syndicate of local business and civic leaders known as the "Happy Hundred" for $300,000. Businessmen James P. Clark and Frank McNamee led the group, which also included entertainers Bob Hope and Frankie Lane and future Eagles president Leonard Tose.

Steve Van Buren, Unstoppable Running Back

Of the many fine football players who have adorned Philadelphia gridirons in the 20th century, there was no one else quite like Steve Van Buren. He not only stood helmet and pads above every other running back, but was the best of a group of superb athletes who performed in Philadelphia during the 1940s.

Although not terribly big (200 pounds), Van Buren was a running back who combined unbelievable strength and power with speed and extraordinary balance. He could run around opponents or through them. Elected to the Pro Football Hall of Fame in 1965, Steve was too good to be stopped by just one tackler. He had to be gang-tackled, and even that often didn't work.

Steve Van Buren was considered one of the best running backs in NFL history.

A native of Honduras, Van Buren had come out of Louisiana State, after leading his club to a 19–14 victory over Texas A&M in the Cotton Bowl, to become the Eagles' first-round draft pick (fifth overall) in 1944. His first contract gave him a salary of $4,000, a high amount for the time, but a bargain well worth the price.

During Van Buren's eight years with the Eagles, the team won three division titles and two NFL championships, finishing second three times and third once. It was the best era in Eagles history.

To be the best athlete of the 1940s, Van Buren had to beat out some stiff competition. Teammate Pete Pihos, Joe Fulks, Paul Arizin, Jack Kelly, Jr., Joe Verdeur, Bob Montgomery, and Chuck Bednarik were all in the running. But none quite measured up to the amazing Van Buren.

Many compared Van Buren favorably with Jim Thorpe while rating him better than Red Grange. Elusive one time, a battering ram the next, "Wham Bam" Van Buren led the NFL in rushing four times, twice going over 1,000 yards. He made the All-NFL team five times. And he set numerous records (many since broken) such as most touchdowns rushing in one season (15) and in a career (69), and most yards rushing (205) in one game. Nineteen times he rushed for more than 100 yards in one game. He is the only Eagle in history ever to rush for more than 200 yards in one game. During his career, he scored 458 points, nearly twice as many as the next-closest Eagle of that era.

Van Buren didn't waste any time acclimating to the pros. In his rookie season in 1944 he ranked fifth in the NFL in rushing and made the all-NFL first team. The following year he set an NFL record when he led the league in scoring (110 points) and touchdowns (18) while capturing his first rushing title. Steve led the league in rushing again in 1947, 1948, and 1949, setting an all-time record in 1947 with 1,008 yards, then breaking it in 1949 with 1,146 yards.

Steve was spectacular in the Eagles' two championships. In 1948, with the field covered with snow and in the midst of a 98-yard rushing total, he plunged across from the five-yard line to give the Birds their only touchdown in a 7–0 victory. One year later, in mud and torrential rain, he set a playoff record with 196 yards on 31 carries as he led the Eagles to a 14–0 win.

Van Buren also caught passes and returned punts and kickoffs. In one game in 1944 he returned a kickoff 97 yards for a touchdown. In 1945 he ran a kickoff back 98 yards for a TD.

Van Buren's playing days ended prematurely when injuries forced him to the sidelines during training camp in 1952. Subsequently he was released, bringing a glorious career to an end. It was a career of incomparable brilliance.

The First Big All-Sports Decade

The 1950s could be characterized as the decade during which sports in Philadelphia blossomed more fully than ever before.

Unlike previous decades when a few sports dominated the city's athletic landscape, the 1950s marked the first time that a wide variety of sports flourished at once. Collectively, they produced the city's first big all-sports decade of the 20th century.

Whether it was at Shibe Park, Municipal Stadium, Convention Hall, Franklin Field, the Arena, the Palestra, or elsewhere, major events occurred with regularity throughout the decade, giving reason to proclaim Philadelphia one of the leading sports centers in the world. And good teams, as well as superb players, were plentiful.

Baseball was still king. But even it produced mixed emotions among fans as the Phillies won their first National League pennant in 35 years with a team affectionately called the Whiz Kids, and the Athletics abruptly left town after playing in the city for 54 years. The Philadelphia Stars, a long-standing staple of Negro League baseball, also came to an end in the early 1950s.

The Eagles spent much of the decade trying to regroup, after dominating pro football in the late 1940s, while pro ice hockey still strove to gain a foothold in the city with the minor league Ramblers. College football remained a major force at Penn in the early part of the decade, and even Drexel, West Chester, and PMC captured part of the spotlight with undefeated teams.

The biggest boost to the local scene came from the growing sport of basketball. Once played in dingy gyms by a select few, the game was gaining rapidly in popularity at all levels, and the 1950s served as the springboard from which it really took off. The city had back-to-back national collegiate scoring champs in Paul Arizin and Bill Mlkvy. During the decade, not only did the Big Five come into existence—in the process, elevating the Palestra to a place as one of the most revered venues in the country—but La Salle won an NIT championship in 1952 and an NCAA title in 1954, and later in the decade teams from Temple advanced twice to the Final Four of the NCAA tournament. To help emphasize Philadelphia's claim as the "Basketball Capital of the World," the professional Warriors won the NBA championship in 1956.

Track, too, was on the rise. Villanova had the first of its great teams in the 1950s, the Penn Relays continued to flourish, and the United States met the Soviet Union at Franklin Field in a highly charged appendage of the cold war. In the same decade the Dad Vail Regatta found a permanent home on the Schuylkill River, Penn won its first NCAA fencing championship, and Drexel captured a national soccer title. The richest horse race in the world was held at Garden State Park in New Jersey, and auto racing was at the height of its local popularity with major races at Langhorne Speedway and stock car races at a number of small tracks in the area.

Events of national, even worldwide, importance happened throughout the decade in Philadelphia. In golf Ben Hogan came back from a nearly fatal auto accident to win the U.S. Open at Merion in 1950, Patty Berg won the Women's Western Open at Whitemarsh Valley in 1951, and Sam Snead fell apart in the final round to lose the 1958 PGA at Llanarch. Among numerous high-level boxing matches in the city, Sugar Ray Robinson twice won middleweight championship fights in Philadelphia in 1950, and Jersey Joe Walcott defeated Ezzard Charles in a heavyweight championship bout at Municipal Stadium in 1951, then 13 months later lost the crown to Rocky Marciano at the same place.

The Philadelphia area produced an abundance of outstanding athletes in the 1950s. A 7-foot, 1-inch giant named Wilt Chamberlain began to carve a niche in basketball that would lead to his becoming the greatest athlete ever to come out of the city. Vic Seixas dominated tennis in the 1950s, winning at Wimbledon, at Forest Hills, and in the Davis Cup and ranking number one in the world three times. Roy Campanella, rejected by local baseball teams because of his color, won the Most Valuable Player award three times while playing in Brooklyn. And Harold Johnson,

Gil Turner, and Joey Giardello in boxing; Tom Gola, Arizin, Guy Rodgers, and Larry Foust in basketball; Bobby Shantz, Del Ennis, Eddie Stanky, and Ray Narleski in baseball; Francis (Reds) Bagnell and pros Emlen Tunnell, Lou Ferry, and the Eagles' Jack Ferrante, Bucko Kilroy, and Mike Jarmoluk in football; George Fazio and Skee Riegel in golf; Walt Bahr in soccer; and Horace Ashenfelter in track all represented the Philadelphia area well as native sons.

They were joined by a profusion of other superb athletes who came to Philadelphia to play. Robin Roberts established himself as one of baseball's premier pitchers. Richie Ashburn and Ferris Fain each won two batting titles. Neil Johnston led the NBA in scoring three times. Chuck Bednarik solidified his place as one of football's greatest players. Temple's Mlkvy was an All-American, once registering 73 points in a single game. And Ron Delaney came from Ireland to help launch Villanova track on a course of spectacular success.

Along with all the good athletes, there were many great coaches, too, particularly at the college level. Harry Litwack, Jack Ramsay, and Jack McCloskey all began hugely successful careers in basketball in the 1950s. Jumbo Elliott in track, George Munger in football, and Al Severance and Ken Loeffler in basketball continued to turn out fine teams during the decade.

The 1950s also magnified another element of the sports world for which Philadelphia became famous. Although it had long been in existence, the practice of fans booing the men on the field was elevated nearly to an art form in the '50s. Especially frequent targets were the Phillies' Ennis and the A's Gus Zernial, who was even booed once while he lay injured on the field. Not to be outdone, Eagles fans in 1953 staged what was thought to be their first snowball attack when they pelted referees during a particularly contentious moment at Shibe Park.

Overall, however, the decade of the 1950s was as interesting as any in Philadelphia's history. It was a decade in which the good news far outweighed the bad.

PHILLIES WIN THE PENNANT

After years of dreary teams and dismal failures, the Phillies captured their first National League pennant in 35 years when the 1950 team won the flag on the last day of the season on Dick Sisler's 10th inning home run. It was only the Phillies' third first-division finish since 1917.

Named the Whiz Kids by sportswriter Harry Grayson, the team featured mostly fresh, young players led by pitchers Robin Roberts and Curt Simmons, center fielder Richie Ashburn, right fielder Del Ennis, shortstop Granny Hamner, and third baseman Willie Jones. A few seasoned veterans such as first baseman Eddie Waitkus, who came back from being shot the previous year, catcher Andy Seminick, left fielder Sisler, and pitcher Jim Konstanty were also key members of the team.

Managed by a patient, scholarly, part-time college professor named Eddie Sawyer, the Whiz Kids were originally not considered major contenders for the pennant. But after moving in and out of first place during the early months of the season, they went into first place to stay on July 25. Eventually, the club built a huge lead, and, despite an early September slump—aided by Simmons' induction into the Army—held a seven-game cushion with 11 games left in the season.

The Phils, however, went into a tailspin, losing eight of 10 games. Their lead fell to one game over the second-place Brooklyn Dodgers, managed by ex-Phils skipper Burt Shotton. It all came down to the final game of the season against the Dodgers at Ebbets Field.

The Phils sent a dead-tired Roberts to the mound to face Brooklyn's Don Newcombe. Both pitchers were seeking their 20th win of the season. Each team scored once, and with the score tied 1–1 in the bottom of the ninth inning, the Dodgers had men on first and second with none out and Duke Snider at bat. Snider ripped a line single to center. Ashburn fielded the ball on one hop and threw it to the plate, where Cal Abrams, waved home by Dodger third base coach Milt Stock—ironically, the Phillies third baseman in 1915—was tagged out 15 feet up the line by Phils catcher Stan Lopata. Roberts then escaped the jam, sending the game into extra innings.

In the top of the 10th with two men on base, Sisler—his dad George, a Hall of Famer and Brooklyn scout, watching from the stands—crushed a Newcombe pitch into the left field bleachers for a three-run homer. Roberts retired the Dodgers in order in the bottom half, and the Phillies danced away with a 4–1 victory and the National League pennant.

Konstanty, soon to be named the league's Most Valuable Player after winning 16 games and saving 22 while making a record 74 appearances in relief, was a surprise starter in the first game of the World Series against the New York Yankees. The bespectacled veteran, who called on an undertaker friend named Andy Skinner for help when he was having trouble with his pitches, hurled valiantly but lost, 1–0. The Phillies then lost each of the next two games by one run, 2–1 and 3–2, with Joe DiMaggio's 10th-inning home run beating Roberts in Game Two. They then fell to their fourth straight defeat, 5–2, to get swept in the Series.

Although expected to be a contender in the ensuing years, the Phillies faltered after 1950 and were never in the running for the rest of the decade. Weak teams and a parade of managers haunted the club, and by the late 1950s, with the Whiz Kids, having aged or been traded, the Phils had tumbled to the bottom of the standings. It would be 30 years before the team made another appearance in the World Series.

Heroes of the Phillies pennant-winning victory, Robin Roberts (left) and Dick Sisler (right), celebrated with manager Eddie Sawyer.

HOGAN HEROICS AT MERION

When Ben Hogan had a head-on collision with a Greyhound bus that came into his lane while it was trying to pass a truck on a lonely highway in East Texas, in February 1949, he not only came perilously close to death, but it was feared he would never walk again, much less play golf. Hogan, who had saved his wife Valerie from being injured by throwing himself across her as she sat on the passenger side, emerged from the wreck with a double fracture of the pelvis, broken collarbone, ankle, and ribs, and a damaged bladder.

Sixteen months later, however, in June 1950, Hogan, the world's best golfer, won the U.S. Open at Merion East in one of the most memorable golf tournaments ever held. He did it not only by overcoming nearly fatal injuries and a blot clot, followed by surgery and long months of rehabilitation, but also with a spectacular finish that ranks as one of the most thrilling in golf history.

Limping noticeably and with his legs and ankles heavily bandaged, Hogan, who soaked his ailing limbs for an hour before each round, shot 72 and 69 on the first two days of the tournament despite severe cramps that nearly forced him to withdraw. He was just two strokes off the lead as he began the 36 holes of the last day (In those days in the Open, golfers played 18 holes in the morning and 18 in the afternoon on a marathon final day.)

After shooting another 72 in the morning, Hogan was still two shots back as the last round began. A 37 on the front nine briefly gave Ben the lead, but as he came into the 458-yard 18th hole, he needed a birdie to win the tournament.

Exhausted and walking and painfully and slowly, Hogan realized his second shot would be the key. For that, he pulled out a one iron. It is said that only God can hit a one iron, but Hogan hit his onto the green, a marvelous shot that landed 40 feet from the pin. A two-putt would give him a tie for the lead, sending the tournament into a special playoff round.

Hogan two-putted to finish the round with a 74 and a four-round total of 288. That

Ben Hogan (center) received his Open trophy as wife Valerie, George Fazio (left) and Lloyd Mangrum (right) watched.

put him in a three-way tie for the lead with Lloyd Mangrum and George Fazio, a prominent touring pro from Norristown.

The next day, the Open staged the sixth three-way playoff in its history. With 6,000 in the gallery, Hogan led by one shot after 15 holes. But a two-stroke penalty assessed against Mangrum for picking up his putting ball to blow off a bug and Hogan's 50-yard putt for a birdie two on the 17th sent the lithe Texan to the clubhouse with a 69, four strokes ahead of Mangrum's 73 and six ahead of Fazio's 75.

Hogan won the $15,000 prize that went with winning his second Open title. He also won a spot in sports annals for one of the most courageous comebacks ever staged.

PHILLY IS A BIG-FIGHT TOWN

There had been numerous headline boxing matches in Philadelphia over the years. But in the 1950s the city had more big-time fights than in any other decade, and it earned a place as one of the leading centers of boxing in the nation.

Philadelphia boxing made its biggest mark the early 1950s, first when Sugar Ray Robinson twice defended his middleweight championship in the city, again when Jersey Joe Walcott twice fought for the heavyweight crown, and finally when Kid Gavilan had two welterweight title bouts.

Walcott, a well-traveled veteran of the fight game, whose real name was Arnold Cream, was a special local favorite because he was a native of Camden, New Jersey. Walcott became the Philadelphia area's first fully recognized and boxing's oldest heavyweight champion in August 1951 when at age 37 he won a 15-round decision over defending champ Ezzard Charles at Municipal Stadium. It was Walcott's fifth attempt at winning the heavyweight title, with two losses to Joe Louis and two to Charles preceding this fight.

Thirteen months later on September 23, 1952, the 38-year-old Walcott was back in the same ring to defend his title against a strong young fighter named Rocky Marciano. Undefeated in 42 pro bouts, the favored Marciano had never been knocked off his feet.

His invincibility crumbled in the first round when Walcott knocked him down with a crushing blow to the head. Marciano, however, got back up, and for the next 12 rounds he and Walcott waged one of the most brusing battles ever seen. It ended in the 13th round when a bloodied Marciano uncorked the devastating right he called Suzy Q, which sent Walcott crashing to the canvas for the count of 10. The knockout ended Walcott's brief reign as heavyweight champ and elevated Marciano to the top of the boxing world, from which he would later retire without a defeat in 49 fights. Walcott, who fought from 1930 to 1953, retired with a 53–18–1 record.

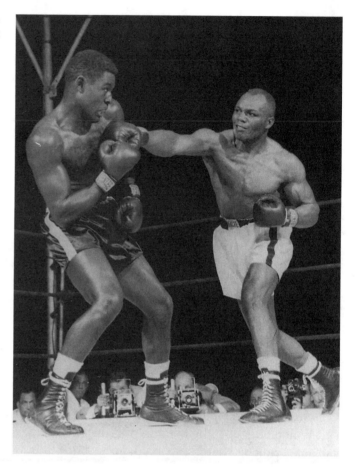

Camden's Jersey Joe Walcott (right) finally won the heavyweight title when he defeated Ezzard Charles in 1951.

The graceful and gifted Robinson, perhaps the finest fighter in boxing history, was no stranger to Philadelphia. On July 11, 1949, he had won a 15-round decision over Gavilan for the welterweight crown in a classic bout at Municipal Stadium. Then, moving up a class in 1950, Robinson won two middleweight title fights in Philadelphia, beating Robert Villemain on a 15-round decision on June 5 at Municipal Stadium and knocking out Carl (Bobo) Olson in the 12th round of an October 26 match at Convention Hall.

Still another prominent championship battle occurred on July 7, 1952, again at Municipal Stadium. A crowd of 39,025, a record for a welterweight fight, watched as the Cuban-born Gavilan kayoed undefeated Gil Turner from Philadelphia's Strawberry Mansion section in the 11th round. Gavilan would later lose a 15-round decision to Johnny Saxton in a welterweight title bout October 20, 1954, at Convention Hall.

Turner, who beat Ike Williams in a fierce fight in 1951 at Shibe Park, was one of many local pugilists who made the term "Philadelphia fighter" familiar throughout boxing circles. In the 1950s fighters such as Harold Johnson, Joey Giardello, Sugar Hart, Charley Scott, and Percy Bassett gave the city a national reputation for producing top-level boxers. And Philadelphian Zack Clayton, a one-time member of the Harlem Globetrotters, was considered one of the top boxing referees in the nation.

In addition to Municipal Stadium, Convention Hall, and Shibe Park, fights were held at the Arena and at smaller venues such as Toppi Stadium, the Met, and the Cambria in North Philadelphia, as well as clubs such as the Alhambra and the Plaza in South Philadelphia.

PENN FOOTBALL'S LAST GREAT ERA

Going back to its early days in the late 1800s, football at the University of Pennsylvania had always been one of the major sports in Philadelphia. The Quakers featured outstanding coaches, talented players, and big-time schedules, and whenever they played, they always drew huge crowds.

One of the most glorious eras of Penn football followed World War II. Annually Penn had one of the best teams in the country. Quaker opponents were some of the nation's top teams, including squads from Notre Dame, California, Army, Navy, Michigan, Ohio State, Georgia, and Penn State. Some 70,000 fans jammed Franklin Field each game to watch. And Penn always held its own under the highly respected head coach George Munger, whose 82–42–10 record during a 16-year reign included only one losing season between 1938 and 1953.

Every year the Quakers lineup featured All-Americans. Tackle George Savitsky (a four-time choice), center Chuck Bednarik (a two-time selection), halfback Skippy Minisi, and guard John (Bull) Schweder had set the stage in the mid to late 1940s. The tradition continued into the 1950s when halfback Francis (Reds) Bagnell, guard Bernie Lemonick, linebacker Gerry McGinley, end Eddie Bell (a two-time selection), and tackle Jack Shanafelt gave Penn at least one first-team All-America each year between 1950 and 1953. Bagnell also won the Maxwell Club award in 1950.

Between 1946 and 1953, Penn beat Navy seven times with one game a tie. The Quakers beat Alan Ameche–led Wisconsin, 20–0, in 1950. That same year Bagnell, the brilliant all-around tailback from West Philadelphia, set an NCAA record with 490 total yards as Penn clobbered Dartmouth, 42–26. The Quakers tied third-ranked Notre Dame, 7–7, in 1952 on a touchdown pass caught by Bell. In 1953 they beat

All-American tailback Francis (Reds) Bagnell excelled at Penn as both a runner and passer.

Penn State, 13–7, before losing to Ohio State, Notre Dame, and Army by one touch-down each.

In the early 1950s, Penn was close to being at the top of the collegiate football heap. But the glory ended suddenly. In 1954, Penn president Gaylord Harnwell signed an agreement with other Ivy League presidents creating a formal football league of Ivy colleges. Penn football was never the same again. From 1953 through 1971, the Quakers had just two winning seasons out of 19 under five different head coaches.

Under the restrictions imposed by the new Ivy League, Penn's top-level pro-gram came to a screeching halt. Munger retired, and his successor, Steve Sebo, went 0–18 in his first two seasons (1954–55). Big-time opponents were dropped from the schedule as Penn settled into a watered-down Ivy League slate. Although the Quakers had a brief reprise when they won the Ivy League championship in 1959, even that campaign was tarnished when it became known that before the season had begun Penn had secretly hired a new coach (John Steigman) to replace Sebo in 1960.

La Salle Joins Basketball Elite

College basketball as a popular sport was still very much in its infancy when the 1950s began. By the time the decade ended, though, the sport had grown into one of the most popular domains on the Philadelphia athletic scene.

Much of the reason could be attributed to the success in the early 1950s of La Salle College basketball teams. The Explorers were the first team in the Philadelphia area to experience a sustained level of success on a national scale.

La Salle had fielded successful teams before, particularly in the late 1940s when the Explorers won 61 of 78 games over a three-year period. But in 1949, when Ken Loeffler took over as head coach, the program went into high gear. Loeffler's first two teams registered 21–4 and 22–7 records, each time playing in the National Invitational Tournament (NIT), the first time beating Arizona, 72–66, before losing to Duquesne, 49–47, and the second time bowing to St. Louis, 73–61.

La Salle's 1951–52 team had something none of the others did. His name was Tom Gola.

As a freshman, Gola led La Salle to a 25–7 record and a berth in the NIT. Playing at Madison Square Garden in New York, the Explorers defeated Seton Hall, 80–76, in the first round as Gola scored 30 points and Fred Iehle added 25. St. John's was La Salle's next victim, 51–45. Then Duquesne fell, 59–46, as Norm Grekin scored 21, Gola 14, and Jackie Moore 12.

That victory put La Salle in the final against Dayton. With Gola (22), Iehle (18), Grekin (15), and Buddy Donnelly (11) all hitting in double figures, the Explorers captured the NIT championship with a stirring 75–64 victory on March 15, 1952.

The following season the Explorers posted a 25–3 record but lost in the first round of the NIT, 75–74, to St. John's. Then La Salle had the best season in its history in 1953–54 when it streaked to a 26–4 record, entering the NCAA Tournament for the first time.

The Explorers got 28 points from Gola to beat Fordham in overtime, 76–74, in the first round at Buffalo, New York. Then 26 points each by Gola and Charley Singley led La Salle to an 88–81 win over North Carolina State in the Eastern Regional semifinal at the Palestra. Gola's 22 points and 24 rebounds sparked the Explorers to a 64–48 victory over Navy in the Eastern Regional final.

Moving to the Final Four at Kansas City, Missouri, La Salle smashed Penn State,

La Salle College climaxed a highly successful era by winning the NCAA championship with a team led by (bottom row) Frank Blatcher (3), Frank O'Hara (5), and Tom Gola (15), and (top row) Fran O'Malley (4) and Charley Singley (10).

92–54, in the national semifinal as Frank Blatcher and Gola each scored 19. An equally easy victory followed in the final as La Salle clobbered Bradley, 92–76, behind 23 each by Blatcher and Singley and 19 by Gola, voted the tournament's Outstanding Player and later the NCAA Player of the Year.

In Loeffler's final season of 1954–55, La Salle posted a 26–5 record (giving the coach a 145–30 career mark) and again advanced to the NCAA final after a 76–73 victory over Iowa in the semifinal. But this time the Explorers bowed in the final, 77–63, to a San Francisco team led by Bill Russell and K. C. Jones. It was the end of a very special era. With NIT and NCAA titles, plus another NCAA finalist and three other NIT appearances in a six-year period, La Salle had put together the most spectacular run in the history of Philadelphia college basketball.

Tom Gola, a Star at Three Levels

Whenever Philadelphia basketball is discussed, the name Tom Gola usually enters the conversation. That's because Tom Gola *is* Philadelphia basketball.

Since basketball made its local entry, countless numbers of outstanding players have graced the city's hardwoods. None, however, has been more representative of the city's rich basketball heritage than Gola. To basketball aficionados, he is the ultimate embodiment of a magnificent tradition.

Gola stood out locally at three levels of the sport, first while attending La Salle High School, then at La Salle College, and finally in the pros with the Warriors. Even today, he is viewed as one of the finest players ever to perform in Philadelphia.

When Tom attended La Salle High, the school was housed at the same location as the college. In his junior year Gola, who grew up in nearby Olney, led his team

Tom Gola was the embodiment of a Philadelphia basketball tradition.

to the city title with a 55–31 victory over Overbrook after it had built a 27–5 halftime lead. Although he was heavily recruited by some of the top basketball colleges in the country, he chose to stay home and enroll at La Salle College.

For the next four years Gola was the Explorers' leading scorer and a three-time All-American who led his team to both NIT and NCAA championships and eventually was named to the College Basketball Hall of Fame. Although he played in an era prior to the formation of the Big Five, he is generally considered the best all-around player ever to come out of La Salle.

Gola could score from the outside as easily as he could from the inside. He stood 6 feet, 6 inches, but he passed and handled the ball like a small guard. Yet he could maneuver inside with the best of the big men. Moreover, he was a fierce competitor.

In four years at La Salle, Gola averaged a remarkable 20.9 points and 19.0 rebounds per game. His 2,461 career points, at the time far and away the highest total in Explorer history, now rank third on the school's all-time list behind modern shooting machines Lionel Simmons and Michael Brooks.

Gola was a territorial draft pick of the Warriors following his career at La Salle, and in his rookie season, playing guard, he helped his new team win the NBA championship. Tom spent six seasons with the Warriors. In 1959–60 he scored 1,122 points while dishing out 409 assists and averaging 10.4 rebounds per game.

Tom made the all-NBA team five times during his career, which saw him move with the Warriors to San Francisco in 1962, then join the New York Knicks in 1963. He finished his pro career in 1966 with 7,871 points (11.3 average).

One final laurel was added to Gola's basketball career when he returned to La Salle to coach the team for two years from 1968 to 1970. His '69 team, which compiled a 23–1 record and was ranked second in the nation, is regarded as one of the best in Explorer history.

An accounting major in college, Gola served as a state representative and as Philadelphia's city controller after leaving coaching. He also ran unsuccessfully in 1983 for mayor of the city.

VIC SEIXAS RULES TENNIS

Given the enormous popularity of tennis in Philadelphia dating back to the 1870s, it is small wonder that the area has produced more than its share of outstanding players. Quite a few of them made their marks on the national as well as the international level.

One of the most prominent in that category was certainly a handsome native of the Overbrook section of the city whose name was E. Victor Seixas, Jr.—Vic to his

Vic Seixas was ranked first in the nation three times and second three other times.

friends. During the 1950s, Vic Seixas was one of the top players on the international circuit.

Seixas played in his first national championship at Forest Hills in 1940 while he was a student at Penn Charter. Later, after graduating from the University of North Carolina, his career went into high gear, and in 1951, 1954, and 1957 Seixas was ranked the number-one player in the United States. He was ranked second three other times.

Those rankings came during what is generally considered the golden era of tennis when many great players adorned the courts of the world. Along with Seixas and Tony Trabert of the United States, Australians Lew Hoad and Ken Rosewall were regarded as being among the finest players the sport of tennis had ever produced.

Seixas's greatest triumph during that period occurred in 1953 when he defeated Kurt Nielson, 9–7, 6–3, 6–4, to win the Wimbledon championship. A year later, after losing in the finals to Trabert, he won the U.S. title at Forest Hills by beating Rex Hartwig, 3–6, 6–4, 6–4, 6–4. That same year, he and Trabert led the United States to victory over a powerful Australian team in the Davis Cup. Seixas's singles victory over Rosewall and his doubles triumph with Trabert over Hoad and Hartwig paved the way for the American victory.

Between 1952 and 1956, Seixas won 15 grand-slam tournaments. After the 1957 season he gave up full-time tennis to pursue a business career, but he continued to play in selected major events into the 1970s. Altogether, he competed at Forest Hills 28 times. In 1966 at age 42 he played in the sixth-longest match in tennis history, beating 23-year-old Bill Bowrey of Australia in a 94-game match in the third round of the Pennsylvania Grass Championships. Seixas won by the staggering score of 32–34, 6–4, 10–8.

Elected to the International Tennis Hall of Fame in 1971, Seixas during the 1950s was the best Philadelphia tennis player there was.

ATHLETICS LEAVE TOWN

For 54 years, Philadelphia had the luxury of being a two-team baseball town. The Phillies performed in the National League, and the Athletics played in the American League. The beauty of was that there was always a baseball game going on.

During most of their years in Philadelphia, the Athletics were the dominant team. Under Connie Mack, the A's won nine pennants and five World Series. They also finished in last place 18 times, which figures out to exactly one-third of their seasons, the highest percentage of cellar-dwellings of any team in baseball history.

The A's had their last big season in 1948, when the team contended for the pennant until mid-August. The club slipped rapidly downhill after that, and when the Phillies won the National League flag in 1950, the allegiance of Philadelphia's baseball fans shifted heavily to the Whiz Kids.

Mack, at age 88, had finally retired as manager in 1950, his 50-year tenure by far the longest anyone ever piloted a big league team. The venerable Connie was revered by fans and players, and said to be a good judge of talent. But often overlooked was the fact that twice he had jilted loyal A's fans by unloading his best players after pennant runs, claiming poverty each time. In his later years, this supposedly astute baseball man had dumped two future Hall of Famers, George Kell and Nellie Fox, almost before they got started. Eventually, his health fading rapidly and control of the team now in the hands of his sons, Mack would deliver the ultimate disservice by sanctioning the relocation of the A's to Kansas City.

That was a low blow to A's fans, who despite their dwindling numbers, staunchly backed the team through thick and thin. Attempts were made to keep the team in Philadelphia by finding new ownership. Several groups of local businessmen attempted unsuccessfully to buy the team, one failing to raise sufficient funds, the other unable to win league support. One of Mack's sons, Roy, also tried, but came up short financially.

On September 19, 1954, before a sparse crowd of 1,715, the A's lost to the New York Yankees, 4–2. No one fully realized it at the time, but it was the club's last game in Philadelphia.

That winter the club, which had been one of the charter members of the American League when it was formed in 1901, was sold to businessman Arnold Johnson and moved to Kansas City. Johnson paid slightly less than $2 million for the stock owned by Mack and his sons, while assuming another $2 million in accumulated debt.

By then few seemed to care. Attendance had dropped in 1954 to a mere 305,362. The A's were so awful on the field and the Macks so financially strapped off of it that the team was a poor excuse for a big league franchise.

The A's lasted just 13 seasons in Kansas City, accomplishing virtually nothing before moving to Oakland in time for the 1968 season. There, at least, brighter days lay ahead for this once-proud Philadelphia baseball team.

PALESTRA MADNESS BEGINS

Prior to the mid-1950s the major college basketball teams in Philadelphia basically went their own ways. Some—but not all—of the teams played each other, often at campus gyms, but there was no organization, no structure binding them together.

Great players had been plentiful among the college ranks in Philadelphia. But over the years standout performers—including Paul Arizin, Tom Gola, Larry Foust, Bill Mlkvy, Ernie Beck, George Senesky, Herb Lyon, Ike Borsavage, Larry Hennessy, and numerous others—seldom if ever played against each other. And there were no great rivalries between teams.

That all changed on November 23, 1954, when University of Pennsylvania president Gaylord Harnwell—joined by the presidents of La Salle, St. Joseph's, Temple, and Villanova—announced the formation of what would become known as the Big Five. The new creation would feature games in which all five colleges played each other in a continuous yearly series. All five would share equally in the profits, secure a television contract, and play games at the storied Palestra on the Penn campus.

It was a marriage made in heaven. In the ensuing nearly 40 years—or until the union basically disintegrated in 1991—the Big Five was followed avidly. Inspiring the kind of passionate performances and devout loyalties that existed in few other sports, the Big Five was not only synonymous with Philadelphia but also known throughout the country for its fierce competition, frequent upsets, and basketball-crazy fans.

Doubleheaders at the Palestra were a staple of the Big Five schedule. The first one under the new organization was held December 3, 1955, with Muhlenberg defeating La Salle in the first game, 69–58, and St. Joseph's beating Rhode Island in the nightcap, 84–72. On December 14, 1955, the first Big Five game took place with St. Joe's downing Villanova, 83–70. The Hawks won the first Big Five title, winning all four games while recording a 23–6 record under coach Jack Ramsay.

In the years that followed, Big Five games at the Palestra took a back seat to nothing in Philadelphia sports. Great players, superb teams, brilliant coaches, spectacular games, and the ever-present packed house of raucous and often overzealous fans combined to make Big Five games some of the most memorable events anywhere.

Banners flew, mascots strutted—and sometimes fought with each other—cheerleaders tried to outdo each other, bands blared, and several generations of colorful characters like Yo Yo (Bernie Schifren), Boulevard Bernie Cohen, Sam the Drummer, and hot dog vendor Charlie "Franks" helped to turn every Big Five event into a spectacle with a carnival-like atmosphere.

It was a special time for basketball in Philadelphia. Unfortunately, the round-robin format held at the Palestra was changed in 1986 when the five college presidents signed a new 10-year agreement that allowed for games to be played on the various campuses. The format underwent additional changes in 1991, effectively putting an end for the rest of the century to the Big Five as it had originally been configured. While the Big Five lasted, though, there was nothing in the world quite like it.

WARRIORS WIN THEIR LAST TITLE

Of the great professional basketball teams that have played in Philadelphia, one of the best was a powerful Warriors club that ran rampant through the NBA during the 1955–56 season. The Warriors easily won the league championship with a team that not only was strong in every department, but also fielded some of the finest individual talent ever seen on a Philadelphia basketball court.

Playing their home games at Convention Hall in an eight-team league in the days when the NBA often featured doubleheaders with four different teams participating, the Warriors were led by two of the top scorers in the league, forward Paul Arizin and center Neil Johnston. The two ranked second and third in the NBA in scoring that year, the league's 10th season.

Johnston, who early in his career had dabbled as a minor league pitcher in the Phillies organization, was a 6–8 center out of Ohio State with a deadly accurate hook shot who led the NBA in scoring and in shooting percentage three times each. Despite a bad knee that eventually cut his playing career to eight seasons, he twice

Center Neil Johnston (right) was a three-time NBA scoring champ and a key player on owner Eddie Gottlieb's last championship Warriors team.

was first in minutes played and once led the circuit in rebounds. Johnston ended his career with 10,023 points.

Arizin, who had led the nation in scoring in 1949–50 while playing at Villanova, after failing to make the team at La Salle High, would eventually also top the NBA in scoring twice and would earn a spot in the Basketball Hall of Fame. Just back in 1956 after missing two seasons because of military service, he specialized in line-drive jump shots and strong drives to the basket. Later in his 10-year pro career, when he scored his 10,000th point en route to a final total of 16,266, he was only the fifth man in NBA history to do so.

The Warriors also featured rookie and future Hall of Famer Tom Gola in the back-court. Set-shooting Joe Graboski was the other forward, Jack George the second guard, and Ernie Beck the first man off the bench. The Warriors had a strong local flavor with not only Arizin, Gola, George, and Beck coming out of the Philadelphia area, but also reserves Jackie Moore, the club's first black player, and Larry Hennessy. Even the coach, George Senesky, was a local product.

Paul Arizin won two NBA scoring titles and a national college scoring crown during a fine career with Villanova and the Warriors.

With Gola providing superb all-around play and George, who was second in the league in assists, setting up the big men, the Warriors cruised home first in the Eastern Division during the regular season, finishing the campaign with a 45–27 (.625) record, six games ahead of the second-place Boston Celtics.

The Warriors, who had finished last in the division the year before, although Johnston and Arizin ranked one-two in the league in scoring, drew a first round bye, then defeated the Syracuse Nats, three games to two, in the playoff semifinals. Their opponent in the finals was the Fort Wayne Pistons, runner-up to Syracuse in the NBA finals in 1954–55 and winners of a weak Western Division regular season title with a 37–35 mark. The Pistons, featuring high-scoring George Yardley, ex–La Salle great Larry Foust, forward Mel Hutchins, and former Warriors playmaker Andy Phillip, had the best defensive team in the league. They had edged the St. Louis Hawks, three games to two, in their semifinal match.

The Pistons were no match for the Warriors, losing four out of five games. Beck came off the bench to score 23 points to lead the Warriors to a 98–94 victory in the first game. After losing Game Two, 84–83, the Warriors won the next three. Arizin (27) and Johnston (20) sparked a 100–96 win, then Arizin's 30 and George's 20 led a 107–105 triumph in Game Four. In the clincher, Graboski, firing in set shots from the corner with uncanny accuracy, scored 29 points, and Arizin added 26 to pace the Warriors to a 99–88 triumph at Convention Hall.

The championship proved to be the last for the Warriors, who had also won the NBA crown in 1947. After the 1961–62 season, owner Eddie Gottlieb moved the club to San Francisco. Although gone, the Warriors, especially that splendid 1955–56 team, would not be forgotten.

OTHER TOP STORIES OF THE DECADE

An excessive number of big stories in Philadelphia's major sports distinguished the 1950s from other decades, but a lot more was happening during the period. Headline news was being made in many other areas of the city's busy world of sports.

Professional soccer was hugely popular, particularly in the northern sections of the city, and Philadelphia teams were enormously successful, winning seven championships in the American Soccer League during the decade. Led by Walt Bahr, a member of the 1948 U.S. Olympic soccer team, the Philadelphia Nationals, who had won the title in 1949, also won crowns in each of the next two years and again in 1953. They were coached by Scotsman Jimmy Mills, a fixture in local soccer circles since his playing days in the 1920s and like Bahr a future member of the Soccer Hall of Fame. The Philadelphia Americans captured the title in 1952. They became the Uhrik Truckers the following year, and with Bahr setting the pace in 1955 and 1956 they claimed championships, followed in 1958 by the city's victorious Ukrainian Nationals.

In the 1950 World Cup matches, Bahr of Kensington got the assist on a goal by Joe Gaetjens that gave the United States an upset win over England, 1–0, in one of the most memorable World Cup victories for the United States. Bahr, who had started with the Nationals in 1942 as a 15-year-old and was later a highly successful coach at Temple and Penn State, was one of the finest soccer players ever to come out of the Philadelphia area. Two of his sons, Chris and Matt, both excellent soccer players, became placekickers in the NFL.

Another important figure in the 1950s was bowler Sylvia Wene Martin. A Philadelphian elected to the Women's International Bowling Congress (WIBC) Hall of Fame in 1966, she was one of the world's top bowlers. After finishing second in the top women's tournament, the U.S. Open, in 1951 and 1954, she won the event in 1955 and again in 1960. In 1956 she was named the nation's top woman bowler of the year. Between 1952 and 1954 she averaged 206, one of the highest marks in WIBC history. She posted 700 series 14 times during her career, a record that ranks among

Walt Bahr, one of the city's finest soccer players, led the Philadelphia Nationals to three titles in the 1950s.

the WIBC's all-time leaders. Twice in one season she rolled 300 games, and in 1959 she teamed with Adele Isphording, also of Philadelphia, to win the WIBC doubles championship with a near-record 1,263 score.

Racing, both four-legged and vehicular, was also prominent in the 1950s. Garden State Park in Cherry Hill, New Jersey, attracted the best horses and staged top thoroughbred racing throughout the decade. Atlantic City and Delaware Park also entered the thoroughbred scene, while Brandywine Raceway opened for harness racing. Langhorne Speedway was the top track for auto racing in the area, but in the '50s stock car racing was also highly popular at small tracks such as Sanatoga, Hatfield, and Atco, as well as at Municipal Stadium. Regular NASCAR races began at Langhorne in 1950 with Curtis Turner winning a 150-mile event in an Oldsmobile. He averaged 69.4 miles per hour.

In 1950, Henry Williams, Jr., club pro at Tully-Secane in Delaware Country, finished second in the PGA at Columbus, Ohio. Satchel Paige pitched briefly for the Philadelphia Stars of the Negro American League. The Phillies' Del Ennis led the National League in runs batted in with 126, and Jimmy Dykes was named manager

Sylvia Wene Martin was one of the world's top bowlers during a career that led to the Hall of Fame.

of the Athletics, becoming only the second pilot in the team's history. Connie Mack, who had retired at the close of the '50 season, ended his long managerial career with a 3,731–3,948–75 record, the most wins and the most losses of any pilot in history.

Another legend also departed the local scene as the Philadelphia Eagles fired coach Earle (Greasy) Neale at the end of the 1950 season after he had feuded with the club's new owners. Neale, who has the most wins of any Eagles coach, left with a 66–44–5. record. Although the Eagles had started the decade with high hopes, their optimism was dashed by a string of mediocre teams. With no less than five different head coaches after Neale left, the Birds could never do better than four second-place division finishes during the decade. Also included were five losing teams.

Equally disappointing were the Phillies. After their pennant-winning season in 1950, the club stumbled home fifth in 1951, then never got higher than a third-place tie the rest of the decade. Many key players never again performed up to their 1950 levels, and by the end of the 1950s, the team had staggered to four straight last-place finishes.

The one team that did gain a measure of success was the Warriors. They finished first in the Eastern Division in 1951, but that year and the next lost in the first round of the playoffs to Syracuse. In 1952–53 they won just 12 games (losing 57), despite Johnston's leading the NBA in scoring and placing second in rebounds. Johnston and Arizin combined for five scoring titles over a six-year period. After their championship year in 1956, the Warriors faced Syracuse twice more in the postseason, losing in the first round in 1957 and winning in the first round in 1958. That victory, however, was followed by a four-games-to-one loss to the Boston Celtics in the semifinals.

Basketball had started to become a major force in Philadelphia in the 1950s, and it wasn't just because of the Warriors. College hoopsters had begun to attract a sizable amount of attention.

None attracted more attention than a sharpshooter from Temple, whose nickname—the Owl Without a Vowel—was one of the most colorful in sports. Bill Mlkvy, out of Palmerton, Pennsylvania, was a dazzling all-around performer who would be named first team All-American in 1951 after leading the nation with a 29.2

Known as the Owl Without a Vowel, Temple's Bill Mlkvy led the nation in scoring while setting an NCAA record with 73 points in one game.

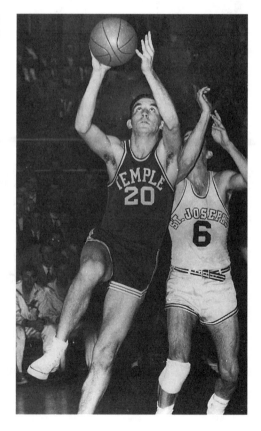

scoring average while tallying 731 points. Remarkably, that year, Mlkvy, a junior, also ranked second in the country in assists and rebounds, and in a 99–69 Temple win over Wilkes College scored an NCAA record 73 points. Netting 55 consecutive points at one stage, he shot 32-for-69 from the field.

Mlkvy eventually became the first territorial draft pick in the NBA after that process was instituted in 1952. He signed with the Warriors—his bonus was a hamburger and a milk shake at a White Tower—and played part-time his first year while attending Temple Dental School. A two-year hitch in the service during the Korean War and continuing dental studies kept him from furthering his pro career.

There were other special performances in 1951. Three years before he broke the four-minute mile, England's Roger Bannister won the mile race at the Penn Relays in the record time of 4:08.3. Defensive back Emlen Tunnell, Radnor High School's gift to the Green Bay Packers, was named to what would become the first of four All-NFL defensive teams during a stellar, Hall of Fame, 14-year career in which he ranks second in league history in interceptions (79) and first in return yardage (1,282).

Athletics first baseman Ferris Fain won the American League batting title with a .344 average, and left fielder Gus Zernial led the junior circuit in home runs (33) and RBI (129). In the National League, Roy Campanella, a native of the Nicetown section of Philadelphia and a one-time Simon Gratz High student, won his first of three Most Valuable Player awards while catching for the Brooklyn Dodgers. Campy, who would win the award again in 1953 and 1955 en route to a berth in the Baseball Hall of Fame, had been a veteran Negro League player before becoming one of the first blacks signed by organized baseball in 1948. As a teenager Campanella had practically begged for tryouts with the Phillies and A's, but because of his color, he had been repeatedly turned away.

Also in 1951, Patty Berg won the Women's Western Open golf tournament at Whitemarsh Valley Country Club, the only time that event was held in the Philadelphia area, and Robert (Skee) Riegel, a club pro and two-time Pennsylvania Open winner from Upper Darby, nearly won the Masters at Augusta, Georgia. After Norristown's George Fazio had led the field at the end of one round, Riegel was tied with Sam Snead for the lead after the third round. He finally finished second by two strokes to Ben Hogan. Riegel, who carded a 282 for four rounds, collected a check for $1,875.

Riegel and Fazio were among the many fine pro golfers who came out of the Philadelphia area. Others included Stan Dudas, Henry Williams, Jr., Ed (Porky) Oliver, George Griffin, and touring pro Al Besselink. The amateur ranks featured top players such as John Dyniewski, Howard Everritt and Billy Hyndman III.

There was continuing news on the baseball front in 1952. Elfin lefthander Bobby Shantz out of Pottstown was voted the American League's Most Valuable Player

The Athletics captured the American League's Triple Crown in 1951 when Ferris Fain (left) won the batting title and Gus Zernial led in home runs and RBI.

after ringing up a spectacular 24–7 record, Fain won his second straight batting title with a .327 average, and pitcher Harry Byrd was named Rookie of the Year with a 15–15 mark as a solid A's club made its last respectable showing in Philadelphia with a fourth-place finish. Across the corridor, the Phillies' Robin Roberts won more games than any National League hurler since 1934 as he registered a 28–7 mark but was deprived of his own MVP when the award went to outfielder Hank Sauer of the Chicago Cubs.

Baseball's All-Star Game was held at Shibe Park in 1952 with the Phillies' Curt Simmons starting on the mound for the National League. Despite being halted after five innings because of rain, the game featured Shantz striking out Whitey Lockman, Jackie Robinson, and Stan Musial in the fifth inning, along with a two-run homer by Sauer that gave the Nationals a 3–2 victory.

In another flirtation with the unusual that summer, the Phillies played an exhibition game at Haverford College. It wasn't baseball they played, though. It was cricket.

Ennis connected on one ball, sending it over the roof of a nearby house. Meanwhile, Charles Moore, Jr., of Coatesville, a student at Cornell, won a gold medal in the 400-meter hurdles and a silver in the 1,600-meter relay in the 1952 Olympics at Helsinki, Finland. Penn State grad Horace Ashenfelter from Collegeville set a world record in winning Olympic gold in the 3,000-meter steeplechase. He then captured the Sullivan Award as the nation's top amateur athlete. Between 1952 and 1956, Ashenfelter won five straight national indoor championships in the two-mile race. In women's lacrosse, Mary Fetter (Semanik), playing at Temple and later with local club teams, made her first of what would be nine straight All-American field hockey teams, reaching all the way to 1961, by which time she was well on her way to a 37-year career as a coach and administrator at Drexel.

A new ice hockey team, known as the Philadelphia Falcons, joined the Eastern Hockey League, but the team folded after just one season. And 23-year-old amateur Arnold Palmer made his first appearance in the Philadelphia area, tying with Green Valley Country Club pro George Griffin for first place in the 36-hole Pennsylvania Open. Palmer then lost to Griffin by three strokes in an 18-hole playoff at Gulph Mills.

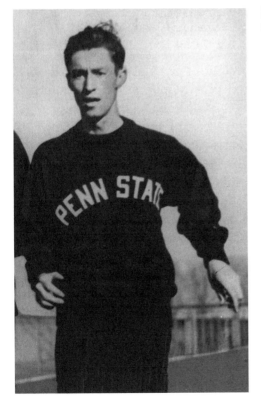

Horace Ashenfelter of Coatesville set a world record in the Olympics and won five straight national two-mile titles.

Mary Fetter (center), an All-American and later long-time coach at Drexel, led a U.S. lacrosse touring squad that also featured (from left) Philadelphians Gertrude Dunn, Jane Oswald, Gayle Meachum, and Barbara Heylman.

On another golf front, Fazio, the Norristown touring pro, finished fifth in the U.S. Open before ending the season 20th on the PGA money list with earnings of $7,164.67. The following year Fazio, the winner of five Philadelphia Opens, tied for fourth in the U.S. Open. He would retire from the tour in 1959 at the age of 47 to launch a career as a full-time golf course designer, eventually becoming one of the world's foremost members of his profession. He designed some 35 courses, including Kimberton, Squires, Moselem Springs, Waynesboro, Atlantic City, and Langhorne in the Philadelphia area.

The long-overdue integration of baseball had an adverse effect on the Negro Leagues as an increasing number of black players moved into the major leagues. While Negro League baseball lingered in a weakened condition for several more years, the 1952 season marked the end of the line for the Philadelphia Stars. Playing on their home field at Penmar Park at 44th and Parkside, as well as at Baker Bowl, Shibe Park, and Passon Field at 48th and Spruce, the Stars had been a Philadelphia fixture since 1933. With players such as Gene Benson, Bill (Ready) Cash, Mahlon Duckett, and Jud Wilson, the Stars had a large and extremely loyal following. But financial problems, helped along by the departure of their best players, made continued operation impossible.

Another Philadelphia institution departed in 1952 when the great running back Steve Van Buren retired from the Eagles after seriously injuring a knee in training camp. But as the future Hall of Famer was leaving, others were coming that year. Drexel hired a new basketball coach named Sam Cozen, and he would go on to lead the Dragons for 17 years, compiling the best coaching record (213–94) in the college's history. At Temple, assistant coach Harry Litwack was elevated to the head position, a post he would hold for 21 years, building a 373–193 record before retiring to membership in the basketball Hall of Fame. And at Penn, brilliant All-American Ernie Beck scored a still-standing record 47 points against Duke. Beck, who led the Quakers in scoring three straight years and the nation in rebounding in 1951, finished his career in 1953 with 1,827 points, still the most in Penn history.

Also joining the local sports landscape was the Dad Vail Regatta. Started with three colleges in 1934 by Penn crew coach Rusty Callow, who named the event after his friend Harry (Dad) Vail, the long-time coach at the University of Wisconsin, the Regatta was originally held in Ohio, but each year thereafter was staged at the home river of the defending champion. In 1953 it found a permanent home in Philadelphia on the Schuylkill River. Since then, the race has grown to a two-day, 18-event affair in which some 100 high schools and colleges and as many as 3,500 athletes compete over the 2,000-meter, six-lane course. As many as 70,000 spectators line the banks to watch what has become the largest regatta of its kind in the world.

La Salle College was the dominant team in the Dad Vail in the 1950s. Led by coach Tom (Bear) Curran, the Explorers won the varsity eight championships in 1951, 1952, 1953, 1956, 1957, and 1958. In that same era, Jack Kelly lost in a photo finish in the single sculls championship in the 1952 Olympics. Four years later, Kelly won a bronze medal in the same Olympic event.

Touring pro Al Besselink added his name to Philadelphia sports lore in 1953 when he put down a $500 bet on himself to win the Tournament of Champions golf tournament at Las Vegas. Getting 25-to-1 odds, the flamboyant Merchantville, New Jersey, resident astonished onlookers by winning the tournament by one stroke. Besselink, a regular on the tour for 15 years and winner of eight tournaments overall, collected $10,000 from the tournament and $12,500 from oddsmakers.

Big money was also passed out at Garden State Park that year when the richest race in the world was run. It was the $100,000-added Garden State Stakes for two-year-olds, run for the first time. Turn-To romped across the line first as a crowd of 42,205 watched.

The crowd had a different perspective at an Eagles home game in 1953. When fans didn't agree with a referee's call, they pelted the officials with snowballs during a 37–28 loss to the New York Giants. It was the first recorded snowball attack by Eagles fans, and netted the team a five-yard penalty. In their next game the Eagles

Pete Pihos made the Pro Football Hall of Fame as one of the top ends in Eagles history.

suffered their first shutout in 11 years when they bowed, 10–0, to the Washington Redskins. It was a quixotic season for the Birds as quarterback Bobby Thomason passed for a then-record 437 yards in a 30–7 win over the Giants before the Eagles ended the season with a 42–27 decision over the Cleveland Browns that nullified the loser's chance for a perfect 12–0 season. End Pete Pihos, one of the great receivers in Eagles history and a member of the Pro Football Hall of Fame, ended the season as the league leader in receptions (63) and receiving yards (1,049). He would repeat that distinction in 1954 and 1955.

In other developments in 1953, Philadelphia got something it never had before—a black major league baseball player—when pitcher Bob Trice joined the Athletics. Trice would win nine of 18 decisions during his two years in Philadelphia. Shibe Park was renamed Connie Mack Stadium by the A's board of directors. Penn under legendary coach Lajos Csiszar won its first NCAA fencing championship, an achievement it would repeat in 1969 and 1981. Brandywine Raceway became the area's first harness-racing track. Villanova resident Straight Clark, who would complete in 10 U.S. national championships, at Wimbledon, and in the Davis Cup, ranked fifth in the nation in tennis. And at Langhorne Speedway, the track's first 250-mile NASCAR race was held with Dick Rathman winning in a Hudson Hornet while averaging 67 miles per hour.

Racing of the horse variety made headlines in 1954 when Nashua, one of the greatest thoroughbreds of all time, lost the first race of his career, finishing second by a neck to Royal Note in the Cherry Hill Stakes at Garden State. Later in the year Philadelphian William Knox was elected to the American Bowling Congress Hall of Fame, and the Phillies hired Roy Hamey as their first general manager since 1948. Eagles quarterback Adrian Burk tied an NFL record with seven touchdown passes in a 49–21 victory over the Redskins and end and placekicker Bobby Walston led the league in scoring with 114 points. Phillies owner Bob Carpenter purchased Connie Mack Stadium for $1,657,000. And Pennsylvania Military College (later to be called Widener) in Chester, coached by George Hansell and led by quarterback Yommie Costello and future pro tackle Jack Klotz, had its first undefeated football season of the 20th century when it went 7–0.

Also in 1954, Mount St. Mary's College in Emmitsburg, Maryland, hired La Salle High and La Salle College graduate Jimmy Phelan as head basketball coach. A fine player with the Explorers and their assistant coach in 1953–54, Phelan had a 22–3 record in his first season with the Mountaineers. He would go on to have 19 more 20-plus-win seasons, and in his 45th season in 1999 would win his 800th game, putting him third in wins on the all-time list of college basketball coaches. One of only five men to coach in more than 1,110 basketball games, the Philadelphia native won the NCAA Division II championship in 1962 and captured NCAa College Division Coach of the Year honors four times

Nineteen fifty-five was a big year for sports in Philadelphia. Richie Ashburn won his first batting crown, hitting .338 to beat both Willie Mays and Stan Musial by 19 points. Penn's rowers, in their second of seven appearances in the Henley Royal Regatta in England, won the Grand Challenge Cup. The pro golf tour returned to Philadelphia with a tournament called the *Daily News* Open, held at Cobbs Creek. Ted Kroll beat Doug Ford in a sudden-death playoff, while new pro Arnold Palmer finished out of the money. The tournament lasted just two years.

Also in golf, Jenkintown native Billy Hyndman III made his first splash nationally by finishing second in the U.S. Amateur tournament. Over the next 30 years, Hyndman would become one of the nation's top amateur golfers, playing on five Walker Cup teams, winning three British Amateur championships, placing runner-up in another U.S. Amateur, winning numerous state and local tournaments, and winning two U.S. Senior Amateur championships—in 1973 and in 1983 at the age of 67.

In a basketball game in 1955, La Salle's Gola grabbed an amazing total of 37 rebounds in a 112–70 victory over Lebanon Valley. A future pro teammate of Gola's also had a big game. Wilt Chamberlain, a senior at Overbrook High, poured in 90 points in a 32-minute game against Roxborough for an all-time city record. Chamberlain went on to score 2,252 points during his high school career, the highest in Philadelphia schoolboy history. Two years later, he would score 121 points in four games to win MVP honors in the NCAA tournament, although his Kansas University team would lose a 54–53 triple-overtime game to undefeated North Carolina University in a memorable final.

Another big story in 1955 took place in West Philadelphia where Drexel, then known as Drexel Institute of Technology, achieved the only undefeated football season in the college's history, posting an 8–0 record under coach Eddie Allen, a former Penn and Chicago Bears fullback. Led by two-time Little All-American tackle

Wilt Chamberlain scored 90 points in a 32-minute high school basketball game.

Vince Vidas, a Korean War veteran, and stellar quarterback Bill Zador, the team allowed an average of less than nine points per game while scoring big wins over powerful West Chester, 7–0, previously undefeated Franklin and Marshall, 23–6, and Pennsylvania Military College, 20–6, in the snow in the last game of the season.

That winter Philadelphia got a new ice hockey franchise when the Ramblers joined the minor league Eastern Hockey League. Playing home games at the Arena, traveling to road games by automobile with most players getting paid $75 a week, and only once finishing as high as second place, the Ramblers' brand of hockey would not be terribly skillful. But players such as Rocky Rukavina, Reggie Meserve, Ray Crew, goalie Ivan Walmsley, and one of the first black skaters, Art Dorrington, would become fan favorites as the Ramblers hung around through 1964.

The first Big Five season ended in 1956 with both St. Joseph's and Temple ruling the spotlight. Ending a 23–6 season, the Hawks gained a 93–82 victory over St. Francis (New York) to finish third in the NIT in Jack Ramsay's first year at the helm. Ram-

The Ramblers, with players such as Gil MacNeil, Reggie Meserve, and Ivan Walmsley (from left), were a popular attraction for local ice hockey fans.

Jack Ramsay became the winningest coach in St. Joseph's history during his 11 years at the helm.

say would become the winningest coach in Hawk history, posting a 234–72 record for a sizzling .765 percentage. In his 11 seasons at St. Joe's, Ramsay's Hawks made 10 postseason appearances.

Temple, with the dazzling lefthanded backcourt duo of Hal Lear and Guy Rodgers, won the NCAA's Eastern Regional final with a 60–58 triumph over Canisius as Lear sank two foul shots at the end and Rodgers scored 22 points. Advancing to the Final Four, the Owls lost to Iowa, 83–76, in the first game before Lear scored 48 points to spark a 90–81 victory over Southern Methodist to give Temple third place in the tournament. Lear, who scored 745 during the season, then the fifth-highest total in college basketball history, was named Final Four MVP.

Connie Mack died at the age of 93. Very much alive was Villanova's track team. Wildcat runners captured three gold medals in the Olympic Games at Melbourne, Australia, marking the first of an eventual seven gold medals for Villanova trackmen. Charley Jenkins won golds in the 400 meters and for running the third leg of the 1,600-meter medley relay team, while Irishman Ron Delany finished first in the 1,500 meters, his first of four NCAA outdoor titles in distance races.

Guy Rodgers led Temple to two trips to the Final Four and a third-place finish in the NIT.

Villanova's success carried over into 1957 when coach Jim (Jumbo) Elliott fielded one of the best track and field teams in collegiate history. With a well-balanced team led by Delany, Jenkins, sprinter Ed Collymore, high jumper Phil Reavis, and pole vaulter Don Bragg, the Wildcats won every major college and AAU competition, both indoor and outdoor. Also in track, Norristown's Josh Culbreath, running for Morgan State, established himself as one of the great intermediate hurdlers when he set a world record in the 440-yard hurdles. Culbreath had already won three AAU national championships (1953, 1954, 1955), a bronze medal in the 1956 Olympics, and his first of two Pan-American Games titles.

Temple continued as a basketball powerhouse, finishing third in the NIT after a 76–50 victory over St. Bonaventure. With Lear graduated, Rodgers became the Owls' leading player. A superb playmaker and exceptional dribbler, he would eventually become a three-time Big Five MVP and a consensus All-American while averaging 19.6 and scoring the third-highest total of points (1,767) in Temple history. A long and successful NBA career mostly with the Philadelphia and San Francisco Warriors and Chicago Bulls followed for Rodgers after he left Temple.

Langhorne Speedway had perhaps its biggest season in 1957 with the running of five major races, including three NASCAR events. In the second of two Indianapolis car events, Paul Goldsmith won a grueling 300-mile race in a Chevrolet, taking more than four hours to get the checkered flag.

Ten long years after Jackie Robinson became the major league's first black player in the 20th century, the Phillies finally got around to signing African-Americans. Former Negro Leaguer John Kennedy was the first to suit up in red pinstripes in spring training in 1957. Cuban Chico Fernandez, obtained from the Brooklyn Dodgers in a trade, became the first black to perform for the Phillies during the regular season. That same year the Phillies had a Rookie of the Year in Ed Bouchee and a Rookie Pitcher of the Year in Jack Sanford.

Across the Atlantic Ocean, an Air Force sergeant from Havertown named Harold (Red) Ridgley became only the fourth American to win the British Amateur golf championship. Many years later, Ridgley would be the one who hit the golf shots as a stand-in for actor Rodney Dangerfield when the movie *Caddyshack* was filmed on Red's home course in Florida.

In one of the great races at Garden State, the legendary Bold Ruler, with Hall of Fame jockey Eddie Arcaro in the saddle, clinched Horse of the Year honors by defeating both Gallant Man and Round Table in the Trenton Handicap. Althea Gibson was the women's winner in the Pennsylvania Lawn Tennis Championship, an event that was held at Merion Cricket Club for 80 years. And West Chester State football under Glenn Killinger posted a 9–0 record with Jack Harrington, Bruce Shenk, and Jack Wendland leading the way.

In 1957 the Eagles had one of their finest drafts when they picked fullback Clarence Peaks (first round), receiver Tommy McDonald (third), and quarterback Sonny Jurgensen (fourth). After a run of disappointing seasons, the Eagles were plotting their comeback. Within the next few months, they would hire the highly regarded Buck Shaw as head coach, land veteran quarterback Norm Van Brocklin in a trade, claim tight end Pete Retzlaff on waivers, and switch their home games from Connie Mack Stadium to Franklin Field. Although the 1958 Birds lost their first game at the Penn stadium, 24–14, to Washington before a crowd of 36,853, the move proved to be one of the best the club ever made as attendance figures were soon double what they had been for Eagles home games.

In basketball, Temple returned to the limelight in 1957–58 to the limelight as Rodgers teamed with new backcourt mate Bill (Pickles) Kennedy and veteran center Jay Norman to drive the Owls to a 27–3 record, including 25 wins in a row, and another berth in the NCAA tournament. After defeating Dartmouth, 69–50, in the regional final, Temple advanced to the Final Four for the second time in three years. The Owls bowed to Kentucky, 61–60, in the first game, then captured third place with a 67–57 victory over Kansas State. That same season, the Warriors' Woody Sauldsberry was named NBA Rookie of the Year.

That summer, the PGA tournament in its first year of stroke play was held at Llanerch Country Club. Third-round leader Sam Snead fell apart on the back nine of the fourth round, butchering several holes and winding up third, four strokes behind the leader, Dow Finsterwald, whose 276 beat Billy Casper by two strokes. Masters champion Arnold Palmer finished a distant 22 strokes off the lead.

Drexel won the NCAA soccer championship in 1958 in the final year that the title was awarded by vote. Coach Don Yonkers, later to join the Soccer Hall of Fame, guided his team to a perfect 12–0 record. Three All-Americans led the way, including Stan Dlugosz, the squad's top player, who set a still-standing three-year scoring record with 49 goals, Igor Lissy, owner of the one-season record with 22 goals, and goalie Bob Muschek.

By 1958, La Salle's track and field program had begun to build a reputation. The Explorers' Ira Davis set a U.S. record in the triple jump. One year later, Al Cantello moved into the spotlight in the javelin, an event in which he eventually held the world record. Meanwhile, the Phillies' Richie Ashburn won his second batting crown, edging Mays on the last day of the season to finish with a .350 mark. Famed driver Eddie Sachs won a 100-mile race at Langhorne. West Chester, led by quarterback Harrington and running back Bill Shockley, scored a school record 514 points, including an 85–0 win over Cheyney and three other games over 60, while compiling a 9–1 record. And trying out for the Eagles was a young lineman chosen in the 21st round of the draft. A knee injury kept John Madden from making the team, but he would be heard from many times again, first as a coach, then as a network broadcaster.

In the Army-Navy game soon-to-be Heisman Trophy winner Pete Dawkins led the Cadets to 22–6 victory at Municipal Stadium. The following year another legend, Navy's Joe Bellino, scored three touchdowns to guide the Midshipmen to a 43–12 rout. In that game, Springfield (Delco) High grad Bill Carpenter was dubbed "the Lonesome End" for lining up on the far side of the field and not joining huddles in an unorthodox strategy employed by Army.

Two local field hockey standouts began to attract national attention. In 1958, Ursinus player Yvonne (Vonnie) Gros of West Chester was a first-team selection on the U.S. Field Hockey Association team. She would be named to the team every year through 1970. In 1959, Mary Anne Leight (Harris), a Temple All-American, made her first USFHA first team. A resident of Harleysville, she, too, would make the squad every year through 1970.

Track and field made the biggest news of the year in Philadelphia in 1959 with the staging of the first United States–Soviet Union meet held in this country. The previous year the teams had met in Moscow. Taking place at Franklin Field in the blazing heat, the two-day event came at the height of the cold war when the two countries were engaged in their most acrid relationship. Because of the political hostility, the meet drew worldwide attention. But it was conducted without incident, with the American men winning, 127–108, and the Soviet women victorious, 67–40. The only double winner of the meet was Ray Norton, who won the 100- and 200-meter dashes. Norristown's Josh Culbreath in the 400-meter hurdles, Al Cantello in the javelin, Villanova's Don Bragg in the pole vault, Al Oerter in the discus, Parry O'Brien in the shot put, and Dyrol Burleson in the 1,500-meter run were among the American winners.

In 1959 the Eagles' Retzlaff led the NFL in pass receptions. The Phillies had a second baseman who hit just .218 in his only year in the big leagues, but Sparky Anderson went on to a Hall of Fame career as the third-winningest manager in the big leagues with 2,194 victories. The name of Municipal Stadium was changed to Philadelphia Stadium. And the last NASCAR races were held at Langhorne Speedway. A NASCAR race had been held every year since 1950 at the tight little track. But repeated major accidents and dwindling crowds combined with the rapidly growing popularity of the sport in the South (where most of the races had shifted) to make it no longer practical to hold NASCAR events at Langhorne.

Also departing the local sports scene was Bert Bell, founder of the Eagles, NFL commissioner since 1946, and a member of the Pro Football Hall of Fame. Bell, who had almost single-handedly led the NFL from rags to riches, collapsed and died while attending an Eagles game at Franklin Field. He was a towering figure in pro football, and the Philadelphia native and former Penn gridder was one of the most highly respected commissioners in sports.

Robin Roberts Was a Superb Pitcher

In a decade in which as many top athletes performed in Philadelphia as in any other era, Phillies pitcher Robin Roberts was the best of a luminous gathering.

That statement says volumes about the ability of Roberts because to be the best of the 1950s, he had to be better than a group that included football's Chuck Bednarik, Pete Pihos, and Reds Bagnell; basketball's Tom Gola, Paul Arizin, Neil Johnston, Hal Lear, and Guy Rodgers; boxer Joe Walcott; tennis player Vic Seixas; and baseball players Richie Ashburn, Del Ennis, and Ferris Fain. No finer group ever graced the Philadelphia sports scene.

Roberts, though, not only was the best Philadelphia athlete of the 1950s, but was

Robin Roberts had six straight 20-win seasons while recording 234 victories for the Phillies.

one of the best pitchers the city ever had. Playing from mid-1948 to 1961 with the Phillies, the Springfield, Illinois, native was one of the National League's most dominant hurlers. He won 20 or more games six years in a row between 1950 and 1955, and in 1952, when he won 28, he had the highest number of victories in the National League since Dizzy Dean won 30 for the St. Louis Cardinals in 1934.

A big, strong righthander, Roberts threw with a beautifully fluid motion. He had a blazing fastball and a devastating curve, and he threw with pinpoint control. Hitters liked to dig in on him, and because he refused to throw brush-back pitches, Roberts annually gave up a high number of home runs.

But neither that propensity nor the fact that he played mostly for mediocre to poor teams ever kept Roberts from pitching with remarkable success. He won the game in which the 1950 Phillies clinched the National League pennant. He was the starting pitcher in an unprecedented five All-Star Games. He pitched three one-hitters. Once he pitched 32⅔ scoreless innings in a row.

Durability was one of Roberts' strongest traits. Over one stretch in the early 1950s, he pitched 28 consecutive complete games. Eight different times he completed 21 or more games during a season, once reaching 30 and once 33. He led the league in complete games five times. And seven times he made more than 40 starts in a season.

A graduate of Michigan State University, which he attended on a basketball scholarship, Roberts signed with the Phillies in 1948. Assigned to the Wilmington Blue Rocks, he spent just one-half season there before being called to the parent club.

Roberts was named the major leagues' Pitcher of the Year, an award then equal to today's Cy Young Award, four times. He was named to seven All-Star teams. And in 1976 he was elected to the Baseball Hall of Fame.

Overall, during a 19-year career in the major leagues, Roberts posted a 286–245 record. He walked only 902 batters in 4,688⅔ innings while allowing 4,582 hits and striking out 2,357. He had a career earned run average in 676 games of 3.41.

Roberts was one of the finest pitchers ever to grace a mound, not only in Philadelphia, but in all of baseball. In the 1950s, in all of Philadelphia sports, no athlete was better.

CHAPTER 7

1960s

An Era of
Extremes

Under normal conditions, one of the many virtues of sports is that they are seldom static. They are in a state of constant change, with fluctuations that can reach from the highest point to the lowest.

In the 1960s the variability of Philadelphia sports exceeded the normal range. It was perhaps the most volatile decade of the century—a decade of extremes in which the ups and downs were in perfect harmony with the explosive developments occurring throughout the rest of society.

Just as the turbulent '60s were characterized by social unrest all across the nation, the era was marked in Philadelphia sports by major variations and changes. Some were good; some were not. Collectively, however, they made for one big, erratic decade.

The peaks and valleys were everywhere. The Eagles began the decade with a stirring championship, then faded to the slums of the NFL. College basketball opened the decade with a point-shaving scandal, then moved into an era of splendid teams, capped by Temple's NIT championship. The Warriors moved out of town, and the 76ers moved in and, after struggling to gain acceptance, had the best season in NBA history. The Ramblers left, and the Flyers came. A new stadium called the Spectrum was built, and soon after it opened its roof blew off.

There were plenty of other ugly moments. The Phillies lost 23 straight games, then three years later blew the National League pennant in the last two weeks of the season. Phillies fans unmercifully booed superstar Dick Allen, and Eagles fans threw snowballs at Santa Claus. Heading toward a winless season and a sure first-round draft choice of O. J. Simpson, the Eagles won two of their last three games to lose the pick. Philadelphia resident Sonny Liston remained on his seat and lost the heavyweight title to a young boxer then named Cassius Clay. The Phillies traded for outfielder Curt Flood, who refused to come to Philadelphia, then filed a lawsuit that would have a permanent effect on major league baseball.

The 1960s were the era of Joe Kuharich, the Philadelphia Tapers, a bomb threat at the Palestra, the Phillies trading away future Hall of Famer Ferguson Jenkins, and the refusal of a local daily newspaper to cover the newly arrived 76ers.

Surrounding such bleak trappings, however, were an awful lot of high spots. During the decade it was common to see Philadelphia area athletes accepting gold medals at one of the three summer Olympics. The professional golf and tennis tours took over major roles in local sports. Two new horse tracks, Liberty Bell Park and Keystone Race Track, opened. Boxing returned to the Blue Horizon after a long absence. A college basketball tournament came to town. So did a new professional soccer team called the Spartans and a pro football team named the Bulldogs. Approval was given to build a new multipurpose stadium in South Philadelphia. And the second-class status that had long impeded women's sports finally started to lift.

It was also the era when several fierce rivalries were launched. The Eagles and Dallas Cowboys became bitter enemies in an acrimonious rivalry that lives to this day. And the 76ers and Boston Celtics began a three-decade run as hated antagonists in a rivalry which during its height featured ferocious battles not only between the two teams but also between star centers Wilt Chamberlain and Bill Russell.

Villanova vaulted into a spot as the nation's premier producer of track and field excellence, and its football team played in two straight bowl games. The Ukrainian Nationals dominated professional soccer. Penn women had their first undefeated season in basketball. West Chester won the NCAA soccer championship and the first women's basketball title. A quasi-professional men's softball team playing as Flatiron AC was not only the class of the city, but one of the nation's top squads.

Jim Bunning became the first pitcher in 42 years to hurl a perfect game during the regular season. Wilt Chamberlain scored an unbelievable 100 points in an NBA game. Frank Budd broke a Jesse Owens sprinting record. Joe Frazier came to Philadelphia and became heavyweight boxing champion. Harold Johnson won the light-heavyweight boxing title. Jimmy Caras came back from retirement to once again dominate the sport of pocket billiards. The Flyers drafted a young player named Bobby Clarke who came from someplace called Flin Flon, Manitoba.

There were tons of other stars of the '60s. It was a time for Norm Van Brocklin, Timmy Brown, and Bob Brown. Chet Walker and Hal Greer. Joey Giardello and Bennie Briscoe. John Baum and Cliff Anderson. Don Bragg and Vic Zwoluk. Gene Mauch and Alex Hannum. Johnny Callison, Ellie Daniel, and Rueben Navarro, not to mention Bill Campbell, Richie Ashburn, Gene Hart, and Les Keiter in the broadcast booth and quite possibly the finest sports columnist the city ever had, a transplanted North Carolinian named Sandy Grady. And Jack Ramsay, Harry Litwack, Jack Kraft, and Jack McCloskey were all coaching against each other in the Big Five.

A number of Philadelphians went out of town to gain fame and glory. Danny Murtaugh, Mickey Vernon, Reggie Jackson, and Pat Kelly in baseball; Johnny Rauch, Herb Adderley, Leroy Kelly, and Milt Plum in football; Ray (Chink) Scott, Walt Hazzard, and Earl Monroe in basketball all performed special deeds elsewhere. Havertown's Shag Crawford in the National and Chester's Johnny Stevens in the American were considered two of the big leagues' top umpires. And the NBA was dominated by referees from the Philadelphia area, including Ed Rush of West Chester, the youngest man ever to officiate in the NBA, and Jake O'Donnell of Clifton Heights, who for a while was also an American League umpire.

Overall, it was the best—and in some cases, the worst—of times. The extremes were never more conspicuous. But the decade of the 1960s was also a time that would be one of Philadelphia sports' most unforgettable eras.

EAGLES FLY AGAIN

It would be no stretch of the imagination to say that in 1960 the Eagles had the finest season in the club's history. It was a season in which the Birds fielded probably their most exciting team, while capturing their third and last NFL championship of the century in dramatic fashion against the Green Bay Packers.

After capturing the NFL title in 1949, the Eagles had entered a long period of mediocrity. They were no longer contenders, and, in fact, by the mid-1950s they had become downright pitiful. In four seasons between 1955 and 1958, they had won just 13 games.

But in 1958, despite a 2–9–1 record, the future was beginning to brighten. That year the Eagles had hired a first-rate head coach in Buck Shaw. One of Shaw's first moves was to land veteran quarterback Norm Van Brocklin in a trade with the Los Angeles Rams. Shaw also signed end Pete Retzlaff as a free agent to go along with a bumper crop of young players that included Tommy McDonald, Sonny Jurgenson. Billy Barnes, and Clarence Peaks, all 1957 draft choices, and defensive linemen and future Eagles coaches Marion Campbell and Ed Khayat.

In 1959, with Shaw phasing out some of the Eagles' aging players and adding new ones, particularly linemen J. D. Smith, Jim McCusker, Stan Campbell, Gerry Huth, and Joe Robb, linebacker Chuck Weber, and defensive back Jimmy Carr, the Eagles climbed into a second-place tie in the Eastern Conference with a 7–5 record. Then in 1960, with rookies Maxie Baughan, John Wittenborn, and Ted Dean of Radnor and veteran defensive backs Bobby Freeman and Don Burroughs added to the fold, they took off.

Now playing for the third year at Franklin Field, the Eagles dropped their season's opener to the Cleveland Browns, 41–24. They then won nine straight, including a thrilling 31–29 decision over the Browns on Bobby Walston's 38-yard field goal with

Eagles coach Buck Shaw surrounded himself in 1960 with a talented backfield that included (from left) Billy Barnes, Radnor's Ted Dean, Norm Van Brocklin, and Tommy McDonald. Dean scored the winning touchdown in the Eagles 17–13 championship win over the Packers.

10 seconds left to play. All the while, the crafty veteran Van Brocklin was relentlessly driving the Eagles along with his special brand of tough, opportunistic quarterbacking.

The Birds suffered a crucial loss when fullback Peaks broke his leg in the seventh game of the season, but fortunately they had Dean to step in. In Dean's first game as a starter, the Eagles won one of their most memorable games when they beat the New York Giants, their main competition for the Eastern title, 17–10. The key play of the game, occurring as the Giants drove into Eagle territory with two minutes left in the fourth quarter, came when Chuck Bednarik, playing both ways, put a ferocious hit on Frank Gifford at the 30, knocking the Giants' ballcarrier out and causing a fumble. Bednarik danced gleefully over Gifford's prone body as Weber recovered loose ball.

Two games later, after another win over the Giants, the Eagles clinched the Eastern title with a 20–6 victory over the St. Louis Cardinals. They then split their last two games, with McDonald finishing with a club record 13 touchdown receptions and Walston scoring 105 points. Despite having the second-lowest team rushing yardage in the league, the Eagles had advanced to their first championship game since 1949. Van Brocklin, nicknamed "the Dutchman," was named the league's MVP, while he, Bednarik, and defensive back Tom Brookshier were named first-team All-NFL, with Roxborough's Jesse Richardson at defensive tackle and McDonald making the second team.

The championship game was one of the great contests in Philadelphia sports history. Facing the Packers, who under coach Vince Lombardi were just starting to put together the dynasty that would rule the NFL in the 1960s, the Eagles captured a pulsating 17–13 victory before 67,325 at Franklin Field.

After two field goals by Green Bay's Paul Hornung, the Birds went ahead on Van Brocklin's 35-yard TD pass to McDonald and Walston's extra point. A 41-yard pass to Retzlaff set up Walston's 15-yard field goal to make it 10–6 at halftime, but the Packers regained the lead in the fourth quater as Bart Starr and Max McGee combined on a seven-yard scoring pass. On the ensuing kickoff, Dean raced 58 yards to the Packers' 39, then a few plays later burst over from the five to put the Eagles back in front at 17–13.

The Eagles still needed one more big play, and again it came from the 35-year-old Bednarik, who was playing 58 of the game's 60 minutes. On the last play of the game, as Jim Taylor rumbled toward the Eagles' goal after taking a Starr swing pass, Bednarik leveled the Packers fullback with a bone-jarring tackle at the nine-yard line. Concrete Charley then sat on Taylor as time ran out.

In the wake of the Eagles' greatest win, Shaw and Van Brocklin both retired. "I don't think I've ever coached a team that had more desire," Shaw said. After a second-place division finish in 1961, the Eagles entered another long, dreary period of losing. It would be 20 years before they reached a championship game again.

LET THERE BE GOLD

A little more than 100 years after the Gold Rush took place in the West, the Philadelphia area had a gold rush of its own. Never have so many people in the area panned so successfully for the glittering treasure

The gold in this case was Olympic gold. During the 1960s dozens of local athletes sought it, and a record number of them found it. They were helped, of course, by the fact that during the decade there were three summer Olympics—in 1960 in Rome, in 1964 in Tokyo, and in 1968 in Mexico City.

The local gold rush began right at the start of the decade. In the 1960 Olympics, Villanova's Don Bragg from Penns Grove, New Jersey, won the pole vault. Bragg, the last of the great prefiberglass vaulters, had set a world record of 15–9¼ in the tri-

Equesterian Frank Chapot of Camden is one of only four Americans to compete in six Olympics.

als. Ted Nash, who a few years later would begin a long and successful career as Penn's crew coach and was later the coach at Vesper Boat Club, rowed on the winning four without a coxswain team. Frank Chapot of Camden, one of only four Americans to compete in six Olympics, won silver medals in two equestrian events.

Overbrook High graduate Walt Hazzard, having just helped UCLA to an undefeated (30–0) season and its first NCAA championship while being named a first-team All-American, sparked the U.S. basketball team (which included future 76ers Larry Brown, Luke Jackson, and George Wilson, plus Bill Bradley) to a gold medal in 1964. Hazzard would go on to a 10-year career in the NBA. In track, Villanova's Paul Drayton won a gold as his 4 × 100-meter relay team finished first, along with a silver in the 200-meter race.

Still another gold was pocketed when Vesper rowers won the eights with a coxswain with a team that included Joe and Tom Amalong, Boyce Budd, Emory Clark, Stan Cwkinski, Hugh Foley, Bill Knecht, Bill Stowe, and Bob Zimonyi (cox). Knecht, out of La Salle High and Villanova, was one of the area's finest oarsmen, having won numerous national titles as well as three gold medals in the Pan-American Games.

More gold was mined by Philadelphia-area residents in the 1968 Olympics. Most prominent among the winners was swimmer Ellie Daniel. As an 18-year-old swimming for Vesper, where she was coached by Mary Kelly, wife of Jack, she won the gold medal in the 4 × 100 medley relay, plus a silver in the 100-meter butterfly and a bronze in the 200-meter butterfly. Daniel, possibly the finest woman swimmer ever to come out of the Philadelphia area and a gold medal winner in the 100-meter butterfly in the 1967 Pan-American Games, later went to Penn, and in the 1972 Olympics she won a bronze medal in the 200-meter butterfly, an event in which she set world records four different times

Golds were also won in the 1968 Olympics by three other local swimmers. Steve Rerych of Philadelphia won two golds for his participation on the winning 4 × 100- and 4 × 200-meter freestyle relay teams. Jane Barkman of Wayne was on the winning women's 4 × 100-meter freestyle relay team—a triumph she would repeat in the '72 Olympics—and picked up a silver medal in the 200-meter freestyle. Carl Robie of Drexel Hill, having won a silver medal in the 200-meter butterfly in the '64 Olympics, captured the gold in that event in 1968. During his career, Robie won two NCAA titles while at the University of Michigan, nine AAU titles, and a gold medal in the 1963 Pan-American Games. Debbie Meyers, a transplanted Californian originally from Haddonfield, won gold medals in the 200-, 400- and 800-meter freestyle events. Later in the year, she won the Sullivan Award as the nation's top amateur athlete.

Philadelphia native Bill Toomey won the gold in the decathlon. Larry James, a three-time NCAA 440 champion at Villanova, ran a leg of the winning 4 × 400-meter relay team and added a silver medal in the 400-meter race. Mel Pender of the Philadelphia Pioneers track club helped the 4 × 100-meter relay team cross the line first.

Ellie Daniel won gold, silver, and bronze medals in the 1968 Olympics.

PHILLY FIGHTERS

Philadelphia has always enjoyed a reputation as the home of a special kind of fighter. "Philly Fighters" they are called, and among them have been some of the toughest, most talented boxers in the universe.

They were in particular abundance during the middle decades of the century— welterweights, lightweights, and middleweights mostly, fighters who grew up on the streets of Philadelphia and learned their craft in one of the many gyms dotting the city. No decade ever had more of them than the 1960s. It was perhaps the finest era in Philadelphia boxing.

There were champions such as Harold Johnson and Joey Giardello, both members of the Boxing Hall of Fame. And there were strong perennial contenders such as Bennie Briscoe, Stanley (Kitten) Hayward, Eugene (Cylone) Hart, Gypsy Joe Harris, Len Mathews, and Leotis Martin.

Johnson was a master technical boxer out of Manayunk. He had begun fighting professionally in 1946, reeling off wins in his first 24 fights. Johnson was finally stopped by Archie Moore in 1949. He also lost to Jersey Joe Walcott before fighting

Moore three more times within four months, losing twice and winning once. Finally, in 1954 in New York, Johnson fought Moore for the light-heavyweight title. After knocking the champ down in the 10th and being ahead on points through the 13th, Johnson was punched out by Moore in the 14th.

A drugging incident for which he was later cleared slowed Johnson's career in 1955. But in 1961, Harold got a shot at Moore's vacated NBA title against Jesse Bowdry in Miami Beach. Johnson, at the age of 32, became the champ with a ninth-round TKO. Later that year, he beat Von Clay and Eddie Cotton in title defenses while fighting three times in four months, then unified the title in 1962 by defeating world champ Doug Jones in 15 rounds at the Arena. Johnson held the title for another year before losing it to Willie Pastrano on a 15-round decision in Las Vegas. He fought sporadically after that, winding up his career in 1971 with a 76–11 record.

Harold Johnson became light-heavyweight champion at the age of 32.

Giardello had a similar long climb to the top after turning professional in 1948. A self-taught brawler who lived in South Philadelphia, Joey recorded important wins over Billy Graham, Gil Turner, Tiger Jones, and numerous others in the 1950s. He got his first title fight when he challenged Gene Fullmer for the NBA middleweight crown in 1960. In a bruising 15-round brawl in Bozeman, Montana, Fullmer retained his title in a bout that was declared a draw. Each fighter accused the other of dirty tactics.

The title finally came to Giardello in 1963 when he faced Tiger, who had beaten Fullmer for the crown, in Atlantic City. The two had met twice in 1959, each winning once. This time Giardello won a 15-round decision. The crown was his, and he held it for two years, beating Ruben (Hurricane) Carter in 15 rounds in 1964 at Convention Hall. In 1965 in only his second title defense, Giardello lost a 15-round decision to Tiger in New York. Joey, now 35, would have just four more fights before retiring in 1967 with a career record of 100–25–7.

Among the other great fighters of the era, middleweight Briscoe was the best. A

Joey Giardello (left) held the middleweight championship for two years.

relentless body puncher, the North Philly native was one of the most popular boxers and best drawing cards ever to step into a ring in Philadelphia. And he stepped in frequently, often the victim of poor management in his early years. Late in his career, Briscoe, who never gave up his job as a garbage collector for the city of Philadelphia, had title fights in Buenos Aries against defending champ Carlos Monzon of Argentina and twice with Colombia's Rodrigo Valdes, losing twice in 15-round decisions and once on a seventh-round kayo. Bennie fought from 1962 to 1982, compiling a record of 66–24–6.

Harris, who strutted into the ring wearing a red cape and fought with an unorthodox style, was easily the most colorful of the local fighters. He was also very good. He won his first 24 fights, including upset wins over Hayward and welterweight champ Curtis Cokes in a nontitle fight. In 1968 he took part in what many regard as the top local fight of the decade when he lost a 12-round decision to Emile Griffith in a spectacular bout at the Spectrum. Gypsy Joe never fought again. In an examination before his next fight, it was discovered that he could only see out of one eye. He was forced to retire from the ring.

THE BEST OF THE BIG FIVE

When it comes to college basketball, Philadelphia doesn't take a back seat to any city in the country. It has strong programs at both large and small college levels, many of them dating back to the early part of the century.

The cornerstone of Philadelphia basketball is, of course, the Big Five where fierce rivalries and nationally ranked teams were staples for more than four decades. La Salle, Penn, St. Joseph's, Temple, and Villanova usually play more good basketball in a single season than most teams do in a decade.

Of all the fine eras of the Big Five, none surpassed the 1960s. It was truly the golden era of the Big Five when some of the best basketball ever played in the city took place.

Great teams were plentiful. St. Joseph's went to the Final Four in the NCAA in 1961 and lost in the Eastern Regional final in 1963. Villanova placed third in the NIT in 1963 and second in 1965. And Temple won the NIT in 1969. During the decade St. Joseph's made six appearances in the NCAA playoffs and one in the NIT. Villanova went to the NCAA playoffs three times and to the NIT six times. Temple was in the NCAAs twice and the NIT six times. And La Salle made one trip to the NCAAs and two to the NIT. Overall, these teams made 27 trips to postseason tournaments. During the decade the five Big Five teams had a combined record of 897–428.

St. Joseph's won the Big Five title five times during the 1960s. La Salle and Villanova each won the crown twice and Penn once.

No arena epitomized college basketball better than the fabled Palestra.

Great players were in abundance during the decade. Villanova had Jim Washington, Hubie White, Billy Melchionni, Wally Jones, Johnny Jones, and Howard Porter. Temple had Bruce Drysdale, Jim Williams, Eddie Mast, Clarence Brookins, and John Baum. From Penn there was Dave Wohl, Steve Bilsky, Stan Pawlak, Jeff Neuman, and John Wideman. From La Salle, there was Bernie Williams, Frank Corace, Hubie Marshall, George Sutor, Larry Cannon, and Ken Durrett. And St. Joe's featured Matt Guokas, Jr., Jimmy Lynam, Steve Courtin, Mike Hauer, and Cliff Anderson.

The '60 were an era of brilliant coaches, too. The Hawks' Jack Ramsay, the Owls' Harry Litwack, the Quakers' Jack McCloskey, and the Wildcats' Jack Kraft could match minds with anybody who ever drew a line on a chalkboard.

As often happens, though, there was bad news to go with the good news. Early in the decade, the Big Five was rocked by a point-shaving scandal. After the 1961 season it was learned that St. Joseph's Jack Egan, Frank Majewski, and Vince Kempton and La Salle's Ed Bowler had taken part in a point-shaving scheme that included 37 players from 22 colleges around the country. It was devastating news for the Big

Five, and especially the schools involved. In the aftermath the third-place finish that St. Joseph's had achieved in the NCAA finals was taken away.

Another damaging blow was suffered in 1969 when La Salle under coach Tom Gola posted its finest single-season record, winning 23 and losing one and ranking second to UCLA in the nation in the final polls. Some said that this team, led by Cannon, Williams, and Durett, was not only La Salle's best but maybe the finest in Big Five history.The Explorers, however, were barred from competing in the NCAA tourney because the college was on probation, the result of an illegal practice under previous coach Jim Harding in which players weren't performing their summer jobs.

The Big Five had to endure a bomb threat, which occurred in 1965 at halftime of a Hawks-Wildcats game. While the Palestra was evacuated, TV broadcaster Les

Coach Tom Gola got plenty of big games from (from left) Stan Wlodarczyk, Bernie Williams, and Larry Cannon as La Salle had its best single-season record.

Keiter remained at his post high above the stands, providing in melodramatic tones a running commentary on the situation.

But the Big Five withstood these and a few minor setbacks during a glittering decade. It was a decade when Phi Beta Kappa John Wideman, a future Rhodes Scholar and award-winning novelist, led Penn to its first Big Five title in 1963; when an unheralded sub named Steve Donches sank a 29-foot shot at the buzzer to give St. Joe's a pulsating 71–69 win over Villanova in 1966; when Temple's John Baum, La Salle's Larry Cannon, St. Joe's Cliff Anderson, and Villanova's Jim Washington, Wally Jones, and Hubie White each made three straight All–Big Five teams; when Penn emerged a 32–30 winner over the Wildcats in 1969 after holding the ball most of the game; and when Calvin Murphy, one of many great opposing players who visited the Palestra, scored 52 points to lead Niagara to a 100–83 victory over La Salle. Overall, it was the Big Five's finest era.

TOURING PROS STOP TO PLAY

Strange as it may seem, given the abiding interest in golf that exists in the Philadelphia area, the professional tour prior to the 1960s did not play much of a role in local sports. To be sure, a pro tournament would be held in the area once in a while, but there was none on a regular basis.

The pro tour made its first big visit of the 1960s to Philadelphia when the PGA Tournament was held at Aronimink Country Club in 1962. The year's U.S. Open winner Jack Nicklaus and British Open winner Arnold Palmer were both in the field, but the third member of the Big Three stole the show. Gary Player, leading after the third round, held on to beat Bob Goalby by one stroke to win the tournament.

The pros left town quickly, but they soon returned. Just one year later Philadelphia became a regular stop on the PGA tour with the creation of what was originally known as the Whitemarsh Open. Held at Whitemarsh Valley Country Club, it offered a total purse of $125,000, making it the richest event on the pro tour.

Player, Nicklaus, and Palmer were all there for the inaugural tournament. This time it was Palmer who prevailed. Although he blew most of a five-stroke lead on the back nine of the final day, a birdie on the 17th hole helped him win the tournament by one stroke over Lionel Hebert.

It was Nicklaus's turn the following year, and Jack overcame a six-shot deficit that had him in ninth place starting the fourth round to beat Palmer by one stroke. Nicklaus repeated his victory in 1965 when he eagled the 17th with a 45-foot putt to break a three-way tie and set up a one-stroke win over Doug Sanders and Joe Campbell. The legendary Ben Hogan, making his last appearance in Philadelphia, dropped out of the tournament after two rounds.

Arnold Palmer was the first winner of the pro tournament held for 18 years at Whitemarsh Valley Country Club.

By then the tournament's name had become the Philadelphia Classic. It would be called that until 1971 when the name was changed to IVB Golf Classic to reflect the name of its new sponsor.

While it existed, the Classic attracted large galleries and top players, and it featured exciting golf on the challenging Whitemarsh course. It was a major event on the local sports calendar, and it commanded a considerable amount of attention each year. It also attracted many of the area's touring pro players such as Bert Yancey, Jim King, Dick Hendrickson, Charlie Sifford, and upstate Pennsylvania's Art Wall.

Through the remainder of the 1960s, the Classic was won by Don January, Dick Sikes, Bob Murphy, and Dave Hill. The last two were particularly noteworthy. Murphy beat Labron Harris on the third hole in the tourney's first playoff. Hill won when he birdied the first extra hole of a four-way playoff with Gay Brewer, Sikes, and Tommy Jacobs.

In the 1970s, with top players becoming harder to attract despite a total purse that exceeded $200,000, the tournament was won by Billy Casper, Tom Weiskopf, J. C.

Snead, Weiskopf again, Hubie Green, Tom Kite, Jerry McGee, Nicklaus again, and Lou Graham. Doug Tewell won the first tournament of the 1980s. It would, however, be the last one. With the 1981 U.S. Open scheduled at Merion just a few weeks before the Classic, sponsors at IVB, deciding that such a conflict would severely jeopardize their tournament, chose not to renew their contract. No new sponsor was found, and a highly popular event came to an end after 18 years.

THE GREAT COLLAPSE OF '64

Sports teams have folded many times in the heat of battle. None, however, can match the astonishing disintegration of the 1964 Phillies. It was the greatest, most devastating collapse of all time.

You have to reach back into Phillies history to understand the depths of such a tragedy. The Phillies had won only two pennants in their entire history, the last in 1950. The rest of the time the club was mostly a sometimes colorful but usually inept band of losers who specialized in aggravating their already disenchanted fans.

After 1950 the Phillies had slipped from good to bad to terrible, culminating their decline with a horrendous 1961 season in which they not only lost 107 games, but at one point dropped 23 in a row, a major league record. But with new manager Gene Mauch on board and a steadily improving collection of players, brighter days seemed to lie ahead.

Those days arrived in 1964. With the addition of rookie sensation Richie Allen and veteran pitcher Jim Bunning, the Phils finally had a solid club. It had a number of fine players in outfielders Johnny Callison, Tony Gonzalez, and Wes Covington, second baseman Tony Taylor, all-around utility man Cookie Rojas, catcher Clay Dalrymple, and pitchers Chris Short, Art Mahaffey, Dennis Bennett, and Jack Baldschun.

The Phillies started quickly, winning 19 of their first 30 games. On June 21, Father's Day, Bunning pitched the first perfect game during the regular season in 42 years, beating the New York Mets at Shea Stadium, 6–0. A little more than two weeks later on July 7 at the same park, Callison's three-run homer in the bottom of the ninth inning off Dick Radatz gave the National League a 7–4 victory in the All-Star Game.

The Phillies were flying high. Allen was hitting everything in sight on his way to being named Rookie of the Year, and at the All-Star break the Phils had a one and one-half game lead over the San Francisco Giants.

The lead kept getting bigger. The Phillies were doing everything right, including making three triple plays. And general manager John Quinn had picked up a valuable first baseman in Frank Thomas, who immediately got hot with the bat.

Jim Bunning fired a perfect game for the Phillies in 1964, the year the team staged the worst collapse in baseball history.

On the morning of September 21 the Phillies had a six and one-half game lead with 12 games left to play. Even though Thomas had broken his thumb, a pennant seemed certain. World Series tickets were even being printed.

But the Cincinnati Reds beat the Phillies, 1–0, at Connie Mack Stadium as Chico Ruiz stole home with Frank Robinson at bat, handing Mahaffey the loss despite a superbly pitched game. The next day, the Reds pounded Short en route to a 9–2 win, then they swept the series as Vada Pinson homered twice off Bennett to spark a 6–4 victory.

The Phillies then lost four straight at home to the Milwaukee Braves, with Joe Torre's three RBI beating Bunning, 5–3, John Boozer losing in relief in the 12th inning, 7–5, Rico Carty's three-run triple beating Bobby Shantz, 6–4, and Bunning losing again, 14–8, despite three home runs by Callison. The last loss knocked the Phils out of first place, dropping them one game behind the surging Reds.

The losing streak continued as the Phils traveled to St. Louis. Bob Gibson out-pitched Short to give the Cardinals a 5–1 win. Ray Sadecki followed with a 4–2 decision over Bennett. The losing streak reached 10 a day later when former Phil Curt

Simmons hurled the Cards to an 8–5 victory over Bunning, who like Short was making his third start of the losing streak.

After a day off, the Phils visited Cincinnati where Short and Ed Roebuck combined to get a 4–3 win over the Reds. Another idle day followed, then the Phillies came back to crush the Reds, 10–0, behind Bunning. It was, however, too late. The Phils' chance for a pennant was over, crushed under the weight of a mind-numbing 10-game losing streak.

St. Louis won the pennant, while the Phillies and Reds tied for second, one game back. For the Phils, it was a devastating end to what had for the first 142 games been a glorious season. The collapse would leave deep scars on both the Phillies and their fans that would not heal until 1980.

A GOLDEN DECADE FOR VILLANOVA TRACK

Few college teams ever held the spotlight in one sport longer than Villanova did in track and field. From the mid-1950s until the end of the century, the Wildcats were one of the nation's most dominating teams.

Of all the glorious eras during that period, the one that stands out the most was the 1960s. The 1970s and the 1980s were also times of great accomplishment for Villanova track and field teams, but in terms of names, numbers, and wins, the 1960s have the edge.

Jim (Jumbo) Elliott was in the midst of a long and illustrious career at Villanova that stretched from 1935 until his death in 1981. While building Villanova into a national power in both outdoor and indoor track and field as well as cross-country, Elliott's record included eight NCAA, 39 IC4A, and 75 Penn Relays championships. Six of his athletes won Olympic gold medals, 50 set world records, 86 won NCAA titles, and 324 were IC4A champions.

A number of those championships came in the 1960s. Villanova teams captured the men's outdoor IC4A championship seven times, winning each year between 1960 and 1964 and again in 1967 and 1968. They won the men's indoor IC4A title eight times, triumphing every year during the decade except 1961 and 1966. The Wildcats also won the NCAA men's indoor title in 1968 (as well as in 1971 and 1979). In the Penn Relays in 1968, with Larry James becoming the first man ever to run a mile relay leg under 44 seconds (43.9), they became the first and only college ever to win five different relay events, a feat they repeated in 1969 as well as in 1970 and 1978. Villanova won four different relays in the meet in 1964.

Track wasn't the only running sport in which Villanova excelled in the 1960s.

Elliott's cross-country team won the NCAA championship three straight years between 1966 and 1968 (and again in 1970), and the IC4A title in 1962, 1966, 1967, 1968, and 1969.

Villanova's individual talent in the '60s was spectacular. Pole vaulter Don Bragg and sprinters Paul Drayton and James won Olympic gold medals, while Drayton, James, and sprinter Erv Hall also pocketed silvers. Pat Traynor in 1963 and Dave Patrick in 1968 became the second and third Wildcats to break the four-minute mile. And the Wildcats fielded many other top performers, not the least of whom was Frank Budd.

Budd was the premier sprinter of his day who in 1961 broke Jesse Owens' world record with a stunning time of 9.2 seconds in the 100-yard dash and in 1962 was clocked at 20.0 in the 220, both still Villanova records. Six other times he ran the 100-yard dash in 9.3. Although he had not played football since high school, Budd's speed was so remarkable that the Eagles signed him in 1962. Frank spent one year unsuccessfully trying to adapt to pro football as an end.

Don Bragg (left) and Frank Budd were two of Villanova's premier track stars during the 1960s.

A Villanovan who did make the jump to pro football and had a long career in the American Football League was shot putter Billy Joe. A fullback on the Wildcats' football team, Joe still holds Villanova's top five marks in the shot put.

The Wildcats had numerous other stars. Noel Carroll came from Ireland to excel in the 880. Vince Bizzaro still holds the school record in the pole vault. Hall in the hurdles and Earl Horner in the sprints were top performers, as were a number of relay teams, including the 400 meter, the 1,600 meter, and the two mile, which set men's outdoor world records.

Vic Zwolak won the NCAA 3,000-meter steeplechase championship in 1963 and 1964 while also winning the NCAA cross-country crown in 1963. In a great performance at the Penn Relays in 1964, he anchored the winning four-mile and distance relays just two hours apart, then came back the next day to lead off the winning two-mile relay team and to win the 3,000-meter steeplechase.

With Budd winning two 100 titles (1961 and 1962) and one in the 220 in 1961, Patrick the mile in 1966 and the 1,500-meters in 1968, Traynor the 3,000-meter in 1962, Horner the 220 in 1965, Hall the 120 hurdles and Marty Liquori the mile in 1969, and the mile relay team of Ken Prince, Hardge Davis, Hal Nichter, and Larry James in 1968 all winning NCAA outdoor titles, Villanova had more national champions in the 1960s than it had in any other decade.

THE 76ERS MAKE HISTORY

Pro basketball in Philadelphia has had a long and somewhat checkered past. But there was never any doubt about when it reached the summit. It happened in 1966–67. That season the 76ers made NBA history.

The Sixers were relatively new in town. They were playing in just their fourth season in Philadelphia, having moved to the city in the spring of 1963 from Syracuse, where they had been playing since 1946 as the Nats or Nationals.

The move was mandated by several factors. First, Philadelphia's long-time franchise, the Warriors, had left town after the 1961–62 campaign when owner Eddie Gottlieb chose money over loyalty and sold the team for $850,000 to a San Francisco group. That decision left Philadelphia without big league basketball for the first time since 1946.

After one year without NBA basketball—a team called the Tapers, playing in the American Basketball League, tried unsuccessfully to fill the gap—local businessman Irv Kosloff and lawyer Ike Richman came to the rescue by buying the Syracuse club. The Nats were a solid club, which had won an NBA championship in 1954–55, but their fan support in Syracuse was weak, and the club was ripe for a move.

Kosloff and Richman brought the team to Philadelphia. A contest was held to name the team, 76ers won, and the club began play during the 1963–64 season.

The 76ers had a rocky start. Because of petty differences with publisher Walter Annenberg, the *Philadelphia Inquirer* refused to cover the team, instructing editors to give it two paragraphs if it won and three if it lost. Playing at Convention Hall, the team had some excellent players, namely Hal Greer, Chet Walker, and Johnny (Red) Kerr. But starters Larry Costello and Lee Shaffer missed much of the season with injuries. The Sixers also had a weak coach, the aging star Dolph Schayes, who was playing in his final year. As a result, the first 76ers team played well below .500 (34–46), finishing deep in third place before getting bounced out of the playoffs in the first round by the Cincinnati Royals.

Conditions brightened considerably the following season when on January 15, 1965, the 76ers landed superstar Wilt Chamberlain in a trade with the San Francisco Warriors. Chamberlain had gone to San Francisco when Gottlieb sold the Warriors. Now he was coming back in a one-sided deal in which the 76ers gave up Shaffer, Connie Dierking, and Paul Neuman. With Wilt in the lineup, the 76ers improved to 40–40. They made it to the semifinals of the playoffs before losing in seven games to the Boston Celtics in a series made famous when John Havlicek tipped an inbounds pass by the 76ers to teammate Sam Jones with five seconds left to play and Philadelphia trailing by one point in the final game.

Improvement continued in 1965–66 when the 76ers won the division title with a 55–25 record. By now the 76ers had a superb team that included three marvelous players in Chamberlain, Greer, and Walker, as well as Rookie of the Year and future Hall of Famer Billy Cunningham and former Villanova star Wally Jones, who had come to the club in a trade with the Baltimore Bullets for Kerr. Nonetheless, the Sixers were again knocked out of the playoffs by the Celtics, losing in the semifinals in five games. After the season, Schayes was replaced as head coach by veteran NBA player Alex Hannum, who ironically had been the Warriors coach. The Sixers were on their way.

With the addition of rookie forward Luke Jackson and first-year reserves Matt Guokas and Billy Melchionni, the 76ers had the most talented team in the league. It showed when they reeled off 45 wins in their first 49 games. No team, not even Red Auerbach's haughty Celtics, winners of eight straight NBA titles, could match up with the high-flying 76ers.

The 7–2 Chamberlain, of course, was the 76ers—indeed the league's—most dominant player. But it was hardly a one-man team. Walker was an exquisite offensive player with silken moves as smooth as anybody's in the league. Jackson was a powerful asset under the boards, Cunningham was a rally-igniting sixth man, and Jones was a master playmaker. The glue that held the team together, though, was the indomitable Greer, a deadly jump-shot artist and one of the league's most respected players. "He's so good with his jumper that it startles you when he misses," Hannum once said. The 6–2 Marshall University graduate was not flashy, but he almost always got the job done. During a 15-year career that led him to the Basketball Hall of Fame, Greer scored 21,586 points (the 14th highest in NBA history), 19.2 per game. He played in 10 straight NBA All-Star games, and in 1968 he was MVP of that contest.

By the end of the season, the Sixers had a record of 68–13, to that point the best mark in NBA history. Their offense was awesome. En route to being named Most Valuable Player, Chamberlain, persuaded by Hannum to pass more and shoot less, averaged 24.1 points per game but failed to win the scoring title after seven straight crowns. Greer (22.1), Walker (19.3), sixth man Cunningham (18.5), and Jones (13.2) complemented the big man on offense.

In the playoffs the 76ers tore through the first round, thrashing the Cincinnati Royals in three straight games after losing the opener. They then met the hated Celtics of Bill Russell, Sam and K. C. Jones, Havlicek, and Bailey Howell in a heated semi-

En route to earning a spot in the Hall of Fame, Hal Greer (left) anchored a solid 76ers team that ran away with the NBA championship.

final. By now, the rivalry between the 76ers and Celtics had exploded into one of the most fierce in sports. The Sixers won the first three games, 127–113, with Wilt scoring 32, 107–102, and 115–104. After a 121–117 loss at Boston, Philly came back to close out the series with a rollicking 140–116 rout, ending the Celtics' title run.

The finals were almost anticlimactic. Facing the Warriors in what could have been a bitter battle between Philadelphia's old and its new, the 76ers cruised to victory in six games in a quiet series that had none of the excitement or intensity of the previous round. They won the first two games, 141–135 in overtime and 126–95, lost the third game, 130–124, then came back with a 122–108 triumph. The Warriors, led by Rick Barry and Nate Thurmond, captured Game Five, 117–109. Then it was over as the 76ers won the sixth and clinching game, 125–122, at San Francisco.

The victory climaxed a brilliant season for the 76ers. Although their regular-season record would be broken by the Chamberlain–Jerry West–Elgin Baylor Los Angeles Lakers of 1971–72, the team would go down in history as Philadelphia's finest pro basketball team. In 1980, at the NBA's 35th anniversary celebration, the '66–'67 Sixers would be voted the best team in the league's history.

A NEW ICE HOCKEY TEAM

For more years than most people cared to remember, the National Hockey League had consisted of six teams. The same six, year in and year out, two in Canada and four in the United States.

In 1965, however, the NHL, finally convinced that it was time for expansion, decided that 12 teams were better than six. A new six-team division would be created, and applications would be cheerfully accepted.

A group from Philadelphia, led by Eagles executive Ed Snider and including Eagles owner Jerry Wolman, Fitz Eugene Dixon, Jr., and several others, took the bait. And after an intense and demanding selling effort, a franchise was awarded to Philadelphia in 1966 with the local group putting up $2 million.

Off an on, ice hockey teams had called Philadelphia home since the late 1920s. But with one exception, a terrible team called the Quakers that spent one year in the NHL in 1930–31, all the teams had been minor league entries. The new Philadelphia NHL franchise would be one of 12 teams that played in the city in the 20th century.

In the months after the franchise was awarded, the effort to establish the new team was fast and furious. Plans got under way to build a new indoor stadium at Broad Street and Pattison Avenue. A former minor league coach and player named Keith Allen was hired as the new head coach. It was decided to call the team the Flyers and dress it in orange and black colors. Gene Hart was hired as the team's first play-by-play announcer, and he would go on to a legendary career that stretched into the 1990s. And Allen and new general manager Bud Poile set about laying the groundwork for a roster that would come largely from an expansion draft.

Two separate drafts were held, one for goalies and one for the rest of the roster. Picking second in the goalies draft, the Flyers raised some eyebrows when they passed over some available veterans and chose a 22-year-old with little NHL experience named Bernie Parent. Who could have guessed that 18 years later, after a marvelous 13-year career, Parent would be the first Flyer inducted into the Ice Hockey Hall of Fame?

With their second goalie pick, the Flyers chose Doug Favell, who like Parent, also came from the Boston Bruins farm system. Then in the regular draft, picking fifth, they nabbed defenseman Ed Van Impe from Chicago. The Flyers then selected defenseman Joe Watson from Boston, center Brit Selby from Toronto, center Lou Angotti from Chicago, and right wing Leon Rochefort from Montreal.

The Flyers held their first training camp at Quebec, where the team had its first farm club. In their first exhibition game the Flyers suffered an embarrassing loss to that farm club, 6–1. By then the Flyers ownership group had already changed, with Wolman pulling out to focus his efforts on finding financing for the new stadium, beer distributor Joe Scott entering the fold, and Snider winding up with 60 percent of the shares and club president Bill Putnam owning 25 percent.

When the season started, the Flyers weren't expected to do much. That assumption looked about right when they dropped a 5–1 decision to the expansion California Seals in Oakland on October 11, 1967, in the first game in Flyers history. Gary Sutherland scored the Flyers' first and only goal, but the team didn't look good.

The Flyers then lost, 4–2, to the Los Angeles Kings before traveling to St. Louis, where they won their first game with a 2–1 decision over the Blues on goals by Angotti and Ed Hoekstra. One day later, on October 19, with the new stadium, which had been named the Spectrum, barely ready for action despite the increasing financial problems of Wolman, the Flyers staged their home opener before a crowd of 7,812. With Favell, who had beaten out Parent for the job, in goal, the Flyers shut out the Pittsburgh Penguins, 1–0, on a shot by Sutherland.

Eventually, the Flyers got better, and the crowds got bigger. At one point they lost eight straight games to the old teams, but they battled back, began attracting sellout crowds, and in early 1968 had climbed atop the West Division standings. On March 1, the Flyers express was derailed when large sections of the Spectrum roof blew off, forcing the building to be shut down and sending the Flyers on an extended road trip in which they played all away games during the final month of the season. But the Flyers overcame that ordeal and finished in first place in the expansion-team division with a 31–32–11 record.

With the Spectrum finally reopened, the Flyers first-round playoff opponent was St.

Pat Hannigan (right) scored a goal for the Flyers early in the team's first season in Philadelphia.

Louis, a team that had become a bitter rival after several bloody brawls during the season. The Flyers lost their first playoff game, 1–0, at the Spectrum. They won the second game, 4–3, on Rochefort's tie-breaking goal, but then lost the next two games, 3–2 and 5–2. Game Five turned into the longest game in Flyers history before Don Blackburn's goal gave the Flyers a 2–1 victory at 11:18 of the second overtime period. The Flyers then lost the sixth and deciding game, 3–1, bringing to an end their first season.

TEMPLE WINS THE NIT

Since it began fielding basketball teams in 1894, Temple has been no stranger to postseason tournaments. The Owls won the very first NIT in 1938, reached the Final Four of the NCAA tourney twice in the 1950s, and numerous other times ventured into one or the other of the big season finales.

In 1969, Temple added another notch to its long list of basketball achievements when it won the NIT at Madison Square Garden. The Owls did it with a team of mostly seniors, led by John Baum, one of only two Temple players (the other was Jim Williams) ever to complete their careers with more than 1,000 points and 1,000 rebounds.

The 6–5 Baum, a 1,544-point career scorer at Temple, was the captain and big

Under coach Harry Litwack (center), Temple won its second NIT title in 1969 with a team that included (back row from left) Tony Brocchi, Tom Wieczerak, John Richardson, Pat Cassidy, and Bill Strunk, and (front row) Joe Cromer, John Baum, Jim Snook and Eddie Mast.

star on the Owls, but he was by no means playing by himself. A solid, workmanlike cast surrounded him, including 6–8 center Eddie Mast, forward Joe Cromer, and guards Tony Brocchi and Bill Strunk, a sophomore, the only nonsenior starter on the team. All five starters came from the Philadelphia area.

As they had been for 21 years, the Owls were coached by Harry Litwack, who was on his way into the College Basketball Hall of Fame with a 373–193 record between 1952 and 1973. His chief assistant was Don Casey, who succeeded Litwack as head coach and piloted the Owls for nine years before embarking on a long career as an NBA coach.

Temple had started the 1968–69 season slowly, winning just five of its first nine games. Two of the four losses were in tournament finals, the Owls bowing to New Mexico, 83–70, in the Lobo Tournament at Albuquerque and to Detroit, 87–76, in the Motor City Tournament. Starting the new year, though, Temple went on a winning streak, ultimately capturing 12 decisions in 14 games.

Ironically, the Owls would lose two of their four Big Five games, the only triumphs coming on a 107–83 victory over Penn and a 79–59 win over St. Joseph's. But the Hawks were not opposed to exacting revenge, and less than two months after that loss, they came back to beat Temple, 68–67, in overtime in the Middle Atlantic Conference championship game at the Palestra.

That loss knocked the Owls out of the NCAA tourney, but the NIT quickly filled the void when it gave a bid to Temple. It was the seventh time a Litwack team had been invited to the tournament.

Temple wasted little time getting established. In their first outing, the Owls whipped Florida, 82–66, with Mast bagging 20 points. Next, behind 31 points and 23 rebounds by Baum, the Owls clobbered St. Peter's, 94–78. In the semifinal, Temple stunned Tennessee, 63–58, to reach the last round against Boston College led by ex-Boston Celtics star Bob Cousy in his last year of coaching.

BC, coming off the nation's longest winning streak of the year at 19 games and featuring All-American Terry Driscoll, was favored. But before a screaming crowd of more than 17,000, the Owls hung close throughout. With four minutes left to play, the lead had changed hands 11 times.

Late in the second half, with Temple trailing, 67–64, Litwack made his only substitution of the game, inserting Tom Wieczerak for Strunk, who was hobbling on a bad ankle. Wieczerak's two quick goals sparked the Owls on a 25–9 run, and Temple won going away, 89–76, giving it a 22–8 record for the season. Baum, although deprived of the tourney MVP award, which went to Driscoll, finished with 30 points and 10 rebounds. Cromer added 19 and Brocchi 15. Mast, who chipped in with 22 rebounds, wound up with 68 points for the tourney.

It was a magnificent win for a team that had no expectations of reaching such lofty heights. "This is the happiest day of my coaching life," said Litwack.

THE LAST AGE OF INNOCENCE

With each decade of the 20th century, sports in Philadelphia stretched into increasingly broader areas. Every decade offered more than the last, and by the 1960s the city had plunged into a wider variety of different sports endeavors than at any previous time.

The 1960s also might have been the last era when sports demonstrated a reasonable degree of sanity, particularly of the fiscal variety. In the remaining decades of the century, athletes, especially the professional ones, would start to lose their innocence and begin the inflation of self-esteem so common today. With that process came escalated salaries and financial madness that eventually permeated almost every area of sports.

In the 1960s sports figures for the most part did not seem bigger than life. Chester residents could watch with pride as native son Danny Murtaugh managed the Pittsburgh Pirates to the National League pennant and an improbable win (on Bill Mazeroski's dramatic home run) over the New York Yankees in the 1960 World Series, then reminisce with the former Phillies second baseman while he worked at his winter job in a men's clothing store.

Large numbers of pro basketball players, used to performing before big crowds in fancy arenas, could be seen testing their skills in the summer in a church gym in North Philadelphia where a unique brand of competition called the Baker League held forth. The combination of pro players and graduated college seniors made the league, played for many years at Bright Hope Baptist Church, one of the best-known summer leagues in the country. Summer basketball leagues were also prominent during the era in various other parts of the city. Especially noteworthy were the ones at Narberth Playground and at A Street and Champlost Avenue where college and high school players honed their games with stiff competition. Later, the Sonny Hill League arrived. It was one of many basketball activities that over the years would be guided by Sonny Hill, a former player who became one of the most important figures in the sport over the next three decades.

Perhaps Phillies manager Eddie Sawyer set the tone for the decade when he quit his job after the first game of the 1960 season. "I'm 49 years old, and I want to live to be 50," he said. The statement was not only a reflection of the unhealthy status of the Phillies, but an indication that sports did not yet have a choke hold on all of its participants.

Sawyer's sudden resignation had one other consequence. It paved the way for the debut of Gene Mauch as Phillies manager. The fiery former utility infielder would lead the Phils for nearly nine stormy seasons, managing in more games (1,331), winning more games (645), and losing more games (684) than any other pilot in the club's history. A brilliant strategist and master manipulator of his lineup, Mauch fell short of the success he deserved, but he is usually considered the smartest skipper the Phillies ever had.

The '60s were also a time when several teams that had begun essentially as neighborhood teams rose to prominence. The Ukrainian Nationals won American Soccer League titles four straight years starting with the 1960–61 season and again in 1967–68, while also winning the U.S. Open Cup in 1960, 1961, 1963, and 1966.

A fast-pitch softball team named Flatiron AC after a section in Kensington won its first of five straight Central Atlantic regional championships in 1960. Flatiron, which paid its pitchers but none of the other players, became the dominant softball team in the Philadelphia area, winning numerous local titles, particularly in the Philadelphia Major Softball League. It was annually one of the best teams in the Atlantic Seaboard League, the top circuit on the East Coast, and a frequent participant in national championships. The team's most prominent player was pitcher George Ulmer, whose risers, drops, and change-ups were virtually unhittable. While hurling numerous no-hitters, Ulmer averaged nearly 500 innings pitched per year and two strikeouts per inning. Catcher Ed Hengy was also a key player, as were pitcher Tommy Thomas and infielder Dick Stout. Flatiron, which played home games before big crowds at the Max Myers Playground at Bustleton and Magee Avenues in Northeast Philadelphia, compiled a 254–45 record between 1960 and

George Ulmer was viritually unhittable while pitching for Flatiron in the 1960s.

1963. In 1964 the team went 76–21. Flatiron ruled the high levels of local softball for 17 years until the team was dissolved in the late 1970s.

Rowing ranked at one of its highest levels with the Schuylkill River serving as a training site for some of the best oarsmen in the world. One of the driving forces behind the sport was Ted Nash, the winner of two Olympic medals, who became coach at Penn. Under Nash, the Quakers maintained their national status, and at one point during the decade won three straight Intercollegiate Rowing Association championships in eight-oared shells. After he left Penn in 1982, Nash played a major role as coach at Penn AC and a number of national teams, including the 1992 Olympic crew.

The decade was not without some other notable events. In 1960, 20-year-old Jack Nicklaus, a junior at Ohio State and fresh from placing second in the U.S. Open, shot a remarkable four-round 269 at Merion East to lead the U.S. team to victory in the World Amateur Team Championship. Also on the victorious team was Bill Hyndman III of Huntington Valley. Some 50,447, the largest crowd ever to attend a horse race in New Jersey, bet a track record $4,008,799 at Garden State during a nine-race program that featured Bally Ache's victory in the Jersey Derby, American's oldest derby. Later that year, 1961 Kentucky Derby and Preakness winner Carry Back gave a hint of his greatness with an easy victory in the Garden State Stakes.

In one of the best individual performances in an Army-Navy game, Heisman Trophy–bound Joe Bellino ran for 85 yards, caught two passes for 16 yards, returned two kickoffs for 46 yards, and ran back an interception for 45 yards to lead the Middies to a 17–12 victory over the Cadets at Municipal Stadium. West Chester under coach Jim Bonder had its last undefeated (9–0) football team. Penn graduate and future fencing coach David Micahnik, a three-time Olympian, won the 1960 U.S. national title in the epee before finishing second in 1964, 1966, and 1968. George Grudza of Penndel won the men's national roller skating championship, a title that he would win again in 1964 and that Ted Rendfrey of Riverside, New Jersey, would win in 1966. And in the NBA All-Star Game held at Convention Hall, rookie Wilt Chamberlain was named MVP after scoring 23 points and grabbing 25 rebounds to lead the East to a 125–115 victory over the West.

Penn football started the decade under a new coach, John Stiegman. He would have five straight losing seasons before being replaced by Bob Odell, who added four more losers to the decade. Temple football wasn't much better under George Makris, who would have four winning seasons out of 10, his best being 7–2 marks in 1964 and 1967. In the Philadelphia area's highest scoring basketball game, Pete Cimino, a future major league pitcher, tallied 114 points for Bristol High School in a game against Palisades.

Nineteen sixty-one was a big year, topped off by coach Mel Lorback's West Chester State team finishing the season with an unbeaten 12–0 record after capturing the men's Division I NCAA soccer championship with a 2–0 victory over St. Louis

University, winner of the title in the previous two years and in five of the first seven years the tournament was held. It would be the only NCAA soccer title ever won by a Philadelphia area team since tournament play was initiated in 1959.

St. Joseph's, closing fast with 15 straight wins at the end of the season, gained a berth in the NCAA tournament. After beating Princeton, 72–67, and Wake Forest, 96–86, the Hawks advanced to the Final Four where they lost to Ohio State, 95–69. Then, in a memorable consolation game in which Jack Egan scored 42 points and Jimmy Lynam 31, St. Joe's nipped Utah State, 127–120, in four overtimes in what was up to that point the highest-scoring game in NCAA playoffs. The Hawks ended the season with a 25–5 record, but their third-place finish in the playoffs was taken away after it was revealed that three Hawks were involved in a point-shaving scandal.

Marcus Hook's Mickey Vernon became the first manager of the expansion Washington Senators. Phillies pitcher Art Mahaffey set a club record and tied a National League mark (since broken) when he struck out 17 Chicago Cubs while hurling a four-hit shutout at Connie Mack Stadium. The Phillies set a much more dubious record that same year by losing 23 games in a row, a feat never equaled by a major league team. The streak finally came to an end when John Buzhardt beat the Milwaukee Braves, 7–4, in the second game of a doubleheader.

Later in the year the defending champion Eagles launched their season when speedy running back Timmy Brown ran back the opening kickoff 105 yards for a touchdown in a 27–20 win over the Cleveland Browns. Brown would become one of the most exciting backs ever to wear the Eagles' green during a splendid eight-year career. At the end of the season, Sonny Jurgensen had passed for an NFL record 3,320 yards and club record 32 touchdowns; Tommy McDonald, after snaring a record 237 yards of passes in one game, had broken his own club record in pass reception yardage with 1,142; and the Eagles had lost, 38–10, to the Detroit Lions in a Playoff Bowl for each division's second-place teams.

Villanova, concluding its best season of the decade with an 8–2 record under coach Alex Bell, captured a 17–9 victory over Wichita State in the Sun Bowl in El Paso, Texas, with Billy Joe and Lou Rettino scoring touchdowns and Sam Gruneisen kicking a field goal and two extra points. Woodbury, New Jersey, native and Penn State alumnus Milt Plum led the NFL in passing for the second straight year while quarterbacking the Cleveland Browns. A. J. Foyt won his first of four straight 100-mile races for Indy cars at Langhorne Speedway. West Philadelphia High's Ray (Chink) Scott began a fine NBA career as a rebounder and scorer. And Philadelphia began an eight-year term as home of a roller derby team.

In 1962, with the Warriors having departed for the West Coast, Philadelphia got a new pro basketball team. Called the Tapers, the team was relocated from New York and played at both Convention Hall and the Arena in the American Basketball

League, a six-team circuit that featured three-point goals and a 30-second shot clock. Coached by Mario Perri, previously the athletic director at Technical Tape Corporation, the team's Long Island–based sponsor, the Tapers were manned by players such as former Warrior Andy Johnson and ex–college players Charlie Tyra, Sylvester Blye, Bruce Spraggins, Roger Kaiser, and Bill Chmielewski. Mayor James Tate threw out the first ball as the Tapers launched what was scheduled as a 72-game season with a 116–98 win over the Chicago Majors. After averaging crowds of 5,000 in the early home games, the Tapers soon started to slip at the gate, and at one point just 394 attended a game. Finally, with the Tapers holding a 10–8 record, the league folded in December. Hardly anyone mourned its passing.

Two other newcomers came to town in 1962. The Quaker City Basketball Tournament began that year. It brought in some of the top college teams in the nation, first to the Palestra and later to the Spectrum, before ceasing in the mid-1970s. The U.S. Pro Indoor Tennis Tournament also began with Stanford All-American quarterback Jon Douglas winning the first trophy. An idea of Philadelphia lawyer and tennis player Leif Beck, the event was originally held at St. Joseph's Field House before moving to the Arena, Cheltenham High School, and finally the Spectrum. Directed by Marilyn and Ed Fernberger since 1962, the tournament has grown into a hugely successful event that attracts the top players in the world. Four-time winners of the tourney include Rod Laver, Jimmy Connors, and John McEnroe. Philadelphia was also the site for the only time of the professional bowling national championship with Carmen Salvino beating Don Carter for the title.

Also in 1962, the Penn Relays held the first event for women, a 100-yard dash. In its last bowl game and after snow had been shoveled off the field, Villanova's football team bowed, 6–0, to Oregon State as Heisman Trophy winner Terry Baker raced 99 yards for the game's only score in the Liberty Bowl at Municipal Stadium. Richie Richman quarterbacked the Wildcats in that game, then played that night for the Villanova basketball team, which was headed for a fourth-place finish in the 1963 NIT. Chuck Bednarik retired to end a 14-year career with the Eagles. Sonny Jurgensen completed 33 passes in one game and threw five touchdowns in another, but the Eagles lost both games in the first season of a swoon that would send them to the depths of the NFL. They would have 14 losing seasons over the next 16 years.

Liberty Bell Park joined the local sports scene in 1963 when it opened for harness racing in Northeast Philadelphia. Meets were sponsored by the William Penn Racing Association owned by Pittsburgh Steelers owner Art Rooney and his family. In the ensuing years, Liberty Bell became one of the leading raceways for standardbreds, a track where all the top stables, horses, and drivers, including such towering figures as Herve Filion, Stanley Dancer, Bill Haughton, and Eddie Davis, performed. The track's signature event was the Colonial, a race for trotters that was

Herve Filion was one of the major drivers when harness racing flourished at Liberty Bell Park and Brandywine Raceway.

comparable to the world-famous Hambletonian. Thoroughbred racing was added to the Liberty Bell menu in 1967, and through the Continental and Eagle Downs meets, the track hit its peak from the late 1960s through the 1970s. For the 1969 season, harness racing attendance averaged 10,000 with wagering slightly under $1 million a night. Poor management and an inability to keep up with the times eventually led to the demise of Liberty Bell. The reopening of Garden State in 1985 took the final toll, and the once-premier track closed forever that year, yielding to developers who built a large shopping mall on the site.

Something else was new in 1963. Former Phillies center fielder Richie Ashburn quit the New York Mets to become the color analyst in the Phillies broadcast booth. Ashburn would wind up behind the mike for 35 years, longer than any other Phillies broadcaster, in a career that elevated him to the summit of popularity in Philadelphia. Also joining the Phillies broadcast team that year was Bill Campbell. He would call games of Philadelphia sports teams for more than 50 years, including both the Eagles' 1960 title match and Wilt Chamberlain's 100-point game in 1962. At the request of Mayor Tate, Municipal Stadium was renamed John F. Kennedy Stadium after the assassination of the president. Timmy Brown set a then-NFL record for total offense with 2,436 yards, including 841 rushing, 487 receiving, 945 on kickoff returns, and 152 on punt returns. But that didn't keep the Eagles from being sold to Washington, D.C., developer Jerry Wolman and Earl Foreman, who paid $5,505,000. Wolman hired Ed Snider as the team's treasurer, two years later naming him CEO.

The following year, Wolman hired former Chicago Cardinals and Washington Redskins leader Joe Kuharich as head coach and general manager. It quickly became apparent that Kuharich was not the man for the job, especially after he traded away some of the top Eagles players, including Jurgensen. The Eagles, despite the presence of splendid All-Pro offensive tackle Bob Brown, played poorly, and eventually the fans and press began severely criticizing the hapless Kuharich. During some games, airplanes hired by fans flew over Franklin Field pulling banners that carried such slogans as "Joe Must Go." The Eagles plunged into one of their worst periods in history, yet Wolman awarded Kuharich a 15-year contract. Joe was fired after a 1968 season in which the Eagles lost 11 games in a row.

An equally dismal event occurred in the boxing ring in 1964. Sonny Liston, who as a youth had spent time in prison for armed robbery and who later had moved to the Philadelphia area to be near his manager, Jack Nilon of Ridley Park, lost the heavyweight title. in a controversial match in Miami Beach. (Liston had taken the title from Floyd Patterson with a first-round knockout in 1962.) Fighting a brash, young Cassius Clay, Liston refused to budge from his stool when the bell rang to start the seventh round. He later contended that he'd injured his shoulder, although that claim was never clearly proved. In equally murky circumstances one year later, the hard-punching Liston lost again to Clay, now Muhammad Ali, in a first-round knockout in Lewiston, Maine. After moving from Philadelphia to Denver, Liston revealed his dislike for the city. "I'd rather be a lampost in Denver than mayor of Philadelphia," he said.

At Germantown Cricket Club, the United States team, featuring a fast-rising young star named Billie Jean Moffitt, lost in the final round to Australia in the first Federation Cup tennis tournament held in Philadelphia. Swarthmore College tennis coach Ed Faulkner was named coach of the U.S. Davis Cup team for the seventh time. The 76ers' Johnny Kerr set an NBA record by playing in his 745th consecutive game. Eagles owner Jerry Wolman bought Connie Mack Stadium from the Phillies' Bob Carpenter. A new pro football team playing at Temple Stadium and calling itself the Bulldogs hired ex–Navy head coach Wayne Hardin, signed well-traveled quarterback Bob Broadhead, and went to work in the Continental League, lasting just two seasons. And it was the last season in Philadelphia for the Ramblers, who after playing in the Eastern Hockey League since 1955, moved across the Delaware River where they became the Jersey Devils, playing at the Cherry Hill Coliseum.

St. Joseph's was back in the limelight in 1965. In their fourth consecutive post-season appearance, the Hawks, led by Anderson and Guokas, lost in the third round of the NCAA regionals, 103–81, to North Carolina, to finish the season with a 26–3 record, good for a third-place final ranking in both wire service polls. Meanwhile, Villanova, sparked by Melchionni, Washington, and George Leftwich, reached the Final Four of the NIT before losing in the championship game to St. John's, 55–51. And in the Army-Navy game that year, the Middies gained a 7–7 tie when quarterback John Cartwright of Sharon Hill threw an eight-yard touchdown pass to Terry Murray just before halftime.

In a brutal bout at Convention Hall, heavyweight Sonny Banks never recovered from a ninth-round knockout by Leotis Martin and died several days later. The track at Langhorne Speedway was paved for the first time, an improvement that was to Jim McElreath's liking, as he won both a 100-mile and a 125-mile race. The Camden Bullets won the championship of the fast-paced Eastern Basketball League after fin-

Cliff Anderson set a single-season scoring record for St. Joseph's while playing for coach Jack McKinney.

ishing runner-up the year before. And in the only time it was held in Philadelphia, professional bowling's U.S. Open was won by Dick Weber in the men's division and Ann Slattery in the women's.

Richie Allen had his finest season in a Phillies uniform in 1966 when he hit .317 with 40 home runs, 110 RBI, and 112 runs scored. Unfortunately, the brilliant slugger had become one of the city's most controversial sports figures. The year before he had engaged in a pregame fight with teammate Frank Thomas after some needling had turned nasty. Thomas was dismissed from the team, but fans never forgot Allen's role in the incident. From then on, he was often subjected to loud and frequent boos. Allen, now calling himself Dick, became more withdrawn as the years passed, and having been switched from third to first base often wrote messages in the dirt with his feet. In 1967 he appeared with a severely slashed hand and wrist, the result, he said, of jamming his hand through a headlight while trying to push an old car. Allen was often accused—falsely he would later claim—of being late or absent, but his remarkable ability as a hitter never waned, and he had six splendid seasons with the Phillies.

Nineteen sixty-six was the year in which Jim Williams became the first Temple player to score more than 1,000 points and snatch more than 1,000 rebounds in his career. On the gridiron, the Owls' John Waller, entering the game late in the first half, threw a school-record six touchdown passes to lead Temple to an 82–28 annihilation of Bucknell. Also that year, Villanova finished third in the NIT after beating Army, 76–65. The Eagles made it all the way back to second place in Kuharich's only winning season before losing, 20–14, to the Baltimore Colts in the Playoff Bowl. In one of the worst swaps in club history, the Phillies traded seldom-used young hurler Ferguson Jenkins to the Chicago Cubs as part of a deal for two aging pitchers. Jenkins would wind up in the Hall of Fame. Mario Andretti won a 150-mile race at Langhorne, and Canadian Gary Cowan edged Deane Beman to win the U.S. Amateur golf championship at Merion. And St. Joseph's set a Big Five record by averaging 91.1 points per game. The Hawks were led by All-American Cliff Anderson, who after a glittering career departed as St. Joe's all-time leading scorer (1,728 points) and rebounder (1,228), the latter a record that still stands.

New stadiums were the big stories in 1967. The city of Philadelphia approved funds for the construction of a new multipurpose stadium that would house the Phillies and Eagles at Broad Street and Pattison Avenue, and a groundbreaking ceremony was held shortly thereafter. Across the street, the doors to the $12 million, 17,000-seat Spectrum opened. Until the mid-1990s, the oval structure, which *Evening Bulletin* columnist Sandy Grady wrote resembled a "fish can," would be home to the 76ers, Flyers, Wings, Freedoms, college basketball tournaments, tennis tournaments, boxing matches, and an assortment of other teams and events that made it one of the busiest sports venues in America. Of course, it didn't help that early in 1968, a portion of the roof fell on fans during a performance of the Ice Capades, and then several weeks later after some hasty repairs, a larger section of the roof blew away, causing the building to be shut down for nearly one month. The problem forced the 76ers to play home games at Convention Hall and sent the Flyers on the road for all their games.

Philadelphia got a new professional team in 1967 when the Spartans of the North American Soccer League set up shop at Temple Stadium. The team, a collection of players from different countries, drew 14,000 for its home opener. One writer said covering the team was "like covering the Tower of Babel. They spoke every language but English." The Spartans ended the regular season tied for first place in the Eastern Division but lost in a playoff to the Baltimore Bays. The Spartans' Rueben Navarro was named the league's most valuable player. But neither that honor nor a strong team could save the Spartans from extinction. They folded after just one season.

It was a big year for the Kelly brothers from Simon Gratz High School in 1967. Pat made his debut with the Minnesota Twins, launching a big league career that would span 15 years as an outfielder with five American League teams, during which he produced a .264 lifetime batting average. Leroy, Jimmy Brown's successor as the Cleveland Browns fullback, won his first of two consecutive NFL rushing titles while also leading the league in touchdowns. Leroy would go on to a dazzling career in which he was named six times to the NFL Pro Bowl and eventually ushered into the Pro Football Hall of Fame.

Jimmy Caras was another local guy who had a banner year in 1967. A Scranton native who lived for many years in Springfield (Delco), Caras came out of 11 years of retirement to win his fifth pocket billiards world championship in St. Louis. The 58-year-old Caras beat Luther Lassiter in the final round. Caras, a member of the Billiards Hall of Fame, had been shooting pool since he was five years old. At 17 he earned the nickname "Boy Wonder" after beating the great Ralph Greenleaf in an exhibition. Caras had won world titles in 1936, 1938, 1939, and 1949.

Philadelphia College of Textiles and Sciences made a major move in 1967 when it hired former player and assistant coach Herb Magee to guide the basketball team. A two-time Little All-American and at the time the leading scorer in Textile history with 2,235 points, Magee would become one of the most successful coaches in the college ranks, finishing the 20th century with 670 (252 losses) and leading the Rams to 19 NCAA playoffs, three regional championships, and one national title. During 32 years at the helm leading up to the 21st century, Magee's teams won 20 or more games 20 times and experienced just three losing seasons.

Numerous other major developments occurred in 1967. A Cheltenham High School grad named Reggie Jackson broke in with the Oakland Athletics, thus starting a 21-year big league career in which he would hit 563 home runs, become a fixture in World Series with the A's and New York Yankees, often become embroiled in controversy, and eventually gain a spot in the Baseball Hall of Fame. Upper Darby native Bobby Lloyd was named first-team All-American while playing basketball at Rutgers.

Another former local schoolboy, Earl Monroe out of Bartram High, made his pro basketball debut with the Baltimore Bullets after winning MVP honors while leading Winston-Salem to the NCAA Division II title. Earl the Pearl, as he was called, had led the nation in scoring in 1967 with what would be the second-highest point total (1,329) in collegiate history. Monroe's pro debut began what would become a long and dazzling career as one of the NBA's most electrifying players, most notably dur-

Philadelphia produced outstanding basketball players in droves, including Earl Monroe (33), Wilt Chamberlain (13), and Chink Scott (back).

ing a stint with the New York Knicks, for whom he was a key member of the 1973 championship team. Monroe was elected to the Basketball Hall of Fame in 1990.

West Chester football, coached by Bob Mitten and led by Bert Nye and Don Wilkinson, scored 50 or more points four times while compiling a 10–1 record marred only by a 25–8 loss to Tennessee-Martin in the Tangerine Bowl. Penn's women's basketball team under coach Faye Bardman had its first undefeated season, an achievement it would repeat in 1969. The Flyers assumed ownership of their first minor league team when they purchased the Quebec Aces of the American Hockey League.

The new year in 1968 began on a high note for Yeadon native Johnny Rauch. The former Georgia University All-American quarterback coached his Oakland Raiders into the second Super Bowl after they'd captured the American Football League championship in 1967 with a 13–1 record. Rauch, who would pilot the Raiders for five seasons, wound up on the losing side of a 33–14 scrap with the Green Bay Packers. One of the Packers' stars was former Northeast High standout Herb Adderley, a five-time All-Pro defensive back and now a member of the Pro Football Hall of Fame. An All-American running back at Michigan State, Adderley had few peers during his days as a pro defensive back.

Another All-American of the era, Southern California's O. J. Simpson, would have become a Philadelphian had it not been for a strange reversal by the Eagles. After losing their first 11 games of the 1968 season, the hapless Birds were in line for the first pick in the college draft. Instead, they won two of their last three games and lost Simpson to the Buffalo Bills. They had to settle for Purdue running back Leroy Keyes. During the last game of the season Eagles fans demonstrated their displeasure with the team by pelting Santa Claus with snowballs as he arrived in his sleigh for a halftime show.

Alex Hannum led the 76ers to a 62–20 record and their third straight first-place finish in the NBA's Eastern Division, but the team lost to the Celtics in a seven-game conference final. Afterward, Hannum resigned to join the American Basketball Association. Jack Ramsay, who had left St. Joseph's in 1966 to become the first general manager of the 76ers, took over as head coach of the team, a spot he would hold for four seasons. Gene Mauch was dismissed as Phillies manager after nearly nine stormy seasons. Hal Greer was the MVP in the NBA All-Star Game after scoring 21 points to lead the East to a 144–124 victory. And a long tradition ended at Penn when the university introduced its first women cheerleaders at sporting events.

The Eagles underwent still another change of ownership in 1969 after Wolman's empire fell apart and he ended in bankruptcy. Out of that came the purchase of the team for $16.1 million by trucking company owner Leonard Tose. Tose's first moves were to fire Kuharich after paying him off for the last 10 years of his contract and to name former Eagles Pete Retzlaff as general manager and Jerry Williams as head coach. The Eagles, however, still didn't have a winning season between 1967 and 1977.

A landmark event took place in 1969 when West Chester State played host to the first women's national basketball tournament. The brainchild of Golden Rams coach Carol Eckman, 16 teams participated. West Chester won the event, beating Iowa, 70–30, in the semifinals behind 25 points by Pat Ferguson, and Western Carolina, 65–39, in the final as Ferguson added 20 more points. Eckman, who would later be elected to the Women's National Basketball Hall of Fame, guided her team to the national finals in each of the next three years while compiling a five-year record of 67–7.

More horse racing entered the picture that year with the opening of Keystone

Carol Eckman launched the first women's college national basketball tournament, and her West Chester team won the event.

Race Track in Bensalem Township just north of the city. A track for thoroughbred racing, Keystone was renamed Philadelphia Park in the early 1990s after new ownership took over. Later, plagued by a decline in attendance, the track became one of the leaders in simulcasting after a British company bought it and opened six related OTB sites at strategic locations around the fringes of the city.

In 1969 the Flyers chose a skinny kid from Flin Flon, Manitoba named Bobby Clarke in the second round (17th overall) of the NHL draft. Under the direction of former sportswriter J. Russell Peltz, the Blue Horizon reopened after a long period of inactivity. The former Moose Lodge would become a mecca for local fighters, with Peltz promoting numerous cards each year for the rest of the century. Penn replaced the grass surface at Franklin Field with Astroturf. Monsignor Bonner and Villanova alumnus Al Atkinson stood out as a linebacker on the New York Jets as they won the third Super Bowl with a 16–7 upset victory over the Baltimore Colts. Dick Allen hit home runs in five straight games, but after the season the Phillies swapped him and two others to the St. Louis Cardinals for four players, including outfielder Curt Flood. A 12-year veteran, Flood refused to report to the Phillies, calling Philadelphia "the nation's northernmost southern city" and claming the system that allowed teams to trade players "indentured one man to another." Linking the system with slavery, Flood, with former Supreme Court Justice Arthur Goldberg as his attorney, filed suit against major league baseball. The case advanced all the way to the Supreme Court, which voted 4–3 against Flood. Although he lost the case, Flood's claim that players had the right to be free agents led to further cases and finally paved the way for the free agent system that exists today.

Wilt Chamberlain, One of a Kind

Wilt Chamberlain never did anything in moderation. That was amply reflected in his career as an athlete.

During a long and astonishingly brilliant career, Chamberlain did virtually everything a basketball player could possibly accomplish. His achievements made him not only the greatest basketball player of all time, but arguably America's greatest athlete of the 20th century.

Unquestionably, Wilt was Philadelphia's finest athlete of the century. And in the

Throughout the 1960s, Wilt Chamberlain's battles with Bill Russell and the Boston Celtics were legendary.

decade of the 1960s when Dick Allen, Jim Bunning, Tommy McDonald, Timmy Brown, Sonny Jurgensen, Hal Greer, Joe Frazier, Harold Johnson, Joey Giardello, Frank Budd, Don Bragg, and Ellie Daniel gave the city the biggest gathering of top athletes that it ever had, Chamberlain was easily the best of the group.

Wilt probably could have been a success at almost any sport. In fact, he was a top high jumper and runner in high school, as well as a fine volleyball player, and he toyed with the idea of becoming a boxer. But he chose basketball, a wise decision for a guy who stood 7 feet, 2 inches tall.

That choice didn't take long to produce rewards. As a senior at Overbrook High, Chamberlain scored 90 points in a 32-minute game while averaging 44.5 for the season. His 2,252 career points are by far the highest any Philadelphia schoolboy ever scored. In his two varsity seasons at the University of Kansas, where he landed after being one of the most heavily recruited players in college annals, he averaged 29.9 points a game, making the All-American team each year and leading the Jayhawks to a two-year record of 42–8 and a berth in the NCAA final in 1958.

After taking one year off to play with the Harlem Globetrotters, Chamberlain arrived back in Philadelphia in 1959 as the Warriors' first-round territorial pick, signing to play for $30,000. He was Rookie of the Year, averaging 37.6 points. Wilt played three seasons with the Warriors, then moved with them to San Francisco where he played for two and one-half years before returning to Philadelphia as a member of the 76ers.

Chamberlain's return to Philadelphia solidified the 76ers and made them at that point the best team in NBA history in 1966–67. The only team with a better record was the 1971–72 Los Angeles Lakers led by none other than Wilt Chamberlain, who had gone west again in another trade.

During a 14-year career that put him in the Basketball Hall of Fame, Wilt led the NBA in scoring seven times, in rebounding 11 times, and in field goal percentage nine times. When coach Alex Hannum insisted he shoot less, Wilt led the league in assists, the only NBA center ever to do so. He was the league's Most Valuable Player four times. He holds 43 NBA records, including most career rebounds (23,924) and highest career scoring average (30.1). He has 10 of the 11 highest-scoring games in 76ers history and the team's top 21 highest rebounding games, including a club record 43. He scored 31,419 career points during the regular season, once averaging 50.4 points per game (1961–62). In 122 games he scored 50 or more points, and in 1961 he tallied 50 or more points seven games in a row.

Chamberlain's greatest individual effort came on February 2, 1962, when he scored an NBA-record 100 points, including 31 in the last quarter, in a 169–147 victory over the New York Knicks in Hershey, Pennsylvania. Wilt shot 36-for-63 from the floor and 28-for-32 from the foul line while pulling down 25 rebounds. That season, Chamberlain averaged 50.4 points and 27.2 rebounds per game. In another memorable game, Chamberlain registered the only triple double in NBA history when he scored 22 points, snatched 25 rebounds, and dished out 21 assists in a 1968 game against the Detroit Pistons. And in a game in 1960 he grabbed 55 rebounds against the Celtics.

One of the most remarkable aspects of Chamberlain's career is that he never fouled out of a game. Yet he played virtually every minute of every game, rarely coming out and almost never missing a game because of injury. He led the NBA in minutes played eight times. One season he missed only eight minutes the entire season—occurred when he was ejected on technical fouls.

Wilt was truly one of a kind. There never was and there probably never will be anyone like him.

A Galaxy of Superstars

Every decade in Philadelphia sports has had its share of superstars. They were ones who stood high above the crowd in both performance and presence. They captured the headlines and the hearts of fans. They led their teams and usually their leagues. And long after all the others were forgotten, they would be remembered for their special deeds.

No other decade in the 20th century in Philadelphia had a profusion of superstars that could match that of the 1970s. It was an era when great players flocked to the city and performed with such elevated skill that many of them wound up in halls of fame.

Bobby Clarke and Bernie Parent wore the orange and black of the Flyers. Steve Carlton and Mike Schmidt came to town to play with the Phillies. George McGinnis and Julius Erving joined the 76ers. Wilbert Montgomery, Ron Jaworski, and Harold Carmichael performed with the Eagles. And Joe Frazier and Matthew Saad Muhammad in boxing, Mark Donohue in auto racing, and Billie Jean King in tennis gave the area the most illustrious collection of superstars it ever had.

Illustrious teams were also part of the picture. The Flyers won two Stanley Cups.

Immaculata, the first of the great modern women's basketball teams, won three straight national championships. Philadelphia Textile and Cheyney State both won NCAA Division II men's basketball titles. Penn had probably the best decade any Big Five team ever had and went to the Final Four in the NCAA tournament, as did Villanova. Glassboro State won a Division II baseball crown, and Widener won a Division III football title. Temple's football team went to three bowl games. West Chester's women won four consecutive national field hockey titles. The 76ers reached the NBA final. And the Phillies escaped an extended entombment at the bottom of the National League standings to win three division titles in a row.

There were numerous top players in the college ranks, too. Penn's Corky Calhoun, La Salle's Ken Durrett and Michael Brooks, Temple's Ollie Johnson, and Villanova's Howard Porter and Chris Ford were among the featured stars of the era in basketball. To that list was added Immaculata's Theresa Shank and Marianne Crawford in women's basketball, Villanova's Marty Liquori and Sydney Maree in track, and Temple's Bill Singletary and Steve Joachim in football.

As always, some local stars did their good deeds out of town. Penn State running back John Cappelletti became the first player from the area to win the Heisman Trophy. Geoff Petrie of the Portland Trailblazers was named the NBA's co–Rookie of the Year. Tom Lasorda began a long career as manager of the Los Angeles Dodgers. Reggie Jackson hit three memorable home runs in the World Series. And Widener's Billy (White Shoes) Johnson, Villanova's Mike Siani, Temple's Randy Grossman and Joe Klecko, and Penn State's Franco Harris and Lydell Mitchell launched big careers in pro football.

The 1970s were the decade of the Phillies' Paul Owens, perhaps the best general manager the city ever had. The decade was also one of fine coaches and managers such as Fred Shero, Cathy Rush, Wayne Hardin, Dallas Green, Dick Vermeil, Billy Cunningham, Rollie Massimino, Chuck Daley, Don Casey, Jack McKinney, Paul Westhead, Herb Magee, John Chaney, Skippy Wilson, Gene McDonnell, and Bob Seedon.

New teams and events landed in Philadelphia about as often as April showers. The 1970s saw the Firebirds, Atoms, Fever, Fury, Freedoms, Blazers, Bell, and A's come to town, some lasting little more than one season. The Virginia Slims tennis tournament and an LPGA golf tournament arrived. With Title IX now in effect and changing the scope of women's sports, the Big Five was expanded to include women's basketball. Major league baseball and basketball held their All-Star Games in Philadelphia. So did the men's and women's U.S. Open in golf. There was a NCAA basketball Final Four here. Philadelphia opened a new multipurpose ballpark called Veterans Stadium.

Philadelphia sports also earned a place in fiction. In 1977 a low-budget movie starring a relatively unknown actor from the Philadelphia area named Sylvester Stallone was filmed in the city. With its unforgettable scenes of boxer Rocky Balboa, the main character, running up the steps of the Art Museum and through the Italian Market while training for his big fight, the movie *Rocky* became the hit of the year. Philadelphia had worldwide exposure like it never had before. The first *Rocky* gave birth to a series of others, and eventually a statute of Rocky was cast. It would stand at the Art Museum for many years before being transferred to the Spectrum, where it remains to this day as a symbol of the city's enduring sports heritage.

The '70s were the decade when the "Miracle of the Meadowlands" occurred. Pete Rose brought his exuberance to town. Mike Rossman won a boxing title. The term "Broad Street Bullies" became famous. Temple went to Tokyo to play a football game. Fans of the 76ers booed a pig. And Harry Kalas, Kate Smith, and the Phillie Phanatic made their local debuts.

Of course, there was a downside, too. Barry Ashbee, who had become a Flyers coach after a career as one of the team's most popular players, died tragically of leukemia. Connie Mack Stadium shut down after 62 seasons and was eventually destroyed by fire. Langhorne Speedway closed for good, and Garden State Park also burned down.

Drexel dropped football from its list of varsity sports. The 76ers went through a season winning just nine of 82 games for the worst record in NBA history. Steve Carlton stopped talking to the press. Villanova had a runner-up spot in the Final Four taken away. And Kiteman crashed at the Vet.

The 1970s were a decade when something was always happening. Most of the time, it was quite exciting. Especially when one of the era's many superstars was involved.

SMALL COLLEGE TEAMS ERUPT

Most of the time, prior to the 1970s, small college basketball teams in the Philadelphia area had just hung around the fringes as distant cousins of the local big-time powers, staying out of the way and taking whatever crumbs were thrown their direction. Those habits changed dramatically in the eighth decade of the century.

In the 1970s small college basketball moved boldly into the mainstream of local basketball. The move was led by Philadelphia Textile, Cheyney State, and Widener, the best of many fine area teams. The Rams and Wolves both won Division II NCAA championships.

Textile's title was the first of its kind ever won by a Philadelphia team. It came in 1970 when the Rams defeated Tennessee State, 76–65, in the final at Evansville, Indiana.

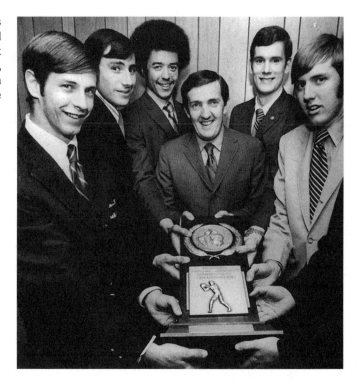

Philadelphia Textile won the area's first small college national basketball crown in 1970 with a team that included (from left) Mike O'Rourke, John Pierantozzi, Carl Poole, coach Herb Magee, Jim McGilvery, and Bruce Shively.

Textile, which first fielded a team in 1919, had had a strong small college program for many years. In Bucky Harris's 13-year tenure as head coach, the Rams posted a 242–56 record. When Herb Magee took over in 1967, Textile's domination at the small college level continued, and in 1969–70 the Rams stormed through the playoffs to take the national title, ending the year with a 29–2 record

The Rams beat Youngstown State, 79–52, then Ashland, 45–28, in the Mideast Regional final. Next to fall was American International, 101–53, and UC-Riverside, 79–63. That win sent Textile to the championship match where the Rams won their 28th straight game, finishing the season by outscoring opponents by an average of 24.5 points.

Ironically, Cheyney knocked Textile out of the playoffs the following year with a 60–58 win in the regional final. Both teams, however, would visit the playoffs many times again.

The Wolves had been playing high-caliber basketball since the 1960s when Hal Blitman became coach and quickly pushed the team to national prominence. In 1972, Cheyney hired a young coach named John Chaney, and over the next 10 seasons he would produce a 225–59 record and make eight trips to the NCAA Division II tournament.

The high point came in 1977–78 when Cheyney stormed to the national title, first beating Adelphi, 78–64, then Textile, 73–60, for the regional crown. The Wolves followed with a 59–57 win over Sacred Heart and a 79–63 decision over Florida Tech in the semifinals. In the final at Springfield, Missouri, Cheyney broke from a 20–20 halftime tie to beat Wisconsin–Green Bay, 47–40, with tourney MVP Andy Fields leading the way with 11 points. The Wolves ended the season with a 27–2 record.

The following season Cheyney again advanced to the Final Four but lost in the semifinals to Green Bay, 46–45. The Wolves had to settle for third place after beating Bridgeport in the consolation game, 81–78, as George Melton scored 22 points and All-American Fields added 15.

Widener just missed out on a national title in 1978 when it bowed to North Park, 69–57, in the NCAA Division III final at Rock Island, Illinois. The Pioneers, coached by Alan Rowe, had defeated Stony Brook, 48–38, in the semifinals

BOBBY CLARKE, THE FLYERS' PEERLESS LEADER

It is a special athlete who blends brilliant performance with inspirational leadership. Much more common is the athlete who excels in one area but not the other.

In the case of Bobby Clarke, though, extraordinary achievements were accomplished in both aspects of his career as the greatest of all Flyers players. Clarke was the most prolific scorer in Flyers history and a peerless leader who guided the team to two straight Stanley Cup victories.

During a 15-year career that wound up with Clarke being elected in 1987 to the Hockey Hall of Fame, there was little the hard-charging skater didn't do. He won the Hart Trophy as the NHL's Most Valuable Player three times (1973, 1975, 1976), played in nine NHL All-Star games, and twice made the all-league first team and twice the second team at the end of the season.

Clarke led the Flyers in scoring eight times, and he is the team's all-time leading scorer with 1,210 points, which comes out to an average of more than one point per game. In 1973 he became the first Flyer and only the ninth NHL player to score more than 100 points in one season. In 1981 he became the 13th NHL player to reach 1,000 career points. He currently ranks 25th on the NHL's all-time scoring list. He's also the Flyers' leading playoff scorer with 119 points.

The Flyers' captain through much of his playing career, Bobby was not just an offensive standout. He was regarded as one of the best defensive forwards ever to play the game. When he was on the ice, nobody worked harder than Clarke.

Bobby Clarke ranks as the Flyers'
greatest player of all time.

"He worked so hard night after night," Flyers coach Fred Shero once said. "I thought, no one should have to work that hard."

Clarke was just a skinny 20-year-old kid from Flin Flon, Manitoba, when the Flyers made him their second-round draft pick (17th overall) in 1969. Within three years of being drafted, Bobby's fiery leadership and relentless style of play had made him one of the NHL's top players.

When the Flyers won the Stanley Cup in 1974 and again in 1975, Clarke was the heart and soul of the team. Time after time, he came through with clutch plays. "Some players were bigger and faster and had harder shots," said Shero, "but nobody accomplished more than Bobby."

Clarke, who won numerous other awards, including honors for sportsmanship, for outstanding service to hockey, and for defensive excellence, was a master at having a sense of the other 11 players on the ice. And he played with boundless courage, often taking the brunt of opponent's jabs. He took the ice despite the encumbrances of a lifelong case of diabetes.

After his playing days ended in 1984, Clarke became the fourth general manager of the Flyers. He served in that position until 1990 when he joined the front office of the Minnesota North Stars. Clarke returned to the Flyers in 1992, then left for a brief stint as an executive with the Florida Panthers. He came back once again to the Flyers in 1994 as president and general manager, a position he held for the rest of the decade. During his tenure as Flyers GM, the club has played in the Stanley Cup finals four times. As an executive, Clarke preferred to be called Bob.

MIGHTY MACS MAKE THEIR MARK

Of all the women's teams that have graced the Philadelphia sports scene, none was more successful or more important that the Mighty Macs of Immaculata College. They pioneered a whole new concept in women's sports, bringing it to a level never reached before.

Prior to the 1970s women's college basketball—indeed, most women's sports—were widely perceived as being generally insignificant. Women were considered lacking as both athletes and as competitors, and their participation in sports was viewed as an endeavor designed merely to fill a few idle hours every once in a while.

Immaculata College's basketball team changed those stereotypes forever when it won three consecutive national women's collegiate (AIAW) championships, then was runner-up in two more during a spectacular decade in which the Mighty Macs became the first nationally prominent women's team in college sports.

A tiny school on the upper Main Line with a student body of 450, Immaculata's was a success story that was almost too good to be true. In 1970 it had hired as basketball coach 22-year-old Cathy Rush, a one-time West Chester State athlete with no prior coaching experience. In her first season, her team posted a 10–12 record.

"We had no bleachers," she recalled. "People brought their own chairs. The players were all just girls coming out of high school looking for an education. The first three years, all the players were commuters. We didn't do any recruiting at first."

Rush taught her players the full-court press, trapping defenses, and various other tactics that no women's teams had ever used before. At games her then-husband Ed, an NBA referee, sat at the top of the stands, using a walkie-talkie to relay advice to the bench. In the 1971–72 season Immaculata, in the first AIAW tournament ever held, beat West Chester, 52–48, in the final at Normal, Illinois, to finish the season with a 24–1 record. The Mighty Macs, led by Theresa Shank and Rene Muth, were on their way.

Rush recruited her first player the following season. Her name was Marianne Crawford, and she was an immediate sensation with her behind-the-back dribbles.

Coach Cathy Rush (right-center), All-American Theresa Shank (left), and teammates celebrated their first national title after returning home to Immaculata College.

With Shank making her first of two All-American teams, Immaculata again won the national title, this time downing tourney host Queens College in the final, 59–52. It was the Macs' 20th win that season without a loss.

Mary Scharff joined Shank, a senior, on the All-American team in 1973–74, and while running up a 20–1 record, Immaculata again won the national crown with a 68–53 victory over Mississippi College in the final at Kansas State. The win gave the Macs a three-year record of 64–2.

Immaculata reached the AIAW finals in both 1975 and 1976, losing to Delta State each time, 90–81 and 69–64. Crawford was All-American both years. By then the Macs had set a number of other precedents. They were the first women's team (with Maryland) to play in a nationally televised game, they were the first women's team (with Queens) to play at Madison Square Garden, and they played in the first all-women's doubleheader at the Spectrum.

The Mighty Macs had one more moment of glory when they finished fourth in the AIAW tourney in 1977 after losing to Louisiana State in the semifinals and Tennessee in the consolation game. After that season Rush, still with no scholarships and watching other women's teams zoom past hers, decided to heed the handwriting on the wall and leave Immaculata. Her record in seven seasons was an astounding 149–15.

The Mighty Macs never entered the national spotlight again. But several of their former players did. Shank (by now Theresa Grentz) became a highly successful coach, first at St. Joseph's, then at Rutgers and Illinois, and in 1992 she coached the U.S. women's team to a bronze medal in the Olympics. Muth (Rene Portland), who also started coaching at St. Joseph's, has been the long-time coach at Penn State, and in 1996 she took her team to the Final Four. Crawford (Marianne Stanley) coached Old Dominion to three national championships before piloting teams at Stanford, Penn, and the University of California (Berkeley). Despite numerous offers, Rush never returned to coaching, but she has been heavily involved in women's sports for more than 20 years, especially helping to develop young players for the game she helped elevate to its present level.

SMOKIN' JOE IS SIZZLING

Of all the heavyweight boxers who called Philadelphia home, none could match Joe Frazier. And he had the record—not to mention the punches—to back up that claim.

Smokin' Joe came to Philadelphia shortly after winning a gold medal in the 1964 Olympics. A native of Beaufort, South Carolina, he had been beaten in the Olympic trials by Buster Mathis, but he got a second chance when Mathis broke his thumb while training. Frazier also broke a thumb in the semifinals but prevailed to capture the heavyweight title.

A savage puncher who packed extraordinary power into his wallops, Frazer quickly turned pro, and in his first fight, at Convention Hall in 1965, he knocked out Woody Goss in the first round. Joe then knocked out 10 more nobodies in a row before meeting his first bona fide challenger, Oscar Bonavena. Frazier captured a 10-round decision.

Joe stretched his unbeaten streak to 18 when he kayoed Tony Doyle in 1967 in the second round in the first boxing match at the Spectrum. Two fights later, in 1968, he reached the summit when he knocked out old rival Mathis in the 11th round at Madison Square Garden to win the vacated New York–World heavyweight title.

Fighting under the banner of a sponsoring consortium known as Cloverlay, Frazier successfully defended his title twice more during the year, knocking out Manuel Ramos in the second round in New York and winning a 15-round decision

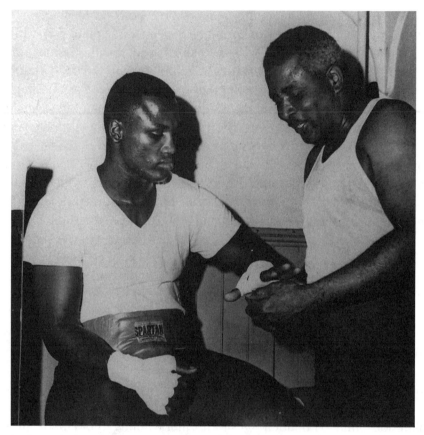

Joe Frazier (with trainer Yank Durham) was one of the towering figures in boxing for a decade.

over Bonavena at the Spectrum. He followed those bouts with knockouts of Dave Zyglewicz and Jerry Quarry before also capturing the vacated World Boxing Association (WBA) heavyweight crown with a fifth-round TKO of Jimmy Ellis in 1970.

Fighting out of his adopted Philadelphia throughout his career, Frazier was undefeated in 26 bouts when he had his first of three memorable fights with Muhammad Ali in 1971 at Madison Square Garden. The former champ, having just been cleared to fight again after a bout with his draft board, bragged about his prowess and chided Frazier for being "a pawn of the white man." The bout was dubbed the Fight of the Century.

With some 300 million fans watching on closed-circuit TV, the two staged a magnificent fight. Ali battered Frazier in the early rounds, but Joe rallied, finally knocking his opponent down for only the third time in his career and winning a 15-round decision. It was the first loss in Ali's career.

In 1973, after 29 straight wins, Frazier lost his crown to George Foreman on a second-round TKO in Kingston, Jamaica. He would lose two title fights to Ali in now-famous bouts, one in 1974 in New York on a unanimous 12-round decision, and one in 1975 on a 14th-round TKO in the memorable "Thrilla in Manilla" in the Philippines, one of the most bruising and widely discussed fights of the century.

Frazier retired after one fight in 1976 (a loss to Foreman), although he staged a brief comeback in 1981. He ended his career with a 32–4–1 record. Joe was elected to the Boxing Hall of Fame in 1990.

NEW TEAMS GALORE

If you want to start a new professional team, put it in Philadelphia. That was the battle cry of sports entrepreneurs during the 1970s.

New teams seemed to flock to Philadelphia about as often as pigeons landed at City Hall. Most of them came, left quickly, and were never heard from again. Usually, they left a trail of debt in their wake.

During the decade Philadelphia provided a brief resting place for the Firebirds and the Blazers in ice hockey, the Atoms, Fever, and Fury in indoor soccer, the Freedoms in tennis, the Bell in football, and the A's in softball. About the only one that met with any success was the Atoms.

The Atoms arrived in 1973 as new members of the indoor North American Soccer League. Coached by Al Miller, they won the league title in their first year after defeating Toronto, 3–0, in the semifinals and Dallas, 2–0, in the championship game with Bob Rigby of Ridley Township starring in goal for the winners. The Atoms were the first expansion team in major league sports ever to win a league title in its inaugural season. After the season the Atoms had perhaps their most memorable game when they played the Soviet Army team at the Spectrum. Some of the Atoms' top players were performing at the time in England, and the team had to borrow players to fill out the roster. With 11,790 in the stands, the teams were tied, 3–3, with 17 minutes left to play when the Russians exploded to capture a 6–3 victory. After that, the Atoms never challenged for another league title. Following the 1976 season, the team folded.

Before the Atoms, there were the Blazers. With much fanfare, they came to town in 1972 as members of the new World Hockey Association. In a big move to grab some headlines, the team signed Boston Bruins star Derek Sanderson to a 10-year, $2.65 million contract, said to be the largest amount ever paid an athlete. They also lured goalie Bernie Parent away from the Toronto Maple Leafs, who had acquired him from the Flyers. In the Blazers' first home game at Convention Hall, ice cracked under a Zamboni, and the game had to be canceled. Many of the 6,000 fans in attendance fired their souvenir pucks onto the ice in disgust. The team never quite recovered from that and, with Sanderson a bust, finished third during the regular season, then lost four straight in the playoffs with Cleveland. The best performance on the Blazers was provided by former Flyer Andre Lacroix, who led the WHA in scoring with 124 points. After the season the Blazers moved to Vancouver.

The Freedoms, led by player-coach Billie Jean King, arrived in 1974 to compete under a new concept called World Team Tennis. King, a six-time Wimbledon and four-time U.S. Open champion, was one of many marquee players in the league. The Freedoms, also featuring Fred Stolle, drew 14,000 on opening night at the Spectrum. But it was all downhill after that, and early in 1975, the red, white, and blue–clad Freedoms were sold to a group that moved the team to New York and called it the Apples.

Tennis great Billie Jean King came to Philadelphia to coach and play for the short-lived Freedoms.

The Bell also arrived in 1974 as an entry in the new World Football League. Playing at JFK Stadium in the summer and giving away tickets by the truckload, the Bell drew crowds of 50,000–60,000, of which only 6,000–15,000 were paid. In their first game, the Bell beat the Portland Storm, 33–8, but it turned out that less than 14,000 of the announced crowd of 55,000 had bought tickets. Later in the season, following 24 hours of rain that turned the playing field into a swamp, the Bell fell to Shreveport, 30–25, before just 750 spectators. Summer football turned out not to appeal to fans, and the league folded midway through the following season.

A team called the Firebirds played at Convention Hall in the North American Hockey League from 1974 to 1976, when the league folded, and in the American Hockey League from 1977 to 1979, after which it moved to Syracuse.

The A's came back to Philadelphia in 1978, but they were a softball team playing in the American Professional Slow-Pitch League. In a weekend league that featured pitches with a 6-to-10-foot arc, the A's were originally managed by ex-Phillies outfielder Johnny Callison and included players such as pro football star Billy (White Shoes) Johnson, newspaper columnist Ray Didinger, and home run slugger Larry (Boom Boom) Hutchinson. The league featured a number of other former major leaguers and played a 60-game schedule. The A's played home games at Veterans Stadium in their first year, when they made it to the playoff final before losing to Cleveland. Later, they had home fields in Claymont, Delaware, and Berlin, New Jersey, before the league disbanded after the 1980 season.

Two new soccer teams made their debuts in 1978. The Fury played in the North American Soccer League from 1978 to 1980. The team's Fred Grgurev led the league in scoring with 74 points the first season. After the 1980 season the team moved to Montreal where it became the Manic. The Fever became a member of the Major Indoor Soccer League and in its first season finished fourth. In the playoffs the Fever defeated the Houston Summit, 6–3, to move to the final where the team lost 14–7 and 9–5 to the New York Arrows. The Fever remained in Philadelphia through 1982 when it became the Los Angeles Lasers.

STEVE CARLTON, MASTER LEFTY

When John Quinn in his last deal as Phillies general manager sent Rick Wise to the St. Louis Cardinals for Steve Carlton in an exchange of pitchers, he was harshly condemned for making a bad trade. How ironic that the swap would someday be regarded as the best deal the Phillies ever made!

At the time, though, the trade made little sense. Wise was coming off a fine year as the Phillies' top hurler, and Carlton was still in the early stages of his career. But both pitchers were unhappy with their contract offers, and the deal was struck. It worked out well for both clubs.

Carlton went on to become the second-winningest lefthanded pitcher in baseball history, the owner of a 329–244 career record, four Cy Young Awards, the second-highest strikeout total (4,136) ever registered, six 20-win seasons, a National League record six one-hitters, and in 1994 a spot in the Baseball Hall of Fame. Only four other pitchers in big league history started more games than Carlton, only eight others pitched more innings, and only 13 others fired more shutouts.

While pitching with the Phillies from 1972 to 1986, Carlton was one of the most dominant hurlers of his or any other era. Mixing a crackling fastball with a slider that broke as sharply as any ever thrown, the powerful southpaw was simply too good for most opposing hitters.

During a glorious career with the Phillies, Steve Carlton won four Cy Young Awards while becoming the second-winningest lefthander of all time.

Few baseball players could match Carlton in intensity or strength. He was focused to the point of being fanatical, and his strenuous workouts with Phillies conditioning guru Gus Hoefling were legendary. Equally legendary was his total abstinence from talking with the media. After several unpleasant experiences with writers, Carlton refused to give interviews throughout the rest of his career, even though privately he was an extremely articulate and personable fellow.

Carlton had perhaps his greatest season in his maiden year with the Phillies in 1972. That year the last-place Phils won just 59 games, but Steve won 27, including 15 in a row, while leading the league with a 1.98 ERA and a career-high 310 strikeouts, then a club record. Such an accomplishment was almost too astounding to be believed.

Carlton won the Cy Young Award that year and again in 1977, 1980, and 1982. Along the way, he was a key figure in the Phillies' resurgence from doormat to perennial National League contender. His 24–9 record in 1980 was one of the major factors in the Phillies' drive to their first World Series victory. Carlton won twice in the Series.

He also won four out of six decisions in League Championship Series, including two games in 1983 when the Phils again won the National League pennant. Overall, Steve won more games (241) than any other Phillies pitcher. He started in a league record 14 opening day games, was named to 10 All-Star squads, and even won one Gold Glove.

Carlton struggled after his release from the Phillies in 1986, pitching with four other teams before finally retiring at the age of 43 in 1988. While he was with the Phillies, though, he was as invincible as any hurler the team ever had.

FLYERS WIN STANLEY CUPS

They were known as the Broad Street Bullies, a belligerent bunch who would fight at the drop of a puck. Their coach was an oddly aloof taskmaster who combed through libraries in search of inspirational quotes. An aging singer was their good luck charm. And many of them came from tiny Canadian towns such as Smithers, Flin Flon, and Moose Jaw.

But, oh, could they play hockey!

The Flyers gave Philadelphia its first taste of real ice hockey, and then they gave Philadelphia a sparkling sip from the Stanley Cup—not once, but twice in a row. It was unlike anything that had ever happened to the city before.

The Flyers, of course, weren't the first Philadelphia team to win back-to-back championships. But when they won Stanley Cups in 1974 and 1975, they became the first team that made virtually a whole city crazy. The parade in '74 down Broad Street before two million wide-eyed fanatics attested to that.

After arriving in the NHL as an expansion team in 1967, the Flyers didn't have a winning season until 1972–73. But by then, with Fred Shero holding the coaching reigns, Bobby Clarke coming into his own, and a solid cast of talented players surrounding him, the Flyers were obviously a team on the rise.

When the 1973–74 season began, Bernie Parent had returned to the Flyers from the defunct WHL Blazers. Rick MacLeish, Bill Barber, Gary Dornhofer, Barry Ashbee, and Andre Dupont were among the top offensive players, with Ed Van Impe, Joe Watson, Dave Schultz, and Don Saleski anchoring a tough, unforgiving defense. It was a team that refused to knuckle under to anyone. It pounded opponents relentlessly, often with its fists. Especially notable in that regard was Schultz, the baddest of the Bullies, who led the NHL in penalty minutes three years in a row between 1973 and 1975.

The Flyers opened the season at the Spectrum with singer Kate Smith making her first live appearance. Previously, the Flyers had played her recorded rendition of *God Bless America* before games, and they had won most of the time. This time was no exception, and it launched a season in which the Flyers brawled and skated through opponents, finishing with a 50–16–12 record and their first of four straight first-place Eastern Conference finishes.

In the playoffs, with Ashbee out after getting hit in the eye with a puck, the Flyers swept the Atlanta Flames in four games, then downed the New York Rangers, four games to three, winning the seventh game, 4–3, with the help of two goals by Dornhofer. In the final against the Boston Bruins, the Flyers dropped the opener, 3–2, then won three straight by scores of 3–2 in overtime, 4–1, and 4–2. After a 5–1, loss, the Flyers came back to win the deciding game, 1–0, at the Spectrum on a first-period goal by MacLeish and a brilliant shutout by Parent, the playoff MVP (Conn Smythe Trophy) and winner of the season's Vezina Trophy as the year's top goalie. Shero won the Jack Adams Award as coach of the year.

The Flyers were the first expansion team to win the Stanley Cup. Philadelphians went crazy. A night-long celebration was staged in all corners of the city, followed by a gigantic parade down Broad Street the next day.

The following season was more of the same. With Reggie Leach joining a team that was otherwise pretty much the same, the Flyers dashed off a 51–18–11 record to win the division crown. In the playoffs, they took four straight from the Toronto Maple Leafs, then won a tough seven-game series with the New York Islanders as MacLeish got a hat trick in the last game to give the Flyers a 4–1 win.

In the final series against the Buffalo Sabres, the Flyers jumped out to a two-game advantage with 4–1 and 2–1 wins, but then lost 5–4 in overtime and 4–2. Philadelphia came back to capture a 5–1 victory in Game Five. Two days later at Buffalo, goals by Bob Kelly and Bill Clement gave the Flyers a 2–0 victory and their second straight Stanley Cup. This time, nearly 2.5 million turned out for the parade on Broad Street. Par-

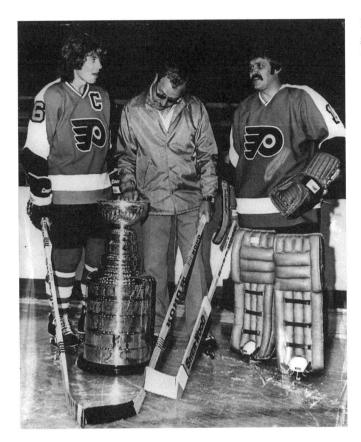

Bobby Clarke, coach Fred Shero, and goalie Bernie Parent admire the Flyers' first Stanley Cup in 1974.

ent became the first player to win two straight MVP awards in the playoffs, and he again won the Vezina Trophy while Clarke bagged the Hart Trophy as league MVP.

The Flyers made it back to the Stanley Cup final in 1975–76, but this time they lost in four straight to the Montreal Canadiens. They reached the semifinals in each of the next two years before getting swept in four games by Boston in 1976–77 and losing in five games to the Bruins in 1977–78. They were bounced in five games in the quarterfinals by the Rangers in 1978–79, bringing a marvelous era to an end. It was a most memorable decade.

Phillies Rediscover Winning

After nearly a quarter-century of defeat, disappointment, and distress, the Phillies finally produced a winner again in the 1970s. The decade would launch the team's greatest era during which it won a World Series, two National League pennants, and five division titles.

The seeds for that success were planted in the '60s when the club began rebuilding its tattered farm system under the direction of Paul Owens. Eventually numerous good, young players were signed, including Larry Bowa, Bob Boone, Greg Luzinski, and Mike Schmidt. When Owens was elevated to the general manager's post in 1972, another dimension was added. One of baseball's most astute traders, Owens brought in players such as Garry Maddox, Bake McBride, Jay Johnstone, Dave Cash, Tug McGraw, and Jim Lonborg. By the mid-1970s, Owens had assembled a team as solid as any in the league.

Owens and Ruly Carpenter, who had ascended to the presidency of the team after his father Bob retired in 1972, pulled a surprise in 1973 when they named an unknown Los Angeles Dodgers coach named Danny Ozark as the Phillies manager. But with talented players, Ozark had the club all the way up to second place in the Eastern Division by 1975.

The following year, inspired by second baseman Cash's "Yes We Can" slogan, the Phillies made their first postseason appearance since 1950 when they roared to the division title, winning a club-record 101 games and finishing nine games ahead of the second-place Pittsburgh Pirates. After years of frustration Philadelphia fans took to the team like bears take to honey, and for the first time in club history Phillies home attendance went over the two million mark (2,480,150).

Maddox (.330), Johnstone (.318), Luzinski (.304–21–95), and Schmidt (38–107) had big years at the plate, and Carlton and Lonborg won 20 and 18, respectively. Unfortunately, regular season performances have no value in the playoffs, and the Phillies were swept in three straight by the Cincinnati Reds' Big Red Machine in the LCS.

But the Phillies surged back with a fury in 1977 with what many consider the finest club in franchise history. With Ted Sizemore now playing second and Richie Hebner taking over for Dick Allen at first, the Phils again won 101 games. Luzinski (.309–39–130) had a monster year, finishing second in the MVP voting, while Carlton (23), Larry Christenson (19), and a superb bullpen led by McGraw, Ron Reed, and Gene Garber headed a strong pitching staff.

Once again, though, the Phils faltered in the LCS. This time, facing the Dodgers, they lost in four games, the only victory coming as the Phillies scored twice in the ninth-inning to win the first game, 7–5. In Game Three, after Phillies fans had hooted Dodger pitcher Burt Hooton from the mound during a streak of wildness, Ozark failed to send in Jerry Martin as a ninth-inning defensive substitute in left field for Luzinski—as he had done throughout the season—and when Manny Mota's catchable drive bounced off Luzinski's glove, followed one play later by a blown call at first by umpire Bruce Froemming, the Phillies were doomed. They lost that game, 6–5, then dropped the deciding contest, 4–1, when Tommy John beat them in a game played entirely in pouring rain.

The Phillies had another shot in 1978 when they won their third straight division title. As he did every year, Owens got help in a trade when he picked up pitcher Dick Ruthven, who won 13. The Phils won 90 games and finished just one and one-half ahead of Pittsburgh as the race went down to the next to last day of the season before the Phillies clinched the flag on pitcher Randy Lerch's two-homer, 10–8 victory.

Again, however, the Phils lost in a four-game LCS to the Dodgers. The Phils' only win was Carlton's 9–4 victory in Game Three. The following day, Maddox, usually an extraordinary defensive player, dropped Dusty Baker's 10th inning, two-out fly, setting up what became the winning run in a 4–3 Dodger triumph.

It was a disappointing end to the Phillies' exciting three-year run. But better days were ahead.

PENN'S EXTRAORDINARY DECADE

Especially during the second half of the 20th century, college basketball was one of the most prominent sports in Philadelphia. The city was known far and wide for its teams, coaches, and players, and it enjoyed a reputation as a kind of mecca of basketball superiority.

No team exhibited more superiority over a sustained period than Penn did during the 1970s. It was a decade that the Quakers dominated from start to finish. They did it in a way that has never been matched by any other Big Five team.

From a perfect 28–0 regular season at the beginning of the decade to a spot in the Final Four at the end, Penn put together a spectacular record. Over 10 seasons the Quakers posted a 223–56 record, winning 20 or more games every year but two. They won or tied for seven Big Five titles, captured eight Ivy League championships, and eight times played in the NCAA tournament. The Quakers' Ivy League record was 127–13, and their Big Five mark was 32–8, which included four undefeated seasons.

Remarkably, Penn had three different coaches during that period. Dick Harter was winding up a five-year stint while piloting the Quakers in the first two seasons of the decade. Chuck Daly handled the reigns for six seasons in the middle, and Bob Weinhauer led Penn for the last two years in the start of his own five-year term. All three were superb coaches, and all three went on to lengthy careers in the NBA, with Daly guiding the Detroit Pistons to two league titles on his way to the Basketball Hall of Fame.

Penn's run began with a 25–2 record in 1969–70. But that was nothing compared to the following campaign when the Quakers had what many call the best Penn team ever put together. Led by Corky Calhoun, Dave Wohl, Steve Bilsky, and Bob Morse, the Quakers reeled off 26 straight wins during the regular season, outscoring opponents by almost 17 points per game. Penn, who had a young assistant coach named Rollie Massimino, beat Syracuse, Utah, and Temple to win the Quaker City Tournament, then cruised to its second straight unbeaten season (14–0) in the Ivy League. In the NCAA playoffs the Quakers downed Duquesne, 70–65, and South Carolina, 79–64, to reach the Eastern Regional final, where in an incredible shocker Penn was crushed by Villanova, 90–47. Penn ended the season with a 28–1 record and a third-place ranking in the final poll of the Associated Press.

The following season, Daly's first, Penn's regular season winning streak reached 48 before it was stopped by Temple. In the playoffs the Quakers avenged the previous year's loss to Villanova with a 78–67 win but lost to North Carolina, 73–59, in the regional final and finished with a 25–3 record.

Penn then went 21–7, 21–6, 23–5, 17–9, 18–8 and 20–8 over the next six years with players such as Phil Hankinson, Ron Haigler, John Engles, and Kevin McDonald leading the way. In 1974–75, Haigler scored 606 points, the most for a Quaker since Ernie Beck in 1952–53. Then in the final season of the decade (1978–79), in Weinhauer's second year of coaching, the Quakers had their most satisfying if not finest overall season.

After winning 21 of 26 during the regular season, Penn rolled into the playoffs with a 73–69 win over Iona, coached by Jim Valvano. North Carolina fell next in a 72–71 shocker in Raleigh. Tony Price and Matt White then sparked the Quakers to an 84–76 victory over Syracuse and a 64–62 decision over St. John's in the Eastern Regional final.

It was off to the Final Four in Salt Lake City for the Quakers where they met a Magic Johnson–led Michigan State in the semifinals. Penn was no match for the Spartans, who prevailed, 101–67. The Quakers then bowed to DePaul in the consolation game, 96–93, in triple overtime as Price scored 31 to lead the tournament in scoring with 142 points.

Although they lost in their final game of the decade, it had been a marvelous run for the Quakers. Only two major college teams—UCLA and Marquette—had better records than Penn in the 1970s.

WOMEN'S SPORTS MOVE FORWARD

The decade of the 1970s displayed no similarity whatsoever with previous decades in Philadelphia sports. It was a decade with its own distinctive flavor, one in which there were more unprecedented developments and a greater accumulation of idiosyncrasies than in any other period.

One of the many distinctive elements of the century's eighth decade was the arrival of women's sports in the mainstream of athletic competition. Women's sports were raised from second-class status and elevated to an unprecedented level. Although that process had started much earlier, the passing in 1972 of Title IX, which mandated equal funding for women's and men's college athletics, hastened the growth of women's sports into a substantive athletic activity.

In Philadelphia in the 1970s women made sports news like never before. West Chester's basketball team lost, 56–55, to Mississippi in the final of the Women's National Invitational Collegiate Tournament in 1971, and its field hockey team won four straight national AIAW championships. Little Immaculata College won three straight national women's basketball titles. Women participated in the Dad Vail Regatta for the first time in 1976. The Big Five was expanded to include women's basketball games in 1979. And women's teams throughout the area began awarding scholarships, hiring first-rate coaches, and fielding teams that were more interested in good competition than a good time.

Women were carving numerous other inroads in the area, too. In 1970 the Ladies Professional Golf Association made its first appearance in the Philadelphia area with a tournament called the George Washington Classic at Hidden Springs in Horsham. The Virginia Slims women's pro tennis tournament began a seven-year run at the Palestra in 1973. Women joined men on a pro tennis team called the Philadelphia Freedoms in 1974. The Federation Cup returned to Philadelphia in 1976 at the Spectrum. That same year the U.S. Women's Open golf tournament was held at Rolling Green in Springfield.

Women's sports were advancing in every direction. Overall, the world of sports would never again be the same.

Something else that was being raised to a new level was men's college baseball. Previously a sport on which there was little emphasis locally, it made a sudden ascent on the scale of importance in the 1970s. Temple became the first area team ever to participate in the College World Series when it played in the tournament in 1972, winning twice and losing once before getting knocked out by Arizona, 1–0. The Owls ranked sixth in the nation that season, finishing with a 33–5 record, the best in the college's history. Temple would return to the tournament in 1977 when it ranked eighth in the nation with a 34–9 mark.

Glassboro State, coached by Mike Briglia, won the Division III NCAA baseball championships in 1978 and 1979, beating Marietta, 5–3, in the final of the former and Cal State–Stanislaus, 3–0, in the last game of the latter. Glassboro pitcher Bob Ffeffer and second baseman Tak Upshur were MVPs in '78 and '79, respectively. In 1975, Penn won its first Ivy League baseball title since 1943 with its most overall wins

(25) up to that point. The Quakers were coached by Bob Seddon, who in 1971 had launched a career in which he would join Temple's Skip Wilson and La Salle's Gene McDonnell as the winningest college baseball skippers in Philadelphia history. Seddon entered the 21st century with a 532–458–11 record. Wilson ran up a 901–652–23 mark between 1960 and 1999, while McDonnell was 503–494–8 from 1959 to 1988 and 1991 to 1995.

The decade of the '70s was hardly under way when things began happening. The inaugural George Washington Classic was held with Judy Rankin beating Sandra Haynie by one stroke. In subsequent years, the tournament would be won by Jane Blaylock, Kathy Ahern, Carole Jo Skala, Haynie, and Carol Mann before it came to an end after the 1975 season. The Eagles played their last game at Franklin Field. The Ukrainian Nationals won the American Soccer League title. Drew Gordon set a school record when he passed for 395 yards and three touchdowns to lead Villanova to a 31–26 decision over Temple. The 76ers beat the San Diego Rockets, 159–131, in the highest-scoring game in club history. In the second NBA All-Star Game held in Philadelphia, the East beat the West, 142–135, with Willis Reed winning the MVP trophy. Temple opened a new indoor sports arena, McGonigle Hall.

The first year of the '70s also marked the end of Connie Mack Stadium. After 62 years, the ancient ballpark held its final game on October 1. Throughout the game, many of the 31,822 fans in attendance ripped souvenirs from everywhere including the bathrooms. After the Phillies had beaten the Montreal Expos, 2–1 in 10 innings, fans poured onto the field, tearing up the turf and grabbing whatever else they could find. Much of the park was destroyed by fire in 1971, and in 1976 it was demolished.

Both the Phillies and Eagles moved into a brand new stadium in 1971. The city-owned Veterans Stadium was built at a cost of $52 million, more than double the amount voters had originally approved in a referendum in 1964. During a tour of the park before it opened, baseball commissioner Bowie Kuhn was momentarily found to be missing when he accidentally locked himself into a closet. The new park, erected on marshland in South Philadelphia, opened with the Phillies beating the Expos, 4–1, before the largest crowd (55,352) ever to see a baseball game in Pennsylvania. In the years that followed the Vet would house numerous games of special significance, plus an assortment of promotional activities of varying levels of success. Of particular note were two pregame crashes into the stands by a stuntman called Kiteman, and the breathtaking walk across the top of the stadium by high-wire artist Karl Wallenda. Golden-voiced Harry Kalas began his Phillies broadcasting career the day the Vet opened. In their first game at the Vet, the Eagles bowed to the Cincinnati Bengals, 37–14, despite seven catches for 118 yards and two touchdowns by Ben Hawkins and a 301-yard passing day by Pete Liske.

In 1971, Villanova's basketball team concluded the regular season with a 23–6 record, with Howard Porter, Chris Ford, and Hank Siemiontkowski leading the Wildcats to their 10th straight postseason appearance. Villanova then whipped through the NCAA playoffs by beating St. Joseph's, 93–75, Fordham, 85–75, and Penn, 90–47, in the Eastern Regionals. That string of victories vaulted the Wildcats into their first Final Four,where coach Jack Kraft's club defeated Western Kentucky, 92–89, to advance to the championship game against UCLA. Coach John Wooden's Bruins had four future pros in the starting lineup and a 28–1 record on the table, and they heavy favorites to win their fifth straight NCAA title. But the Wildcats hung close, and after leading at one point, 22–21, trailed 45–37 at halftime. Late in the second half, Porter field goals twice cut UCLA's lead to three, the last at 63–60. Although UCLA pulled away in the end to win, 68–62, it had been a marvelous performance by the underdog Wildcats. Porter finished with 25 points and Siemiontkowski had 19. The Wildcats stopped Sidney Wicks and Curtis Rowe, but Steve Patterson bagged 29 and Henry Bibby 17. Later, however, it was revealed that Porter had signed a pro contract during the season. Villanova was stripped of its playoff record, and its spot as NCAA runner-up was expunged from the books.

That disappointing development ruined an otherwise glittering season for the Wildcats. But Philadelphia sports had some other bright spots during the year. The Phillies' Rick Wise did something no other major leaguer ever did by hitting two home runs in the same game in which he pitched a no-hitter, beating the Cincinnati Reds, 4–0. Ken Durrett won his third straight Big Five Player of the Year award while averaging 27 points per game as he led La Salle to a 20–7 record. Villanova's Marty Liquori beat the nation's top distance runner Jim Ryun in a spectacular mile race at the Martin Luther King Games in New York. Liquori also won three straight NCAA outdoor mile titles between 1969 and 1971.

Palmer Page of Penn won the National Squash Association championship. Temple hired John McDonald as golf coach, and by the time he left in 1985 he had produced nine undefeated teams, three Atlantic 10 titlists, 10 touring pros, and a career record of 139–9. After catching 12 passes in two different games, future pro Mike Siani was named All-American wide receiver at Villanova. Army beat Navy, 24–23, in the first game in the series decided by one point. The Flyers fired Vic Stasiuk, replacing him with an unknown minor league coach from the New York Rangers system. Fred Shero would direct the Flyers to two Stanley Cups while compiling an overall 308–151–95 record in eight seasons before quitting in 1978.

The U.S. Open was held once again at Merion, and Lee Trevino prevailed by three strokes in an 18-hole playoff with Jack Nicklaus after the two had finished regulation tied at even par with 280 scores. "I didn't beat Merion, I just compromised with her," Trevino said later. Beset by numerous crashes on its accident-prone track and boycotted by drivers who were scheduled to compete two weeks later for a much richer purse at the new Pocono Speedway, Langhorne Speedway officials decided to close the track for good in 1971. There wasn't much racing left in the area after that except a few midget car events at JFK Stadium.

There was, however, still a racer in the area. In 1972, Mark Donohue, now living near Media—in fact, across the street from Mike Schmidt—and racing under the Roger Penske banner, won the Indianapolis 500, driving his McLaren-Offenhauser to victory while averaging a record speed of 162.962 miles per hour. It was the first time a driver had exceeded 160 mph in the 500. Donohue, who was runner-up in the 1970 Indy race, was one of the world's top drivers and became a member of the International Motorsport Hall of Fame after his untimely death in a race in 1975. Meanwhile, Penske, a former driver himself, would go on to produce more 500 winners (10) than any other race car owner in history.

Also making news in 1972 was Springfield (Delco) athlete Geoff Petrie, a former Princeton basketball star. The first draft choice of the new Portland Trailblazers,

Mark Donohue resided near Media when he became the area's fifth Indianapolis 500 winner.

Petrie was named co–Rookie of the Year in the NBA with the Boston Celtics Dave Cowens. He is one of only three NBA guards (the others are Oscar Robertson and Michael Jordan) ever to have scored more than 2,000 points in his rookie season. Petrie would average nearly 22 points per game during a six-year career that was cut short by a knee injury. In 1999 he was named NBA executive of the year for his work as general manager of the Sacramento Kings.

In 1972, Ollie Johnson helped Temple to a 23–8 record in basketball. Mike Bantom concluded a fine three-year career at St. Joseph's during which he averaged 20 points per game and which was followed by a nine-year stint in the NBA. Tim McKee of Newtown Square won three silver medals in the Olympics in swimming. The Eagles' Bill Bradley became the first NFL player to lead the league in interceptions in two consecutive seasons. Franco Harris, in his first year with the Pittsburgh Steelers after starring at Penn State and Rancocas Valley High in Mount Holly, New Jersey, pulled off what become known as the "immaculate reception" when he snatched off his shoetops a deflected pass by Terry Bradshaw and rumbled 40 yards for a touchdown with only seconds remaining in the first round of the AFC divisional playoffs. The 60-yard play gave the Steelers a stunning 13–7 victory over the Oakland Raiders. Harris would go on to have a fine 13-year pro career as a running back, gaining more than 1,000 yards eight times and leading the Steelers to four Super Bowl victories.

Another area resident attained prominence in 1973 when Penn State All-American running back and former Monsignor Bonner star John Cappelletti became the first local player ever to win the Heisman Trophy after rushing for 1,522 yards and scoring 17 touchdowns for the undefeated (12–0) Nittany Lions. In a tear-inducing speech, the Upper Darby native dedicated the award to his little brother Joey, who was dying of leukemia. Cappelletti, also winner of the Maxwell Club Award, went on to play nine years in the NFL for the Los Angeles Rams and San Diego Chargers, and in 1993 he was elected to the College Football Hall of Fame.

Widener's Billy (White Shoes) Johnson also captured headlines in 1973 when he made the Little All-American team for the second straight year. By the time he was done, Johnson had set nine NCAA records and 31 Widener marks, 29 of which he still holds. Rushing for 1,556 yards in 1972 and 1,496 in 1973, Johnson of nearby Boothwyn, where he attended Chichester High, recorded the two highest totals in Widener history. The 5-foot, 9-inch speedster joined the Houston Oilers in 1974, and in a 14-year NFL career spent mostly with the Oilers and Atlanta Falcons, Johnson became one of the top punt returners in NFL history while leading the league in that category in 1975 and 1977 and setting an all-time record of 279 punt returns for 3,291 yards.

The first women's pro tennis tournament held in Philadelphia began at the Palestra in 1973. Called various names but mostly known as the Virginia Slims tour-

John Cappelletti became the Philadelphia area's first Heisman Trophy winner when he won the award in 1973 while playing at Penn State for coach Joe Paterno (right).

nament, the first event was won by Margaret Court. During the seven years it lasted, the tourney was won twice by Chris Evert, once over Martina Navratilova and once over Billie Jean King. Evert also finished runner-up twice, losing to Virginia Wade and to Evonne Goolagong.

Also in 1973, the Eagles' Harold Carmichael, as had Harold Jackson the year before, led the NFL in pass receptions. The 6-foot, 8-inch Carmichael would put in 13 outstanding seasons in an Eagles uniform, at one point catching passes in a record 127 straight games, three times exceeding 1,000 yards in pass receptions, and ranking first on the Eagles' all-time list in receiving yardage and touchdown receptions. Another receiver making a name for himself was Temple's Randy Grossman. The Owls' tight end from Haverford High had a banner season in 1973, then entered the pros and in eight seasons with the Pittsburgh Steelers would be the recipient of four Super Bowl rings. Also in 1973, Drexel football, stymied by a lack of interest and a shortage of funds, was dropped from the college's athletic roster. Navy crushed Army, 51–0, in the most one-sided game in the series. And in a basketball game in the Volunteer Classic between Temple and Tennessee, the Owls dropped an 11–6 decision after holding the ball almost the entire game.

Dropping that game was not nearly as bad as what the 76ers dropped. After five straight years of atrocious number-one draft picks, the club had become one of the worst in the NBA. In 1972 the club had hired Roy Rubin as coach after Kentucky's Adolph Rupp wisely rejected a job offer. Rubin, previously the coach at Long Island University, was in miles over his head. He was fired after the club had lost 47 of its first 51 games. His replacement, guard Kevin Loughery, could do no better, and when the season ended, the 76ers sported a dreadful 9–73 record, the worst in NBA history. At least there was one consolation. The 76ers got the first draft pick, and with it they chose Doug Collins, who would go on to a fine eight-year career as a high-scoring guard.

The 76ers' luck in the draft didn't last. In 1974, after again finishing with the worst record in the NBA, although it improved to 25–57, the Sixers and Portland flipped a coin to determine who would get the first draft choice. This time the 76ers lost the toss and the opportunity to choose UCLA star Bill Walton. Former Penn State running back Lydell Mitchell from Salem, New Jersey, led the NFL in pass receptions while playing with the Baltimore Colts in 1974. That was also the year that Mr. Prospector set a track record of 1:08 at Garden State in the six-furlong Whirlaway Stakes. Temple moved its football games to Veterans Stadium and, with but a few exceptions, seldom filled more than a fraction of the seats.

Temple football was on a decided upswing after a long period in the doldrums. In 1970 the Owls had hired former Navy coach Wayne Hardin, and in 1972, Temple had a first-team All-American in offensive guard Bill Singletary. By 1973, Temple had climbed to a 9–1 record. The following year the Owls were 8–2 as quarterback Steve Joachim became the only Temple player ever to win the Maxwell Club award. In 1975, with tackle Joe Klecko out of St. James High School in Chester on his way to a 12-year pro career, Temple faced Penn State for the first time since 1952 and nearly pulled off the upset of the decade before losing a 26–25 thriller at Franklin Field. A repeat performance occurred the following year when the Owls lost to the Nittany Lions, 31–30, after scoring on the last play of the game, then failing to make a two-point conversion. Temple finished the decade with three straight bowl appearances, losing 35–32 to Grambling in the Mirage Bowl in Tokyo, beating Boston College, 28–24, in the same game in 1978, and downing California, 28–17, in the Garden State Bowl at the Meadowlands. The Owls completed the decade with a 67–33–3 record, their best mark since the 1930s, and when Hardin left after the 1982 campaign, he'd won more games (80) and coached more years (13) than any other Temple football coach.

Neither Penn nor Villanova was in that class in football. Nor were the Eagles, who had suffered 14 losing seasons out of a possible 15 between 1962 and 1976. That year, though, they had at least taken a step in the right direction when they hired

UCLA coach Dick Vermeil. A tireless worker with boundless energy and enthusiasm, Vermeil inherited Pro Bowl players Bill Bergey and Charley Young, but little else. His first team went 4–10, but in 1977 the Eagles traded Young to the Los Angeles Rams for quarterback Ron Jaworski. Then a dashing young running back named Wilbert Montgomery would land a starting job in 1978. The Eagles were on their way. They had their first winning season (9–7) since 1966 before ending the decade with a 12–4 mark, just one step from the Super Bowl.

Joe Bryant scored 25 points to help La Salle beat Penn, 67–65, to end the Quakers' 12-game Big Five winning streak in 1975. The Explorers posted a 22–7 record that year. Fans, who had booed a pig a year earlier during a halftime show at a 76ers game, had more reason to cheer in 1975 when the team signed George McGinnis, one of the top players in the ABA. With Collins and McGinnis setting the pace, the Sixers managed to land back in the playoffs by 1976, although they lost in the first round to the Buffalo Braves.

That, however, was just a tiny part of the picture in 1976, the year of Philadelphia's Bicentennial celebration and unquestionably one of the greatest years in the city's sports history. It was a year when the city played host to more major events than ever before.

The U.S. Women's Open was one of the major events of the summer and one of the most exciting. Jo Anne Carner won an 18-hole playoff with Sandra Palmer by two strokes after the two had tied in the regulation 72 holes with eight-over 292s. Furman University senior Betsy King of Reading, who would eventually become the all-time leading money winner in women's pro golf, was low amateur. The NBA held its All-Star Game at the Spectrum, and led by MVP Dave Bing and Bob McAdoo's 22 points, the East took a 123–109 decision. Baseball had its All-Star Game at the Vet with MVP George Foster's three RBI powering the National League to a 7–1 victory.

The Flyers defeated the Red Army, the perennial Soviet champs, 4–1, in a bruising ice hockey game at the Spectrum. The game was delayed for 17 minutes in the first period when Red coach Konstantin Loktev pulled his team off the ice in protest of a referee's decision. When order was restored, the Flyers went on to outshoot the Soviets, 49–13, to claim a rousing victory. And the Final Four came to the Spectrum with Bobby Knight's Indiana team ending an undefeated (32–0) season with an 86–68 victory over Michigan in the final. Kent Benson was named MVP. In the consolation game UCLA downed Rutgers, 106–92.

In 1976, Mike Schmidt hit four home runs to lead the Phillies to an improbable 18–16, 10-inning victory over the Chicago Cubs at Wrigley Field in a game in which the Phils had trailed, 12–1, after three innings. The 76ers made a major leap forward just before the 1976–77 season when, soon after Fitz Eugene Dixon, Jr., bought the team, they signed ABA star Julius Erving to a $6 million contract. Philadelphia's

Tyrone Everett survived a vicious head-butting but lost a controversial 15-round decision to defending junior-featherweight champ Alfredo Escalera at the Spectrum. Eamonn Coughlan was winning distance races regularly for Villanova. The Flyers' Reggie Leach became only the second NHL player ever to score 60 goals in one season and the first to score 80 in the entire campaign (counting playoffs). The Federation Cup returned to Philadelphia for the second time, and the United States emerged victorious in the 32-team match as Billie Jean King and Rosie Casals led the U.S. team over Australia in the final, beginning a reign of seven straight titles for the winners. In the Olympics at Montreal, gold medals were won by Bruce Davidson of Unionville in the equestrian, Donald Haldeman of Souderton in trap shooting, and, representing the Philadelphia Pioneers track club Steve Riddick in the 4 × 100 relay and Herman Frazier and Fred Newhouse in the 4 × 400 relay. Davidson

The Flyers' Reggie Leach was only the second NHL player to score 60 goals in one season.

would go on to win another gold in the 1984 Olympics while winning silvers in 1972 and 1996. And in the worst Big Five season in history, no team finished above .500, and for the first time no team went to a postseason tournament.

Philadelphia was not without tragedy in that period. In 1976, Eagles defensive end Blenda Gay was stabbed to death while sleeping. His wife was charged with the murder. One year later highly popular former Flyers player Barry Ashbee, who, forced by an eye injury, had retired the year before to become a coach with the team, succumbed to leukemia. And Garden State Park, a fixture in horse racing for nearly 40 years, was destroyed after faulty wiring in the clubhouse kitchen caught fire. More than 10,000 people were at the track when the fire broke out. All but 18 escape unharmed. The blaze could be seen as far away as Trenton. Clerks returned $200,000 to track officials, but several hundred thousand dollars were never found and another $800,000 was burned or damaged by water.

The 1977 season was the year that Widener's football team captured its first NCAA Division III championship. The Pioneers were in the midst of their most successful era in football and would finish the decade with a sparkling 83–15 record,

Widener gained its first NCAA football championship in 1977 during a decade when the Pioneers posted an 83–15 record. Chip Zawoiski (23) scored for Widener in a mud-soaked playoff win over Albany.

which included eight seasons in which they would lose just one game each year. Under coach Bill Manlove, the '77 Pioneers won eight of their nine regular-season games, then won two playoff games to reach the championship match against Wabash in Phenix City, Alabama. Widener won, 39–36, clinching victory on a 70-yard scoring pass from Mark Walter to Walker Carter in the closing minutes. After finishing at 11–1 that season, the Pioneers would post 8–1, 10–1, and 11–1 marks over the next three years.

Another Division III NCAA winner was the Swarthmore College tennis team, which defeated Claremont, 15–12, to win for coach Bill Cullen. It was also a big year for the 76ers, who with Erving and McGinnis—ironically the co-MVPs in the ABA in 1975—forming a powerful frontcourt tandem that combined for an average of 40 points per game, won the East Division title. Victory over the hated Boston Celtics in a stormy seven-game first-round playoff vaulted the 76ers into the division final, where they beat the Houston Rockets in six games. That sent the Sixers to the final for a meeting with the Portland Trailblazers coached by Jack Ramsay and led by Bill Walton. The Sixers won the first two games, but then lost four straight.

Matthew Saad Muhammad, previously known as Matthew Franklin, won the vacated NABF light-heavyweight championship with a 12th round kayo of Marvin Johnson at the Spectrum. The new Philadelphia champ had been boxing professionally since 1974. He fought until 1992, compiling an overall 39–16–3 record. Saad Muhammad successfully defended his NABF title in Philadelphia matches against Billy Douglas in 1977 and Richie Kates and Yaqui Lopez in 1978. He then beat Johnson for the WBC crown in Indianapolis in 1979, and over the next two years he won title bouts eight more times, taking all but one by knockouts. Saad Muhammad finally lost his crown in late 1981 when the referee stepped in in the 10th round of a bout with fellow Philadelphian Dwight Braxton (later Dwight Muhammad Qawi) in Atlantic City. Saad Muhammad was badly battered in a rematch with Braxton in 1982 at the Spectrum and lost on a sixth-round TKO. He fought for 10 more years but had only one other title fight, an 11th round TKO by Willie Edwards in 1984. Saad Muhammad was inducted into the Boxing Hall of Fame in 1998.

Meanwhile, Rollie Massimino, in his fourth season as head coach at Villanova, guided the Wildcats to third place in the NIT after beating Alabama in the consolation game, 102–89. During the season the Wildcats had beaten St. Joseph's, 92–78, at the Spectrum in the first Big Five game not played at the Palestra. Michael Brooks launched a splendid career at La Salle by making his first of four straight All–Big Five teams. Roberto Duran won a 15-round decision over Edwin Viruet to capture the lightweight championship at the Spectrum. Gene Banks, one of the most widely heralded high school players ever to perform in Philadelphia, ended a marvelous career at West Philadelphia High by leading his team to two undefeated seasons and a 79–2 record over three years before accepting a scholarship to Duke, then embarking on a six-year career in the NBA. Cheltenham High's Reggie Jackson, who would eventually win four home run titles, hit three of the biggest four-baggers of his life in the sixth and deciding game of the World Series. The blows gave Jackson's New York Yankees an 8–4 win over the Los Angeles Dodgers, managed by Norristown's Tom Lasorda. And a new group called the Flyers Wives was formed to raise money for the research and treatment of cancer, blood diseases, and later AIDS. By the end of the century the group had raised $11.65 million.

Another winner surfaced in 1978 when Philadelphia Textile went to the Final Four in soccer after going undefeated in 14 games during the regular season. Coached by former Ram All-American Barry Barto, Textile beat La Salle, Temple, and Brown in the playoffs before losing, 2–0, to Indiana in the semifinals and 6–2 to Clemson in the match for third place. Villanova hired Harry Perretta to coach its women's basketball team, and by the end of the century he had compiled a 380–221 record, making him by far the winningest women's cage coach in the area.

Yet another victorious team was West Chester's women's field hockey squad, which in 1978 claimed its fourth straight AIAW national championship. The team had won the 1975 and 1976 national titles under coach Vonnie Gros, who in 13 seasons had compiled a 100–6–17 record. The Golden Rams continued to dominate hockey when Robin Cash became coach in 1977. That year, with Jane Glass leading the team in scoring, West Chester posted a 20–0–1 record to win another national title. The Rams repeated in 1978 with a 20–1–2 mark as all-time leading West Chester scorer Gail Smith Rockey tallied a school record 62 points.

The Eagles also made 1978 a year to remember with the "Miracle of the Meadowlands." With 31 seconds left to play, the Eagles were out of timeouts and trailing the New York Giants, 17–12, when Giants quarterback Joe Pisarcik incredibly tried to make a handoff to fullback Larry Csonka. The ball was fumbled, and Eagles defensive back Herm Edwards caught it on a bounce and raced 26 yards for a touchdown that gave the Birds a most improbable 19–17 triumph. The Eagles, recording their first winning season since 1966, went on to make the playoffs for the first time since 1960, but they lost, 14–13, to the Atlanta Falcons in the wild card game after leading, 13–0. Tim Mazzetti, cut by the Eagles in training camp and a bartender in West Philadelphia for the first half of the season, kicked the winning PAT for the Falcons.

That year Wilbert Montgomery, in his first season as a starter, rushed for 1,220 yards to break Steve Van Buren's 29-year-old team record and become the first Eagle in 28 years to rush for more than 1,000 yards. Montgomery would become one of the great running backs in Eagles history, and the following year he stretched the record to 1,512 yards. In his eight years with the Eagles, the sixth-round draft choice

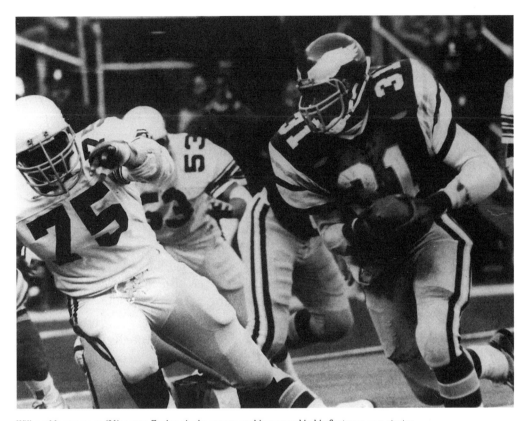

Wilbert Montgomery (31) set an Eagles single-season rushing record in his first year as a starter.

out of Abilene Christian would lead the team in rushing seven times while becoming the Birds' all-time leader in rushing yardage (6,538) and carries (1,465). When he retired after a 1985 season with the Detroit Lions, he was the 16th leading all-time rusher in the NFL.

In 1978 the 76ers, with former star Billy Cunningham now ensconced as head coach, finished first in the division again. But after sweeping the New York Knicks in the conference semifinals, they lost in six games to the Washington Bullets. After the season, the Sixers decided that Erving and McGinnis didn't work well enough together. McGinnis was traded to the Denver Nuggets for defensive wizard Bobby Jones in a move that turned out to be a stroke of genius for the Sixers. Jones would become a major force in future Sixers teams, and Erving as the undisputed leader would become the league's top player while guiding the team through the '80s and its finest era.

Philadelphia got another boxing champ when Mike Rossman ended Victor Galindez's 41-win streak with a 13th round TKO to win the WBA light-heavyweight title in a bout in New Orleans. Three months later, Rossman knocked out Aldo Traversaro in the sixth round at the Spectrum. He held the title for one year before finishing his career with a 44–7–3 record. A new character stepped onto the turf at the Vet in 1978. Dressed in a comical green costume, the Phillie Phanatic would become a fixture at Phillies games for the rest of the century, with Dave Raymond playing the role through 1993 and Tom Burgoyne taking over after that.

Another newcomer joined the Phillies in 1979. Signed as a free agent after Phils vice president Bill Giles convinced a local television station to help pay the $3.2 million, four-year contract, Pete Rose would prove his worth many times over in the years immediately ahead. Although the Phillies missed the playoffs that year, they had a memorable Shootout in Chicago when they won a 23–22 decision over the Cubs in a game that featured 49 hits and 11 home runs. The Phillies had blown a 21–9 lead before Schmidt ended it with his second homer of the day in the 10th inning. It was the highest-scoring one-run game of the 20th century.

Villanova track remained in high gear as Sydney Maree set an NCAA record in the 1,500 meters and all-time Wildcat marks in the 3,000 meters, the 5,000 meters, and the three mile. Over the next two years, he would also set new school marks in the 1,500 meters, the mile, and the 10,000 meters. Don Paige won the NCAA outdoor 800- and 1,500-meter races and over a three-year period between 1978 and 1980 would win the NCAA indoor title in the 1,000. Wildcat women won their first event, a 3,200-meter relay, at the Penn Relays. The same Penn Relays were memorable because of the brilliant performance of Maryland University's world class sprinter Renaldo Nehemiah, who anchored wins in the shuttle hurdles and the 4×200 and 4×400 relays.

Also in 1979 tennis player Barbara Jordan of King of Prussia, a three-time All-American at Stanford and runner-up in the NCAA tournament in 1979, came from the fifth seed and a 68th overall ranking to win the Australian Open. Her sister Kathy ranked fifth in the world. Whitemarsh Valley pro Sam Trahan set a PGA record (since tied) when he used just 18 putts in a round at the IVB Golf Classic. Penn four-time All-American Ed Edwards won the National Intercollegiate Squash Championship. Coach Don Casey's Temple team ran its two-year record in basketball to 49–9, but the Owls' football team was headed in the opposite direction. Over the next 20 years Temple, under five different head coaches, would manage just two winning seasons in what became an embarrassingly futile attempt to compete at a level far above its means. The Phillies fired laconic manager Danny Ozark and replaced him with the team's fiery minor league director Dallas Green. The Eagles finished the season with an 11–5 record, then beat the Chicago Bears, 27–17, in a wild card playoff as Jaworski threw three touchdown passes. In a lackluster perfor-

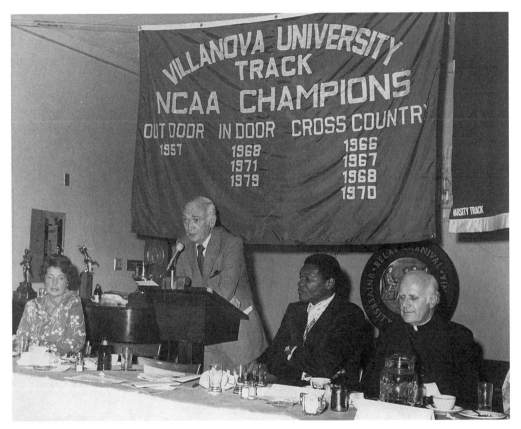

Jumbo Elliott (standing) continued to produce track and field and cross country champions at Villanova throughout the 1970s.

mance in their next playoff outing, however, the Eagles were upset by the Tampa Bay Bucs, 24–17. For the Eagles, as well as some of Philadelphia's other sports teams, better days were just around the corner.

Mike Schmidt, the Century's Greatest Slugger

There was no shortage of great power hitters in Philadelphia during the 20th century, but one stood out above the rest. Mike Schmidt was the best the city ever had at knocking a baseball out of the park.

During all or parts of 18 seasons with the Phillies, Schmidt clubbed 548 home runs. That not only ranks as the most any third baseman or any Philadelphia batter ever hit, but it's also the seventh-highest total in baseball history.

Schmidt led the National League in home runs seven times—in 1974, 1975, 1976, 1980, 1981, 1983, and 1986. Only Babe Ruth won more home run crowns (nine) than Schmidt. Eleven times during his career Schmidt laced 35 or more homers, a figure that ties with Hank Aaron and is one behind Ruth. Mike is one of just 11 players who hit four home runs in a single game. His 11th-inning four-bagger clinched the division title for the Phils in 1980, and his 48 homers that year are the most any Phillies player ever hit.

Mike Schmidt hit more home runs than any other third baseman in baseball history while winning seven outright home run crowns.

The native of Dayton, Ohio, was not just a power hitter. Nine times he drove in 100 or more runs in one season. He ranks 14th on the all-time list in walks and 19th in extra-base hits. And he won 10 Gold Gloves, recording a lifetime fielding percentage of .955.

For all his accomplishments, Schmidt ranks as Philadelphia's finest athlete during the decade of the 1970s. It was a decade packed with superstars, including Steve Carlton, Bobby Clarke, Bernie Parent, Julius Erving, Joe Frazier, and Wilbert Montgomery.

Schmidt had a lifetime batting average of .267 and a slugging percentage of .527. He was selected for 12 All-Star Games, of which he started eight. He was a three-time National League MVP (1980, 1981, 1986).

Mike was elected to the Baseball Hall of Fame in 1995, a fitting climax to a brilliant career. It was a career that had started slowly, but which picked up quickly.

Signed off the Ohio University campus by famed scout Tony Lucadello, Schmidt was a second-round draft choice of the Phillies in 1971. He was a second baseman during most of his one and one-half years in the minors, but by the time he arrived in Philadelphia in late 1972, he had been switched to third.

The young infielder struggled during his first full year in the majors, hitting just .196 and striking out 136 times in 367 at-bats. Strikeouts plagued Schmidt throughout his career, and his total of 1,883 ranks third on the all-time list. But when Mike won the home run crown with 36 swats in his sophomore season, he was on his way.

Although frequently booed in his early years by fans who had trouble dealing with his strikeouts and his seeming nonchalance, Schmidt's many banner seasons—during which he was the offensive leader as the Phillies won five division titles, two pennants, and one World Series eventually won people over to his side. He hit .381 to lead the Phils to victory in the 1980 World Series.

After hitting his 500th home run in a memorable game in 1987, Schmidt retired in 1989. A longtime resident of the Philadelphia area, he later moved to Florida to focus on a pro golf career, which he was still pursuing as the 21st century began.

1980s

What a Way to Start

There are times in sports when outcomes are predictable. And there are times when they are not. The 1980s began as a time when not even the wildest dreamer could have imagined what was about to take place in Philadelphia sports.

It was unpredictable. It was unprecedented. It was unbelievable. It was unquestionably the most amazing start of any decade in the 20th century, either in Philadelphia or any other place where people played games for fun or profit.

What made it that way were the performances in 1980 of the city's four major professional teams, the Phillies, Eagles, Flyers, and 76ers. All four won their division titles. All four won their league or conference crowns. And in a collective achievement that was truly astounding, all four played in their league's championship game or series. That never happened in any other city.

The first year of the ninth decade began with the Flyers advancing to the Stanley Cup final and the 76ers competing in the NBA final. Later the Phillies played in the World Series. And finally the Eagles made it to the Super Bowl.

All occurred within the space of less than one year. Ultimately, the Phillies became the lone winner when they defeated the Kansas City Royals in six games to win their only World Series in club history. But the mere fact that all four clubs reached the final rounds of their respective league playoffs gave the decade of the 1980s a start that almost defied description.

It was a start that set a high standard for the rest of the decade. While the rest of the 1980s didn't quite reach such lofty elevations, it was, nonetheless, a decade of considerable accomplishment.

The 76ers won an NBA championship in 1983 and went to the championship round one other time during the decade. The Phillies appeared in a second World Series. The Flyers played in two other Stanley Cup finals.

At the college level, Villanova won an NCAA basketball title. Glassboro won five straight men's outdoor track titles and a soccer crown, and Temple and Ursinus each won two women's lacrosse crowns. Widener in football, Villanova in women's cross-country, Swarthmore in tennis, La Salle in field hockey, and Penn in men's and women's fencing also won national championships. La Salle's basketball team played in the men's NIT final, and Cheyney's women hoopsters made it to the NCAA final. Penn had an undefeated football team, and Temple's men's basketball team briefly ranked number one in the nation.

As always, the area was richly endowed with extraordinary individual talent. Carl Lewis won six Olympic gold medals during the decade as well as the Sullivan Award. Michael Brooks and Lionel Simmons completed oustanding four-year careers at La Salle. Mike Rozier gave the area its second Heisman Trophy winner. Villanova's Vicki Huber and Sydney Maree reigned as two of the nation's top runners. Jay Sigel won two U.S. Amateur golf championships.

Philadelphia had a rash of boxing champions with Tim Witherspoon, Meldrick Taylor, Muhammad Qawi, Jeff Chandler, Charlie (Choo Choo) Brown, Gary Hinton, Buster Drayton, and Robert (Bam Bam) Hines all winning a version of some boxing title. Scott Hamilton moved to town to train for the Olympic gold medal he'd win in figure skating. And Marilyn Stephens at Temple and Shelly Pennefather at Villanova were without peer in women's basketball.

As in the previous decade, the great pros of the area were still performing their special feats. Julius Erving with the 76ers, Mike Schmidt and Steve Carlton with the Phillies, Bobby Clarke and Bernie Parent with the Flyers, and Wilbert Montgomery, Ron Jaworski, Harold Carmichael, and Bill Bergey with the Eagles continued to dominate the pro ranks with the help of others such as Pete Rose, Maurice Cheeks, Bobby Jones, Charles Barkley, Reggie White, and Randall Cunningham.

Many new developments occurred during the decade. The Bell Atlantic Classic became a stop on the senior PGA tour, and the McDonald's Kids Classic began as an LPGA tournament. After owning the team for 37 years, the Carpenter family sold the Phillies to a group headed by club vice president Bill Giles. Likewise, the Eagles were sold by Leonard Tose to Norman Braman, and Fitz Eugene Dixon, Jr., peddled the 76ers to Harold Katz. Garden State Park reopened after being closed for eight years. Philadelphia got a new indoor lacrosse team called the Wings and a new pro football team known as the Stars. Villanova dropped football, then reinstated it five years later.

The U.S. Open was played again at Merion. The Walker Cup came to Pine Valley. The men's NCAA basketball finals came back to Philadelphia. The Flyers went 35 straight games without a loss. The 76ers won 33 of their first 37 games one season. During the decade Jim (Jumbo) Elliott died, Dick Vermeil and Billy Cunningham resigned, and Dallas Green switched to the Chicago Cubs. Some exciting, not to mention colorful, new personalities such as Marty Stern, John Chaney, Speedy Morris, and Buddy Ryan took up some of the slack in the coaching ranks.

No decade, of course, is perfect. And the 1980s certainly weren't. Pro baseball and football had devastating strikes. The United States did not participate in the 1980 Olympics. Flyers goalie Pelle Lindbergh was killed in an auto accident. Some Phillies players were involved in a drug scandal. Guard Gary McLain also admitted he was involved with drugs during Villanova's NCAA title season. Temple forfeited six football victories after it found out that star running back Paul Palmer had signed a pro contract prematurely. The IVB Golf Classic folded. And Brandywine Raceway closed.

The decade ended quite differently from the way it started. No team was a candidate for a league championship. But how could the end of the decade possibly be expected to duplicate anything as improbable as the first year?

STANLEY CUP REVISITED

Vying for the Stanley Cup in the final round of the NHL playoffs is an experience that can never happen too often. The Flyers, though, were fortunate. In their first two decades, they got to that point more than most teams.

The Flyers had won the Stanley Cup twice during the 1970s, and reached the final one other time. In 1980 it was time to go back. It would be the first of three times during the decade that the Flyers reached the Stanley Cup final.

In the 1979–80 season the Flyers were in their first full year under Pat Quinn, who won the Adams coach of the year award. Although goalie Bernie Parent had been forced to retire the previous season after getting hit in the eye with a stick, the team still had Bobby Clarke, Rich MacLeish, Bill Barber, Andre DuPont, and Reggie Leach from the last Stanley Cup winner. Plus, they'd added some other fine players such as Brian Propp, Ken Linseman, Mel Bridgman, and Paul Holmgren.

Shortly after the season started, the Flyers beat the Toronto Maple Leafs, 4–2, at the Spectrum. The team would not lose another game until early January. In the interim the Flyers played 35 games, winning 25 and tying 10. It was the longest unbeaten streak in professional sports history.

The Flyers won the Patrick Division title with a 48–12–20 record, with Leach becoming the team's first player to score 50 goals in two straight seasons. In the play-offs the Flyers swept the Edmonton Oilers in three games in the opening round, then beat their old coach Fred Shero's New York Rangers and the Minnesota North Stars, both four out of five. Those triumphs put the Flyers in the Stanley Cup final, where they met the New York Islanders in a bruising six-game series.

The Flyers lost the first game, 4–3, in overtime, but came back to win the next one, 8–3. With Quinn switching back and forth between goalies Pete Peeters and Phil Myre, losses of 6–2 and 5–2 followed before the Flyers won again, 6–3. Game Six went to the Islanders, 5–4, on Bob Nystrom's goal in overtime, and the Flyers went home to lick their wounds.

But they'd be back. After making it past the first round of the playoffs only once in the next four seasons, the Flyers in 1984–85 with Mike Keenan in his first year as coach and winning the Adams Award as top skipper of the year, set a club record with 53 wins, which included a 13–2 victory over the Vancouver Canucks and an 11-game winning streak. Finishing with a 53–20–7 mark, the Flyers swept the Rangers in three games in the first round with Tim Kerr scoring four goals in the second period in the clinching 6–5 victory. They then downed the Islanders in five and topped the Quebec Nordiques, four games to two, with goalie Pelle Lindbergh, later named the Vezina Trophy winner, registering a 3–0 shutout in the deciding game. The Flyers got blown out in the Stanley Cup final, however, winning the first game but losing the next four as Edmonton and Wayne Gretzky captured their second straight championship.

The Flyers matched their previous victory record with a 53–23–4 mark the following year, but it was not accomplished without major heartbreak. Early in the season Lindbergh was leaving a party with some friends and teammates in the wee hours of the morning when he drove his Porsche at a speed estimated to be 120 miles an hour into a wall in Cherry Hill, New Jersey. He died later that morning of massive injuries.

Lindbergh's death cast a pall over the Flyers' season. But they set a team record with 14 straight wins, and with Kerr leading the way, they won the division title but lost in the first round of the playoffs. In 1987 the Flyers won their third straight division crown, with rookie goalie Ron Hextall making his debut and ultimately winning the Vezina Trophy, Kerr scoring 50 goals for the fourth straight season, and Mark Howe recording his 1,000th career point.

In the playoffs the Flyers beat the Rangers in six games and the Islanders in seven to win the Patrick Division. A four-games-to-two win over the Montreal Canadiens put them in the Stanley Cup final once again with Edmonton. This time the Flyers lost the first two games, split the next two, then won two to even the series at three wins apiece. J. J. Daigneault's goal with 5:32 left to play gave Philadelphia a 3–2 win in the crucial sixth game. In the seventh game a superior Oilers team led by Gretzky and Mark Messier gained a 3–1 victory and the coveted Cup.

Although they lost the Cup again, it had been a good run for the Flyers. Three Stanley Cup finals in one decade was a record most teams would envy.

PHILLIES ARE WORLD CHAMPS

Ninety-seven years after they entered the National League, the Phillies finally reached the promised land. Nothing in all the years of Philadelphia sports was more exciting.

It had been 30 long years since the Phillies last reached the World Series. When they finally got there again in 1980, it was the culmination of years of frustration and disappointment. It was the crowning achievement for this long-suffering ball club and its fans, as well as the highlight of the decade.

The Phils had been building for this moment throughout the 1970s. General manager Paul Owens had been carefully laying the groundwork, and when the club signed first baseman Pete Rose and traded for second baseman Manny Trillo in 1979, all the pieces were finally in place.

The Phils began the 1980 season slowly, then drifted in and out of first place through much of the first half. It was a solid club, which included future Hall of Famers Mike Schmidt and Steve Carlton, as well as Greg Luzinski, Garry Maddox, Bake McBride, Larry Bowa, and Bob Boone; a superb bench led by Del Unser, Greg Gross, and Lonnie Smith; pitchers Dick Ruthven and rookie Bob Walk; and an excellent bullpen led by Tug McGraw and Ron Reed. But it was hardly playing up to its potential.

In mid-August the team was six games back and seemed to be out of the race. But after stormy team meetings held by fiery manager Dallas Green and later Owens, the team began to respond. Coming down the stretch, the Phils had won 19 of 25 games entering a three-game series on the final weekend of the season against Montreal.

The Phillies won the first two games in Montreal to clinch the Eastern Division title with Schmidt's two-run, 11th inning home run providing the clincher, 6–4. That landed the Phils in the League Championship Series against the Houston Astros.

In one of the great LCSs of all time, the Phils got the jump as 24-game winner Carlton posted a 3–1 decision in the opener. A four-run 10th-inning rally handed Houston a 7–4 win in Game Two. Joe Morgan tripled and scored in the 11th to give the Astros a 1–0 win in the third game. Rose, a spark plug all season, belted Astro catcher Bruce Bochy with his forearm while scoring the winning run in the 10th in a 5–3 Phillies victory to even the series. Then in a heart-stopping fifth game, the fourth straight that went extra innings, the Phillies, trailing 5–2 in the eighth inning against Nolan Ryan, exploded for five runs to take a 7–5 lead. Houston came back with two runs in the bottom half before Maddox doubled home Unser in the 10th to whip the Phils to an 8–7 victory and a trip to the World Series.

In just their third trip in club history to the fall classic, the Phillies completed a memorable year by defeating the Kansas City Royals in six games for their first World Championship. Walk and McGraw combined to pitch the Phils to a 7–6 win

After 97 years, the Phillies finally won the World Series. Commissioner Bowie Kuhn presented the trophy to general manager Paul Owens (left), manager Dallas Green, and president Ruly Carpenter (right).

in the opener. Carlton followed with a 6–4 decision. Moving to Kansas City, the Phillies then lost two straight, 4–3 and 5–3. In the second of those losses, Phils reliever Dickie Noles knocked down Royals star hitter George Brett with a brush-back pitch, a play that many consider the turning point in the Series. The Royals were never the same after that. Schmidt's homer and two RBI and McGraw's winning relief helped the Phils to a 4–3 verdict in Game Five. Back at the Vet, the Phillies then scored the clincher with a 4–1 victory behind timely hitting and the pitching of Carlton and McGraw, who after Rose had caught a foul pop that jumped out of Boone's glove, struck out the Royals' Willie Wilson to end the game.

It was the greatest moment in Phillies and perhaps Philadelphia sports history. Police had taken the field with guard dogs to keep the fans in their seats, a move for which the city was later ridiculed. But that was the only damper on the night as hundreds of thousands of fans piled onto the streets of the city and suburbs to celebrate. The next day the city held a mammoth parade in which the Phils traveled from City Hall to JFK Stadium with three million fans lining the route.

Eagles' Only Super Bowl

There is no date more special in Eagles history than January 25, 1981. That was the day the Eagles played in their only Super Bowl.

There were 33 Super Bowls played in the 20th century. Although they had appeared in four NFL championship games before the Super Bowl began, neither before 1981 nor since then did the Eagles ever come close to making an appearance in the single biggest game in sports. But in the climax of Philadelphia's greatest year in sports, the Eagles met the Oakland Raiders at the Superdome in New Orleans at the end of a thrilling 1980 season.

It had been a long, hard climb back for the Birds. Between 1962 and 1977 they had achieved just one winning season (1966). But with Dick Vermeil taking the reigns in 1976, the Eagles had started to fly again, and after winning seasons in 1978 and 1979 the team was primed for a run at the title.

The team was packed with top players, led by running back Wilbert Montgomery, wide receiver Harold Carmichael, offensive tackles Stan Walters and Jerry Sisemore, and quarterback Ron Jaworski, along with a defense led by linebackers Bill Bergey, John Bunting, and Reggie Wilkes, ends Carl Hairston and Claude Humphrey, middle guard Charlie Johnson, and defensive backs Herman Edwards and Randy Logan.

Jaworski, one of the NFL's most durable quarterbacks, who once started 116 straight games, was a solid although not spectacular passer who had a knack for finding open receivers. In his 10 seasons with the Eagles, he would set seven club passing records, including ones for completions (2,088), touchdowns (175), and yards (26,963). Named the NFL Player of the Year in 1980 after leading the league in passing, he would spark the Eagles to the Super Bowl in the pinnacle of his fine career.

The Eagles began the season with a rush, easily winning their first three games, including a 42–7 whipping of Minnesota, their first win over the Vikings since 1962. A 24–14 loss to the St. Louis Cardinals ended the streak, but the Eagles got back on track with eight wins in a row, including a 17–10 victory over the Dallas Cowboys and a 10–7 decision over Oakland. The Eagles then lost three of their final four games to end the regular season with a 12–4 record and a first-place tie with the Cowboys in the NFC East Division. Based on a complex ruling, the Eagles were awarded the division title.

The Birds thrashed Minnesota, 31–16, taking advantage of eight Vikings turnovers to win the division playoff at Veterans Stadium. That win vaulted them into the conference championship at the Vet, where a fierce defense and Montgomery's 194 yards rushing led the Eagles to a 20–7 victory over the Cowboys.

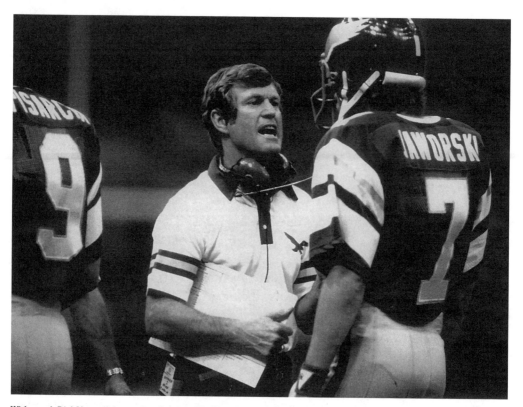

With coach Dick Vermeil (center) and quarterback Ron Jaworski leading the way, the Eagles visited the Super Bowl in 1980, but lost 27–10 to Oakland.

It was on to New Orleans, where the Eagles were favored to beat Oakland with its "bad guy" image. But it didn't happen. The Eagles played a flat and uninspired game. And with Raiders' quarterback Jim Plunkett riddling the Birds defense to become the game's MVP, Oakland, with a 27–10 victory, became the first wild card team to win a Super Bowl.

The loss proved to be a major disappointment for the Eagles. Equally disappointing, they would fall into another funk. After a 10–6 record and a wild card playoff loss to the New York Giants in 1981, they would not have another winning season until 1988. By then Vermeil had become the victim of his own workaholic habits and resigned, replaced first by Marion Campbell, then Buddy Ryan. The Eagles would go 10–6 in 1988 and 11–5 in 1989, but would lose wild card playoffs each time. Vermeil remained out of coaching until returning in 1997 with the St. Louis Rams with whom he would win that long-coveted Super Bowl in 2000.

PRO GOLF RETURNS TO LOCAL LINKS

When the popularity of golf climbed to unprecedented heights in the 1980s, it was only a matter of time before golf in the Philadelphia area joined the surge. Having long ago established itself as one of the nation's leading golf havens, the area was a natural for taking part in the upswing.

That fact was not lost on the powers who ran professional golf. Taking particular notice were two of the fastest-growing entities in pro golf, the Ladies Professional Golf Assocation (LPGA) and the Senior PGA Tour.

Pro golf was hardly new to the Philadelphia area. Numerous tournaments had been held over the years, including an LPGA event called the George Washington Classic, which ran for six years before closing in 1975. For 18 years the men's PGA had made a local stop each year at the variously named Whitemarsh/Philadelphia/IVB Golf Classic.

The IVB was held for the last time in 1980. Its closing—largely because the sponsoring bank withdrew its support and no new sponsor could be found—left a huge void in local golf. But the Philadelphia area had too many golf fans and was too steeped in golf tradition to remain idle for very long.

First to step into the void was the LPGA. There was a time when the women's golf tour generated little interest among the sport's fans, but that was no longer the case. Having heavily promoted and glamorized itself, the LPGA had become hugely popular. The time was ripe to bring it back to Philadelphia.

The first McDonald's Classic was held at White Manor Country Club near Malvern in 1981. Played from the outset as a tournament that benefited the Ronald McDonald House, the total purse in the original tournament was $150,000 with the winner getting $22,500.

Among an attractive field of top-level golfers, Canadian Sandra Post won the first tournament with a six-under 282 for a two-stroke lead over Amy Alcott. The following year the purse was raised to $250,000, the tournament name was changed to McDonald's Kids Classic, and Jo Anne Carner won with a four-round 276.

From there, the tournament got bigger and better. Beth Daniel beat Carner on the first hole of sudden death in 1983. In 1987 the event was moved to DuPont Country Club just outside of Wilmington where it has since remained. Big name winners included Daniel again; and Betsy King, Patty Sheehan, Laura Davies, and Julie Inkster each twice claimed tournament victories. By 1994 the total purse had exceeded $1 million. Eventually becoming one-fourth of the LPGA's Grand Slam, the tourney was still going strong entering the 21st century.

Meanwhile, the Senior PGA Tour had also carved a place for itself in the area. Originated in 1980, the Senior Tour made its first visit to the Philadelphia region in 1985 when it held what was called the United Hospitals Senior Championship at Chester Valley Country Club, with a total purse of $200,000, Don January won the $30,000 first-place prize in the inaugural event.

Each year the tournament got bigger and stronger. In 1989 its name was changed to Bell Atlantic Classic, and St. Christopher's Hospital for Children became the sole beneficiary. Eventually all the great senior players peformed in the tournament, including Arnold Palmer, Jack Nicklaus, Lee Trevino, and Gary Player. Trevino and Dale Douglas both won the tournament twice, with the latter defeating Player in a playoff in 1990 in one of the great finishes of the event.

The tournament was switched to White Manor in 1991, then moved back to Chester Valley where it was held through 1997. With a purse having reached $1.1 million, first place money worth $165,000, and crowds of up to 125,000 in attendance, it was then relocated to Hartefeld National near Kennett Square for a two-year stint before transferring out of the area to Princeton in 2000.

MOSES, DOC, AND A BIG BROOM

Over a six-year period between 1977 and 1982 the 76ers reached the NBA final three times. Each time, however, they lost in six games—in 1977 to the Portland Trailblazers, and in 1980 and 1982 to the Los Angeles Lakers.

There was a good reason for the losses. The Sixers had no big man in the middle to compete with the likes of Bill Walton and Kareem Abdul-Jabbar.

That problem was remedied in September of 1982 when the 76ers obtained

Moses Malone from the Houston Rockets. A free agent, Malone had signed an offer sheet with the 76ers. Houston matched it, then traded Malone to the Sixers for Caldwell Jones and a draft choice.

With Malone in the fold, the Sixers had the big center they sorely needed. Malone was a powerful 6-foot, 10-inch strongman, an outstanding rebounder and scorer who had a knack for controlling the boards like few others. With no college experience, he had joined the pro ranks at the age of 18, then gradually became one of the most dominant centers in the NBA.

Malone spent five years altogether in Philadelphia during a sparkling 20-year pro career, but the 1982–83 season was by far his finest. He had lots of help, though. First and foremost there was Julius Erving. Dr. J had become the premier NBA player and was without peer as both scorer and showman. The 76ers also had one of the great defensive players in NBA history, the always-hustling Bobby Jones. In the

The acquisition of center Moses Malone paved the way for a 76ers NBA championship in 1983.

backcourt they had high-scoring Andrew Toney and the clever playmaker Maurice Cheeks. Coached by ex-Sixers star Billy Cunningham, a future member of the Basketball Hall of Fame, who during his eight-year career would win more games (454) than any other 76ers mentor, it was a team marked for success right from the start.

The Sixers won 13 of their first 16 games and never looked back. After ending 1982 with a 24–5 record, they lost just one of 15 games during the entire month of January and only one of 12 in February. Despite losing five of their last 10 games and 10 of their final 26, they breezed home with a 65–17 record, the second-best mark in franchise history and a nine-game lead over the second-place Boston Celtics.

Malone was spectacular. He led the league in rebounds with 15.3 per game, was fifth in scoring with a 24.5 average, and was named the league's Most Valuable Player. Erving scored at a 22.4 clip, and Toney hit 19.7 points per game. Jones and Cheeks also had glittering seasons, while Marc Iavaroni and Clint Richardson played key roles, too.

"The difference was Moses," Cunningham said. "He gave us the consistency inside that we didn't have before."

As the playoffs got under way, Malone made no attempt to hide his views of the outcome. "Fo, Fo, Fo," he chanted, waving a big broom to help endorse his prediction of a clean sweep.

He was right on target in the first playoff series, as the Sixers, after drawing a first-round bye, made short order of the New York Knicks in four games in the Eastern Conference semifinals. In the conference final, the Sixers won the first three games, including a 111–109 overtime decision in the opener, but the Milwaukee Bucks slipped in a 100–94 triumph in Game Four to disrupt Malone's prediction. It mattered little as the Sixers captured the fifth and deciding game, 115–103.

Back in the championship match against the Lakers once again, the 76ers this time did not squander their opportunity. They knocked down the Lakers in four straight, winning by scores of 113–107, 103–93, 111–94, and 115–108. The last win came after the Sixers stormed back from 11 points down at the start of the fourth quarter. Malone, who had averaged 26 points during the playoffs, was named MVP of the final series.

As other recent Philadelphia champions had been, the Sixers were feted with a parade down Broad Street. It was a fitting conclusion to a glittering season.

THE WHEEZE KIDS TAKE OVER

Good things don't last long. The Phillies proved that adage in 1983 when they took the field with a team that was vastly different from the one that won the World Series in 1980.

Gone were many of the brightest stars from that championship club. In just three seasons, top players from that team had departed, including Greg Luzinski, Bob Boone, Manny Trillo, Larry Bowa, Bake McBride, and Dick Ruthven. Their places had been taken by an odd assortment of rookies, aging veterans, and players acquired in trades from other teams.

The Phils still had Mike Schmidt, Garry Maddox, Steve Carlton, Tug McGraw, and a few others. But in the years that followed the 1980 victory, they had added outfielders Gary Matthews, Joe Lefebvre, and Sixto Lezcano, shortstop Ivan DeJesus, catcher Bo Diaz, and pitchers such as John Denny and Al Holland in trades. Outfielder Von Hayes had come from Cleveland in a controversial five-for-one deal. And joining Pete Rose were two of his old teammates, Joe Morgan and Tony Perez, aging veterans from the days of Cincinnati's Big Red Machine.

The team was quickly dubbed the Wheeze Kids. No one took them seriously as pennant contenders, but by mid-July the Phillies were in first place, although they were not playing very well and were barely above .500 with a 43–42 record.

Then a funny thing happened. General manager Paul Owens, one person who did think the Phils were pennant contenders, fired manager Pat Corrales, relinquished his GM duties, and installed himself as manager. It may have been one of the few times a manager was fired when he had his team in first place.

Owens, never one to suffer fools—or inept performers—hounded the Phillies until, lo and behold, they caught fire in September. With Morgan's season-long quiet bat suddenly coming alive and rookie Len Matuszek getting numerous timely hits, the Phils won 11 in a row and 14 of their last 16 games. With three games left to play in the season, they clinched the division flag with a 13–6 victory over the Chicago Cubs at Wrigley Field.

Denny wound up the season with a 19–6 record and the National League's Cy Young Award. With 25 saves and eight wins, Holland was the league's top relief pitcher. No Phils hit over .300 except reserves Lefebvre and Greg Gross, but Schmidt led the NL with 40 home runs while driving in 109. And the Phils got sporadic help from youngsters Charlie Hudson and Kevin Gross as well as a late-season call-up, Juan Samuel.

The Phils met the Los Angeles Dodgers in the League Championship Series. Carlton, who had won 15 but lost 16 during the season, combined with McGraw to win the first game, 1–0. Denny lost the second game, 4–1, to Fernando Valenzuela, then Matthews took over the LCS. Gary, who had clubbed a solo homer in Game Two, homered again and drove in four runs to spark Hudson and the Phillies to a 7–2 victory in Game Three. In the fourth and final game, Matthews' three-run homer in the first inning led Carlton and the Phils to another 7–2 triumph and the National League pennant. For his .429 average, three homers, and eight RBI, Matthews was named the series MVP.

Nicknamed the Wheeze Kids because of veterans such as Pete Rose, Tony Perez, and Joe Morgan (from left), the Phillies won the National League pennant again in 1983.

Unfortunately, the Phils' hot hand cooled off in the World Series. Facing the Baltimore Orioles, the Phils won the first game behind Denny and home runs by Morgan and Maddox, 2–1. But then they lost four straight. Mike Boddicker beat Hudson, 4–1, in Game Two. Then Carlton lost, 3–2, with Jim Palmer getting the win in relief despite solo home runs by Matthews and Morgan. Denny was on the losing end of a 5–4 verdict in the fourth game. Finally, the Phils' fate was sealed in Game Five when Scott McGregor pitched a five-hit shutout while Eddie Murray laced a pair of home runs as the Orioles clinched the Series with a 5–0 victory.

The loss put the lid on what had been the Phillies finest period. Between 1975 and 1983, during the golden era of Phillies baseball, the team had won five division titles, two pennants, and one World Series.

KING CARL IS GOLDEN

Of all the many athletes who came out of the Philadelphia area to win Olympic medals, none did it so successfully or over so long a period as Carl Lewis. Put simply, the once shy, skinny kid from Willingboro, New Jersey, is the king of Olympic victories and competitive longevity.

Lewis won nine Olympic gold medals. No one else from the Philadelphia area ever came close to winning that many. In fact, in Olympic history, no one from anywhere ever won more gold medals. And only swimmer Mark Spitz, gymnast Larysa Latynina, and distance runner Paavo Nurmi won as many.

The remarkable record compiled by Lewis while competing in four different Olympics is a mark that even Carl might have had trouble envisioning had he not set his sights at an early age on making a strong mark in track and field. Lewis was

Carl Lewis came out of Willingboro, New Jersey, to win nine Olympic gold medals.

already performing on a local track club at the age of 10. By the time he was a senior in high school, he had set a national schoolboy long jump record with a leap of 26–8.

Lewis attended the University of Houston, and in 1981 he ranked first in the world in the 100 meters and the long jump. That year he won the Sullivan Award as the nation's top amateur athlete. Two years later he became the first person since 1886 to win three national championships when he captured the 100, 200, and long jump.

In the 1984 Olympics at Los Angeles, Lewis won four gold medals, a feat last accomplished in track and field in 1936 by his idol, Jesse Owens. He won the 100-meter race by eight feet, the largest margin in Olympic history, with a record time of 9.99 seconds. Then he took the long jump. Next, he won the 200 in then-record time of 19.80. Finally, he anchored the winning 4 × 100 relay team to victory.

The 6-foot, 2-inch speedster returned to the Olympics in 1988 in Seoul, Korea, and became the first person ever to successfully defend his titles in both the 100 and the long jump. He won the long jump just 55 minutes after running a preliminary race in the 200. He won the 100 after being beaten at the finish line by Canadian Ben Johnson, who was soon after disqualified for failing a drug test. Lewis's time of 9.92 was a world record. Carl also lost by just 0.04 second in the 200 final.

Lewis went unbeaten for 10 years in the long jump, winning 65 straight times before his streak was snapped in the 1991 World Championships in Tokyo despite the fact that he jumped 29 feet for the first time in his career. But in the same meet Carl set a world record in the 100 when he won in 9.86.

Two more gold medals were added to Lewis's trophy case in the 1992 Olympics in Barcelona. Carl won the long jump again and ran the anchor leg of the record-setting 4 × 100 relay team. Then in 1996, at the age of 35, he won another gold in the long jump in the Olympics in Atlanta.

No one had ever won the long jump in four straight Olympics. But then, no one was ever quite the track and field performer that Carl Lewis was.

REGGIE WHITE, THE MINISTER OF DEFENSE

Had he been anything other than a football player, Reggie White might have spent his Sundays delivering sermons. Instead, White, an ordained minister, could usually be found on the Sabbath delivering bone-crunching tackles to enemy ball arriers.

Battering opponents wasn't exactly a way to preach the Gospel. But White's ferocious play as a defensive end with the Eagles was not without a religious connotation. More than one opponent was known to have prayed for mercy.

With good reason, too. A gigantic 6-foot, 5-inch 300 pounder, White was as good

The Eagles never had a better defensive lineman than Reggie White.

as any defensive lineman ever to grace a football field. And for eight seasons he anchored an Eagles defense that was one of the best in the NFL.

An All-American at the University of Tennessee, White had spent his first year in pro football in 1984 with the Memphis Showboats of the United States Football League. Nine days before the start of the 1985 season, the Eagles purchased the rights to White, and a glittering career in Philadelphia was launched.

In his first season with the Eagles, the Chattanooga native was named National Football Conference Rookie of the Year. He was Most Valuable Player in the Pro Bowl in 1986, the first of seven straight years in which he was named to the all-NFL first team.

As the leader of a rugged band of Eagles defenders that for the most part included Jerome Brown, Clyde Simmons, Seth Joyner, Andre Waters, and Wes Hopkins, White was nicknamed the Minister of Defense. His specialty was sacks. In 1987 he led the league with 21 sacks, just one short of the NFL record. That year he also scored his first NFL touchdown, rumbling 70 yards after stealing the ball from Doug Williams of the Washington Redskins.

White was named NFL Defensive Player in 1987 and 1991, and NFL Defensive Lineman of the Year in 1990. In 1991 he anchored an Eagles defense that was first in the league in allowing the fewest yards rushing, passing, and overall.

In 1993, White signed with the Green Bay Packers as a free agent, ending what had been a superb career with the Eagles during which he gained recognition as the best interior lineman ever to play for the club. The Packers gave him $17 million over four years. The deal paid off when White helped Green Bay to victory in the Super Bowl in 1997.

Always outspoken, White became embroiled in controversy in 1998 when he made disparaging comments about gays and minorities. He retired in 1999, the all-time NFL leader in sacks with 192½, nearly 100 more than the total held by the previous record-holder, Lawrence Taylor. He was also the only NFL player ever to record double digits in sacks nine straight years.

VILLANOVA IS NEARLY PERFECT

At a press conference the day before Villanova met Georgetown in the 1985 NCAA final, Wildcats coach Rollie Massimino was asked what it would take for his team to beat the heavily favored Hoyas. "It would probably take a perfect game," Massimino said.

The Villanova coach wasn't just making idle conversation. He knew that in their first NCAA championship game, the Wildcats were going up against the best college team in the country. After all, Georgetown was the defending national champ, it had the best defense in the country—holding opponents to 39 percent shooting—and it fielded a team with three future pros, including Patrick Ewing, the best player in the nation.

Furthermore, the Wildcats had already lost twice during the season to Georgetown, 52–50 and 57–50. Villanova, seeded just eighth when the tournament began, had an unspectacular 19–10 record during the regular season, and most observers figured the Wildcats must have possessed an ample load of rabbits' feet just to reach the final.

Villanova was no stranger to NCAA playoffs. It had made the big dance every year since 1980. But it could never get to the Final Four during those years.

The 1984–85 Wildcats didn't even win the Big East title that season. But they gained a bid to the playoffs, and in their first three games barely survived. Villanova inched by Dayton, 51–49, Michigan, 59–55, and Maryland, 46–43, before sliding into the Final Four with a 56–44 win over North Carolina in the Southeast Regional final. The Wildcats then edged Memphis State, 52–45, in the semifinals at Rupp Arena in Lexington, Kentucky.

Villanova had a nice starting five consisting of Ed Pinckney, Harold Pressley, Harold Jensen, Dwayne McClain, and Gary McLain. But they appeared to be no match for the haughty Hoyas led by their exalted coach John Thompson.

Georgetown jumped out to an early lead, at one point going up 20–14. But Villanova fought back, and Pressley's follow-up shot sent them to a 29–28 advantage at halftime. The Wildcats held the lead until the Hoyas went ahead, 42–41, with 10:41 left in the game.

The lead then changed hands five times before Villanova pulled to a 53–48 edge. Georgetown regained the lead at 54–53, but Jensen's 16-foot shot with 2:36 left put the Wildcats back on top at 55–54.

Villanova never trailed again. Pinckney blocked a shot by David Wingate, then made two free throws to put the Wildcats up, 57–54. With 18 seconds to play, Villanova had a 65–60 lead. Although Georgetown closed with a rush, the Wildcats held on to win, 66–64.

The win was hailed as one of the greatest upsets in college basketball history. David had once again beaten Goliath. "Everyone wrote us off, didn't think we had a chance," said Massimino. "But I did, and so did they [his team]."

Ed Pinckney went over Patrick Ewing for a shot as Villanova defeated Georgetown to win the NCAA championship.

The Wildcats, as their coach had said they must, played nearly perfect basketball. Led by McClain's 17 points, 16 by Pinckney, and Jensen's 14, they sank 22-of-28 field goal shots for an incredible 78.6 percent. On the free-throw line, which really told the story, they hit 22-of-27 attempts, including 11-of-14 in the final two minutes. Villanova's defense was equally stellar, controlling the tempo of the game, forcing the Hoyas to a 29-for-53 shooting mark from the floor, and holding Ewing to 14 points, Wingate to 16, and Reggie Williams to 10.

It was, in Massimino's words—and there were no challenges to the statement—"the greatest moment in Villanova basketball history." It was one of the greatest in Philadelphia area history, too.

The only blemish on the Wildcats' season occurred several months later when in an article in *Sports Illustrated* guard Gary McLain detailed his extensive drug use.

A POTPOURRI OF SPORTS ACTIVITY

With each passing decade, sports in Philadelphia got bigger, better, and broader. The athletes were bigger and better that those of the previous decade. In many cases, so were the teams. But of all the improvements, none was more pronounced than the breadth of sports in the city.

In the decade of the 1980s, Philadelphia had something for everybody. It had pro teams in baseball, football, basketball, ice hockey, and lacrosse. The area had pro golf tournaments and major boxing matches. Horse racing was back. The Big Five was thriving. So were numerous other college sports, both men's and women's. Track was big. Women's basketball was growing by the year. Football was still strong in certain places. And soccer, field hockey, lacrosse, fencing, and a lot of other sports were playing an increasingly larger role on college campuses.

Philadelphia was a veritable potpourri of sports activity with more happening than ever before. If there wasn't a game going on in one place, there was surely one going on in another. It was a good time to be a sports fan.

Along with the main events of the decade, there were many other highlights. One was the performance of La Salle's field hockey team, which in 1980 won the AIAW national championship with a 3–2 victory over Southwest Missouri State in the final. La Salle, coached by Joan Broderick, who succeeded Kathy McNally that year, and led by All-American Kathy McGahey, finished with a 19–6 record after winning its last 12 games, including four playoff verdicts before the final. Glassboro State's outdoor track team won the Division III NCAA title after being runner-up the two previous years. The championship was the first of five straight for coach Oscar Moore's team. Another winner was Penn's undefeated women's crew team, which, led by

Hope Barnes, won the varsity eight national championship. Navy walloped Army, 33–6, in the first game of the series played at Veterans Stadium. And the Broad Street run was initiated. Still going strong at the end of the century, the 10-mile race grew to a point where it attracted nearly 8,000 runners from all over the world.

La Salle's Michael Brooks ended a marvelous four-year basketball career by being named a consensus All-American and the NCAA Player of the Year. Brooks, who led La Salle in scoring and rebounding in each of his four years there, finished as the college's all-time leading scorer with 2,628 points. A four-time All–Big Five selection, he was named captain of the 1980 U.S. Olympic basketball team. Penn's Julia Ann Staver was named captain of the Olympic field hockey team. And Philadelphia native Anita DeFrantz, at the time a Penn law school student, qualified for the women's crew team, thus becoming the first black Olympic rower. None would compete, however, as the United States, under orders from President Jimmy Carter, refused to participate in the summer games of the Olympics. In place of the Olympics, U.S. track and field performers participated in the Liberty Bell Classic that summer at Franklin Field.

The summer was also a time when a drug scandal involving the Phillies broke out. An unofficial team physician of the Reading Phillies was accused of supplying members of the parent club with illegal prescription drugs. All parties denied the charges until later that year when under the threat of perjury several players admitted they had been given amphetamines by the doctor and two others.

Also in 1980, the 76ers, after finishing second in their division, advanced to the NBA championship final before losing in six games to the Los Angeles Lakers. The Sixers took two straight in the first round from the Washington Bullets, then won four of five from both the Atlanta Hawks and Boston Celtics. After splitting the first four games with the Lakers, they lost two straight, bowing in the final, 123–107, as rookie Magic Johnson scored 42 points while Kareem Abdul-Jabbar was idled with an injury.

Kevin Lynam's field goal gave La Salle an 84–83 victory over Villanova in triple overtime in one of the great Big Five games in history. Meanwhile, 1980 was the first year of the women's Big Five. Villanova won the title with the Wildcats' Lisa Ortlip winning honors as the first MVP. In one other piece of news on the Villanova campus, the Wildcats canceled varsity football following the 1980 season after playing the sport since 1894. Wrapping up a four-year career with the Wildcats was tackle Howie Long, later a 13-year pro standout with the Raiders before becoming a prominent network football broadcaster.

Philadelphian Jeff Chandler became the first American-born bantamweight champion since 1950 when he won a 14th round TKO over WBA champ Julian Solis in Miami Beach. Chandler went on to defend his title in 1981 with a 15-round decision over Jorge Lujan at Franklin Plaza and a seventh-round knockout of Solis in Atlantic City. Later, he defeated fellow former Bok Tech student Johnny Carter on a six-round TKO at the Civic Center. Despite a later arrest for possession of marijuana and cocaine and a stab wound in the back from a street fight, Chandler went on to post a 33–2–2 career record, never losing a fight in nine title bouts. He held the crown until 1984 when he was stopped in the 15th round of his final fight by Richie Sandoval. He was inducted into the Boxing Hall of Fame in 2000.

In 1981 the U.S. Open returned to the Philadelphia area to be played for the fourth time at Merion East. George Burns had a three-stroke lead after the third round, but Australian David Graham shot a 67 in the final round for a seven-under 273 to win by three strokes. The NCAA men's basketball final was also held in the area, with MVP Isaiah Thomas leading Indiana to a 63–50 victory over North Carolina for the title at the Spectrum. Virginia topped LSU, 78–74, in the consolation round.

Glassboro, posting an overall record of 19–1–3, captured the NCAA Division III soccer title for coach Dan Gilmore with a 2–1 decision over Scranton in four overtimes with tourney MVP Scott Salisbury scoring both goals. Mike Mullan's Swarthmore tennis team tied for the NCAA Division III crown after a 9–9 deadlock with Claremont in the title match. Led by three-time saber All-American Paul Friedberg, Penn won the Division I NCAA fencing crown under coach Dave Micahnik, who in 25 years of coaching never had a team under .500 while posting a 213–63 overall men's record. Temple's field hockey team ranked second in the nation in the final ratings.

Philadelphia's pro teams fared poorly in postseason playoffs. After starting with a 33–4 record, the 76ers finished the season tied for first and with one of their best records (62–20). But after eliminating the Indiana Pacers in two games and the Milwaukee Bucks in seven, and leading the Boston Celtics three games to one in the Eastern Conference final, they lost three straight by a total of five points, including the clincher as Larry Bird's jumper in the final minute gave the Celtics a 91–90 victory. The Eagles came back from their Super Bowl appearance to finish at 10–6 during the season. But they were quickly eliminated in the playoffs after losing a wild card contest to the New York Giants, 27–21, with the help of two disastrous kickoff fumbles by Wally Henry.

Major league baseball players went on strike in 1981. When they came back 50 days later, the Phillies Pete Rose singled to break Stan Musial's record for most National League hits. Because of the strike, the season was divided into halves, and the Phillies were awarded the division's first-half title. In a special playoff, however, to determine the overall division winner, the Phillies lost a five-game series to the Montreal Expos with Steve Rogers pitching a six-hitter to beat Steve Carlton and the Phillies, 3–0, in the deciding game.

Both the 76ers and Phillies were sold in 1981. Weight-loss magnate Harold Katz bought the Sixers from Fitz Eugene Dixon, Jr., and a group headed by vice president Bill Giles purchased the Phillies from the Carpenter family. Dallas Green left the Phillies to become general manager of the Chicago Cubs. Once there, he enticed the Phils into making possibly their worst trade ever when he got them to give the Cubs slick-fielding shortstop Larry Bowa and a young player named Ryne Sandberg for journeyman shortstop Ivan DeJesus. Sandberg would go on to become a National League MVP and a certain Hall of Famer. Meanwhile, Neshaminy High School alumnus Len Barker of the Cleveland Indians hurled the major leagues' first perfect game in 13 years when he blanked the Toronto Blue Jays, 3–0, striking out 11 in the process.

In other events in 1981, St. Joseph's in a big upset defeated number-one-ranked DePaul, 49–48, on John Smith's layup at the buzzer in a second-round game of the NCAA playoffs. Coach Jimmy Lynam's Hawks then defeated Creighton, 59–57, and Boston College, 42–41, before losing, 78–46, to eventual champion Indiana in the regional final. Villanova's Sydney Maree set an NCAA record in the 5,000 meters and Don Paige established a world mark (which he broke the following year) in the 1,000 meters. A high school player named Linda Page from Dobbins Tech set an all-time record with 100 points in a women's basketball game in a 131–37 win over Mastbaum.

Widener won its second Division III NCAA football title in five years when it defeated Dayton, 17–10, on Tony Britton's fourth-quarter touchdown to finish the season with an undefeated 13–0 record for coach Bill Manlove, the winningest coach in the school's history. Manlove had a 182–53–1 mark over 23 seasons. Philadelphia Textile made the Final Four in Division II NCAA soccer before losing, 4–2, to Eastern Illinois (which later vacated the spot) in the consolation game. And local players dominated women's squash with Penn graduate Barbara Maltby winning her second straight national championship, after which she would also win five national doubles titles and one national mixed doubles crown, and Alicia McConnell of Penn winning national junior, intercollegiate, and national titles during a single month in 1982. The leading women's player of the '80s, she won seven national titles and three world doubles championships.

Only two schools were playing major college football in Philadelphia in 1982. Temple had slipped into a dreadful period in which after 1979 it would have five different coaches but only two winning seasons over the next 20 years. Penn, however, was having a resurgence and would win or tie for six Ivy League titles during the 1980s, including in 1986 its first undefeated, untied season (10–0) since 1904.

Another team that came up big was Cheyney's women's basketball team. Coached by Vivian Stringer, who had no paid assistants and no scholarships, the Lady Wolves

Sydney Maree set several world records during a splendid career at Villanova.

won 23 straight during the regular season in 1982. Advancing to the first NCAA women's basketball playoffs (and having to borrow money for travel expenses), Cheyney beat North Carolina State, 74–61, and Kansas State, 93–71, to reach the Final Four. Cheyney topped Maryland, 76–66, behind 20 points by two-time All-American Valerie Walker in the semifinals, but dropped a 76–62 decision to Louisiana Tech in the championship match. For Stringer, it would be the first of three Final Fours, including later ones with Iowa and Rutgers.

The 76ers were back in the playoffs in 1982, and this time they reached the championship series. After finishing second in their division, they swept the Atlanta Hawks in two games, beat Milwaukee in six, and after jumping out to a 3–1 lead, took four wins out of seven games with the Celtics in a series marked by the fierce rivalry of Julius Erving and Larry Bird. The final turned into a repeat of the '80s title match, however, as the Sixers lost four of six games to the Lakers, with none being very close.

The 1982 season also featured the first of two consecutive wins in the U.S. Amateur Golf Championship for Jay Sigel of Berwyn. Sigel, winner of the 1979 British Amateur, low amateur in the 1980 Masters, and a member of three Walker Cup teams, had become the best amateur player in the country. He would be heard from many times again. Meanwhile, Villanova's women's basketball team set a Big Five team record for most wins (29) while finishing third in the AIAW tournament with a 90–81 decision over Wayland Baptist. Penn's four-oared women's crew won the national AIAW championship. Dick Vermeil bowed out as Eagles coach after the Birds had the first of what would become six straight losing seasons. And Allen Lewis, who covered the Phillies for more than two decades during nearly 40 years with the *Philadelphia Inquirer,* became the first local writer inducted into the writers' wing of the Baseball Hall of Fame.

As the 1982–83 basketball season got under way, the Big Five had a new coach in its ranks. John Chaney, previously the long-time pilot at Cheyney State, became the head coach at Temple. By the end of the century Chaney would have a 380–160 record with the Owls and a 605–219 overall mark. The winningest coach in Temple and Big Five history, in his 27 seasons with the Owls he had guided them into 15 NCAA tournaments, reaching the Elite Eight four times, winning five regular-season and four tournament titles in the Atlantic 10, and winning or tying for 12 Big Five crowns.

In 1983, Camden native Mike Rozier, an All-American running back at the second-ranked University of Nebraska, became the second player from the Philadelphia area to win the Heisman Trophy. Rozier, who led the nation with 2,148 yards rushing and 29 touchdowns, also won the Maxwell Club Award and became the Cornhuskers' all-time rushing leader. Ex-Eagles quarterback Sonny Jurgensen was inducted into the Pro Football Hall of Fame. Villanova's Sydney Maree set a world record in the 1,500 meters, while Wildcat grad Eamonn Coughlan set an indoor world record in the mile with a time of 3:49.78. Temple began a run of 15 victories in 16 years in the Dad Vail Regatta under coach Gavin White, Jr., while participating seven times in the Henley Regatta. And in the biggest fight of his brief career, Joe Frazier's son Marvis was stopped in the first round by defending IBF heavyweight champ Larry Holmes.

A new pro football team called the Stars made its debut in the new United States Football League in 1983. Playing in the spring and summer at the Vet and coached by Jim Mora, the Stars featured running back Kelvin Bryant, who gained 4,055 yards rushing in three seasons, and quarterback Chuck Fusina. In their first season, they romped to a 15–3 overall record, beating the Chicago Blitz, 44–38, in overtime to reach the championship game, where they lost to the Michigan Panthers, 24–22. The Stars came back to win the title in 1984, defeating the Arizona Wranglers, 23–3, to end the season with a 16–2 record. In 1985 the league decided to switch the season to the fall. Although Stars' attendance had grown from 18,000 to 28,000 in their two years, team owner Myles Tanenbaum, realizing he couldn't compete with the Eagles, was forced to move the club to Baltimore, where there was then no pro football team. The Stars played games at the University of Maryland but practiced in Philadelphia. They won the USFL title again in 1985, but after the season the league folded, and so vanished a brief but bright franchise.

Another football franchise threatened departure in 1984 when Eagles owner Leonard Tose, deeply in debt, announced he was moving the team to the more lucrative environs of Phoenix, Arizona. Philadelphia Mayor Wilson Goode came to the rescue by inducing Tose to stay with the promise of a new practice facility, numerous improvements at Vet Stadium, and a plan to add revenue to the Eagles coffers. Four months later Tose sold the Eagles to Norman Braman for $65 million.

Former goalie Bernie Parent, forced to retire in 1979 after getting struck in the eye with a stick, became the first Flyer inducted into the Ice Hockey Hall of Fame in 1984. In 10 seasons with the Flyers, Parent recorded 50 shutouts, including ones in the deciding games in both Stanley Cup victories, while allowing an average of just 2.42 goals. In the Olympics, Philadelphia boxer Meldrick Taylor won a gold medal in the welterweight division. Scott Hamilton, who in 1978 had relocated to the area to train at Philadelphia Skating Club under Don Laws, won a gold in figure skating while also capturing his fourth straight U.S. men's championship. The Flyers' Bobby Clarke retired and was named general manager of the team. And Charlie (Choo Choo) Brown of Philadelphia won a 15-round decision over Melvin Paul to win the IBF lightweight title in Atlantic City.

Also in boxing, Philadelphian Tim Witherspoon, who began his pro career in 1979 and lost a heavyweight title fight in 15 rounds to Larry Holmes in 1983, won the vacant WBC crown in 1984 with a 12-round decision over Greg Page in a bout in Las Vegas. Six months earlier, Witherspoon had knocked out James Tillis in the first round to capture the vacant NABF heavyweight crown. Later in 1984 the man called Terrible Tim lost his WBC title to Pinklon Thomas on a 12-round decision before winning it back in 1986 with a 15-round decision over Tony Tubbs in Atlanta. After knocking out Frank Bruno in a title match in London, Witherspoon again lost the WBA title later in 1986 on a first-round TKO by James Smith. Witherspoon had won two NABF championship bouts in 1985 on a second-round kayo of James Broad and a 12-round decision over Smith. Witherspoon went on to fight until 1998, finishing his career with a 44–4 record.

It was a big year for Temple women in 1984. First team All-American basketball player Marilyn Stephens wound up a four-year career as the then–most prolific scorer in Owls history (men's and women's) with 2,194 points, while also setting a

When she graduated, Marilyn Stephens was Temple's all-time leading scorer.

Big Five record with 1,519 rebounds. Temple, coached by Tina Sloan Green, won the NCAA lacrosse championship with a 6–4 victory over Maryland. The Owls had lost in the finals in 1983, 10–7, to Delaware, and would fall again in 1987, 7–6, to Penn State.

Horse racing returned to Garden State Park in 1985, seven years after the track was destroyed by fire. A lavish $150 million showcase of the racing industry was opened with 27,053 in attendance. Bill Shoemaker rode Hail Bold King to victory in the feature race. Soon after, the great horse Spend a Buck, who in 1985 would run the third-fastest Kentucky Derby in history, won three big races at Garden State, including the Garden State Stakes, which he won by 9½ lengths, just two-fifths of a second off Secretariat's world record. Passing up the Preakness to run in the Jersey

Derby, Spend a Buck also won that race and the $2.6 million purse while going off at odds of 1–20.

Only a few days before Garden State reopened, Liberty Bell Park, which had been spiraling downward for a decade, closed permanently. That summer marked the return of the Walker Cup to Pine Valley after a 49-year absence. In one of the best Walker Cup matches in history, the United States, led by captain Jay Sigel and including Davis Love III and Scott Verplank, defeated Colin Montgomerie and Great Britain/Ireland, 13–11. In a far more one-sided contest, the Phillies slammed 27 hits, including two first-inning home runs (one a grand slam) by Von Hayes to trounce the New York Mets, 26–7, in a record-breaking slugfest. That was one of the last bright spots of the decade for the Phils, who failed to contend for the pennant after 1983.

A new cycling race, the U.S. Pro Championship, began in Philadelphia with riders competing over a 14.4-mile loop (plus starting and finishing straightaway) from Benjamin Franklin Parkway to Manayunk and back 10 times. A special feature of the 156-mile race is the half-mile climb up Levering Street, otherwise known as the Manayunk Wall, a wicked, 17-degree ascent. Olympic ice skating gold medalist Eric Heiden won the first race in 1985. World-class cyclist Lance Armstrong won in 1993. By the end of the century the race had become an enormously popular attraction, drawing thousands of spectators and some 140 men and 100 women from all over the world competing for a purse that had grown to more than $120,000.

Kathy Jordan of King of Prussia teamed with Elizabeth Smylie to win her second doubles championship at Wimbledon. One of the top woman tennis players in the country in the 1980s, Jordan had won the Wimbledon doubles crown with Anne Smith in 1980. An Upper Merion High School and Stanford graduate, Jordan ranked among the top 10 players in the nation every year from 1979 through 1987, reaching a high of fourth in 1984. Among numerous other victories, she also won the U.S. Open doubles crown with Smith in 1981, the Virginia Slims tourney with Smylie in 1990, and the Canadian, Australian, French, and Japan opens during the decade.

In 1985, after a strong lobby by students and alumni, Villanova resumed varsity football following a four-year hiatus. Andy Talley was named head coach. The Wildcats beat Iona, 27–7, in their first game. Meanwhile, the Eagles suffered one of the most humiliating losses in their history when they blew a 23–0 fourth-quarter lead and bowed to the Minnesota Vikings, 28–23. Senior Napoleon McCallum had another dazzling afternoon as he gained 217 yards on 41 carries to lead Navy to a 17–7 win over Army. Philadelphia's Muhammad Qawi won an 11th-round TKO over Piet Crous to grab the WBA cruiserweight title in Sun City, Africa. Swarthmore again won the men's NCAA Division III tennis championship with a 5–4 win over Kalamazoo. And at Temple offensive guard John Rienstra became the first Owl ever named to the Associated Press All-American first team in football.

Sisters Kathy (left) and Barbara Jordan of King of Prussia were two of the world's top-ranked tennis players, winning numerous major tournaments.

Penn regained some of the spotlight in 1986. Coach Ed Zubrow's football squad posted a 10–0 record for the Quakers' first undefeated, untied season since 1904. The women's fencing team captured the NCAA championship for coach Dave Micahnik, with Jane Hall being named first-team All-American in the foil. Led by its all-time career point leader Michael Anderson (2,208 points), Drexel sent its first basketball team to the NCAA playoffs, losing in the opening round to Louisville, 93–73. Ursinus, after losing in the final the year before, won the Division III women's lacrosse title with a 12–10 victory over the College of New Jersey. Coach Betsey Meng Ramsey's team would be runner-up again in 1987 before winning the crown once more in 1989 with an 8–6 decision over New Jersey. A $15 million, 6,500-seat basketball arena later named The Pavilion opened its doors at Villanova. Following a 10-year NBA career as a player, Wildcat alumnus Chris Ford was named coach of the Boston Celtics. Over the next decade he would coach several NBA teams. And at the world rowing championships in Nottingham, England, Penn AC's team of Ted

Swinford, Dan Lyons, John Riley, and Bob Espeset won the title in the straight four division.

In 1986, Philadelphia had two new boxing champions. Gary Hinton gained a 15-round decision over Reyes Cruz in Lucca, Italy, to win the IBF junior welterweight title. And Buster Drayton decisioned Carlos Santos in 15 rounds to capture the IBF junior middleweight crown at the Meadowlands. The 76ers parted company with Moses Malone, sending him in an ill-advised trade to the Washington Bullets for the oft-injured Jeff Ruland, who played just 18 games in two years for the Sixers. The Phillies released Steve Carlton. The Eagles hired Buddy Ryan as head coach. And the '86 record of Temple's football team was changed from 6–5 to 0–11 after it was learned in 1988 that star running back Paul Palmer had turned pro before the season. Although his '86 records were expunged, Palmer remained the Owls' all-time leading ground gainer with 3,029 yards in two seasons.

Football was affected by more bad news in 1987. That was the year amateur players were brought in to take the spots held by striking NFL players after the second game of the season. Against his wishes, Eagles coach Ryan halfheartedly fielded a team of replacement players that lost three games. One game drew just 4,074 fans, the smallest crowd in modern NFL history. The regular Eagles came back when the strike ended, and defensive end Reggie White wound up being named NFL defensive player of the year.

With Bill (Speedy) Morris, who would become La Salle's winningest coach with 215 victories by the end of the century, serving as the Explorers' new head basketball coach, the 1987 Explorers had their best postseason tournament since 1955 as they finished second in the NIT. After beating Villanova, Niagara, Illinois State, and Arkansas, La Salle, led by freshman Lionel Simmons, lost in the final, 84–80, to Southern Mississippi. Meanwhile, Temple set a school record with 32 wins, its first of two straight 32-win seasons. And in one of the great races of all time, teams from Georgetown, Villanova, and Mount St. Mary's all broke the world record in the distance medley relay at the Penn Relays, the Hoyas arriving first in 9:20.96.

At Villanova, Shelly Pennefather was completing a brilliant four-year basketball career in which the two-time All-American was named the nation's top woman player and for the third straight time was Big East and Big Five player of the year. She scored more points (2,408) than any other woman in Philadelphia history.

The Wildcats also featured a superb distance runner in Vicki Huber, who not only won three straight NCAA outdoor 3,000-meter championships starting in 1987, captured the 1989 NCAA cross-country title, and was twice named Most Valuable Woman Athlete at the Penn Relays, but also triumphed in numerous other 1,500-meter, mile, and two-mile races and in 1988 became the first woman from Villanova to appear in the Oympics.

Although Huber won no medals there, others from the Philadelphia area in addi-

Villanova's Shelly Pennefather scored more points than any other woman in Philadelphia basketball history.

tion to Carl Lewis did. David Berkoff of Huntington Valley ran a leg of the winning 400-meter medley relay team, and Penn grad Jonathan Fish took home a gold in rowing.

Flyers owner Ed Snider was elected to the Ice Hockey Hall of Fame. Lee Thomas was named general manager of the Phillies. And Cherry Hill High School's Orel Hershiser, pitching for the Los Angeles Dodgers, won the National League's Cy Young Award with a 23–8 record.

It was a good year for Temple. Led by All-American Kim Ciarroca (a future Owls coach) and all-time leading scorer Gail Cummings, Temple, while finishing the season with an undefeated 19–0 record, won its second NCAA women's lacrosse championship of the decade with a 15–7 victory over Penn State. During the 1987–88 season, the Owls men's basketball team became the only Philadelphia quintet ever to be ranked number one in the nation as it rolled up the best record (32–2) in Temple history despite losing in the Eastern Regional final to Duke, 63–53. John Chaney was named NCAA Coach of the Year. And the Owls' Jane Catanzaro was named All-American in field hockey, one of four straight years she would make that team.

The 1988 season was also the year of the infamous Fog Bowl. After registering

Gail Cummings (left) and Mandee Moore helped coach Tina Sloan Green's Temple team win its second NCAA lacrosse championship of the decade.

their first winning season in seven years, the Eagles gained a wild card spot in the NFL playoffs against the Chicago Bears at Soldier Field. Early in the game, however, dense fog rolling in off Lake Michigan began engulfing the field. With visibility eventually reduced to little more than the distance of a first down, the teams spent the last three quarters groping their way around before the Bears stumbled away with a 20–12 victory.

In boxing, Philadelphian Robert (Bam Bam) Hines won a 12-round decision over Matthew Hilton in Las Vegas to grab the International Boxing Federation (IBF) junior middleweight championship. A few months earlier, Meldrick Taylor made his 21st consecutive pro victory a good one when he knocked out Buddy McGirt in the 12th round to win the IBF junior welterweight crown. Taylor would successfully defend his crown twice more before losing it in 1990 to Julio Cesar Chavez in a hotly disputed TKO in which the referee stopped the fight with two seconds left in the 12th round. Taylor came back to win the WBA version of the welterweight title in

1991 with a 12-round decision over Aaron Davis. He held the crown through two more title bouts before losing it in 1992 to Crisanto Espana on an eight-round knockout. Taylor eventually fought until 1998, finishing with a 36–7–1 record.

Several long streaks began in 1989. Villanova launched a string of six straight women's NCAA cross-country championships, the first five under Marty Stern, who had taken over track and cross-country in 1984 and would add men's track and cross-country in 1990. Stern, a six-time NCAA coach of the year, guided those squads through 1994, leading them to five NCAA and 22 Big East team championships while producing 21 Penn Relays titles, 21 NCAA individual champions, nine Olympians, and 12 world record-holders. At Temple, the men's gymnastics team began a streak of nine consecutive Eastern Intercollegiate Gymnastics League (EIGL) titles with Fred Turoff as coach, and the women's basketball team collected a record 22 wins.

The men's U.S. Amateur golf championship returned to Merion in 1989 with 300-pound Clemson University student Chris Patton defeating Danny Green in the final, 3 and 1. Bill White, a Phillies first baseman in the 1960s and later a New York Yankees broadcaster, was named the first black president of the National League, a post he held for six years. The Flyers began a string of five straight seasons without making the NHL playoffs. In an incredible football game that went six overtimes, Villanova defeated Connecticut, 41–35. Local harness racing suffered a severe blow when Brandywine Raceway, where some of the world's top drivers and horses had performed for nearly four decades, shut its gates for the final time. The track, which had tried unsuccessfully to get permission to install slot machines, soon became a shopping center.

Randall Cunningham etched his name in Eagles history as he led the team in rushing for what would be the third of four straight years. No quarterback had led his team in rushing in the NFL since 1972. Cunningham, a scrambling, electrifying player, would also set a number of team passing records, including throwing for 447 yards (34-for-66) and five touchdowns in a 42–37 victory over the Washington Redskins. Rowdy Eagles fans would reach an all-time low in sportsmanship during the 1989 season when they pelted opposing players and coaches, officials, police, and other fans with snowballs during a 20–10 win over the Dallas Cowboys. The efforts of Cunningham and defensive ace Reggie White led the Eagles to another wild card spot in the playoffs. This time, playing on the last day of the decade and in the first playoff game at the Vet since 1981, the Birds dropped a 21–7 decision to the Los Angeles Rams, putting an end to a decade that had had a little bit of everything.

Julius Erving, the High-Flying Doctor

Before he came along, professional basketball had never had a player quite like Julius Erving. He soared higher, performed with more grace, was more acrobatic, and could do more different things with the ball than any player before him. Furthermore, he had more talent.

Dr. J, as he was often called, was the complete package. And during his 11 years in the NBA with the 76ers, he was not only the best player of his era, he was one of the best who ever launched a shot at a basket.

Erving was not a big man. He stood just 6 feet, 6½ inches tall. But he could outjump

Julius Erving propelled himself and the 76ers to new heights during a highly productive career in Philadelphia.

just about anybody. When he did, he soared well above the rim, often gliding seemingly measureless distances through the air to get to the hoop.

No player was ever more exciting to watch than Erving. And none was tougher to guard. He scored 18,364 points in the NBA. Add to those his five-year ABA total, and Erving accumulated 30,026 points during his career, only one of three players (the others are Kareem Abdul-Jabbar and Wilt Chamberlain) to score more than 30,000 in the 20th century.

A native of Long Island, Erving played in 11 NBA All-Star Games, twice being chosen MVP. He was a five-time All-NBA first-team selection, was the NBA's MVP in 1981, and was regularly among the league leaders in rebounds and blocked shots.

Philadelphia had no finer athlete in the 1980s than Erving, who gets the nod over teammate Moses Malone, the Eagles' Reggie White, Bill Bergey, Ron Jaworski, Wilbert Montgomery, and Harold Carmichael, runners Carl Lewis and Vicki Huber, Mike Schmidt, and boxer Matthew Saad Muhammad.

Erving played in college at the University of Massachusetts where he became one of only five players in NCAA history to average 20 points and 20 rebounds during his career. Leaving after his junior year, he joined the Virginia Squires of the ABA, then played with the New York Nets. During his five ABA years, he led the Nets to two championships, won two MVP awards, and tied for another, and captured three league scoring titles.

Clearly the star of the ABA, Erving joined the 76ers in 1976, with his new team forking over $6 million for his services in a complex transaction after the ABA folded and the Nets were one of four teams to join the NBA. Instantly, the 76ers became one of the NBA's top teams. During Erving's 11 years with the team, it never finished below second place during the regular season and went to the playoffs every year. Seven times the 76ers advanced to the Eastern Conference finals, and four times they made it to the championship round, winning the title in 1983.

Erving retired after the 1987 season, having averaged 22.0 points. He ranks as the club's third all-time leading scorer and the leader in blocked shots. In 1993 he was elected to the Basketball Hall of Fame. He was later named to the NBA's 50th anniversary all-time team.

CHAPTER 10

Individual Performances
Save the Decade

The final decade of the 20th century was not without some significance. But it could hardly be said that the century saved its best for last.

Compared to the noble and sometimes momentous accomplishments of most other decades, the 1990s were a study in mediocrity. The decade wallowed in the ordinary, for the most part avoiding the spectacular and in the end sending the century out like a lamb.

Among the shortcomings of the 1990s, none was more conspicuous than the lack of success of Philadelphia's four main professional teams. None won a championship. With the exception of the Phillies in the 1993 World Series and the Flyers in the 1997 Stanley Cup final, none even had a shot at a championship. The city's big four spent most of the decade stumbling somewhere between highly average and downright poor.

That is not to say the area was without winners. The Wings won four professional indoor lacrosse titles in the 1990s. The Phantoms won a Calder Cup in ice hockey. Villanova's basketball team claimed the NIT, and its women's cross-country team won five NCAA titles. And Rowan in soccer and basketball, Swarthmore in tennis, Temple in women's fencing, and Ursinus in women's lacrosse captured NCAA championships.

The Phantoms were among several new teams in the '90s. Philadelphia also gained the Kixx in pro indoor soccer, the Rage in women's pro basketball, and the Bulldogs in pro roller hockey. The last two didn't last long.

One of the true highlights of the 1990s was the Phillies'—and Philadelphia's—presence at the Baseball Hall of Fame inductions in Cooperstown, New York. Foremost among several ceremonies were the 1995 inductions of Richie Ashburn and Mike Schmidt. Inductions in 1994 of Steve Carlton, in 1996 of Jim Bunning, and in 1997 of Norristown's Tom Lasorda put the Philadelphia area in the spotlight four years in a row. In other halls of fame, coaching genius Jack Ramsay was inducted in basketball, Bill Barber, Keith Allen, and Gene Hart in ice hockey, and Jeff Chandler in boxing.

The 1990s also featured the special milestones of three events that had long held places of prominence in the city. The Army-Navy game, the Penn Relays, and the Devon Horse Show all celebrated 100th anniversaries.

The decade had perhaps more tragedy than any other period with the sudden deaths of Wilt Chamberlain, basketball star Hank Gathers, Eagles defensive end Jerome Brown, the Flyers' Dmitri Tertyshny, Ashburn, and Hart. Flyers coach Roger Neilson was diagnosed with cancer. Adding to the somber news was the collapse of a railing at the 1998 Army-Navy game in which nine students were injured.

Team sales were popular during the decade, with the Eagles, 76ers, and Flyers acquiring new ownership. Baseball had a devastating strike in 1994. Strikes or lockouts also caused shortened seasons in pro basketball and ice hockey. The Big Five canceled, then nine years later resumed its round-robin format. A glittering new arena opened in South Philadelphia, as did one at Temple. And football returned to La Salle after an absence of 55 years.

If there was one area that gave real substance to the decade and saved it from almost total anonymity, it was the considerable success of a number of individuals. The 1990s had a full share of noteworthy performers, many of them women. Tara Lipinsky won an Olympic gold medal in figure skating. Mary Ellen Clark reached a special plateau in diving. Dawn Staley in basketball, Lisa Raymond in tennis, and Carrie Tollefson in track also brought special honors to the area.

Among men, the '90s produced Curt Schilling, Darren Daulton, Lenny Dykstra, John Kruk, and Scott Rolen in baseball, Allen Iverson in basketball, and Eric Lindros and John LeClair in ice hockey. Jay Sigel continued his wondrous exploits in golf, as did Carl Lewis in track, Reggie White in football, and Charles Barkley in basketball. Jockey Tony Black won his 4,000th career race, and Lionel Simmons became the first local college player ever to score 3,000 points. The area had two more Heisman Trophy winners in Eddie George and Ron Dayne. David Reid won an Olympic gold medal in boxing, then captured the WBA superwelterweight title. Bernard Hopkins and Charles Brewer also won boxing crowns. Richard Hamilton led his team to the NCAA basketball crown. Leroy Burrell and Chip Jenkins in track, Ed Dougherty and Gordon Brewer in golf, and Duce Staley in football all inspired special headlines during the decade. And New York Rangers goalie Mike Richter from Flourtown, Phoenixville catcher Mike Piazza of the Los Angeles Dodgers, Detroit Tigers outfielder Bobby Higginson from Frankford, Kansas City Royals pitcher Mark Gubicza from Roxborough, and Lower Merion basketball player Kobe Bryant with the Los Angeles Lakers carried on the tradition of fine Philadelphia-area athletes.

It was a decade that gave us Larry Brown, Terry Francona, and Roger Neilson on the one hand, and far too many incompetents on the other. As the century ended, Philadelphia teams were floundering. And so were attempts to build new stadiums for the Phillies and Eagles. It had been that kind of a decade.

CHARLES BARKLEY DOMINATES THE COURT

There was never anything inconspicuous about Charles Barkley. When he was in a game, everybody knew it.

Barkley, or Sir Charles as he was sometimes called, was one of the most dominating players ever to wear the uniform of the 76ers. He wasn't particularly tall for a basketball player, and he certainly wasn't svelte. But the 6-foot, 6-inch, 250-pound bundle of energy could take over a game like few others.

Barkley came to the 76ers out of Auburn University as the fifth overall pick in the 1984 draft. By the time he left Philadelphia in 1992, he had become one of the 76ers' all-time greats. During his eight years with the Sixers, Barkley averaged 23.3 points and 11.6 rebounds per game, which placed him third on the team's all-time scoring list and first in rebounds. His 14,184 points as a 76er rank behind only Hal Greer and Julius Erving.

Charles also ranks in the top 10 with the Sixers in steals, assists, and scoring average. He was all-NBA first team five times, and played in six All-Star Games, including one in 1991 when he was named Most Valuable Player after his 17 points and 22 rebounds led the East to a 116–114 victory.

After the 1989–90 season, Barkley, who led the Sixers in rebounds seven straight years and the NBA in that category in 1986–87, was named Player of the Year by sev-

Charles Barkley gave the 76ers eight years of exciting play.

eral sports publications. He ranked second to Magic Johnson in the NBA's MVP voting. The following year he set a career high by averaging 27.6 points per game.

Never one to hide his views, Barkley was a controversial figure throughout his stay in Philadelphia. Charles's often colorful and sometimes outrageous statements frequently made newspaper headlines. So did some of his off-court exploits, including several well-documented barroom incidents.

The always quotable Barkley, a member of the winning U.S. Olympic basketball team in 1992, parted company with the 76ers after the 1991–92 season as a result of an ill-conceived trade with the Phoenix Suns. Having made it known that he wanted to leave Philadelphia, Barkley was swapped for Jeff Hornacek, Tim Perry, and Andrew Lang. Only Hornacek made any substantial contribution to the 76ers, and he was dealt away during his second year in Philadelphia.

Barkley went on to play eight more seasons with the Suns and Houston Rockets, but his career ended in 1999 after he tore up his knee during a game in Philadelphia. (He returned to play six minutes of the final game in 2000.)

In 1,073 games during his 16-year career, Barkley, the NBA's Most Valuable Player in 1993, scored 23,757 points to rank 13th on the league's all-time scoring list. His 12,546 rebounds and 4,215 assists make him only the second player in NBA history (the other is Wilt Chamberlain) to top 23,000 points, 12,000 rebounds, and 4,000 assists. Barkley, who added 1,648 career steals, was named one of the 50 greatest players in NBA history in 1996.

GYPSIES, TRAMPS, AND THIEVES

There was nothing ordinary about the team the Phillies put on the field for the 1993 season. It was a team that had no parallel in the club's long history.

Catcher and club leader Darren Daulton said the team "was a bunch of gypsies, tramps, and thieves." Others called the squad a throwback to another era. The team was alternately described as a band of rollicking crazies, a collection of blue-collar dirtballs, and assorted other names not fit for print.

Whatever the description, the '93 Phils were sometimes lovable, often irascible, occasionally disgusting, and always exciting. And led by a group of seedy veterans who sat together at one end of the clubhouse in an area dubbed Macho Row, they walked off with a National League pennant they weren't supposed to have.

Throughout most of the 1990s the Phillies weren't much. Both before and after 1993 they resided most of the time at the lower levels of the standings. But for one sparkling season everything went right.

With a club composed largely of players picked up in trades made by general manager Lee Thomas, the '93 Phillies became only the third team in the 20th century to leap from last place the year before to the pennant. No one expected them to do it. And only an abrupt end to the World Series brought about by Joe Carter's home run marred what was otherwise one of the best seasons the Phillies ever had.

The Phillies went into first place right at the outset, and except for one day, they remained there the entire season—a league record. Along the way there was one memorable game after another. In one of the most remarkable, the Phillies lost to the San Diego Padres, 5–2, in a game that after three rain delays ended at 1 A.M. Unfortunately, that was merely the first game of a doubleheader. The second game wasn't over until an unlikely single by Mitch Williams gave the Phils a 6–5 victory in 10 innings. The clock read 4:40 A.M., the latest time at which a major league game had ever been finished. Five nights later the Phillies beat the Los Angeles Dodgers in a 20-inning game, 7–6.

With Jim Fregosi practicing a hands-off style of managing, the Phillies had a new hero almost every day. Daulton, Lenny Dykstra, John Kruk, Dave Hollins, Mickey Morandini, Mariano Duncan, Jim Eisenreich, Wes Chamberlain, Kevin Stocker, Milt Thompson, and Pete Incaviglia all provided offensive heroics. On the mound the Phils had a solid starting rotation led by 16-game winners Curt Schilling and Tommy Green and including Terry Mulholland, Danny Jackson, and Ben Rivera. Williams was a highly effective reliever.

While drawing more than three million fans for the first time, the Phillies clinched the East Division title as Duncan's grand slam—the team's eighth of the year—fueled a 10–7 win over the Pittsburgh Pirates. The Phils' 97 wins, good for a three-game lead over the Montreal Expos, were the third-highest total in club history.

In the League Championship Series the Phillies were huge underdogs to the Atlanta Braves, a team that had won three straight division crowns and two National League pennants in a row. But in a thrilling series the Phillies won four of six games. They won Game One, 4–3, in 10 innings on Kim Batiste's RBI single, then got annihilated in the next two outings, 14–3 and 9–4. But they came back to win three straight with Jackson beating the Braves, 2–1, in the fourth game, Schilling's arm and Dykstra's homer gaining a 4–3 decision in 10 innings in Game Five, and Greene hurling the Phils to a 6–3 triumph in the clincher.

It was on to the World Series against the Toronto Blue Jays, and the excitement continued. Again the Phillies were big underdogs. The Blue Jays not only were the defending world champions, but also had played in five LCSs since 1985 and were the dominant team in the American League.

This time it wasn't to be for the Phillies. Toronto beat Schilling, 8–5, in the opener. Eisenreich's three-run homer sparked a 6–4 Phils win in Game Two before the Blue Jays pounded out a 10–3 verdict in the third game. Game Four was one of the most bizarre in World Series history with Toronto capturing a 15–14 victory in a 31-hit marathon that included two home runs by Dykstra. Schilling, who pitched masterfully throughout the postseason, came back to fire a gritty five-hit, 2–0 shutout in Game Five to keep the Phillies alive.

Then came the fatal sixth game. Dykstra's fourth home run of the Series helped the Phils rally to take a 6–5 lead in the seventh inning. The lead was still holding in the bottom of the ninth when Fregosi brought Williams in from the bullpen. The Wild Thing, as he was called, had saved a club-record 43 games for the Phils in 1993. But he was dead tired, and his arm was out of gas. Williams served up a three-run homer to Carter in the ninth inning that gave Toronto an 8–6 victory and the Series.

In the aftermath Fregosi was heavily criticized for bringing in Williams instead of a fresher reliever. Williams became such an anti-hero that he was traded during the winter. But except for that one dismal moment, it was a season when the Phillies had it all.

True to their personality, the Phillies had a raucous celebration after winning the 1993 National League pennant.

New Teams Deliver Titles

There has never been a shortage of new teams in Philadelphia, especially during the last three decades of the 20th century. Most, however, barely lingered long enough to taste the scrapple or visit the Liberty Bell. Here today, gone, if not today, surely tomorrow, was the modus operandi of most of the city's short-lived and now long-forgotten itinerants.

There have, however, been exceptions, rare instances when new teams came to town and actually stayed around. And in some cases they even did well, attracted a following, and became an important part of the local sports scene.

Such was the case with the Wings and Phantoms, two teams that stayed long enough to sample not only the scrapple, but the hoagies and soft pretzels as well, and that solidified their status with league championships.

The Wings are an indoor lacrosse team that plays in the National Lacrosse League (NLL). They've won five league titles since their arrival in 1987.

Lacrosse, of course, would not be found among the most popular sports in the Philadelphia area. In Baltimore, Long Island, and Canada it would be, but not Philadelphia, making the Wings' success all the more remarkable.

Consisting of players who have full-time jobs elsewhere, the Wings were original members of the new Major Indoor Lacrosse League (MILL) when it was formed in 1987. Playing at the Spectrum, they won their first championship in 1989, beating the New York Saints, 11–10.

The Wings, led by such standouts as Chris Bates, Paul Deniken, Dallas Eliuk, Kevin Finneran, Chris Flynn, Scott Gabrielsen, Gary Gait, Tom Marechek, John McEvoy, Adam Mueller, and John Tucker, won four more titles during the 1990s. They beat New England, 17–7, for the crown in 1990, thrashed Buffalo, 26–15, in 1994, edged Rochester in overtime, 15–14, in 1995, and defeated Baltimore, 17–12, in 1998, by which time the MILL had been absorbed by the NLL and the team was playing at the First Union Center. Three other times (1992, 1993, 1996) the Wings went to the championship game but lost.

The Phantoms arrived in Philadelphia in 1996 as a farm club of the Flyers and a member of the American Hockey League. Coached by former Flyer Bill Barber, they won their first game, beating the Springfield Falcons, 6–3. Before their first season was over, they had triumphed in 19 straight home games and won the league's regular season title. The Phantoms' 49 wins set a league record for most victories by a first-year franchise, and Peter White won the AHL scoring title with 105 points.

After beating the Baltimore Bandits in three straight in the first round of the Calder Cup playoffs, the Phantoms advanced to the final, where they lost in seven games to the Hershey Bears, including 3–2 in the third overtime in the sixth game and 3–2 again in the last game.

The Phantoms came back even stronger in 1997–98. With crowds who couldn't find tickets for Flyers games flocking to the Spectrum to watch them, the Phantoms drew 472,392 for the season, by far the largest attendance in the 62-year history of the AHL.

Again the Phantoms won the regular season title, only the second AHL franchise to win back-to-back crowns in its first two years of operation. With White again winning the scoring title, the Phantoms moved into the playoffs where they beat the Rochester Americans in three games with Jim Montgomery recording back-to-back hat tricks. The Phantoms then swept defending champion Hershey in four games

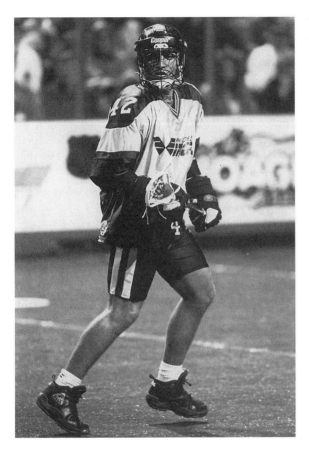

Tom Marechek was one of the Wings' top players as the team won four championships in the 1990s.

with goalie Neil Little posting a 3–0 shutout in the final. The winning streak stretched to nine straight playoff victories as the Phantoms downed the Albany River Rats, four games to two, in the Western Conference final. Then, in the championship series, the Phantoms behind playoff MVP Mike Maneluk wrapped up the Calder Cup in six games with the St. John Flames, winning the final, 2–0, before the largest crowd (17,380) ever to watch a Calder Cup playoff.

AN UNEXPECTED VICTORY FOR VILLANOVA

Every once in a while a team comes out of nowhere to do something totally unexpected. In 1994, Villanova became such a team when it won the National Invitational Tournament.

Big things had definitely not been expected of the Wildcats during the 1993–94 season. It would be a gross understatement to say the team was inexperienced. It had no seniors and only two juniors, with the rest of the squad evenly divided between eight sophomores and freshmen.

The Wildcats were coming off a horrendous 8–19 season the year before. In fact, Villanova hadn't really had a sterling season since it won the NCAA title in 1985. Most of the teams since then had featured mediocre records and uninspiring play.

The experts made dire predictions for the 1993–94 Wildcats. Last place in the Big East, they forecast. Another loser, they groaned.

Villanova was in its second year under coach Steve Lappas, who had taken over after Rollie Massimino moved to Nevada–Las Vegas. Lappas wasn't quite as pessimistic as the experts. He apparently knew something nobody else did.

The Wildcats proved Lappas right when they got off to a good start. They beat Georgetown, 76–75, in their second game of the season, then lost to Providence by one and to Temple by five. After their first 11 games, the Wildcats had won six. By the end of the season, Villanova had a 15–11 record, with a 10–8 mark in the Big East, good for fourth place.

Villanova was abruptly bounced from the Big East playoffs when it bowed to Providence, 77–66, in the first round. But the Wildcats got a bid to the NIT. In their first game they reached Villanova's highest point total since 1982 with a 103–79 whipping of Canisius. The Wildcats then blasted Duquesne in Pittsburgh, 82–66, as Eric Eberz scored a career-high 22. That win vaulted Villanova into the quarterfinals where it beat Xavier, 76–74, on Eberz's game-winning basket, 19 points by Kerry Kittles, and 17 points and 15 rebounds by Jason Lawson.

Next up was Siena. In front of a hostile crowd at Madison Square Garden, Villanova rode 21 points by Kittles and 17 by Alvin Williams to a 66–58 victory. All that was left was Vanderbilt in the final.

Vanderbilt jumped out to an early lead and was up by as much as 17 in the first half before taking a 41–26 cushion into intermission. While Vanderbilt could do no wrong, shooting 52 percent from the field, the Wildcats were stumbling all over themselves.

The story changed drastically in the second half. With Kittles scoring 11 points and Eberz eight, Villanova outscored the Commodores, 30–16, over a 12-minute segment to take a one-point lead with 8:22 remaining. The lead then seesawed back and forth. Kittles's three-pointer tied the score at 70–70 with 4:19 left. Then two steals by Williams led to four points, including a three-point goal by Jonathan Haynes. Villanova had a 74–70 lead, and from there coasted in with an 80–73 victory as Haynes finished with 19 points, Kittles 18, and Eberz 16.

It was a magnificent climax to an unexpected season for the Wildcats. In winning, Villanova became the 15th major college to win both the NIT and the NCAA.

Eric Eberz was one of the top scorers as Villanova captured the NIT.

Philadelphia Invades Cooperstown

Cooperstown, New York, was never more a part of Philadelphia than it was in the mid-1990s when a parade of Phillies were inducted into the Baseball Hall of Fame. It was as though a section of the city had moved to upstate New York.

Prior to the '90s, the Phillies were not heavily represented at the Hall of Fame. Only a handful of players who spent their best years with the Phillies had been were enshrined there.

But then Steve Carlton was inducted in 1994. Then Richie Ashburn and Mike Schmidt entered in 1995. And finally Jim Bunning joined in 1996. All entered the baseball shrine on days that ranked high on the list of special moments in Philadelphia sports.

None was more special than the Ashburn/Schmidt induction. For those in attendance, it was an occasion never to be forgotten.

The inductions of Mike Schmidt and Richie Ashburn into the Hall of Fame brought thousands of Phillies fans to Cooperstown.

Throughout the weekend, Phillies fans scurried to Cooperstown. The roads from Philadelphia were packed with carloads and busloads of people heading north. When they had all arrived, the tiny village of Cooperstown virtually burst at the seams with so many people.

On the day of the ceremony, a record crowd estimated to be as high as 28,000 flooded the Clark Sports Center. Most of them seemed to be wearing Phillies red. Phillies red erupted from the grounds virtually as far as the eye could see.

Ashburn, a .308 hitter with two National League batting titles to his credit during a 15-year big league career, had always been among the most popular players in Phillies history, and now Schmidt had become one also. Fans sat mesmerized in a boiling sun as first Ashburn, then Schmidt were inducted. "I'm so happy to be here, I just can't believe it," said Ashburn, who was elected by the Veterans Committee after many years of hard lobbying by his supporters.

Schmidt, baseball's seventh-leading all-time home run hitter with 548, was elected in his first year of eligibility by the Baseball Writers' Association of America. At the time he attracted the highest number of votes (444) in the history of the balloting.

The previous recordholder was Carlton, who entered the Hall of Fame one year earlier in his first time on the ballot. Baseball's second-winningest lefthanded pitcher had garnered 436 votes from the BBWAA.

Carlton's induction, while not as one-sidedly a Phillies affair, was a memorable occasion in its own right. One big reason was the ex-hurler's willingness to speak. He had shunned interviews since the mid-1970s and had made few public pronouncements since then. Some 20,000 attended the induction ceremony.

The induction of Bunning, also the work of the Veterans Committee, climaxed a glorious three-year run for the Phillies. Bunning, then a U.S. congressman from Kentucky, would soon become a U.S. senator. He posted a 224–186 record over slightly more than 16 years, with two no-hitters, including a perfect game.

As a final touch for Philadelphia's Hall of Fame run, the 1997 ceremony included the induction of former Los Angeles Dodgers manager Tom Lasorda. A one-time

Norristown native Tom Lasorda joined the Baseball Hall of Fame after a successful career as manager of the Los Angeles Dodgers.

Phillies minor league pitcher who led the Dodgers to two World Championships (1981, 1988) and four National League pennants during a 21-year managerial career in which he won 1,599 games, Lasorda seemingly attracted most of the residents of his native Norristown to the affair. Also inducted that day in yet another Philadelphia connection was the late Nellie Fox, an Athletics infielder in the 1940s.

ERIC LINDROS, ONE OF FLYERS' FINEST

When Eric Lindros won the Hart Memorial Trophy as the most valuable player in the National Hockey League in 1994–95, the award provided conclusive confirmation that sometimes it pays to stretch the levels of reality.

That, of course, is what the Flyers had done when they acquired Lindros in 1992. After the then-19-year-old phenom had turned down a $50 million offer from the Quebec Nordiques, making it clear that he would not play for them, the Flyers acquired the rights to Lindros in a deal that was unprecedented in professional sports. The deal cost the Flyers $15 million, six players, including Mike Ricci and all-star goalie Ron Hextall, a first-round 1993 draft choice, and draft picks from 1994.

That may be a fair price to pay if you're buying a country. But for a teenage hockey player, who although he was regarded as the finest young player in Canada, had no experience beyond the Ontario Hockey League, it was so high, it was almost beyond comprehension.

The Flyers, however—an organization that over the years had demonstrated superior intelligence—knew exactly what they were doing. And since then, their seemingly extravagant purchase proved more than justified, for it brought to Philadelphia a player who would become one of the finest the team ever had.

In a city that ranks its best professional athletes almost on a par with deity, Lindros became one of the all-time favorites. By the end of the century when he left the team after major disagreements with management, he had performed in seven seasons with the Flyers, and despite frequent injuries, trade rumors, and the ability to lead the team to the Stanley Cup final only once, Lindros was worth every penny it cost to get him.

The London, Ontario, native quickly established his value right at the start. In 1992–93, after scoring his first goal in his first game, he became one of the top rookies in the NHL. Two years later, at the age of 21, he was named captain, tied for the NHL lead in points with 70, and won the Hart Trophy, the second-youngest player ever to win it.

Lindros was a finalist for the Hart Trophy again in 1995–96, when his 115 points

By the end of the century Eric Lindros had become one of the top players in Flyers history.

were the fourth-highest total ever recorded by a Flyer. The following season, the 6-foot, 4-inch, 236 pounder led the Flyers to the Stanley Cup final, where they lost in four games to the Detroit Red Wings.

By the end of the century, despite missing numerous games because of injuries, especially in 1994–95, 1996–97, and 1997–98, Lindros had one of the five highest points-per-game career averages (1.408) in NHL history. He was the Flyers' sixth all-time leading scorer. In 1998, with a game-winning goal against the New York Rangers, he became the fifth-fastest player in the NHL to reach 500 points, trailing only Wayne Gretzky, Mario Lemieux, Peter Stastny, and Mike Bossy.

Lindros has recorded 11 hat tricks during his career. He has played in five All-Star Games. In 1997 he recorded a team-record six assists in one game. It has all added up to a splendid career for Lindros, one that was well worth the price to acquire him.

GOING, GOING, GOING, GONE

Hey buddy, you want to buy a team?

That probably wasn't quite the way it was put, but it was hard to avoid imagining some little character lurking in the shadows trying to peddle Philadelphia sports teams during the 1990s. It seemed like every time we turned around, another team was being sold.

These weren't your ordinary fire sales, either. No indeed. The amounts involved in the transactions stretched well into the multimillions. But, of course, this was the '90s, wasn't it—a time when every price tag in sports, no matter how inconsequential the item, contained at least six zeros.

The selling binge included exchange of ownership of the Eagles, the 76ers, the Flyers, and the Phantoms. And just for good measure, the city's two main indoor arenas were part of one of the deals. About the only major team that didn't go on the market was the Phillies, but they had their own version of a switch when president and CEO Bill Giles stepped aside in 1997 and handed the reigns to executive vice president Dave Montgomery.

As for the big ticket items for which someone new signed the checks, the first transaction occurred in 1994 when much-maligned Eagles owner Norman Braman sold the team to Jeffrey Lurie. The Eagles had been decent but not overwhelming for a number of years, but when they started to slip, Braman, who had often been criticized for the way he ran the team and who had become a highly unpopular figure in Philadelphia, figured it was a good time to get out.

He found in Lurie a man with a passion for football, and more importantly, a man with a lot of money. A native of Boston, Lurie had moved to Los Angeles, where in the mid-1980s he launched what became a highly successful movie production company. The fact that Lurie was also involved in several other lucrative businesses was a good thing when it came to buying the Eagles.

The price tag was $185 million, at the time the largest amount ever affixed to a professional sports team. Lurie opened his bank vault, and soon thereafter the Eagles had their third owner in less than 20 years.

That deal was simple compared to the decade's other major transaction. It involved seemingly everything that wasn't nailed down, and it took two years to complete.

The transaction actually had its roots early in the 1990s when Ed Snider and Harold Katz, owners of the Flyers and 76ers, respectively, began negotiating to build a new arena. By 1993 negotiations between Snider and Katz had broken down, and the 76ers owner threatened to move his team first to Trenton, then to Camden.

Finally, however, the two agreed on the deal, and in 1994 ground was broken for what would become a $217.3 million arena. Originally called Spectrum 2, its name was changed to the Core States Center when the bank agreed to kick in $40 million over a 29-year period.

But the wheels were already in motion for a far bigger deal. And in 1996 it was finally announced. At the time, it seemed almost too confusing to comprehend.

It went like this: Comcast Corporation, a locally based *Fortune* 500 conglomerate whose main business was cable television, bought the 76ers from Katz for $125 million. Snider sold 66 percent of the Flyers, their new minor club the Phantoms, the Spectrum, and the Core States Center to Comcast for $250 million. Comcast then put all its new holdings under one company called Comcast-Spectacor, with Snider becoming chairman of the board. Pat Croce, a widely known physical therapist, was named president of the 76ers, and Hall of Fame player and general manager Bob Clarke was appointed president of the Flyers. Comcast also became the marketing arm of the Wings.

As a final piece of the puzzle, Comcast and the Phillies entered into a partnership to create an all-sports television station known as Comcast SportsNet. The new arena opened in 1996. Later, when Core States bank was taken over, the name of the building was changed to First Union Center to match the name of the Charlotte, North Carolina-based sponsoring company.

100TH ANNIVERSARIES

As a place where history flourishes, Philadelphia has always been noted for the longevity of its institutions. No matter what the institution, if it's old, it must belong to Philadelphia.

Longevity is as closely associated with the world of sports as it is with anything else in the city. After all, Philadelphia is a city where people were rowing competitively on the Schuylkill River as early as 1732. Later, the city's competitive juices really heated up when the British came to town in the 1770s.

More than 200 years later Philadelphians were still engaged in combat, albeit a much more gentle form than their Revolutionary War forefathers. And in the 1990s several noteworthy events passed special milestones.

In 1994 the Penn Relays celebrated its 100th anniversary. Originally the idea of Penn track and field coach Franklin Ellis and held as a way to help dedicate the newly built Franklin Field, the meet had begun with nine mile-relay events, four for high schools, four for colleges, and one as a college championship. Over the years, events as well as contestants were added, and the physical surroundings were changed.

Most of the premier track and field performers of the 20th century participated in the Penn Relays. Jim Thorpe, John Woodruff, Jesse Owens, Glenn Cunningham,

Paavo Nurmi, and Roger Bannister were just a few of the many great athletes who entered.

Eventually, the Penn Relays became the longest uninterrupted collegiate meet in the country. By its 100th anniversary, it was attracting more than 20,000 competitors, ages eight to 80, including athletes from 250 colleges and 800 high schools. They performed in some 350 events, with crowds reaching as high as 90,000 for the three-day meet.

Another 100th anniversary was reached by a Philadelphia institution in 1995 at the Devon Horse Show and Country Fair. Started on the old Devon Race Track and Polo Grounds on Lancaster Avenue, it was intended to encourage the breeding of more and better horses. The show was at first a one-day affair with top prize money of $5–10 per event.

Now it is the oldest and largest outdoor, multibreed competition in the nation. Lasting 10 days, it has a paid attendance of more than 100,000. Total prize money in 1999 was $268,820 with 1,750 horses competing in 233 different events. Devon has raised $9.9 million for Bryn Mawr Hospital since it became the beneficiary in 1919.

When the Army-Navy game was played in 1999, it was the 100th year of that game.

The Devon Horse Show has been a popular institution for more than 100 years.

Seventy-five of those games have been played in Philadelphia, including 50 of the last 54. The only games not played in Philadelphia since 1945 were in 1983 (Pasadena, California) and 1989, 1993, and 1997 (the Meadowlands in East Rutherford, New Jersey).

The first game played in Philadelphia was in 1899 at Franklin Field. Later, it was switched to Municipal (JFK) Stadium where crowds of more than 100,000 watched, and finally to Veterans Stadium. Over the years, the game has featured some sensational battles as well as some lopsided affairs. Great players have participated in the skirmishes. Presidents have often attended, and the game has annually attracted nationwide attention.

JUST FOR THE RECORD

Who were the best and worst of Philadelphia's major league teams during the 20th century?

Of those who played more than a couple of seasons, the undisputed winner is the Frankford Yellowjackets. Among Philadelphia's current four teams, the 76ers are far out in front with the Eagles bringing up the rear.

Temple's basketball team has the best record in the Big Five. Among other top records are Philadelphia Textile (now Philadelphia University) in basketball, and West Chester, Widener, and Penn in football. Here's how they look (post-season games included):

MAJOR LEAGUE TEAMS

		Wins	Losses	Ties	Percentage
Yellowjackets	1924–31	69	45	14	.605
76ers	1963–99	1,668	1,484	—	.529
Warriors	1946–62	593	587	—	.503
Athletics	1901–54	3,865	4,190	86	.480
Phillies	1900–99	7,077	8,380	77	.458
Eagles	1933–99	404	490	25	.452

BIG FIVE BASKETBALL

		Wins	Losses	Ties	Percentage
Temple	1900–99	1,447	792	—	.646
Penn	1900–99	1,471	823	—	.641
Villanova	1920–99	1,291	733	—	.638
La Salle	1931–99	1,092	652	—	.626
St. Joseph's	1909–99	1,272	855	—	.596

John Chaney helped Temple post the best record of Big Five basketball teams in the 20th century.

OTHER LONG-TERM TEAMS

		Wins	Losses	Ties	Percentage
Textile basketball	1920–99	1,038	448	—	.699
West Chester football	1920–99	488	214	18	.695
Widener football*	1900–99	507	322	32	.612
Penn football	1900–99	547	367	38	.598
Temple baseball	1926–99	1,175	858	28	.578
Villanova football	1900–99†	457	380	38	.546
Drexel basketball	1900–99	978	834	—	.540
Penn baseball	1900–99	1,332	1,148	35	.537
La Salle baseball	1947–99	714	752	10	.487
Swarthmore football	1900–99	364	408	32	.472
Temple football	1900–99	366	425	51	.463
Ursinus football	1900–99	307	487	46	.387

*originally Pennsylvania Military College
†no team from 1981–1984

The Century Comes to an End

Sports, like every other element of society, are never stationary. Players come and go, teams shift from city to city, rules change, tactics vary, equipment is altered. From year to year, from decade to decade, there are always differences.

Imagine, then, the differences that come to pass over an entire century. As the 20th century came to an end, the contrast between sports in Philadelphia at the beginning and at the end of the century was nothing short of staggering.

In 1900 the city had one professional team—the Phillies. There were no Eagles, no 76ers, no Flyers. Baseball, boxing, tennis, golf, and rowing were the main sports. A number of colleges played football, baseball, basketball, and a few other sports, but there were no big athletic budgets, no scholarships, no women's teams, no glittering arenas and stadiums.

There were no high-salaried players. There were no such people as trainers, or assistant coaches, or equipment managers, or even general managers. Baseball players used large-handled bats and tried to hit singles. Football players wore no helmets and never heard of a forward pass. Basketball was played in cages. Golfers used clubs with names like brassie, mashie, and spoon. And nobody even dreamed there would someday be an aberration known as pro wrestling.

It was a different world, to be sure. And now as a new century gets under way, one can't begin to speculate on the changes that lie ahead. The only certainty is that there will be changes.

The 1990s paved the way for some of these changes while closing a century of magnificent achievements. In Philadelphia it was a decade when rare was the night (or day) when there was no sporting event going on. In some section of the city or surrounding area, a stadium was open, a gym was lit, or a field was in use. Somewhere, there was always a game.

Some of the major stories of the decade took place right at the outset. In 1990 one of the biggest stories involved La Salle. The Explorers had their winningest season when they posted a 30–2 record under Speedy Morris. La Salle was led by Lionel Simmons, who was completing a brilliant four-year college career in which he became only the third player in NCAA history to score more than 3,000 points. While being named first-team All-American and NCAA Player of the Year, Simmons, a three-time Big Five Player of the Year, finished his career with 3,217 points and 1,429 rebounds. He went on to perform seven solid seasons in the NBA with the Sacramento Kings before his career was cut short by a knee injury.

Before losing in the NCAA regionals to Clemson, 79–75, La Salle's only other loss was in a 121–116 barn burner to Loyola Marymount, coached by former Explorers

Lionel Simmons of La Salle was just the third player in NCAA history to score more than 3,000 points.

mentor Paul Westhead. On that California team were two Philadelphians from Dobbins Tech, Hank Gathers and Bo Kimble. Gathers had led the nation in scoring (32.7 average) and in rebounding (13.7) in 1988–89—one of only two players ever to lead in both categories—and Kimble would be the country's scoring champion (35.3 average) in 1989–90 while leading his team to the Elite Eight in the NCAA tournament. Just two months after the La Salle game, Gathers' life came to a tragic end when he collapsed shortly after scoring a basket during a tournament game at Loyola and died a few minutes later. Gathers' death was attributed to a heart disorder called cardiomyopathy, an infectious condition that caused an irregular heartbeat. The 6-foot, 7-inch basketball star had previously been treated for a heart problem, but his death led to several lawsuits, which eventually resulted in a $1.5 million settlement to his family.

The Philadelphia area produced four NCAA champions in 1990. Villanova continued its string of six straight women's cross-country victories, while Sonia O'Sullivan won her first of two individual titles for coach Marty Stern's team. Ursinus, coached by Kim Ciarrocca Lambdin, defeated St. Lawrence, 7–6, to win the Division III women's lacrosse title. Ursinus would lose by the same score to the College of New Jersey in the title match the following year. Coach Mike Mullan's Swarthmore tennis team also won a Division III crown with a 5–1 victory over UC Santa Clara. Glassboro State, which would become Rowan University in 1992, captured the Division III soccer championship with a 2–1 victory over Ohio Wesleyan, with the game-winning goal coming on a penalty-kick shootout after an overtime and two sudden-death periods. All-American Andy Logar had scored the winner's first goal in what was the 11th trip to the NCAA soccer playoffs and the 20th win of the season for coach Dan Gilmore's Glassboro team.

With Charles Barkley having become one of the premier players in the NBA, the 76ers finished the 1989–90 season in first place in the Eastern Conference. During the season, a fight involving Barkley, Bill Laimbeer of the Detroit Pistons, and others had resulted in $162,500 in fines, a record for professional sports. After beating the Cleveland Cavaliers, three games to two, in the first round of the playoffs, the Sixers lost in the Conference semifinals in five games to the Chicago Bulls. Dale Hodges closed out a fine career at St. Joseph's with a school record 2,077 points in women's basketball as coach Jim Foster's Hawks reeled off their sixth straight 20-plus-win season. Terry Mulholland pitched the first Phillies home no-hitter in the 20th century. And, despite his third straight winning season, feisty coach Buddy Ryan (43–35–1 record in five years) was fired after the Eagles lost a wild card playoff game, 20–6, to the Washington Redskins.

The Flyers began a streak of five straight years without making the NHL playoffs, and Bob Clarke was fired as general manager, marking the end of a 21-year association with the team. On the bright side, Bill Barber, who epitomized perfection and during a 12-year career was one of the most reliable players the Flyers ever had, was voted into the Hockey Hall of Fame. At the time Barber ranked 17th on the all-time NHL scoring list.

Big-time tennis returned to Philadelphia in 1991 when the Advanta Championship resumed after a 14-year hiatus. Monica Seles won the first championship held at the Civic Center. Later the tournament would be relocated to the Spectrum, and in 1996 it would move to The Pavilion at Villanova. During the 1990s the tournament attracted the world's top women players, one of whom, Steffi Graf, was a two-time winner.

Phillies fortunes suffered a heavy blow early in the 1991 season. Lenny Dykstra (having one year earlier been admonished by the baseball commissioner for running up big gambling debts) and Darren Daulton, returning home from a bachelor party for John Kruk, were seriously injured in Newtown Square when Dykstra's new luxury car spun and hit two trees. Dykstra, who was later charged with drunk driving, suffered numerous injuries, including a broken collarbone (which he rebroke later in the season). Both he and the less seriously injured Daulton missed a considerable amount of playing time.

Also in 1991, Mark Macon became Temple's all-time leading scorer in basketball when he finished a brilliant four-year career with 2,609 points. The Owls went as far as the NCAA regional final before losing to North Carolina, 75–72. The Eagles, featuring the Gang Green defense led by linemen Reggie White, Clyde Simmons, and Jerome Brown, linebacker Seth Joyner, and cornerback Eric Allen—all members of the Pro Bowl squad at the end of the season—gave up the fewest yards rushing, passing, and overall, only the fifth time an NFL team had led the league in all three categories. Pat Kennedy broke a 41-year-old Villanova rushing record when he collected 249 yards on 21 carries in a 35–21 win over William and Mary. The 76ers, with Barkley finishing fourth in the NBA in scoring, entered their last playoffs until the end of the decade when they swept the Milwaukee Bucks in three games, then lost four games to one to Michael Jordan's Chicago Bulls in the Eastern Conference semifinals

Lansdowne native Leroy Burrell, running for Houston University, set a world record in the 100 with a time of 9.90. Burrell would break that mark in 1994 when he was clocked in 9.85. A member of four world-record-breaking 4 × 100-meter relay teams, he would also win a gold medal in the 1992 Olympics when he (as well as Carl Lewis) ran on the winning and world-record-setting 4 × 100-meter relay team. After a career running professionally in Europe, Burrell became head track coach at Houston in 1999. Another gold medal winner at the Olympics in Barcelona was Villanova's Chip Jenkins, a member of the 4 × 400-meter relay team. Jenkins' father Charlie had won two golds for Villanova in the 1956 Olympics.

The Big Five reached a low point during the 1991–92 season. That's when participating university presidents and athletic directors, prodded by the reluctance of Villanova and Temple to participate fully, decided to eliminate the round-robin format that had been a staple of the Big Five since its inception. The decision effectively killed the Big Five, as over the next eight seasons teams would play just two games against each other.

That wasn't the only blow to local sports as tragedy again entered the picture. In another auto accident, Eagles All-NFL defensive end Jerome Brown was killed in a one-vehicle crash in his hometown of Brooksville, Florida. Brown, a popular team leader, died after his speeding car went out of control and crashed just minutes after he had gotten into it. It was a devastating loss to the Eagles, although they won their first playoff game since 1980—a 36–20 wild card decision over the New Orleans Saints—before bowing to the Dallas Cowboys, 34–10, in the divisional playoffs.

In 1992, Upper Darby native Jack Ramsay was elected to the Basketball Hall of

Fame. Ramsay, who spent 20 seasons coaching in the NBA after 11 years at St. Joseph's, ranked sixth on the all-time NBA list with 864 career wins. Named one of the 10 greatest NBA coaches of all time, he won a championship in 1977 with the Portland Trailblazers and also piloted the 76ers, the Buffalo Braves, and the Indiana Pacers before retiring in 1989 to become a broadcaster.

Another Hall of Fame inductee was former Flyers coach and general manager Keith Allen. The team's first coach, Allen piloted the Flyers for two seasons before taking over as GM, a position in which he played a major role in building the club's only two Stanley Cup winners. He held the GM post through 1983, sending the Flyers to two more Stanley Cup finals before moving up to become the team's executive vice president.

Nineteen ninety-two was also a major year for Darren Daulton. He became only the fourth catcher in major league history to win an RBI title when he led the National League with 109, a club record for a catcher and the highest total for a big league backstop since 1974. Phillies second baseman Mickey Morandini also put his name in the history books when he became only the ninth player and the first National Leaguer in 65 years to record an unassisted triple play.

Dobbins Tech's Dawn Staley wound up a glittering college career at the University of Virginia by being named All-American for the third year and College Player of the Year for the second year in a row. In four seasons at the University of Virginia, she scored 2,135 points while leading the Cavaliers to a 110–21 record, three Atlantic Coast Conference tournament titles, and three appearances in the NCAA Final Four. After college, Staley was named the nation's Female Athlete of the Year in basketball. Later, she played on several winning world tournament teams before turning pro and then becoming head coach of Temple's women's team.

Another woman to hit it big in 1992 was tennis player Lisa Raymond. The Wayne resident won the first of two straight NCAA singles championships while attending the University of Florida. By 1995 she was ranked number five in the country. She reached fourth in 1997. Having turned pro, Raymond ended the century with nearly $2 million in career winnings. She had one singles title and nine doubles crowns, including two at the Advanta Classic, where she teamed with Rennae Stubbs, and the mixed doubles crown in the 1996 U.S. Open.

Army staged the greatest comeback in the history of the series when it overcame a 17-point deficit to capture a 25–24 decision over Navy on Patmon Malcolm's 49-yard field goal with 12 seconds left to play. Carole Zajac won the first of two straight national cross-country titles as she led Villanova to another NCAA women's championship in a meet in which the Wildcats scored the highest point total (123) in the history of the event. Temple's fencing team, led by three-time All-American Muna Bitar, won the NCAA women's foil championship under coach Nikki Franke, a four-time national college coach of the year.

Temple, paced by Aaron McKie and Eddie Jones, who one year later would be the only Big Five teammates ever to be first-round NBA picks in the same year, reached the Elite Eight for the third time in six years in 1993 before losing once again in the regional final, 77–72 to Michigan. Fran Dunphy guided Penn (22–5) to its best season since 1981 behind the standout play of guards Jerome Allen and Matt Maloney. After leading Simon Gratz High School to three straight Public League titles, Rasheed Wallace became one of the most highly coveted basketball players ever to perform in Philadelphia. He wound up at North Carolina, but in a few years he would relocate to the NBA. A March blizzard caused a Flyers game at the Spectrum to be postponed in the first period after glass was broken in the concourse. Unable to leave town, the Flyers game the next night in Hartford was canceled, a rarity for the NHL.

Philadelphia Textile basketball was in the middle of a marvelous four-year run when it won 113 of 126 games and went to four straight NCAA Division II regional finals. Led by David Fields and Eugene Haith, the Rams posted the best mark in the school's history in 1993 when they went 30–2 while winning the regional championship with a 70–62 victory over Millersville before bowing in the quarterfinals to Wayne State, 78–76. Coach Herb Magee's club had lost in the regional final the year before, 90–79, to California (Pennsylvania) State. The Rams also made the regional finals in 1994 and 1995 but lost both times to New Hampshire College, dropping a 79–78 decision in double overtime and an 84–62 tilt.

Rowan, the former Glassboro State, lost in the NCAA Division III football final by a 34–24 count to Mount Union. The Profs would lose again in the same game in 1995, 36–7 to Wisconsin-LaCrosse, and in 1996 to Mount Union, 56–24. Three other times during the decade Rowan reached the semifinals before losing.

The Philadelphia area almost got the prestigious PGA tournament. An invitation in 1993 to play host to the event was accepted by Aronimink Country Club. But it later was revealed that Aronimink did not meet the PGA's timetable for accepting minority members. The club had to withdraw, and the tournament went elsewhere.

Also going elsewhere were major league baseball fans. A strike that eliminated nearly 50 games from the 1994 schedule caused fans to desert the sport in droves. That, coupled with the sudden decline of the Phillies' on-field performance, put the team in a weakened financial condition from which it spent the rest of the century trying to recover.

Labor problems also shattered the NHL's season. When players and the league were unable to come to terms on a new collective bargaining agreement, the start of the 1994 season was postponed by commissioner Gary Bettman. It took more than three months to reach an agreement, and a 48-game season finally got under way in late January 1995.

Penn posted its second straight undefeated season in football in 1994, winning 19 games over a two-year period for coach Al Bagnoli. Drexel, which would post a 118–33 record for Bill Herrion over a five-year period between 1992 and 1997, went to its first of three straight NCAA basketball tournaments. Tammy Greene ended a four-year career at Philadelphia Textile with a school record 2,490 points. Villanova won its sixth straight NCAA women's cross-country title. A new roller hockey team called the Bulldogs, and partly owned by actor Tony Danza, began playing in Philadelphia at the Spectrum. After winning 40 of 69 games in three years, it folded after the 1996 season.

Gordon Brewer of Huntingdon Valley, playing in his first U.S. Senior Amateur championship, won the tournament after beating Dick Siderowf on the 20th hole in the semifinal and medalist Bob Hullender on the 14th hole in the final round in Nicholasville, Kentucky. Brewer would repeat as champ in 1996 when he defeated Heyward Sullivan, 2-up, in Williamstown, Massachusetts.

Golf was a major part of the Philadelphia sports scene in the 1990s. Along with the regular pro tournaments, numerous small pro tournaments, mostly of one or two days' duration, were held. Area golfers such as Jay Sigel, Betsy King, Ed Dougherty, and Jim Furyk, a West Chester native, were prominent on pro tours. And the Philadelphia area also contributed a man widely acclaimed in the '90s as the world's leading course designer, Norristown native Tom Fazio. The nephew of touring pro turned designer George Fazio, Tom had designed nearly 150 courses by the end of the 20th century, including 16 that were ranked as the best public and resort courses in the country.

Dougherty, a native of Linwood in southern Delaware County, had been on the pro tour for 16 years when he won his first tournament in 1995. Affiliated for many years with Edgemont Country Club, the one-time St. James High School baseball pitcher and three-time Philadelphia PGA champ was 47 years old when he won the Deposit Guaranty Classic in Madison, Mississippi. A few years after that, Dougherty went on to become a fixture on the Seniors tour, where he was frequently among the leaders, and in 1999 he placed 15th on the money list with earnings of $951,072.

Another local golfer who met particular success in 1995 was Buddy Marucci of Berwyn. A long-time local standout playing out of Waynesboro, Marucci, a four-time Pennsylvania Amateur champ, lost 2-up in the 36-hole final of the U.S. Amateur championship at Newport, Rhode Island. His conquerer was a 19-year-old phenom named Tiger Woods. That year Marucci became only the sixth player from the Philadelphia area—joining Max Marston, Skee Riegel, Jimmy McHale, Billy Hyndman, and Jay Sigel—to earn a spot on the U.S. Walker Cup team, which lost to Great Britain/Ireland, 14–10.

Ohio State running back Eddie George out of Abington High School won both the Heisman Trophy and the Maxwell Club Award as the year's outstanding college football player after rushing for 1,826 yards and 23 touchdowns. The 1995 season was also the year for high-scoring games in basketball. The 76ers' 5-foot, 11-inch Dana Barros scored 50 points in a game to become only the third NBA player under 6 feet to break that barrier. La Salle's Kareem Townes set an Explorers one-game record with 52 points. St. Joseph's women's basketball team won (with one tie) its sixth straight Big Five title. Meanwhile, Connecticut, coached by Norristown native Geno Auriemma, a former Bishop Kenrick High School and West Chester University player, completed an undefeated (35–0) season when it won the women's NCAA basketball championship with a 70–64 victory over Tennessee in the final. Auriemma would lead UConn to a repeat national title over the Vols in 2000. St. Joseph's Bernard Blount ended a four-year career with 1,985 points to rank as the school's all-time leading scorer. West Chester grad Lee Woodall, a linebacker with the San Francisco 49ers, played in his first of two Pro Bowls. The Eagles, under new coach Ray Rhodes and bolstered by the signing of free-agent running back Ricky Watters, built a 51–7 lead, then battered the Detroit Lions in a wild card playoff, 58–37, in the highest-scoring playoff game in history. The Birds then lost in the divisional playoffs, 30–11, to the Dallas Cowboys.

In boxing, veteran Philadelphia pugilist Bernard (the Executioner) Hopkins won the vacant IBF middleweight title with a seventh-round knockout of Segundo Mercado. Hopkins, who had been fighting since 1989, held the crown for the rest of the decade, with successful defenses against Glen Johnson and Andrew Council in 1997, Simon Brown in 1998, and Robert Allen and Antwun Echols in 1999. His record at the turn of the century was 36–2–1. In another bout in 1995 former heavyweight champ Mike Tyson kayoed Buster Mathis, Jr., in the third round of a fight at the Spectrum.

Nineteen ninety-six was an Oympic year, and as usual, athletes from the Philadelphia area grabbed a share of the medals. Dawn Staley won a gold medal with the women's basketball team. Mary Ellen Clark became the oldest woman to win a diving medal when the 33-year-old from Newtown Square took a bronze in the 10-meter platform. Carl Lewis won the long jump. And Philadelphia welterweight David Reid was the only United States boxer to win a gold. Soon afterward Reid turned pro, and in his 12th fight in 1999 he won the superwelterweight title by defeating Frenchman Laurent Boudouani, the defending champion. Later Reid defeated number-one contender Kevin Kelly, in his first title defense, and former champ Keith Mullings. In early 2000, Reid lost the crown and his first fight in a unanimous 15-round decision to welterweight champ Felix Trinidad in Las Vegas.

Rowan University came up with another winner in 1996 when it won the Division III NCAA basketball championship. Posting an overall 28–4 record,

Rowan defeated Hope College, 100–93, in the final as Antwan Dasher (19), tourney MVP Terrence Stewart (17), Roscoe Harris (17), and Chris McShane (16) all hit in double figures. The Profs, who had finished third in the tournament twice in the last four years, had beaten Illinois Wesleyan, 79–77, to reach the last game. Coach John Giannini, who recorded a 168–38 record in seven years at Rowan, left after the championship season to become head coach at Maine.

With wins over Iona, Providence, Rhode Island, and Alabama, St. Joseph's advanced to the NIT final before coach Phil Martelli's Hawks dropped a 60–56 decision to Nebraska. Penn's 48-game Ivy League winning streak came to an end. Villanova briefly ranked second in the nation while compiling its first back-to-back 25-win seasons since the 1950s. Drexel, led by future pro Malik Rose, had its finest record (27–4) and went to the second round of the NCAA playoffs before losing to Syracuse, 69–58.

After stopping Navy eight times inside the 10-yard line in the final four minutes, Army defeated the Middies, 28–24, in the fifth straight game of the series that was decided by four points or less. Not so fortunate was Temple's football team, which

Rowan coached by John Giannini (center) captured the Division III NCAA basketball title.

Malik Rose led Drexel to its finest basketball season in 1996.

between 1991 and 1996 compiled an unsightly 8–58 record. Penn AC won its first women's international competition when a team of Rosanna Zegarra, Amy Turner, Sara Field, and Emily Dirksen came from behind to beat defending champion Romania in four-oared crew in the world championship at Glasgow, Scotland.

Two new professional teams made their Philadelphia debuts in 1996. An indoor soccer team called the Kixx joined the National Professional Soccer League (NPSL) and went 6–14. The Rage, a women's team, became a member of the American Basketball League with Staley as its centerpiece. Attendance averaged slightly more than 3,200 a game in the team's first year of play at the Palestra, but in 1997–98, Staley left the team, and attendance at its new home at the Apollo at Temple dropped below 1,500. The league folded after that season.

The $107 million, 11,000-seat Apollo was officially opened in 1997. So was La Salle's 4,000-seat Tom Gola Arena, a new part of the Hayman Center, originally opened in 1972. Also experiencing an opening of sorts was La Salle football. Having not fielded a team since 1941, the Explorers returned to the gridiron with former Widener and Delaware Valley coach Bill Manlove serving as head man. Although Manlove would win his 200th career game in 1999, the Explorers struggled, winning only one of nine games in their first year before slowly improving in the ensuing seasons.

Not struggling was Villanova's football team. The Wildcats finished the regular season with an 11–0 record and a ranking as the number-one Division I-AA team in the nation, with Brian Finneran becoming the only wide receiver ever to win the division's Player of the Year award. Coach Andy Talley's team then moved into the NCAA playoffs where it beat Colgate, 49–28. But after leading 21–0 early in the second quarter, the Wildcats lost to eventual champion Youngstown State, 37–34, despite quarterback Chris Boden's passing for 323 yards and four touchdowns.

Allen Iverson became the first 76er to be named Rookie of the Year in the NBA after averaging 23.5 points per game, eighth highest in the league in 1996–97. At one point he scored 40 or more points in five consecutive games, including a career-

Allen Iverson gave the 76ers their first NBA scoring champion in more than three decades.

high 50 in one of them. Iverson, who came to the Sixers after they won the first pick in the NBA lottery, had left Georgetown University after being named first-team All-American in his sophomore year. He would go on to win the NBA scoring title in 1998–99 after averaging 26.8 points per game during the strike-shortened season.

The 1996–97 season was also the one in which the Flyers returned to the Stanley Cup final for the first time since 1987. The Flyers finished second during the regular season with Rod Brind'Amour playing in a club record 288th consecutive game and John LeClair becoming only the second player in the team's history to record back-to-back 50-goal seasons (He would do it again the following year, becoming the first American-born player to score 50 goals three straight times in the NHL.) LeClair, Eric Lindros, and Mikael Renberg gave the Flyers a scintillating line nicknamed "the Legion of Doom." Added to that was a tough defense led by Eric Desjardins and goalie Ron Hextall. Coached by Terry Murray, the Flyers flew through the quarter-finals, beating the Pittsburgh Penguins, four games to one. Next to fall were the Buffalo Sabres and the New York Rangers, both also in five games. In the championship series, however, the Flyers proved no match for the rugged Detroit Red Wings, falling in four straight games to a veteran team that featured the high-scoring Red Line from Russia.

At about the same time the Flyers were pitted in playoff battles, the Phillies were taking the field with a sparkling new third baseman. Scott Rolen was the best player to come out of the Phils' farm system since Mike Schmidt, and he wasted no time proving it. Hitting .283 with 21 home runs and 92 RBI for energetic new manager Terry Francona's club, Rolen was named National League Rookie of the Year. A strong, solid, workmanlike player, Rolen showed maturity far beyond his years. An exceptional fielder, he followed his rookie campaign with a glittering .290–31–110 year in 1998, clinching a spot as one of the top young stars of the league.

Claiming a spot as one of the major leagues' best pitchers was Phillies hurler Curt Schilling. In 1997, while winning a career-high 17 games, he led the major leagues with 319 strikeouts. That was not only a club record, but the most for a righthander in National League history and the 10th highest total ever compiled in the majors. Schilling, a workhorse who thrived on that rare occurrence—a complete game— came back with 300 strikeouts the following season, making him just the fifth pitcher ever to register 300 whiffs two years in a row.

Richie Ashburn, one of the most popular figures ever to grace Philadelphia sports, died suddenly in his hotel room in New York during his 35th year as a Phillies broadcaster. More than 20,000 showed up for Ashburn's viewing at Memorial Hall in Fairmont Park. The Flyers made a blockbuster deal when they landed Chris Gratton in a trade with Tampa Bay. They then signed him to a $16.5 million, five-year contract. Gratton, however, never fit the Flyers' style, and in 1999 he was swapped back to the Lightning. Also in 1997, the 76ers named Larry Brown head coach. The well-traveled Brown, one of the most highly regarded coaches in basketball with the 12th winningest record in the NBA, quickly set about resurrecting a moribund franchise that in recent years had been locked into the lower levels of the NBA standings.

Philadelphia boxer Charles Brewer won the vacant IBF supermiddleweight championship when he knocked out Gary Ballard in the first round of their title fight. Brewer, a pro fighter since 1989, retained his crown later in 1997 with a unanimous 12-round decision over Joey DeGrandis, and again in 1998 with a 10th round knockout of Herol Graham. Haverford College's Karl Paranya, the winningest runner in the history of Division III with nine titles, became the first runner from that division to break the four-minute mile when he finished in 3:57.6 in a race on his home track. Flyers broadcaster Gene Hart was elected to the Hockey Hall of Fame. And Carrie Tollefson of Villanova won the NCAA women's cross-country title, the

Carrie Tollefson won five NCAA championships in the late 1990s at Villanova.

first of five NCAA championships, including 5,000- and 3,000-meter outdoor races, that she would win over the next three years.

A tiny athlete named Tara Lipinsky, a native of Washington Township in South Jersey, became the latest from the area to gain fame when she won the gold medal in figure skating in the 1998 Olympics at Nagano, Japan. At 15 years old, she was the youngest woman ever to win that event. Villanova won its seventh women's cross-country NCAA championship in 10 years, and the Wildcats' Brian Westbrook became the first player in NCAA history to both rush for and receive 1,000 yards when he gained a school record 1,046 yards on the ground and caught 1,144 yards worth of passes. Former Eagles wide receiver Tommy McDonald was inducted into the Pro Football Hall of Fame. And the Kixx, the indoor soccer team, won its first East Division title in the NPSL with a 21–13 victory over the Harrisburg Heat. The Kixx then defeated the Cleveland Crunch, two games to none in the first round of the playoffs, but after defeating the Milwaukee Wave, 9–7, in the first game, lost four straight to them in the American Conference final. Kixx defensive player Matt Knowles was named NPSL Defender of the Year.

The 1998 season also had its downside. Philadelphia suffered nationwide embarrassment when fans threw batteries at St. Louis Cardinals outfielder J. D. Drew, a highly touted young player who had rejected Phillies offers after being the club's first draft choice the year before. During Army's 34–30 victory over Navy at Veterans Stadium, a railing collapsed while Army students were mugging for TV cameras. Nine Cadets were sent hurtling to the ground some 12 feet below. Several serious injuries resulted. Also at Veterans Stadium, drunk and unruly Eagles fans often got so out of control during games that a court was set up at the stadium so rowdies could be tried on the spot.

After not being able to sign Drew, the Phillies got the number-one draft pick again, and this time they chose Pat Burrell, a heavy hitter from Miami University. Ultimately, Burrell signed a five-year, $8 million contract. The draft was also a controversial topic in 1999 for the Eagles and new coach Andy Reid. Instead of picking Texas All-American Ricky Williams, a former Phillies minor league player who at the time was college football's all-time rushing leader, the Birds selected quarterback Donovan McNabb from Syracuse. The choice was not met with a ringing endorsement from Eagles fans, although McNabb would later become a local favorite.

NBA owners locked out players at the start of the 1998–99 season in a labor dispute. When an abbreviated 50-game season finally got started, the 76ers played their best basketball since the beginning of the decade and finished third in the Atlantic Division. In their first playoff venture since 1991, the Sixers took three out of four from the Orlando Magic but were then eliminated by the Indiana Pacers after four straight losses.

Philadelphia jockey Tony Black reached a milestone with his 4,000th career victory.

Philadelphia jockey Tony Black won the 4,000th race of his career, becoming only the 33rd rider in the history of North American racing to reach that level. Black, who dominated Philadelphia-area tracks for 30 years, won his first race in 1970. His milestone victory was achieved in his 27,641st race. Over that span he earned $37,488,414, finished second 3,516 times, and registered 3,510 third-place finishes.

Overbrook (Camden County) High School alumnus Ron Dayne became the fourth Philadelphia-area resident to win the Heisman Trophy as he captured it and the Maxwell Award as the country's top college football player. The Berlin, New Jersey, resident won after a season in which he led Wisconsin to the Big Ten title and its second straight Rose Bowl victory. During his four-year career at Wisconsin, Dayne set an all-time college record in rushing with 6,397 yards, breaking the old mark held by Williams.

The year 1999 was special for many other Philadelphia-area folks. Coatesville's first-team All-American Richard Hamilton was named the Most Valuable Player after scoring 27 points to lead Connecticut to the NCAA basketball championship

Ron Dayne came out of South Jersey to set an all-time college rushing record at Wisconsin.

with a victory over Duke. Enjoying his best season as a pro, golfer Ed Dougherty passed the million dollar mark in earnings in his second year on the Senior PGA Tour while finishing the year 15th on the money list. Former Cheyney coach Vivian Stringer became only the third Division I women's basketball mentor to win 600 games when she reached that mark at Rutgers. Springfield (Delaware County) native Mike Scioscia, a standout catcher for the Los Angeles Dodgers from 1980 to 1992 and the team's career leader in games caught with 1,395, was appointed manager of the Anaheim Angels.

The Eagles' fine running back Duce Staley gained 1,065 yards rushing to join Wilbert Montgomery and Ricky Watters as the only Eagles with back-to-back 1,000-yard seasons. Watters had done it three straight years. Lindsay Davenport, the world's second-ranked woman tennis player, came back after losing in the finals the last two years to win the Advanta Classic, defeating top-rated Martina Hingis. Julie Inkster became only the second golfer to win the LPGA Grand Slam with victory in the McDonald's Championship at DuPont Country Club. And Norristown-based fighter Michael Grant, battered and bloodied, rallied to beat Francois Botha to set himself up as the leading heavyweight contender.

Temple basketball coach John Chaney, the winningest pilot in Owl history, gained the 600th victory of his 27-year coaching career. Chaney, a three-time national coach of the year, had directed Temple to 15 NCAA playoffs, won five Atlantic 10 titles, and won or shared 12 Big Five crowns while compiling a 605–219 career record, including a 380–160 mark at Temple. His 1998–99 team starring the playmaking marvel Pepe Sanchez became the third to make it to the Elite Eight in the NCAA playoffs, beating Kent State, Cincinnati, and Purdue before losing to Duke, 85–64.

Tragedy continued to plague Philadelphia in the 1990s when Russian-born Flyers player Dmitri Tertyshny was killed in a boating accident in northwestern Canada. In 1999, Philadelphia was also saddened by the losses of basketball great Wilt Chamberlain and Flyers broadcaster Gene Hart. Elsewhere, Garden State Park

Ron Hextall won more games and played in more games than any other goalie in Flyers history.

was on the verge of being closed after a tentative deal was struck with a developer who planned to tear down the storied race track. Eagles fans once again showed their crude side when they cheered the Dallas Cowboys' Michael Irvin as he lay injured on the ground.

In one of the strangest games ever held at the Palestra, Princeton rallied from a 40–13 halftime deficit to beat Penn, 50–49. Temple under coach Gavin White won its 15th Dad Vail Regatta in the last 16 years. With his career 233rd win and 487th game played, the Flyers' Ron Hextall moved into first place on the team's all-time list in both categories for goalies, passing Bernie Parent. Penn Charter and Germantown Academy met for the 113th time in 1999 in the longest unbroken schoolboy football rivalry in the country. Penn Charter leads the series, 70–32–11.

In what could be the last Army-Navy game in Philadelphia, quarterback Brian Madden ran for 177 yards to spark the Cadets to a 19–9 triumph over Navy. The Big Five came back to life when school administrators elected to restore in 1999–2000 the round-robin series that had been eliminated at the beginning of the decade. The Kixx behind goalies Peter Pappas and Keith Engelhardt recorded their first shutout, a 16–0 victory over the Florida Thundercats, on their way to capturing a second straight East Division regular season title. And Philadelphia Pharmacy basketball coach Bobby Morgan was approaching his 600th career win.

As the century concluded, the Phillies showed signs of snapping out of their nearly decade-long doldrums as general manager Ed Wade assembled a team that seemed likely to be a contender soon. The 76ers appeared to be on the rise again under the masterful coaching of Larry Brown. Meanwhile, there were still no new football or baseball stadiums in Philadelphia, as had originally been hoped by the Phillies and Eagles. Those would be items to put on the agenda in a new century.

Jay Sigel, From Top Amateur to Top Pro

Back in the 1980s, when Jay Sigel was adding one trophy after another to his collection, one description of him always seemed to surface. Best amateur golfer since Bobby Jones, people called him.

It was a fitting description. No amateur ever won more national tournaments than the big hitter from Berwyn. For nearly three decades Sigel was the cream of the crop in amateur golfing circles, an exceptional player who seemingly had no flaws in his game.

When Sigel turned pro at the age of 50, joining the Senior PGA Tour, his reputation

Jay Sigel became one of the top players on the Senior Tour after a glittering amateur career.

preceded him. But there was no reduction in Jay's game. He immediately became one of the top players on the circuit, a spot he maintained for the rest of the decade.

Because of his extraordinary golfing success, Sigel easily ranks as the Philadelphia area's top athlete of the 1990s. He's accorded that distinction over others, such as the Flyers' Eric Lindros, the 76ers' Allen Iverson, the Phillies' Curt Schilling, jockey Tony Black, and basketball star Dawn Staley, who also produced outstanding work during the decade.

Amazingly, Sigel achieved his success despite accidentally smashing his left hand through a glass door, slashing arteries, nerves, and tendons and slicing off a piece of one finger. The 1963 accident, occurring while Sigel was a sophomore at Wake Forest, required more than three hours of surgery and long months of rehabilitation, and it left Jay with a hand that is mostly numb.

Sigel, however, persevered, and after winning All-American honors went on to a magnificent amateur career that made him the most decorated nonprofessional since—you guessed it—the legendary Bobby Jones.

Jay's major victories are numerous. He won the British Amateur championship in 1979, and consecutive U.S. Amateur titles in 1982 and 1983. He won three U.S. Mid-Amateur crowns and played on seven Walker Cup teams between 1977 and 1993, captaining both the 1983 and 1985 U.S. squads. No player ever made as many appearances or scored as many total points in Walker Cup history as Sigel. He also was low amateur in the Masters tournament three different times, as well as in the 1980 British Open and 1984 U.S. Open.

All the while, Sigel, who finished first in seven Philadelphia and four Pennsylvania Opens, was running an insurance business. When he turned 50, with encouragement from Jack Nicklaus and others, he embarked on a new business: professional golf.

After going to qualifying school, Sigel joined the Senior Tour. In 1994 he was named Rookie of the Year. His biggest achievement that year was a remarkable win in the GTE West Classic in which he came from 10 strokes back to catch Jim Colbert in regulation, then won his first pro tournament on the fourth playoff hole.

Sigel was named the longest hitter on the tour in 1995 with drives averaging 277.4 yards. In 1996 he passed the $1 million mark in earnings after pocketing a $280,000 check—at that point, the largest payment in Senior Tour history—for winning the Senior Tour championship tournament. The following year he finished in the top 10 in 19 tournaments while winning two more tourneys and losing in playoffs of two others. Sigel added the Bell Atlantic Classic to his first-place list in 1998 while shooting a course-record 62. He finished the '98 season fourth on the Seniors tour money list for the year.

As the 20th century concluded, Sigel was still going strong. Unlike most of his touring colleagues who came up through the regular PGA Tour, Jay had arrived late in the pro ranks. But it hardly mattered. On the Senior Tour, he could hold his own against anybody.

PHOTOGRAPH CREDITS

Urban Archives, Temple University, Philadelphia, Pennsylvania–pages 4, 13, 19, 24, 36, 50, 52, 53, 63, 71, 75, 80, 82, 83, 84, 86, 87, 89, 94, 97, 114, 116, 117, 123, 129, 131, 140, 142, 149, 154, 168, 170, 177, 181, 182, 189, 190, 195, 210, 211, 212, 231, 240, 244, 250, 256, 263, 276, 279, 299, 338

Photo courtesy of Vesper Boat Club–page 21 (bottom)

Photo courtesy of Haverford College–page 8

Photo courtesy of Friends Historical Library of Swarthmore College–page 10

Photos courtesy of the Office of Athletic Communications, University of Pennsylvania–pages 15, 21 (top), 47, 49, 113, 153, 172, 214

Photos from the collection of Rich Westcott–pages 6, 18, 33, 42, 54, 73, 77, 99, 134, 136, 144, 155, 167, 194, 196, 201, 217, 219, 237, 260, 282, 290, 298

Photo courtesy of Special Collections Department, Bryn Mawr College Library–page 22

Photos courtesy of Philadelphia Athletics Historical Society–pages 27, 188

Photo courtesy of Richard N. Williams III–page 43

Photo courtesy of Keeneland Raceway, Cook collection–page 61

Photo courtesy of National Baseball Hall of Fame Library, Cooperstown, NY– page 66

Photos courtesy of Betty Shellenberger, U. S. Field Hockey Association, Inc.—pages 104, 150

Photos courtesy of Temple University Department of Sports Information—pages 106, 107, 118, 184, 186, 197, 228, 311, 316, 340

Photo courtesy of Joseph Sweeney—page 111

Photos courtesy of La Salle University Archives–pages 112, 175

Photos courtesy of the Philadelphia Eagles–pages 121, 146, 161, 192, 206, 292, 301

U.S. Army photo–page 138

Photo courtesy of H. Hunter Lott, Jr.–page 152 (left)

Photo courtesy of Merion Cricket Club–page 152 (right)

Photos courtesy of Athletic Communications, La Salle University–pages 157, 174, 215, 342

Photo courtesy of the International Bowling Museum and Hall of Fame, St. Louis, Missouri, USA—page 185

Photo by James Leslie Parker, courtesy of Classic Communications–page 208

Photos courtesy of Villanova University–pages 221, 281, 303, 308, 315, 331, 353

Photos courtesy of the Delaware County *Daily Times*–pages 224, 235, 258, 270

Photos courtesy of the Philadelphia Flyers–pages 227, 252, 275, 335, 357 (The Philadelphia Flyers name, logo and uniform design are trademarks, copyrighted designs and other forms of intellectual property of the Philadelphia Flyers and NHL Enterprises and may not be used, in whole or in part, without the prior written consent of the Philadelphia Flyers or NHL Enterprises. All Rights Reserved.)

Photo courtesy of West Chester University Department of Athletics, Sports Information Office–page 242

Photo courtesy of Immaculata College and the Robert Halvey Collection of the Philadelphia Archdiocesan Archives–page 254

Photo courtesy of Penn State University, Department of Sports Information–page 272

Photos courtesy of the Philadelphia 76ers–pages 295, 318, 324, 351 (The Philadelphia

Photo by Bob Jordan and courtesy of Barbara and Kathy Jordan–page 313

Photos by Alan Kravetz–pages 327, 332, 349

Photo by Ed Mahan and courtesy of the Philadelphia Wings–page 329

Photo courtesy of the Los Angeles Dodgers–page 333

Photo courtesy of Drexel University Department of Sports Information–page 350

Photo courtesy of Philadelphia Park–page 355

Photo courtesy of Ron Dayne–page 356

Photo courtesy of the Bell Atlantic Classic–page 359

INDEX